Continued from first flap

and practices of literary criticism. His book thus has a strict and necessary critical structure of its own that avoids the dangerously easy molds of biography, chronology and genre. In describing the form of his book, which he calls "critical narrative," Field writes: "I have treated Nabokov's novels, poems, stories, plays and essays as characters in a novel, and each has its role and place carefully prefigured and integrated into the whole. The subject of the book is the art of Vladimir Nabokov and, as such, any perceptions and discoveries are necessarily dependent on his creations. But the *form* and *ordering* of these perceptions belong as exclusively to me as the style in which this book is written. The book is successful if the reader senses the harmony between *what* is said, *where* it is said, and *how* it is said. Only in an effort to satisfy all these conditions of content, form and style can literary criticism aspire to be considered an art in any rigorous sense of the term."

In form it is a departure in literary criticism which will cause almost as much comment as its author's fascinating discoveries and interpretations.

Covering the whole of Nabokov's work, including some untranslated novels, plays and poetry, Andrew Field has written a richly rewarding book. NABOKOV: *His Life in Art* is a distinguished critical work which will serve as the definitive interpretation of the great international author for years to come.

Jacket photograph by Horst Tappe

Books by ANDREW FIELD

✖ ✖ ✖ ✖

PAGES FROM TARUSA (*Editor*)

NABOKOV: HIS LIFE IN ART

NABOKOV
His Life in Art

NABOKOV
His Life in Art

�֍ ✖ ✖ ✖

a critical narrative by
ANDREW FIELD

LITTLE, BROWN AND COMPANY · BOSTON · TORONTO

This book is inscribed

to two great literatures which meet at last

to one of America's best literary critics,
Stanley Edgar Hyman

to two readers whom I want, but cannot have—
Vladislav Khodasevich and Andrei Tertz-Sinyavsky

and, most of all, to a future reader,
Andrew Jonathan

NABOKOV
His Life in Art

In Place of a Foreword

✳   ✳   ✳   ✳

N *ah*-buh-kov, *Vlad*-a-mere. Vla-dim-*ear* Na-*bah*-kov. The number of possible mispronunciations of his name grows apace as does his reputation. My own favorite is the one I heard from the receptionist of one of Nabokov's publishers as she announced my arrival to examine a file of reviews: "Mr. Field is here to read Nahba-cocoa's reviews." And this tendency toward transmogrification of his rather simple Russian name — no more unusual, really, than Salinger (Sah-*ling*-er, Sa-lin-*jay*?) — is emblematic of the haze that still surrounds his writings.

Virtually all of the foremost literary critics in the United States and England have written about Nabokov, with enthusiasm often bordering on awe. But their eloquence, where one wants and would expect explication, betrays the fact that they are at least as ill at ease with Nabokov as they are fascinated by him. One of Nabokov's American critics has written: "Nabokov needs no apologia. If you do not get him, you do not get him." To be sure, Nabokov is a singularly independent and idiosyncratic artist, and I suppose there is a certain sort of sensitive and discerning reader whose "taste" is not receptive to Nabokov's art. I suppose this, but I am not prepared to rest with it finally, for two reasons. First, Nabokov is to me as interesting as any poet or writer in this century (or the last, for that matter), and thus to speak of not "getting" or "caring for" Nabokov, unless one cares for literature in only a very conditional way, is not for me an entirely reasonable statement. Second, it is quite clear to me that neither his Russian nor his English readers have ever "gotten" Nabokov in the sense of having access to everything he has written and to the full cultural tradition in which he writes.

The causes are different for his Russian and his English readers, but in both instances they have served to prevent each audience from having a full view of Nabokov's art. In the emigration after 1919 the various cultural centers, primarily Paris and Berlin, tended to be enclaves, and while a Russian living in Paris could in theory follow all the Berlin Russian-language newspapers and literary almanacs, in practice few did. Thus, when Nabokov began to be at all widely known and written about (this was about 1931 or 1932, and Paris by that time had superseded Berlin as the center of émigré culture), his critics were by and large unaware of the poetry, reviews, essays, and short stories that he had been printing fairly regularly for fully ten years in the Berlin Russian-language daily newspaper founded by his father. Typically, in one of the first extensive appreciations of Nabokov, in 1930 when he had published two novels and a book of short stories, the critic notes rather uncertainly: ". . . and it would seem that he has also published two little books of verse."

Then, too, Nabokov is and was from the beginning of his writing career a European or international writer whose "cultural fatherland" extends from London to Moscow. By contrast, the émigré intelligentsia had — for reasons that were complex and two-sided — very little actual contact with and knowledge of contemporary French and German literature, and even less of English. Nabokov's writing seemed to many émigré critics to be somehow "foreign" and "un-Russian," and this banal observation followed him through the critical press right up to 1940 when he emigrated to the United States. Nabokov's novels as they appeared would inevitably be described as "like a translation from the German Impressionists" or "quite unusual for Russian literature perhaps, but standard fare in the French literary monthlies." Who these German Impressionists and French hacks were was rarely if ever even specified, and the matter never got as far as an actual comparison with a specific text. Even in the later years when it became fashionable to speak of Nabokov as a "Proustian," the label was not critically investigated.

Still, by the time his fourth book had been published, Nabokov had achieved an impressive reputation as the most promising young writer in the emigration. In a play on the lines of the Soviet poet Selvinsky (*"The Revolution took place / so that Blok could write The Twelve"*) one émigré critic wrote, half seriously: *"The emigration is justified / because of the appearance of [Nabokov]."* And he did have many perceptive critics — but, again, the diaspora worked to hinder cross-fertilization of opinion: his critics would be in Prague, Warsaw, the Russian colony at Harbin in Manchuria, Berlin, Paris, Estonia and so forth, and their critiques often appeared in newspapers and local almanacs.

For his American readers the terms of the problem were simply reversed. They could easily sense and respond to Nabokov's pan-European culture and, often as not, they were even familiar enough with Gogol to be able to see Nabokov in some sort of Russian tradition. But who was this man? What else had he written? These questions, which have been asked more and more nervously as each succeeding Russian book is translated into English, are by no means idle ones. Nabokov himself has written somewhat sadly: "None of my American friends have read my Russian books and thus every appraisal on the strength of my English ones is bound to be out of focus."

In short, two conditions which did *not* obtain suggest the nature of the present critical confusion over Nabokov. *If* the Russian emigration had had its own "Formosa," a real second Russia in which a literature could have been nurtured and found resonance, America would probably have lost its most important writer of this century. *If* the substantial body of Nabokov's Russian writing and the best critical articles about him had been translated before 1950, it is extremely unlikely that *Lolita* or *Pale Fire* would have been nearly as misunderstood as they were.

This book, therefore, can attempt a service of greater usefulness than can ordinarily be assumed by the literary critic. For the first time all of Nabokov's writing has been gathered together for consideration as an *oeuvre*. This aggregate is imposing in its quantity and quality, and its full extent is certain to astonish even those few — chiefly Russian émigrés with a knowledge of English and French — who were under the impression that they had read most of what Nabokov has written. When I began my work on this book I had a copy of the excellent 1963 bibliography of Nabokov's writing which was printed privately for his friends by his German publisher Rowohlt, and I took this lengthy list to be, for all practical purposes, a "complete bibliography." However, as I dipped into newspapers, journals, and almanacs gathered from six major libraries around the world, I soon realized that the Rowohlt bibliography was anything but complete, and so I went through almost every journal and almanac published in the emigration and approximately three decades of newspapers on microfilm and pages too brown and brittle to turn quickly without seriously damaging them: every page had to be examined closely for that little poem or book review that might be stuck in a corner. Because at this writing there are probably not ten people who have read even eighty per cent of what Nabokov has written, *Nabokov: His Life in Art* is, first of all, in a very real sense, a sea chest containing excerpts from and allusions to hundreds of valuable and precious documents, forgotten or completely unknown. The perplexity that even Nabokov's most fervent admirers have often felt should now — quite apart from my own commentary and opinion — be clarified, for the reader may now place and trace the various Nabokovian motifs which figure throughout his art.

The second unusual aspect of *Nabokov: His Life in Art* is its innovatory nature as a work of criticism: it is *formed*, that is, it is structured in a way roughly corresponding to that of the narrative in fiction. This book starts in the middle and moves steadily forward and backward, in chapters that are parabolic, to the middle again in the third from last chapter; it ends, in a manner of speaking, in the middle yet again — but quite a different middle. In short, I have treated Nabokov's novels, poems, stories, plays, and essays as characters in a novel, and each has its role and place carefully prefigured and integrated into the whole. The subject of this book is the art of Vladimir Nabokov and, as such, any perceptions and discoveries are necessarily dependent on his creations. But the *form* and *ordering* of these perceptions, which in themselves constitute a separate sort of understanding, belong as exclusively to me as the style in which this book is written. The book is successful if the reader senses the harmony between *what* is said, *where* it is said, and *how* it is said. Only in an effort to satisfy all these conditions of content, form, and style, respectively, can literary criticism aspire to be considered an art in any rigorous sense of the term. And I see no reason why it should not. The attempt in this book is necessarily restrained in many respects because of the enormous volume of information that had to be selected and included, and also because of the sufficiently unorthodox personality of the book's subject.

Curiously enough, the very manner in which Nabokov's past Russian works have slowly been revealed between the appearances of his newest English ones is itself a prototype of the form that *Nabokov: His Life in Art* takes. My assumption is that an approach that is strictly chronological or according to genre or language is an unnatural way in which to view and understand any writer of stature. In practice the works of writers whom we know well do not reside in our minds in a neat and simple metal file cabinet, but tend rather to divide and seek affinities and patterns of their own in our remembrance of them. My "narrative criticism" of Nabokov's art is merely an attempt to bring order and symmetry to this natural process. Still, chronology and genre are not without significance — as suggested by certain of my chapter groupings — and so, either before or after reading the book in hand (depending on one's knowledge of Nabokov and need of strict chronology), the reader may turn to Chapter Twelve where he will find, stacked and impersonal, the material from which this book is made. Another help, a terse chronology, precedes Chapter One. *Nabokov: His Life in Art* is sufficiently complected so that serious and amusing distortions will result from spot-reading it. We "read" novels (or we are supposed to), but we spot-read or "use" criticism, and "usefulness" by itself, important though it is, ought not to be cultivated as an ultimate purpose or value in literature or in literary criticism. A skeleton index of Nabokov's works has been included, however (with some misgivings), for the convenience of re-readers and also for an ardent "old index-maker" of my acquaintance.

My critical credo, suitably and oddly, is taken from America's notorious Baltimore sage who wrote very little literary criticism in any proper sense of the term, but who had some brusque and attractive things to say on that and many other subjects:

The assumption that it may be scientific is the worst curse that lies upon criticism. It is responsible for all the dull, blowsy, "definitive" stuff that literary pedagogues write, and it is responsible, too, for the heavy posturing that so often goes on among critics less learned. Both groups proceed upon the theory that there are exact facts to be ascertained, and that it is their business to ascertain and proclaim them. That theory is nonsense. There is, in truth, no such thing as an exact fact in the whole realm of the beautiful arts . . . The critic survives, when he survives at all, mainly as artist. His judgments, in the long run, become archaic, and may be disregarded. But if, in stating them, he has incidentally produced a work of art on his own account, then he is read long after they are rejected, and it may be plausibly argued that he has contributed something to the glory of letters.

Nabokov, I have mastered your themes. (*Nabokov, have I mastered your themes?*) See how your books lie carefully arranged in the window of my critical eye. (*I return your books, neatly packed and unsoiled, but I have kept and cut the pages and taken up the images.*) Each is an essential cubist plane of a bookish portrait that, in the necessary cultural perspective and light, is your truest and most palpable biography. (*Together they form your future monument, the shadow of which even now extends from Moscow to New York.*)

The name of our writer is (say it quickly) Vladee*m*ear Nah*boak*off.

A Brief Chronology

❆ ❆ ❆ ❆

1899 Born St. Petersburg, April 22. Father: Vladimir Dmitrievich Nabokov, eminent jurist and member of the First Duma.
Mother: Elena Rukavishnikov (maiden name), daughter of a
wealthy family, neighbors of the Nabokovs.

1913–1916 Attended the noted St. Petersburg liberal academy,
the Tenishev School. Before leaving Russia he published two
books of verse.

1919 Emigrated with his family from the Crimea on an old Greek
ship carrying dried fruit.

1919–1923 Studied French and Russian literature at Trinity College, Cambridge. Graduated with honors.

1922 His father assassinated by two Russian reactionaries in
Berlin, where he was one of the chief editors of the leading
Russian liberal newspaper, *The Rudder*.

1923 Published two books of poetry, *A Cluster* and *The Empyrean
Path*. Between 1921 and 1931 he published an enormous
number of poems, reviews, chess problems, and short stories in
The Rudder.

1925 Married Véra Evseevna Slonim.

1923–1937 Resident alien in Berlin.

1926 First novel *Mashenka* published. Generally unnoticed.

1928 Second novel *King, Queen, Knave* appears. First stirrings of
interest and controversy.

1929 Third novel *The Luzhin Defense* is published serially, and,
with the 1930 works *The Eye* and a book of stories and poems

The Return of Chorb, Sirin — Nabokov's Russian pseudonym — now begins to be widely written about and discussed as the most important of the younger émigré writers. At no time during his émigré writing career, however, did Nabokov's books ever produce more than a few hundred dollars a year. Nabokov earned his living by giving lessons in tennis, English, and Russian.

1930 The vicious *ad hominem* attacks upon Nabokov's writing begin.

1931 Fourth novel *The Exploit* published.

1932 Fifth novel *Camera obscura* (in English, *Laughter in the Dark*) appears.

1934 The Nabokovs' first and only child, Dmitri, is born. *Despair,* Nabokov's first major novel, appears serially, and a small circle of writers, critics, and readers begins to place Nabokov's name with the great figures of Russian literature.

1935 *Invitation to a Beheading* appears serially, giving rise to much debate and controversy.

1937 *The Gift* begins to appear serially. By this time the Nabokovs have moved to Paris because of the growing Nazi terror in Germany, and between 1937 and 1939 Nabokov does a certain amount of his writing in French and English.

1938 Nabokov publishes two major plays, *The Event* and *The Waltz Invention.*

1940 An extremely important novel which was never completed, *Solus Rex,* begins to appear serially. In May of 1940 Nabokov and his family leave France for America where he takes up citizenship and decides finally to become an English writer.

1941 *The Real Life of Sebastian Knight,* written in English while he was still living in Paris, is published.

1943 Guggenheim Award.

1941–1948 Nabokov lectures at Wellesley: Mr. Nabokov is not at Wellesley in a teaching capacity but as a creative writer, who through his knowledge of writing and literature may participate by lecture and conference in the work of the six departments of English Literature, English Composition, French, German, Italian, and Spanish." From 1942 until 1948 Nabokov is also a Fellow of the Museum of Comparative Zoology at Harvard, and during this time his irreverent *Nikolai Gogol* and his second English novel, *Bend Sinister*, appear.

1948–1958 Nabokov is offered and accepts a professorship at Cornell University by Morris Bishop who has read and admired his stories and poems in *The New Yorker* and *The Atlantic*. While at Cornell Nabokov writes his autobiography *Speak, Memory*, the novels *Lolita* and *Pnin*, and his commentaries to and translations of *The Song of Igor's Campaign* and *Eugene Onegin*.

1951–1952 Nabokov is guest lecturer at Harvard.

1953 Second Guggenheim Award and American Academy of Arts and Letters Award.

1956 Nabokov, who in 1940 tried and was unable to obtain an academic position in England, is proposed for an important chair at a Great University. After heated debate the proposal is defeated: "Gentlemen, even if one allows that he is an important writer, are we next to invite an elephant to be Professor of Zoology?"

1959 With the achievement of bestsellerdom by *Lolita*, Nabokov is able to resign from his teaching position and devote himself full time to creative writing. "I never imagined that I should be able to live by my writing, but now I am kept by a little girl named Lolita." The Nabokovs establish temporary residence in Switzerland in order to be near several members of their family, including their son Dmitri, who is pursuing an opera career in Italy.

1962 *Pale Fire* appears.

1964 *Eugene Onegin* appears in four volumes, and in the course of the following year there is a sharp and protracted controversy between Nabokov and Edmund Wilson.

Since about 1964 Nabokov has been at work on his sixteenth novel, discussed at the conclusion of this book, which will be completed and published no earlier than 1968.

One

❈ ❈ ❈ ❈

THE writing career of Vladimir Nabokov spans slightly more than twenty years in Russian, and by now more than twenty-five years in English. In the brief interstice between 1937 and 1939, while living in France for a few years prior to the Nazi advance, he wrote in French — the third language of which he possesses a native command — in addition to writing in Russian. Nabokov's French output is quite small: a chapter from what was to become his memoirs, some translations of Pushkin's poetry, and a long article, containing translations, on Pushkin in *La Nouvelle Revue Française* (March, 1937). The article is entitled *"Pouchkine ou le vrai et le vraisemblable"* ("Pushkin, or the True and the Probable"), but it is less important for what it says about Pushkin — which, in any case, has been superseded by the imposing 1964 Pushkin Commentary — than for the wealth of literary matters which are called to mind by consideration of Pushkin.

The article begins with a whimsical description of an unbalanced man whom Nabokov once knew. Although he was not even forty, in his own mind the man's birth receded farther and farther into the past, and he was under the impression that he had taken part in important events of the past century. Nabokov speculates on what an intellectual feast a Carlyle might have made of such a madness, but, he says, "unhappily, my man was fundamentally uncultivated and very badly equipped to enjoy a rare psychosis, as a result of which he was reduced to nourishing his imagination with the rubbish of banalities and common ideas which are more or less false." This example leads Nabokov to speculate on the art and manner of biography in general:

At first one sorts the correspondence of the great man, cut out and pasted together again to make a beautiful paper costume, then his works are carefully thumbed over to find some personal traits. And, of course [the biographer] doesn't stand on ceremony. I have chanced to discover some very curious things in these accounts of great lives, for example, the life of a celebrated German poet in which the content of one of his poems entitled *The Dream* is calmly narrated from beginning to end as a dream that the poet in question really had. Indeed what is more simple than to cause the great man to circulate among the people, ideas, and objects which he himself described and which one pulls out half-dead from his books with which to stuff one's own? . . . And then, God preserve us, we have the psychology of the subject, the playful Freudianism, the description choked with what he was thinking at a given moment. . . .

Pushkin's life, full of romantic gusts and vivid flashes of lightning, presents the writers of such popular biographies with as many temptations as traps. There have been many of them written in Russia in recent years, and the few I have seen are quite revolting. But there exists also the pious and disinterested labor of some elite spirits, who, while digging into the past, accumulating precious detail, do not have any desire to construct some spectacle pandering to vulgar tastes. All the same, however, there is a fatal moment at which even the purest scholar becomes involved in composing a novel almost without knowing it, and the literary lie comes to be diffused as thoroughly in this work of a conscientious scholar as in that of the unrestrained compiler.

Nabokov draws the conclusion that the most one can hope to attain via the path of biography is a macabre doll. "Is it possible to imagine in its full reality the life of another, to relive it in oneself and transfer it intact to paper? I doubt it [for] it is only the verisimilar and not the true that our spirit and mind perceives."

Now, as it happens, Nabokov deftly turns on his own point ("I am well aware that this is not Pushkin, but a bad actor whom I pay to play his part. What does it matter! I enjoy myself playing this game, and I come to believe in it") and goes on to convey with some ardor the joys of losing oneself in even this ersatz world of Pushkin, which serves as a poorly painted backdrop for the only *real* Pushkin we can know — the literary one. For Nabokov this simple observation — that, in effect, the emperor has too many clothes, which are not really his anyway, and which prevent us from seeing him at times — is an article of faith that has been held longer and is more significant than his controversial latter-day view on the impossibility of poetic translation, which is, in essence, merely its further extension in regard to a related question.

The proper path for the biographer is the one that moves, with unflagging awareness, through the error-pocked maze of what has been written before, searching for certain "probable truths" but satisfied merely with marshaling all the versions at hand, in the hope that among them *may* be the true one, although we can never know which one it is. This Nabokov did in his remarkable "Abram Gannibal," a sixty-page appendix to his *Onegin* translation, which strives to assemble all the biographical information available on Pushkin's African great-grandfather, about whom comparatively little is known. Nabokov goes back to Ethiopian history and topography, Russian, French, and Islamic history, and languages as exotic as Tigré and Turkish. Two things are accomplished: Pushkin's own account of Gannibal is annihilated, and we get instead a biography that is a phantom centipede. Wholly founded on fact — "Abram Gannibal" would be an honors dissertation in any university — we are left in the end not even sure if Gannibal was dark-skinned. The study ends with certain marginal speculations, and, we are told, "there is nothing in the annals of Russian Pushkinology to restrain one from the elaboration of such fancies." But for all its brilliance, "Abram Gannibal" is finally a tour de force, made possible only by its subject's obscurity. The problem becomes much more difficult with a subject such as a writer, for whom the biographer has ample "givens."

Nabokov's last Russian novel, *The Gift* (1937), and his first one in English, *The Real Life of Sebastian Knight* (written in Paris in 1938), are both concerned in large degree with this very problem of biography. There are two major biographies in *The Gift* — one lyrical and the other hilarious and wholly unrestrained. The novel's hero is a poet, Fyodor Godunov-Cherdyntsev. A sentence about childhood desire from Pushkin, remembrance of how his father had found a rare species in a Petersburg park that he had just before discovered in Siberia, and "thus did he harken to the purest sound from Pushkin's tuning fork — and he already knew exactly what this sound required of him." Thus the biography of his father, a famous explorer and lepidopterist, is begun.

Godunov-Cherdyntsev gives us not a *real* biography of his father, but only the preliminary researches and gatherings that are to go into the biography. Often, however, the one masquerades as the other in the reader's mind, as when, for example, a long passage detailing his father's publications and expeditions (with interspersions of little personal asides) concludes: "Such is the general scheme of my father's life, copied out of an encyclopedia. It still does not sing, but I can already hear a living voice within it." These bare facts are not the narrative thread; they are merely the final string which is tied around the well-padlocked box, to be cut and discarded before opening. Fyodor considers the possibility of what it contains and questions whether or not he ought to pry. When he questions his mother, he receives a long letter that is the most evocative "piece of information" we receive about Fyodor's father (as well as one of the best passages in *The Gift*), but it poses certain problems. Is his mother's account itself to be read as "beautiful fiction"? The elder Godunov-Cherdyntsev *is* a colorful figure and a true eccentric, stories about whom literally permeate the Godunov-Cherdyntsev family, but can a biography — or a life, for that matter — really consist of anecdotes? When Fyodor's mother says: "Now I know that I was always happy, that that unhappiness was one of the colors of happiness," she tells us more about herself than about her husband, although that, too, is certainly not without importance. This personal coloration is still further stressed by the biographical account that Godunov-Cherdyntsev's fiancée, Zina Mertz, gives him about her own father "in a Proustian light."

Finally, Fyodor gives himself up to speculation about his father's inner nature (which would be a direct violation of Nabokov's Pushkin essay except that Godunov-Cherdyntsev is supposedly not actually committing his musings to paper), and a sad romantic image emerges: "It sometimes seems to me nowadays that — who knows — he might go off on his journeys not so much to seek something as to flee something, and that on returning, he would realize that it was still with him, inside him, unriddable, inexhaustible." These speculations, however, are not long sustained.

Fyodor soon passes to an even less palpable, but much more certain facet of his father — the tastes and mental attitudes that have been transferred to him as his son. These come not so much directly from his father as from daydreams in his absence, the presence all around him of thousands of books, and "the precious shimmer of the collections," all of which led him when he was a child to feel that his own travels were about to begin. Godunov-Cherdyntsev's only sure conclusion is that, whatever darkness may have surrounded his father and been transuded to other members of the family, still "our life . . . really was imbued with a magic unknown in other families." This magic, analogous to that famous "certain little something" that Tolstoy called the essential element in all true art, is perfectly conveyed by Fyodor's preliminary musings, which skirt but never fall into the "family sentimentality" that his mother cautioned him against, and thus his biography attains the level of true poetry.

Fyodor conjures up a Siberian expedition at great length and completely effaces the line between himself and his father, but this is art, not life. Immediately after the long Siberian digression, "it shifted and dispersed — and Fyodor saw again the dead and impossible tulips of his wallpaper, the crumbling mound of cigarette butts in the ashtray, and the lamp's reflection in the black windowpane." This abrupt return from (another) reality — a reality attained by means of Fyodor's powerful imagination and his readings of gifted naturalists such as Grum-Grzhimaylo, which supply many of the beautiful descriptive passages in the novel — establishes the great distance between Fyodor's aesthetic demands upon himself and the factual requirements of biography that will finally make the project unattainable. For as he progresses, he sees ever more clearly that "approximate knowledge" gleaned from "hearsay or out of books" cannot be saved by means of "secondary poetization," and he fears that he will wear out the little that he has managed to liberate from the past in the course of the transfer onto paper.

Thus what seems to the reader to be the very fragrance of success is to Fyodor the deceptive perfume of impossibility. Fyodor Godunov-Cherdyntsev is the most sympathetic and subtle of all Nabokov's creations, and thanks to Fyodor's biography-that-is-not-a-biography, his father emerges as only slightly less forceful a fictional presence.

Fyodor's "failure" lays the foundation for the biography that he will write, but not about his father. His experience does not convince him that it is impossible to write a satisfactory biography. It merely points the way toward an artistic metaphrase of the sorry genre, a new form of biography wholly independent of "facts" and responsible only to the poet's muse. This path is prefigured by an account that Fyodor unearths about his grandfather Kirill Ilyich, who had lived outside of Russia for many years and who was fooled by some mischievous boys on his return into thinking that Pushkin was still alive. The joke backfires when a sixty-year-old man in a theater audience *becomes* Pushkin, "in the rich autumn of his genius," in the imagination of one of the little pranksters (the future memoirist). And as the uncompleted biography of his father furnishes the theoretical justification, so this little episode of creative fantasy furnishes the seed which will blossom in Chapter Four of the novel into the singularly extraordinary biography of the famous Russian social figure of the nineteenth century, Nikolai Chernyshevsky. In a very real sense then, the two chapters, however dissimilar they may seem, really represent a single, parabolic line, arching out over the amusing "literary criticism" of Chapter Three.

Chernyshevsky is an unexpected choice for a poet of Godunov-Cherdyntsev's literary sensitivity, but it has its own logic. Godunov-Cherdyntsev is first attracted by the chasm between Chernyshevsky's turgid prose and the exalted place assigned him in Russian literature by Russian literary critics. The fictional Fyodor Godunov-Cherdyntsev and (the semi-fictional) Nikolai Chernyshevsky represent the two hostile lines in the history of modern Russian culture. And the young poet's execution of his task marks the shift of the offensive to the artist — "Firing practice," says Fyodor when he is questioned about his choice of subject — a shift long overdue after more than a century of abuse at the hands of the "utilitarian criticists." (Besides Chernyshevsky, other prominent Russian "criticists" — a term that I am forced to invent for want of a suitable English word that falls between "criticaster" and "critic" — are Belinsky, Dobroliubov, Polevoi, Nadezhdin, Mikhailovsky, and Pisarev.)

It is highly unlikely that the revered Chernyshevsky will ever be the same again — a fact underscored by the astounding refusal of the editors of the liberal émigré journal *Sovremennye zapiski* (*Contemporary Annals*) to print that portion of *The Gift* dealing with him, when the novel was serialized there. The novel appeared in only four chapters, but with the notation "a novel in five chapters."

Contemporary Annals was the most prominent émigré journal, and Nabokov was one of its three or four most frequent contributors. Among the other Nabokov works which appeared there are *The Defense, The Eye, The Exploit, Camera obscura, Despair, Invitation to a Beheading,* and many short stories. A traditional Russian "thick journal" in form, *Contemporary Annals* managed to avoid the political factionalism that one associated with such journals in prerevolutionary times. It also was consistently far more lively than the old stolidly estimable thick journals such as *Russian Thought*. A prominent émigré political figure was certainly right when he said that the existence of such a journal in the emigration and one that was a mouthpiece for no political party was almost an eighth wonder of the world. Every émigré writer, poet, and critic of any note at all appeared in the pages of *Contemporary Annals* during its twenty-year existence, and it must be considered one of the essential basic documents of modern Russian culture. The deletion of the Chernyshevsky chapter by *Annals* editor Mark Vishnyak demonstrates that there was a limit to the liberalism and sophistication of that journal, perhaps merely a faithful reflection of the Russian intellectual's propensity for clay idols.

For many non-Russian readers certainly the lampoon will be a first introduction to Chernyshevsky and thus totally eclipse the traditional biography. Therefore, there is perhaps a need, whether to better appreciate the lampoon or for the sake of "fairness," to set down this now obsolete biography as it is usually presented in encyclopedias and literary histories.

Nikolai Gavrilovich Chernyshevsky died, after a two-day illness, of a brain hemorrhage, during the night of October 16 (Old Style dating), 1889, in bed, in the town of Saratov, in which he had been born sixty-two years before, and to which he had returned only in June from Astrakhan, the farthest point west he had been permitted to come after his Siberian exile. To cite the famous pre-revolutionary Brockhaus-Efron Encyclopedic Dictionary in eighty-six volumes (Chernyshevsky loved encyclopedias and imposing collected works and spent a considerable portion of his life translating them — he was two thirds of the way through Volume XII of Weber when death came): "His death had a significant effect towards returning him to his proper place. The press of various political shades paid him the tribute of respect for his extremely broad and strikingly multi-faceted knowledgeability, his brilliant literary talent, and the extraordinary beauty of his moral character." The Brockhaus-Efron eulogy is also useful for its demonstration of the unquestionable effect that Chernyshevsky did have on the critical rhetoric of the second half of the nineteenth century. The very way in which it is formulated is an echo of Chernyshevsky's customary tone of voice as he praised Tolstoy for his "extraordinary purity of moral feeling," Grigorovich for his "knowledge and love of the people," and so forth.

The marked moral coloration in Chernyshevsky's writings is usually traced back to his childhood, when it was expected that he would follow his father ("a man noteworthy for his striking goodness and nobility") into the priesthood. His schoolmates had "worshipped him." Many years later one of his childhood teachers wrote that as a boy Chernyshevsky had had "a very pure soul," but that he had been seduced by Western European ideas and was "a fallen angel."

And Chernyshevsky's most important role was, in fact, as nineteenth-century Russia's chief importer and adapter of European theories. From John Stuart Mill he took his utilitarianism; in 1846 he entered St. Petersburg University, where he became a Utopian Socialist or Fourierist (except that, unlike Fourier, Chernyshevsky attached great importance to national political questions, and he was indifferent to religion); and, out of dissatisfaction with the inadequacies of the 1861 reform freeing all of Russia's twenty million serfs, he became a Revolutionary Socialist, on the model this time of Louis Blanc. Although his revolutionary stance was, in effect, nothing more than that, tolerance for all extremist politics at this time in Russia was very low in view of what most people felt to be the substantial progress that had been made in 1861 — two years before slavery was abolished in America. The provocative and influential journal that Chernyshevsky edited, *The Contemporary*, was closed down for eight months by government decree in May, 1862, and the following month Chernyshevsky was arrested and sent to Petropavlosk Prison, where he remained for two years. The Senate sentenced him to fourteen years (political prisoners at that time were not made to do hard labor), but this was shortened to seven.

Chernyshevsky's arrest was, really, a symbolic act. His misdeeds were more properly socialist than revolutionary, although it should be kept in mind that mention of socialism then often provoked the same passions that communism was to evoke in the twentieth century. Hard as one searches, Chernyshevsky's misdeeds were no more serious than his goading of Aleksandr Herzen into publishing sharper and sharper articles in his London émigré magazine *The Bell* and his giving Herzen false information wholly misrepresenting the social atmosphere in Russia (these being the accusations of Chernyshevsky's well-known liberal foe Chicherin). But we should not paint too dark a picture of Russian liberal shortsightedness and temper. For one thing, the proper solution to the problem of permissible limitations to civil liberties has yet to be found in practice, and, for another, a year after he was imprisoned the government permitted a second edition of his 1855 St. Petersburg Master's Essay *The Aesthetic Relations of Art to Reality*, though the author's name was not allowed to be printed on the book. Also, there were liberal elements which, although opposed to Chernyshevsky and his journal politically, strongly protested the arrest.

A few words on Chernyshevsky's thought: the substance of *Aesthetic Relations* is that nature is higher than art, and that true beauty can be found only in nature or, the next best thing, in its faithful reflection in art. His next book, *Studies of the Age of Gogol*, is a boldly ventured historical survey of a period that was still very close at hand. The book is notable not for any of its literary judgments, but for its open call for civically oriented criticism and for the importance which he ascribes to his radical predecessor Vissarion Belinsky, whose name had slipped from public view during a period of reactionary dominance. After 1857 he concentrated primarily on social and economic questions. The commune, in Chernyshevsky's eyes, was the means by which the peasants could be saved from turning into proletarians. When, as a result of his revolutionary proclamations, he was imprisoned, his name fell from print just as Belinsky's had before him. Occasionally he would be referred to, but only as "the author of *Studies of the Age of Gogol.*"

It was while he was in prison that Chernyshevsky wrote his famous radical novel *What Is To Be Done?* whose hero Rakhmetov is an idealized and forceful radical of populist persuasion. As a novel *What Is To Be Done?* is generally acknowledged to be weak, but the author forestalls this complaint by disclaiming any artistic talent or intent (these asides are not without a certain charm), and the historian can claim that, in comparison with *other* novels of this sub-genre, *What Is To Be Done?* is indeed a work of major stature. Certainly there can be no question of its enormous influence on Russian radical thought. Chernyshevsky's intellectual and literary shortcomings, frequently contrasted with the gifts of his protégé Nikolai Dobroliubov, were taken into consideration by others before Nabokov (there is, for example, an excellent deprecation of him written by, of all people, the Marxist Plekhanov). But the final estimate in almost all cases is that Chernyshevsky was, as Karl Marx wrote in *Das Kapital,* "a great Russian scholar and critic who brilliantly revealed the bankruptcy of bourgeois economy."

Nabokov's Fyodor Godunov-Cherdyntsev begins his biography with a fragment of a sonnet — his own, but perhaps an imitation of Pushkin's friend Delvig — that denies the possibility of historical science:

> *Alas! In vain historians pry and probe:*
> *The same wind blows, and in the same live robe*
> *Truth bends her head to fingers curved cupwise;*
>
> *And with a woman's smile and a child's care*
> *Examines something she is holding there*
> *Concealed by her own shoulder from our eyes.*

These lines furnish the "secret link" through which the truth of art can replace that of history. Chernyshevsky's father and little Nikolya himself are made to emerge from the pages of history by means of artistic incantation. The poet's incantations play against other historians' accounts rather than turning directly to the personages themselves: "As is invariably noted at the beginning of positively all literary biographies, the little boy was a glutton for books."

Godunov-Cherdyntsev utilizes "facts," to be sure, but with the important difference that *his* facts are the ones which are frequently bypassed. Instead of selecting Chernyshevsky's reverential statements about Pushkin and Tolstoy, Godunov-Cherdyntsev finds quotations much less flattering that show Chernyshevsky in quite a different light — for example, sycophantically flattering Turgenev at the expense of Tolstoy to get him as a contributor to *The Contemporary*, and then insulting Turgenev, too, when he has a falling out with him. A major portion of Nabokov's (Godunov-Cherdyntsev's) "ammunition" comes from the three-volume Soviet *Literary Heritage* (1928–1930), which contains a greal deal of intimate material, including diaries. "His diary, particularly for the summer and autumn of 1849, contains a multitude of most exact references as to how and where he vomited." The public, heroic Chernyshevsky cannot long withstand the evidence of his personal life in which he is humiliated by his wife (Pushkin, we are reminded, handled a very similar situation much better), and he shows himself to be an absurdly nearsighted idealist and bumbler.

Midway through his biography the poet confidently declares: "The motifs of Chernyshevsky's life are now obedient to me — I have tamed its themes, they have become accustomed to my pen; with a smile I let them go." What had been merely a certain playfulness after the manner of Sterne ("Look how this theme takes advantage of a momentary lack of attention and blossoms out. Halt, roll up again. There is, in fact, no need to go so far ahead") gradually becomes full poetic license in the deepest sense of the term. As collaborator in his fantasy biography, the poet furthermore invents a previous biographer named Strannolyubsky (Strangelove) through whom many of the "invented facts" are

introduced and who is at times a foil ("It seems to us that Strannolyubsky is stretching it a bit").

In Godunov-Cherdyntsev's book Chernyshevsky is symbolically
executed when the gendarmes manage only to break an insufficiently incised sword over his neck, but finally, under a shower of
bouquets tossed by the crowd, Chernyshevsky is released and
withdraws from the execution as though it were a Punch and Judy
show: "He thrust his head out of the window, laughed and shook
his finger at the most zealous runners." But the execution is in one
sense not mockery, for it comes at the apogee of Chernyshevsky's
public career, and Godunov-Cherdyntsev quite rightly asks:
"How could one not prefer the death penalty . . . to that funeral
which twenty-five insipid years later fell to Chernyshevsky's lot,"
and which Godunov-Cherdyntsev then proceeds to describe.

Obviously, almost everything about Chernyshevsky is diametri-
cally opposed to Nabokov and his hero. Chernyshevsky's views on
art, butterflies, his (mis)understanding of poetry, his inability to
master foreign languages, his unrestrained and voluminous translation, his failure to tell flowers apart — all this cannot but evoke a
disdainful smile from Vladimir Nabokov — is ridiculed with gay
and delicate savagery:

How poor he was, how dirty and sloppy, how far removed from the
lure of luxury . . . Attention! This was not so much proletarian
chastity as the natural disregard with which an ascetic treats the
prickle of a permanent hair shirt or the bite of sedentary fleas. Even a
hair shirt, however, has at times to be repaired. We are present when
the inventive Nikolai Gavrilovich contemplates darning his old
trousers: he turned out to have no black thread, so what there was he
undertook to soak in ink; an anthology of German verse was lying
nearby, open at the beginning of William Tell. As a result of his
waving the thread about (in order to dry it), several drops of ink fell
on the page; the book did not belong to him. He found a lemon in a
paper bag behind the window and attempted to get the blots out, but
he only succeeded in dirtying the lemon, plus the windowsill where he
had left the pernicious thread. Then he sought the aid of a knife and
began to scrape (this book with the punctured poem is now in the
Leipzig University Library; unfortunately it has not been possible to
ascertain how it got there). Ink, indeed, was the natural element of

Chernyshevsky (he literally bathed in it) who used to smear with it the cracks in his shoes when he was out of shoe polish.

This hilarious passage continues on for a page or so. Its keystone is the book in the Leipzig University Library, a "fact" which effectively subverts any possibility of serious intent — or malice. For it is striking to note how very many of *The Gift*'s most enthusiastic critics have spoken of the author's sympathy, in spite of all, for Chernyshevsky. Perhaps. After thoroughly ridiculing *What Is To Be Done?* the narrator confesses: "And nevertheless it is impossible to handle this old magazine (March, 1863), containing the first installment of the novel, without a certain thrill . . ." Nabokov's own grandfather, Dmitri Nikolaevich Nabokov, was the Russian Minister of Justice who acted on Chernyshevsky's petition to be transferred to Astrakhan (in the same way, a Pushkin appears briefly in *Boris Godunov*), and Fyodor Godunov-Cherdyntsev has a fictional connection with him through his friendship with the Chernyshevsky family in Berlin. Whatever bricks are aimed at Chernyshevsky are, by and large, real bricks, not invented ones, and there are many which could have been used but were not.

In the end, Nabokov's (or Godunov-Cherdyntsev's) attitude toward Chernyshevsky is of only minor import. What matters is the tension that this irreverent life establishes with the other, more conventional lives. By means of a revolutionary overthrow of the basic premises of the art of biography, the revolutionary criticist has been made to live. Although there have been scores of biographers, Chernyshevsky has not been blessed with good ones (in a sense every public figure chooses his own biographers), and the best of them is probably the Marxist Steklov, who is cited many times in the course of Godunov-Cherdyntsev's work. It is, I submit, difficult not to grant that the most outstanding biography of Nikolai Chernyshevsky is precisely the one that Fyodor Godunov-Cherdyntsev has written.

The biographical chapter closes with the first portion of a sonnet, the sestet of which began the chapter. It speculates on what Chernyshevsky's future biographer will say of him, and whereas the sonnet's conclusion stresses the inaccessibility to the historian of the sought object, the initial portion hints that the "dry work" of Chernyshevsky has been redeemed through the miraculous power of art. Thus Fyodor Godunov-Cherdyntsev, flying in the face of everything Chernyshevsky stood for, saves him from the dust pile of history and his own prose.

Several years later, this problem, which occupies such a major place in *The Gift*, became the subject of an entire novel — the first one written by Nabokov in English — *The Real Life of Sebastian Knight*. It is perhaps the weakest of Nabokov's longer works written after 1931, and in a foreword to the Russian version of his memoirs, *Other Shores*, he refers to the "unbearable imperfections" he now sees in *The Real Life of Sebastian Knight*. That judgment is surely unduly harsh — one should recall the high esteem in which the novel was held by such writers as Howard Nemerov and Flannery O'Connor — but *The Real Life of Sebastian Knight* is the only longer work by Nabokov that can be reduced to a single "idea," and it is hard not to notice certain awkwardnesses in the novel.

The research for and composition of the life of Sebastian Knight is undertaken shortly after his death by his half brother, and the novel is almost wholly concerned with that effort. The narrator — identified only as "V" — has had very little contact with his half brother since their childhood. But perhaps this very distance enables V to avoid the constraints of closeness that caused Godunov-Cherdyntsev to abandon his biography of his father. The impetus behind the biography, V informs us, is the life-long affection that he felt for Sebastian and his writing but somehow never expressed. V self-consciously informs us that his mastery of English is unsure (he registers in a writing course to prepare for his task!), but he has an even greater understanding of the nature and dangers of the biographer's task than did Godunov-Cherdyntsev. "Beware of the most honest broker. Remember that what you are told is really threefold; shaped by the teller, reshaped by the listener, concealed from both by the dead man of the tale." This caveat is as necessary to the reader as it is to the biographer, for the line that separates the biographer from his subject is often all but impossible to perceive. In one chapter in *The Real Life of Sebastian Knight* the narrator, with the token help of a certain P. G. Sheldon, conveys with sure hand the inner feelings and motivations of both Sebastian and his mistress Clare. Is it possible that *The Real Life of Sebastian Knight* is not a biography at all, but a fictional autobiography, another of Knight's own novels? It is more than possible.

If we allow Sebastian the fictional freedom needed to fill out the novel and have the trick "work," such an understanding can find considerable justification. The conclusion of the novel, for example, seems to be a clear confession by the author that his biography, to paraphrase the by-now trite formula, contains real people in an imaginary story: "The end, the end. They all go back to their everyday life (and Clare goes back to her grave) — but the hero remains, for, try as I may, I cannot get out of my part: Sebastian's mask clings to my face, the likeness will not be washed off. I am Sebastian, or Sebastian is I, or perhaps we both are someone whom neither of us knows." It has been stressed, as a major motif in Sebastian Knight's art, that "the only real number is one, the rest are mere repetition," and this dictum serves very nicely to reduce the fraction of the half brothers to a single, whole unit.

There are occasional trick mirror reflections which, if we catch them, lead us from descriptions of Sebastian Knight's books back into the novel *The Real Life of Sebastian Knight*. In Knight's story *The Back of the Moon* there is a little man waiting for a train who helps three travelers in three different ways, and subsequently V is aided in his research for *The Real Life of Sebastian Knight* by an extraordinary little man he meets on a train who acts as his private detective and, after some burlesque arithmetic, returns his tiny twenty-franc fee. The plot précis that V provides of Knight's *Prismatic Bezel*, a parody of a detective novel, tells us the book is about a murder, but that just before the stereotyped cockney Holmes is about to unmask the murderer, a character named Nosebag steps forward to remove his wig and dark spectacles, revealing that he is the supposed victim, G. Abeson. ("Nosebag," of course, is an anagram of G. Abeson.) Similarly, in one of the most fanciful flights of *The Real Life of Sebastian Knight*, the noted author is lying spread-eagled on the floor of his study, only to announce from the floor: "I'm not dead. I have finished building a world, and this is my Sabbath rest."

This deceit is abetted by the presence of a hilarious distraction in the person of Mr. Goodman, the author of a rival biography of Knight. Goodman was Knight's secretary for a time, until (according to V) Knight gave him the sack for changing the epigraph to one of his works. He is demolished together with his absurd book, *The Tragedy of Sebastian Knight:* "A black mask covered his face . . . Mr. Goodman's large soft pinkish face was, and is, remarkably like a cow's udder." The excerpts from Goodman's biography and the critical praise it receives are even more riotous than the critical parodies in *The Gift.* But there is this to bear in mind: the lugubrious Goodman serves by way of contrast to lend an air of restraint and seriousness to V's own work, or, to put the same thing another way, Goodman may be one means by which the artist is helped to assume the *appearance* of biographer. The novel's most intriguing moment is a dream that V has in which he sees Sebastian with a black glove on his left hand. Sebastian undoes the glove, and "as it came off, it spilt its only contents — a number of tiny hands, like the front paws of a mouse, mauve-pink and soft — lots of them — and they dropped to the floor." *The Real Life of Sebastian Knight* repeatedly bares its devices, but this dream quite literally bares the hand of the "dream-manager" whose deceit is founded on this very device. V is, I submit, one of those little hands of Sebastian Knight.

The Real Life of Sebastian Knight purports to be a critical biography, and the similarities between Knight's imaginary works and Nabokov's real ones are striking. The fact that Knight demonstrably is an important writer (as Conrad Brenner has noted, the plots of Sebastian Knight's novels have the feeling of Nabokov rejects, "but he writes like an angel"), and one with a close affinity to Nabokov, causes the book to veer from biography toward — but not to — autobiography. There are several clues that tend to corroborate this interaction. There are Shakespearean echoes in the characters' given names, but V, of course, might well stand for Vladimir.

V's critical remarks, however, evoke Nabokov's writing without any need of such substantiation. The following excerpt, for example, is as good as any capsule judgment we have of Nabokov's prose:

As often was the way with Sebastian Knight he used parody as a kind of springboard for leaping into the highest region of serious emotion. J. L. Coleman has called it "a clown developing wings, an angel mimicking a tumbler pigeon," and the metaphor seems to me very apt. Based cunningly on a parody of certain tricks of the literary trade, *The Prismatic Bezel* soars skyward. With something akin to fanatical hate Sebastian Knight was ever hunting out the things which had once been fresh and bright but which were now worn to a thread, dead things among living ones; dead things shamming life, painted and repainted, continuing to be accepted by lazy minds serenely unaware of the fraud . . . *The Prismatic Bezel* can be thoroughly enjoyed once it is understood that the heroes of the book are what can be loosely called "methods of composition." It is as if a painter said: Look, here I'm going to show you not the painting of a landscape, but the painting of different ways of painting a certain landscape, and I trust their harmonious fusion will disclose the landscape as I intend you to see it.

Such auto-criticism made its first appearance in Nabokov's writing in 1927 in a Russian story, *The Passenger*, in which the narrator discusses his artistic manner with a critic. It is thereafter more and more forcefully developed as a theme, particularly in *The Gift*, until it reaches its fullest expression in *The Real Life of Sebastian Knight*. Auto-criticism, it is true, may be found prior to Nabokov. In 1913 Shaw despaired of the inanity of his critics and reviewed one of his own plays under a pseudonym, and Poe wrote about himself in his essay, *The Philosophy of Composition;* more recent auto-critics are Auden and Tate. But such criticism is usually given in separate essays and reviews devoted to the relatively simple task of explication. Nabokov, however, not only "explains" but also *evaluates* his own writing, and he does this as a function of that very writing.

Nineteenth-century Romanticism gave us the artist as prophet and seer. But with all the priestly powers of his art there was one thing the seer was not allowed to see: his own writing which, implicitly or explicitly, was supposed to come to him "from above." This reverence for the artist-as-priest has declined markedly in post-Symbolist literature and literary criticism of this century, but such an attractive article of faith held for over a century dies hard. Nabokov rejects the role of priest, and he claims no more and no less for his art than is customarily granted to music, sculpture, and painting (when he was a child it was expected he would become a painter) — freedom from the sandwich-board message imposed on or willingly worn by many writers. This attitude toward the art of writing does two things. First, it means that the novel or poem itself, rather than society or some "true understanding," acquires greater significance. And the artist, too, becomes more important in a sense, even though he has forfeited his prophetic powers. For he is the sole creator of his art, and consequently also the best critic of what he has created. Art returns to its original Greek meaning.

Even if one accepts the premises of such a position — and its logic is compelling — there still remains that most awkward problem of "modesty." This one potential obstacle to the artist's freedom of expression can be surmounted only by applying a stricter standard to oneself than do any of one's secondary critics. Nabokov has never, to my knowledge, "ranked" himself against the great masters, either in print or in private conversation; he has merely accepted the fact (and why not?) that he *is* a major artist, and not someone who writes "superb and important" books and poems on "problems of the day." In *The Gift* Godunov-Cher-dyntsev reads an unflattering review of another poet, "and when Fyodor realized the infinitely flattering hostility of this article he felt disappointed that no one wrote about *him* like that." In due time Godunov-Cherdyntsev receives an ample supply of just such reviews of his "biography," and they state the most recurrent objections to Nabokov's own art as forcefully as one could wish: "It seems to me — and I am not alone in feeling this — that at the bottom of Godunov-Cherdyntsev's book there lies something which is in essence profoundly tactless, something jarring and offensive [having] a certain arrogant audacity that is bound to repel even the most well-disposed of readers."

Of greater interest and more to the point are the imaginary conversations Fyodor has with another poet, Koncheyev, whom Nabokov has acknowledged to be, in part, "one of my literary impersonators." Fyodor questions Koncheyev about the defects Koncheyev sees in Fyodor's art and imagines the following response:

First, an excessive trust in words. It sometimes happens that your words in order to introduce the necessary thought have to smuggle it in. The sentence may be excellent, but still it is smuggling, and, moreover, gratuitous smuggling, since the lawful road is open . . . you sometimes bring up parody to such a degree of naturalness that it actually becomes a genuine serious thought, but on *this* level it suddenly falters, lapsing into a mannerism that is yours and not a parody of a mannerism . . . One observes in one or two of your transitions something mechanical, if not automatic, which suggest you are pursuing *your own* advantage, and taking the course you find easier . . . and finally, you sometimes say things chiefly calculated to prick your contemporaries, but any woman will tell you that nothing gets lost so easily as a hairpin.

Koncheyev sums up by saying that the real writer thinks only of the future reader, who in the end is synonymous with himself. As if to underscore this autonomy of the artist as both creator and critic, Nabokov steps into *The Gift* in yet another character. But whereas Godunov-Cherdyntsev and Koncheyev are each only partial representations of Nabokov, this character, Vladimirov, is the only clear and acknowledged autobiographical character in all of Nabokov's fiction. Vladimirov's appearance is brief, yet he is depicted only slightly less coldly and "ruthlessly" than any of Nabokov's satirized victims:

Beneath his jacket he was wearing an English sports sweater with a black-and-orange border along its triangular opening; the receding hair on either side of his forehead exaggerated the latter's dimensions, his large nose was strongly boned, his grayish-yellow teeth glistened unpleasantly beneath his slightly raised lip and his eyes looked out with intelligence and indifference — he had studied, it seemed, at an English university and flaunted a pseudo-British manner. At twenty-nine he was already the author of two novels — outstanding for the force and swiftness of their mirror-like style — which irritated Fyodor perhaps for the very reason that he felt a certain affinity with him. As a conversationalist Vladimirov was singularly unattractive. One blamed him for being derisive, supercilious, cold, incapable of thawing to friendly discussions — but that was also said about Koncheyev and about Fyodor himself, and about anyone whose thoughts lived in their own private house and not in a barrack-room or pub.

Thus does biography reveal itself to be only a preamble or flimsy backdrop to criticism. The man's written words are all we have in the end, and they cannot be put to biographical use without resulting in fiction of a lower order.

And, even more important, we should remember that the artist's words may sometimes have a truly startling distance from his own life. A case in point is the delightful 1944 Nabokov story, *A Forgotten Poet*, in which a comical old man causes a "regrettable incident" by appearing at a memorial reading for a poet who had been thought to have drowned many years ago. He claims he is that poet, with the result that he is scorned by those who have come to revere him. Or, to take an even better example, there is the example of the well-known foreign author of a certain best-seller that was proclaimed "repulsive," "exquisitely distilled sewage," and "a provocation to rape and murder," whose marriage to the same woman since 1925 has become something of a legend among those who know them for its uncommon closeness and mutual devotion. In each case the "biography" that has been constructed by and in the public mind is the spurious one — and the one which truth evidently cannot disturb.

Two

⚘ ⚘ ⚘ ⚘

IT is fitting, then, that the "real" Vladimir Nabokov be left as a minor character, showing only intermittently in his writing. Nabokov has managed to make his private self all but invisible, moving from Cambridge to Berlin, to Paris, to the United States, to Montreux, and never leaving more than a puzzled shrug for his potential memoirists. "You will die in dreadful pain and complete isolation," remarked Ivan Bunin after a lunch in which the young Nabokov had steadfastly refused to be drawn into a "heart-to-heart" talk, and, in the same way, one of his colleagues at Cornell who knew him better than most, Arthur Mizener, when asked to comment on Nabokov's years at that university, could say only: "Nabokov never got too close to anybody." The writer's role is that of God to his Art, and, depending upon how one wishes to see God in Nature, he is either seen in his ludicrous "surreptitious peeps and circumlocutions" (the words belong to an atheistic character in one of Nabokov's later novels) or he is a force present at all times but never seen. "Private life" seems somehow out of place. With this in mind, I shall nonetheless venture to collect and comment on some biographical odds and ends in this and later chapters to provide a minimal *mise-en-scène* that will hopefully not be as obtrusive as the traditional chair and stepladder.

Nabokov, of course, has written his autobiography. Or rather, his autobiographies: *Conclusive Evidence* in 1951 (later changed to *Speak, Memory*), which, save for the one French chapter already mentioned, was written in English in chapters that appeared in *The New Yorker, The Atlantic Monthly, Partisan*

Review, and *Harper's,* and were then expanded for the book. Then, in 1954, the Russian version, *Other Shores,* which is not an actual translation, but a close rewriting with many changes and additions; and finally, in 1966, a new expanded version of *Speak, Memory* which more closely resembles *Other Shores,* but has many new things in it, too. A brief Author's Note affirms that "this account of the author's European past is as truthful as he could possibly make it. If there are any lapses, they are due to the frailty of memory, not to the trickery of art." Although this is perfectly true, the many transmutations of the autobiography show there is more that may be said, and I would argue the proposition that *Speak, Memory* is all the same a work of art; it is merely the one Nabokov work in which the narrative course is given, not invented.

The past is not searched out. It is, rather, carefully selected — the changing form may be likened to breathing — and poetically fixed: "The cradle rocks above an abyss, and common sense tells us that our existence is but a brief crack of light between two eternities of darkness. Although the two are identical twins, man, as a rule, views the prenatal abyss with more calm than the one he is heading for (at some forty-five hundred heart beats an hour)." Carefully drawn descriptive passages are present on almost every page, but even in the simple description of a room the evocation of its poetic aura takes precedence over the simple description, which is given as an afterthought ("Some more about that room, please"). Certainly the "facts" are the least important elements in the following whimsical vignette:

Then somebody gave us another pup whose grandparents had been Dr. Anton Chekhov's Quina and Brom. This final dachshund (one of my few connections with the main current of Russian literature) followed us into exile, and as late as 1930, in a suburb of Prague (where my widowed mother spent her last years on a small pension provided by the Czech government), he could be still seen going for reluctant walks with his mistress, waddling far behind in a huff, tremendously old and furious with his long Czech muzzle of wire — an émigré dog in a patched and ill-fitting coat.

Nabokov's splendid disregard for the mundane obligations of the memoirist is shown by the fact that he does not name his brothers and sisters, and, until the 1966 edition of *Speak, Memory*, he did not even say how many he had. (There were, for the record, five Nabokov children: Vladimir born in 1899, Sergei 1900–45, Olga born in 1903 and Elena in 1906, and Kirill 1911–64. Sergei died in a German concentration camp. The youngest brother Kirill published occasional poetry with an unmistakably "Nabokovian" ring in such émigré journals as *The Will of Russia*.) Nabokov's aim is evocation, not the mere reproduction of facts, and his autobiography shows how "free" the autobiographer may be without ever stepping over into *belles lettres*. Nabokov is concerned with the inner world of his childhood, and the world of childhood is composed of fantasy, shadows, and colors. This world is wholly recreated in *Speak, Memory*, a work not inferior to the best Nabokov has written, although peculiarly impervious to what we call "critical commentary." The autobiography has been criticized for its "sentimentality," but Nabokov has succeeded in conveying in cool words the most difficult subject any writer could face — a happy childhood. He sees himself, in his own words, "with interest, with amusement, seldom with admiration or disgust."

One of the most striking "facts" — and the one which it would be most vulgar and coy to conceal or attempt to gloss over — about Nabokov's childhood is the extraordinary opulence in which he grew up. The combination of culture and wealth — during his childhood the young Nabokov inherited two million dollars from an uncle — in the Nabokov family may only be approximated by analogy with similar American families — the Cabots, for example, do not really come close enough in either category — and Nabokov's own attitude toward this wealth — the fifty servants, the mansions, and the elaborate trips abroad — of his childhood is quite singular. He was, in his younger years, oblivious of it, and then, when he was slightly older, resentful of the implication conveyed to him at the "progressive" Tenishev School to which he was sent that there was something unclean about this wealth: "With his face all screwed up in a grimace of disgust, one teacher suggested to me that the least I could do was to have the automobile stop two or three blocks away, so that my schoolmates might be spared the sight of a liveried chauffeur doffing his cap. It was as if the school were allowing me to carry about a dead rat by the tail with the understanding that I would not dangle it under people's noses."

There is a brief passage in *Speak, Memory* in which Nabokov steps downstage for a moment to speak "not for the general reader, but for the particular idiot who, because he has lost a fortune in some crash, thinks he understands me," and declares his complete contempt for those who "hate the Reds" because of lost privilege. Culture is something which *may* accompany wealth, but there is certainly no organic link between the two, and the more frequent occurrence is Philistinism accentuated to a ludicrous degree precisely by wealth.

The detachment of culture from all such base considerations is the basic theme of a 1936 story, *The Circle*, which seems to be a discarded fragment of *The Gift* since it concerns the Godunov-Cherdyntsev family. The story, as its very title indicates, turns in a circle just like Fyodor's Chernyshevsky biography which opens with the end of a sonnet and closes with its beginning. The very first words of *The Circle* are: "In the second place, because a violent longing for Russia had come over him." (Later, James Joyce used the same device in *Finnegan's Wake*.)

The protagonist of the story, Innokenty Bychkov, is the son of a former schoolteacher of the Godunov-Cherdyntsev family in Russia. Bychkov remembers his past with self-pity and class hatred, and this is heightened by the attraction he felt toward young Tanya, Fyodor's sister. Years later the situation has changed radically—the Godunov-Cherdyntsevs have lost their wealth and are living in Paris, where Bychkov, now a successful academic, meets Fyodor and Tanya's mother by chance. When he goes to their apartment, he is shocked by the calm manner in which they discuss the past, and when Tanya's husband returns home she goes to the next room to tell him that "*le fils du maître d'école chez nous au village*" has come to pay them a visit, just as, in their childhood, Bychkov had overheard her speaking about him in French to a girlfriend. Somehow or other the conversation between them remains awkward, and when Elizaveta Pavlovna begins to tell him about her son Fyodor who is living in Berlin, Bychkov gets up and says he must leave. His legs are trembling, and this is because he realizes that the Godunov-Cherdyntsevs have been essentially untouched by the caprices of history, while he has remained a prisoner of his own past. As the story concludes, the circle is closed: "And he was uneasy for several reasons. In the first place, because Tanya had turned out to be just as attractive, just as invulnerable as she had been in the old days."

Consciousness of his own, rather different, "apartness" seems to have been present in Nabokov from a very early age, and later he speaks of himself as "born to be a goalkeeper." But at the same time, he insists upon his normalcy, that is, the puerility which is, after all, the proper accompaniment of everyone's childhood. As it happens, Nabokov's juvenile verse was published in book form prior to the 1917 Revolution. (This was a custom not at all uncommon among wealthy young children of the time.) It was long assumed that both these books had perished, but one, titled simply *Poems* and printed in 1916, has survived, and if I now devote more space to these poems than they merit, that is, of course, because of their enormous historical interest and also because these poems and a few surviving photographs of the young Nabokov included in the 1966 edition of *Speak, Memory* are all that we have to hold up against his autobiography. The reflection is undisturbed.

Nabokov describes the composition of his very first poem during the summer of 1914 in the following manner:

What touched it off? I think I know. Without any wind blowing, the sheer weight of a raindrop, shining in parasitic luxury on a cordate leaf, caused its tip to dip, and what looked like a globule of quicksilver performed a sudden glissando down the center vein, and then, having shed its bright load, the relieved leaf unbent. Tip, leaf, dip, relief — the instant it all took to happen seemed to me not so much a fraction of time as a fissure in it, a missed heartbeat, which was refunded to me at once by a patter of rhymes.

That, of course, is not the poem, but a description of its composition, itself a poem, by the mature artist. On the actual poems he wrote at this age Nabokov is quite frank:

I find it difficult to accept as authentic the recollection of my versifying at a time when I really had no inkling of what it was all about . . . A naïve beginner, I fell into all the traps laid by the singing epithet.

Not that I did not struggle [but] it did not occur to me then that far from being a veil, [my] poor words were so opaque that, in fact, they formed a wall in which all one could distinguish were the well-worn bits of the major and minor poets I imitated.

The specific ingredients of this "miserable concoction" ranged from pseudo-Pushkinian to genuine Apukhtinian (a parlor poet of the late nineteenth century). This very first poem was printed in a little brochure in 1914. It is extremely unlikely that this has survived, nor is it really needed since a reasonable effort of the imagination can conjure it up on the basis of the 1916 poems. In April, 1961 Nabokov told an interviewer for the French newspaper *Nice-Matin* that his juvenile poems had been "*poèmes d'amour dans le style Sully-Prudhomme*," which may be as neat a job of literary assassination as Nabokov has ever performed.

The 1916 book contains sixty-seven poems and was printed in an edition of only 500 numbered copies. There are two epigraphs to the collection. The first is from Alfred de Musset: "*Un souvenir heureux est peut-être sur terre/ Plus vrai que le bonheur.*" (In 1927 and 1928 Nabokov published two excellent poetic translations of de Musset's *La Nuit de Mai* and *La Nuit de Décembre*.) The second epigraph is from Wordsworth:

> *Then fill the bowl! Away with gloom;*
> *Our joys shall always last;*
> *For hope will brighten days to come*
> *And memory gild the past.*

And so we see two things. The theme of memory, often termed the "Proustian note" in Nabokov's art, in fact predates Proust and is present in Nabokov's writing almost from the very beginning, and, secondly, there is the serenity that is to be so characteristic of Nabokov's verse throughout his life — in poverty, obscurity, and emigration — and which is ironic when one stops to consider that this pure positivism (which so annoyed émigré critics and poets indulging themselves in the pessimism and nihilism that ruled Russian émigré verse) belongs to the most scornful adversary of Soviet-style "optimistic tragedy."

The 1916 poems are, with but one or two exceptions, addressed to a girl who was — there's no avoiding it — Nabokov's "first love." In the autobiography she is called Tamara, "to give her a name concolorous with her real one" (the actual name is somewhat longer). "Through all these months, I had kept writing verse to her, for her, about her, two or three poems per week," he writes. "My poems were juvenile stuff, quite devoid of merit and ought never to have been put on sale. The book deserved what it got at the tearing claws of the few critics who noticed it in obscure periodicals." It was this book, according to Nabokov, that forever deprived him of the delights of enjoying critical praise, for a long and treacly review of it was written by a journalist for whom his father had done some favor, and it was read by father and son together "grinding our teeth and shrilly moaning."

In general Nabokov's overall judgment of his juvenilia cannot be contested—the unbroken procession of love poems, unadorned by any symbolism or oblique expression, induces incredulity and then embarrassment in the reader, nor do they even rank very high when placed against the preserved juvenilia of other great writers, except perhaps Lermontov's — but it would be unfair to suggest that the collection is wholly without merit. One poem was accepted for publication in the prestigious "thick journal" *Messenger of Europe* in 1916, and it has at any rate the modest merit that one associates with most of the poetry in that journal.

A more representative poem (like most of them it is untitled) is distinguished by its tom-tom beat repeating the same word (*khóchetsya*) thirteen times in sixteen lines:

> *I want so much, I want so little . . .*
> *I want the smile of a dream come true;*
> *I want your glance to answer*
> *My unspoken question; do you love me?*
>
> *I want so much, I want so little . . .*
> *I want my heart to carry off my thoughts;*
> *I want to be quietly kissed by your*
> *Burning lips on my pale brow.*
>
> *I want so little, I want so much . . .*
> *I want the ecstasy of fiery nights;*
> *I want to see my life and God*
> *In the black jewels of your loving eyes.*

I want so hotly, I want so passionately
Just to hear the echo of my crying . . .
I want without hope, I want in vain . . .
A mad transport of passion . . . and nothing more.

Nothing more, I think, need be added by way of commentary. In other poems we find lines such as "*You, you alone, I promise to love/ All my life, everywhere and always,*" or "*My poor heart until the pale of day/ it seems, shall not survive.*"

Of much greater charm are a series of miniature poems under the collective title *Stained Glass*. Their content is much the same as the rest of the poems in the book, but their delicate form and haiku-like structure are somewhat unusual in Russian poetry. Here are two of them:

Quietly sobbing,
there rings a golden
string . . .
The lane to the garden
is filled
With a limpid chill.

Do you remember what was?
How we were forgotten
By Spring?
Quietly sobbing,
there rings a golden
String . . .

In several of the poems, such as *Colloque Sentimental*, the theme of love cloaks the fact that the poet has been rejected; in others, a more direct emotional note is sounded (in *Speak, Memory* Nabokov tells us he was unaware of it as he wrote the poems), in which love, even as it moves closer to fruition, cannot capture the intense beauty of its initial moments.

Perhaps the most unusual and unmistakably individual feature of the poems is their frequent reference to insects, the dragon-fly appearing to be as important in the young Nabokov's verse as the butterfly at this period in his life. These allusions rise above the deadly cliché of the romantic meditation and constitute perhaps the only true poetry in the book:

The glassy waltz of dreamy dragon-flies

Only the quivering of a dragon-fly suddenly disturbed
the mute harmony of marvelous quiet

Forget-me-nots tease the bluish butterflies,
And elves in the forget-me-nots are laughing sonorously.

Nabokov published one other book of poems before he left Russia. It is a twenty-four page book containing poems by Nabokov and a friend from the Tenishev School named Andrei Balashov, "a little blond chap with a squint, madly in love with poetry." Some copies of the book, *Two Paths*, by chance reached the young Nabokov in the Crimea from Petrograd by mail in 1918 a very short time before the Nabokov family went into emigration. There is a marked advance in poetic technique in the poems in *Two Paths*. One of the poems, written in 1916, has a certain prophetic flavor inasmuch as it concerns the poet's wanderings in foreign cities:

And late at night again in alien cities
I enter, weary and excited,
Deserted, mournful halls,
Where there are no familiar icons in the corners.

Distance calls to the poet from these far-off railroad stations, but as the poem ends he recalls that inevitably there will flash a red light like a railroad semaphor — the end of wandering and exile.

Before following Nabokov on into emigration (through the Crimea to Constantinople on an old Greek ship, *Hope*, which carried, besides Nabokov and his father playing chess as they sailed out of sight of Russia, a cargo of dried fruit), I would pause just a moment longer to include a last curio from the 1916 collection, entitled *Summer Day*:

Who is scattering gold in the grove with his graceful, fiery hand? A violet bird flies by and jests noisily over another and . . . Today I remembered your eyes . . . (Be strong, my heart, grieve not!) In my pained chest there is a name that dies not. First I shall implore the tender, rose-hued insects to bring happiness, and then, lying in the grass amidst the daisies, I shall catch my dreams in the sky's blueness . . . A fragrant chill flows over me . . . Above me are amber clusters

of grapes in the deep blue liquid — The leaves of the birch tree . . .
I've grasped your faithlessness, I know. Sadly I tear up the banal note. I
sit by the window.

   I'll not think. It's too bad. Why happiness was near me . . .

   That's how it always goes. Like a dream, life is free.

This prerevolutionary prose poem — although in the original it is
even closer to poetry than my translation suggests — is the sole
extant Nabokov prose poem as such, and if one wishes to fix upon
the first recognizable hint of Nabokov's émigré prose it is present
in this awkward little childhood effort even more than in his first
émigré short stories. Thus, in *The Gift* the description of one of
Fyodor's poems becomes a prose poem:

Look, children, how they billow and rub against each other, all full of
God's sunshine, in red, blue and green shades. A beautiful sight! Please,
Uncle, I want the biggest (the white one with the rooster painted on it
and the red embryo floating inside, which, when its mother is destroyed, will escape up to the ceiling and a day later will come down,
all wrinkled and quite tame). Now the happy children have bought
their ruble balloon and the kindly hawker has pulled it out of the
jostling bunch. Just a minute, my lad, don't grab, let me cut the string.
After which he puts on his mittens again, checks the string around his
waist from which his scissors dangle, and pushing off with his heel
slowly begins to rise in an upright position, higher and higher into the
blue sky: look, his cluster is no larger now than a bunch of grapes,
while beneath him lies hazy, gilded, berimed St. Petersburg.

Such passages occur almost as a matter of course in Nabokov's
mature works. Here is yet another "prose poem" from *The Gift*,
and note that it is a single sentence:

He was walking along streets that had already long since insinuated
themselves into his acquaintance — and as if that were not enough,
they expected affection; they had even purchased in advance, in his
future memories, space next to St. Petersburg, an adjacent grave; he
walked along these dark, glossy streets and the blind houses retreated,
backing or sliding into the brown sky of the Berlin night, which,
nevertheless had its soft spots here and there, spots that would melt
under one's gaze, allowing it to obtain a few stars.

   In other places one finds rhythmic prose in the manner of Andrei
Bely (whose 1913 *St. Petersburg* was listed by Nabokov as one of

the four great modern novels) or lyric flights in the style of Bunin. Often these slide off into delightful parody, as, for example, in the conclusion of his discussion of his meetings with Bunin in the Russian memoirs *Other Shores:*

After that we would meet at gatherings rather often, and somehow we adopted a friendly bantering tone — and so we never had that talk about art, and now it is too late, and the hero walks out into the usual garden, and the summer lightning blazes, and then he rides to the station, and stars burn menacingly and wonderfully against the sepulchral velvet, and there is a faint bitter odor from the fields, and in the endless responsive remote distance of our youth roosters celebrate the night.

In one of those rare instances in which mention has been made of him in the Soviet press, the "not-un-well-known Nabokov" (an untranslatable Russian adjective, *nebezizvestny*) is reproached by the Soviet poet and editor of *Novy Mir*, Aleksandr Tvardovsky, for this little bit of gentle fun at Bunin's expense.

In Nabokov's first book of short stories (1930) there is a little five-page story *The Storm* — it is undated, but one would guess it was written fairly early — that qualifies as a "poetic" story of sorts. (Sh*iroko i* sh*umno* sh*yol do*sht — *Riotously and raucously ran the rain* is a typical line from it.) But because it is little more than that, it is perhaps the least successful of all his short stories. The principle of poetic prose is, nonetheless, central to Nabokov's fiction, and its success stems directly from its use in such a way that it does not cloy or obtrude itself in any way. As already indicated, it is most important in *The Gift* and *Speak, Memory*, and we find it no less important in Nabokov's English novels. Nabokov has said:

Poetry includes all creative writing; I have never been able to see any generic difference between poetry and artistic prose. As a matter of fact, I would be inclined to define a good poem of any length as a concentrate of good prose, with or without the addition of recurrent rhythm and rhyme. The magic of prosody may improve upon what we call prose by bringing out the full flavor of meaning, but in plain prose there are also certain rhythmic patterns, the music of precise phrasing, the beat of thought rendered by recurrent peculiarities of idiom and intonation. As in today's scientific classifications, there is a

: of overlapping in our concept of poetry and prose today. The
mboo bridge between them is the metaphor.

The brief opening chapter of *Bend Sinister* consists of nothing
but prose poems, and this is indicated by the way in which they are
typographically set off:

An oblong puddle inset in the coarse asphalt; like a fancy footprint
filled to the brim with quicksilver; like a spatulate hole through which
you can see the nether sky. Surrounded, I note, by a diffuse tentacled
black dampness where some dull dun dead leaves have stuck. Drowned,
I should say, before the puddle had shrunk to its present size.

And most important of all, there is the famous opening paragraph
of *Lolita* ("Lolita, light of my life, fire of my loins . . .") which,
in the original 1955 Olympia Press Paris edition, but not in subsequent editions and translations, was actually centered on the page
and thus set off as a prose poem.

Nabokov will frequently suspend his narrative for just a brief
instant during which time he focuses upon a single striking image
which becomes a tiny work of art or "prose poem" in itself:

[She was] in the kitchen engaged in beating an egg in a glass — "goggle-
moggle," we called it . . . The evening sun checkered the kitchen.
Again she started to turn the spoon in the thick yellow stuff, grains of
sugar crunched slightly, it was still clammy, the spoon did not move
smoothly with the velvety ovality that was required . . . "Well — had
a good trip?" asked Lydia as she went on energetically turning the
handle, with the box-part held firm between her knees. The coffee
beans crackled, richly odorous; the mill was still working with a
rumbling and creaking effort; then came an easing, a yielding; gone all
resistance; empty. I have got muddled somehow. As in a dream. She
was making that goggle-moggle — not coffee.

These beautiful and intricate effects are the norm in Nabokov's
mature writing, and understanding of his art should begin with
attention to and appreciation of such "details."

Such a chronology of the development of Nabokov's poetic
prose from prerevolutionary Russia to America is at best tenuous
and contrived, however real and useful, but the enormous importance of childhood as a theme in Nabokov's art in all periods is
beyond any question. The 1916 poems underscore one point which

should have been self-evident but which, without them, is not that easy to keep always in view, namely, that the reality of Nabokov's actual childhood and the childhood of his art are quite distant from each other.

Childhood was the theme (and title) of one of Nabokov's first long poems which appeared in a Berlin Russian almanac, *Facets*, in 1921, that is, when he was just twenty-two. The poem consists of sixteen stanzas of varying length (between five and fifteen lines) and is notable above all for the extraordinary grace and smoothness of its Pushkinian iambic meter. *Childhood* evokes the lost joys of early years by means of a simple enumeration of a day's routine. The subject then could not possibly be less exciting and promising, and the poem's success is necessarily wholly dependent upon the successful conveyance of the poet's real emotion and the purity of the poem's narrative tone. From the specific details it can be seen quite clearly, with the help of *Speak, Memory*, that the poem concerns Nabokov's own childhood. This autobiographical effort is most successful — and *Childhood* was referred to very favorably in almost all the reviews of the almanac — but its success is in the end severely limited by the nature of the task the poet sets himself. For in spite of its affinity to Pushkin's poetic diction, the best that may be said of *Childhood* is that it is like very good Betjeman or middling Wordsworth.

The poem looks back to the time when the poet was eight years old:

> *Could all of this have been?*
> *And we are surprised that our heart has forgotten*
> *What a marvelous life was given us.*

The theme of remembrance is immediately doubled as the poet recalls observing at that age his younger brother playing some sort of childish game and wondering, ". . . *was I really just like him?*" The dream of those days (*"lived without struggle, forgotten without difficulty"*) becomes a distant dream that troubles him. Then in a stanza vaguely reminiscent of Lermontov's famous dream-within-a-dream poem that Nabokov cites in his Introduction to his son's translation of *A Hero of Our Time*, the poet imagines that he awakes from a prolonged dream only as he calls forth those dreamlike years. The poem's concluding lines imagine a future reader who

> *attentively reading through these stormless poems,*
> *will sigh and think: at heart he was a child!*

In a curious way this Pushkinian poem moves directly counter to Pushkin's own dictum: "Our literature will not move forward with remembrances of youth gone by." One detail in Nabokov's list of his activities as an eight-year-old will be useful for those who have confused Nabokov's references to his difficulties in perfecting a distinctive English style with actual mastery of the language:

> *And then till ten,*
> *with back bent over the table*
> *I would write nonsense in the language of Shakespeare*
> *and afterwards be taken for a walk.*

Nabokov's other early long poem, *St. Petersburg*, also written in 1921, treats the city in much the same spirit as *Childhood* does vanished youth — as a golden, insufficiently appreciated past. The city *"proud of the uproar and scope/ of its magic squares"* has died, and only the past lives — *"O city, loved by Pushkin,/ how far-off are those years!"* Life in St. Petersburg now is *"sullen and fearful,"* and the poet remembers *"your last Spring."* (In 1921 this was not so much a political credo as an actual description of conditions in Petrograd where, according to one memoirist, life was so harsh and the weather so cold that "even women's periods stopped.") In this poem the city is seen largely as though one were wandering down various streets from a single, unseen starting-point which is, one gathers, the Nabokov house. The primary virtue of *St. Petersburg* is again its light shading of Pushkin's poetics — it is 184 lines long and written in very regular, close-rhymed four-foot iambs — but here also the total effect sooner recalls certain idyllic nineteenth-century English and Russian poets of minor import. *St. Petersburg* is saved from being a stereotype of émigré recollections, however, by precisely this "nineteenth-century outlook" on the events of 1917. It concludes:

> *There is no lack of such as I. We*
> *wander o'er the world restlessly*

> *and know: the buried city*
> *will rise again; everything in it will be*
> *beautiful, joyful, and new —*
> *but the thing is that the old (city) of our birth*
> *we shall never find anymore . . .*

It would be foolish to think that *Childhood* and *St. Petersburg* could by themselves have a place in the history of Russian literature if they did not enjoy the benefit of their author's subsequent achievement, but by the same token one should not use that same accomplishment to belittle these two poems and relegate them to the rank of juvenilia where they most certainly do not belong.

Nabokov never really abandoned his placid themes. Memories of his childhood and of Russia are a constant motif of his novels and the remarkable personalities of their protagonists tend either to obscure this or present the theme in grotesquely distorted form. In Nabokov's eyes childhood may reassert itself in the adult, and in a 1945 English poem he writes:

> *it came, that sudden shudder,*
> *a Russian something that I could inhale*
> *but could not see. Some rapid words were uttered —*
> *and then the child slept on, the door was shut.*

His most important childhood poems — only because they occur in one of his most important novels — are those he gives to Fyodor in *The Gift.* The poems astound us with their unabashed sentimentality:

> *One climbed a sparkle-splashed platform,*
> *One dashingly fell belly first*
> *On the sled, and it rattled*
> *Down the blueness . . .*

Nabokov has declared that one of these poems "connected with the memory of a young woman, long dead, whom Fyodor has loved when sixteen" is his own favorite among the Russian poems he has written. The nine-line poem is a fairly good one, but it is quite clear that it requires an investment of personal response which must primarily be the poet's own. And this is perhaps the most revealing commentary of all on the nature of the strange relationship which may exist between the actual personality of an artist and the art he creates. Poetry in this vein, even extremely good poetry, easily lends itself to ridicule, and there is a most curious mention of the young Nabokov's poetry in a 1924 survey of Russian émigré literature (at that time the subject could still be written about) in the Soviet journal *Red New Ground*. "The poems of [Nabokov] are very sleek. Earlier the 'thick' journals would gladly have printed him [and] it goes without saying that *maman* and his cousins will be ecstatic with these poems. But this isn't a living voice, it's a gramophone playing a traditional sentimental bourgeois waltz." In historical retrospect, of course, these comments become droll.

A far more satisfactory treatment of his youth is to be found in two delightful, if somewhat melancholy short stories, *The Offense* (1931) and *Goosefoot* (1932). Both stories concern a young boy named Putya Shishkov. As it happens the Shishkovs are a branch of the Nabokov family. The most famous of them was Aleksandr Shishkov, leader of the reactionary circle, *The Concourse of Lovers of the Russian Word*, which advocated pseudo-classical poetic values in opposition to the more eclectic tastes of the Arzamas group with which Pushkin was associated. (In 1925 Nabokov was a founding member of a second, émigré "Arzamas," something like the present day Group 47 in Germany which was designed to be a group to aid and encourage émigré writers.) Shishkov is given a proper roasting — nor is he the only member of the famous Nabokov family to be treated with so little ceremony by Nabokov — in the Commentaries to the translation of *Eugene Onegin* (Vol. 3, pp. 169–173). As for the nickname Putya, we know from Nabokov's footnotes to some published letters (in Russian) by his father that one of Nabokov's uncles by marriage, Ivan de Peterson, was referred to as "Putya" in the Nabokov family. The name Putya Shishkov, then, while it is, strictly speaking, fictional, alerts us to the fact that there is a much narrower distance between author and action than can be found in Nabokov's other stories and novels. Queried about this, Nabokov replied that, yes, the stories were perhaps one tenth autobiographical, which still, of course, leaves one with the problem of deciding *which* tenth.

The childhood chronicle, whether in strictly biographical or fictional form, is an all but obligatory exercise for any Russian writer. The first one that comes to mind is Tolstoy's *Childhood*, his first published work and a mixture of real and imaginary characters and events which he envisioned as forming the basis for a novel. One thinks, too, of Sergei Aksakov's famous *Childhood Years of Bagrov's Grandson*, Goncharov's *The Dream of Oblomov*, Turgenev's *First Love*, Mandelstam's *Noise of Time*, Chekhov's *Steppe*, Boris Zaitsev's *Gleb's Journey*, and Bunin's *The Life of Arsenev*, to mention only a few of the most famous ones.

The Offense (which is dedicated to Ivan Bunin) details a visit by Putya Shishkov to a neighboring estate for the name-day party of a boy his age. The story takes place — if one is to judge by a chalk legend ("Long Live Serbia!") scrawled on a wall the Shishkov carriage passes while Putya is on his way to the party — sometime between about 1910 and 1914. The central device of the story is Russian literature's time-honored *ostranénie* or "making-strange" (Natasha at the opera in *War and Peace* is the most frequently cited example), but in this instance the "strangeness" is not so much a device imposed by the author as a natural expression of Putya's own inexplicable estrangement from literally everyone with whom he comes in contact — servants, adults, and other children, too. The story begins: "Putya was sitting on the coach-box with the driver (he didn't especially like to sit on the coach-box, but the driver and the servants thought he was extremely fond of this, and so Putya didn't want to offend them — he was sitting there then, a sallow, grey-eyed boy in an elegant sailor's suit)." Everyone and everything else appear in a "normal" way, and it is Putya who is "made strange."

Putya Shishkov's passage across the grounds of the estate where he must greet the adults and join the other children at play is described with an impersonality ("One had to cross . . .") that is the narrator's, but also perfectly conveys Putya's aversion to the social situation into which he is being thrust. By means of certain little details of childish cruelty — "Vasya Tuchkov found a small caterpillar with vari-colored tufts of little hairs along its back (something like a toothbrush) and calmly gulped it down to the delight of almost everyone" — the reader is made to share Putya's discomfort. Putya is treated with less interest than the caterpillar by the children, and even the tutor who is directing their play passes over Putya when it falls upon him to be "it" in a game. Thus it is no surprise to anyone but Putya himself when Putya goes off to hide while playing that same game and no one bothers to look for him or even notices that he has not returned. Putya Shishkov's situation is a universal experience shared by all children, even the Vasya Tuchkovs (another branch of the Nabokov family) at some time or other, and it is the remembrance of this that I take to be the autobiographical tenth — and essential core — of *The Offense*. With *Speak, Memory*, *Pnin*, and *Pale Fire* (the poem) this story is one of the comparatively small number of Nabokov's works which seek directly to engage the reader's strong sympathy.

The autobiographical element in the second story, *Goosefoot*, can be fixed with a great deal more precision. The story is about Putya Shishkov's discovery at school, when he sees a journal that is being passed around by the other boys, that his famous father is fighting a duel. Nabokov's father, Vladimir Dmitrievich, who was a famous Russian liberal jurist and political figure, did issue a challenge, and it was when Nabokov was just about Putya's age. His father had been the subject of a basely insulting screed written by a hack journalist of no account and published in the newspaper *New Time*. Since the journalist was considered "unduelable," Nabokov issued his challenge to the paper's prominent editor Aleksei Suvorin. (Suvorin was the close friend and correspondent of Chekhov.) As it happened, Suvorin lost his nerve at the last minute and issued an apology, so there was no duel. At school, however, young Vladimir, knowing nothing of this, had a fight with the perfidious friend who had brought the journal to school, and in the struggle the friend broke his ankle.

Lebedá (*Goosefoot*) represents the emotionally distraught Putya's misunderstanding of a sentence from the poet Maikov being dictated to him at the blackboard; he writes *beda*, which means "tragedy." Putya Shishkov doesn't fight with his unfaithful friend but, I surmise, with the class oaf who, in *Speak, Memory*, was the one who helped carry the friend downstairs after the fight: "The blood from Shchukin's nose continued to run during the Natural Sciences lesson, stopped during the arithmetic lesson, and again started up during the Holy Scriptures lesson. Putya observed it with calm interest." But that, in the story, is before he learns of the impending duel, by means of a newspaper caricature, after which he has all he can do to control his emotions until classes are out.

The usual car has not come to call for Putya that day, and he returns home in a tortuously slow cab — *Goosefoot* and *Speak, Memory* coincide exactly on this particular — to learn that the duel has already taken place, but no one was injured: his father's opponent missed, and — the great romantic flourish — his father fired into the air. (Still another version of the incident is given in the précis of Sebastian Knight's novel *Lost Property*, based, we are told, upon the duel in which Knight's father was killed.) *The Weed* is, to my way of thinking, not as successful a story as *The Offense*, but one regrets that Putya Shishkov was not allowed further scope and development, for the expansion of *Speak, Memory* indicates that there would have been sufficient material for a small volume of Putya Shishkov stories without impinging on the memoirs that were to be written twenty years later.

Nabokov was by no means finished with the name Shishkov, however. Some years later one of the most influential senior émigré critics, Georgy Adamovich, began to take regular potshots at Nabokov's poetry. Nabokov had crossed Adamovich's "circle" several times, the worst offense undoubtedly being a review published in 1937 in which he gently ridiculed some of the critic's verse. Adamovich, who is still alive, is an unreliable but extremely interesting and provocative critic — some of his essays really should be translated — and a quite inept poet. And so, with Adamovich specifically in mind, Nabokov published some poems under the pseudonym Vasily Shishkov. Adamovich took the hook better than Nabokov could have dared to hope, for he wrote an ecstatic notice about the unknown poet Vasily Shishkov, whose name, he predicted confidently, would soon be on everyone's lips:

Every line is full of talent, every word, the sweeping melody convinces one, and everywhere there are scattered those little treasures, now an unexpected and apt epithet, now an unexpected and completely charming repetition, which no amount of experience can give . . . Who is this poet? Where did he come from? It is entirely possible that within a year or two his name will be known by everyone to whom Russian poetry is dear.

Adamovich, of course, had only himself to blame; if he had paid more attention to Nabokov's verse, instead of dismissing it out of hand — knowledge of the Putya Shishkov stories might have helped save him, too — the bait would never have worked. He was not to be let off that easily either. In 1939 Nabokov wrote a short story entitled *Vasily Shishkov*, which was printed in the newspaper for which Adamovich wrote a regular literary column, in which he helpfully supplies a "biography" for his invented poet. When this history behind the story is known, *Vasily Shishkov*, an amusing story in any case, becomes one of the most delightful satirical romps Nabokov has written.

During a literary evening a critic uses the intermission to get up and leave. As he is going down the stairs, he hears a bustling behind him and sees someone chasing after him. The man stops two steps above him and announces: "My name is Vasily Shishkov, I am a poet." Shishkov, after proffering a firm handshake, asks to meet and consult with the critic. When they do meet, Shishkov hands him a notebook of poems written, the critic notes as he opens it, in a hand that bespeaks "health and giftedness." As he begins to read them, though, with Shishkov sitting at his side, immediate disillusionment overcomes him. The poems are hopelessly pretentious, their meter is broken, and the rhymes — numerous examples of which are given — strain belief.

To read them straight through was a torment for a person of nervous disposition, but my goodheartedness was reinforced by the fact that the author was closely keeping watch over me and by that means keeping control over what I was reading, so that it was necessary for me to hesitate over every page. "Well," he asked when I finished, "not too bad?"

The critic looks at Shishkov's unsuspecting face, and, after a long hesitation, tells him that the poems are hopeless. Shishkov then tells him that he wrote all of them in a single day as parodies of a graphomaniac and that his purpose was merely to "test" the critic's sincerity. Here, he says, are my *real* poems, and he thrusts an even thicker notebook into the critic's hands.

The critic, excusing Shishkov's childish urge to obtain a completely sincere opinion, fears that the real poems will all the same contain traces of the gross faults of the first poems, but the poems turn out to be very good. Shortly thereafter Shishkov decides to disappear, and, just as simply as that, he does.

The two sets of poems, the "good" and the "bad" ones, and the "scrupulously honest" critic mock Adamovich caught with his critical principles down, and many of the things that Vasily Shishkov says to the critic are direct parodies of Adamovich's own articles on Nabokov. Adamovich, for example, while confessing that he was not an admirer of Nabokov's writing, allowed (and this is quite characteristic of his style and manner) that, even so, he experienced "an almost physiological pleasure" when reading him. And Vasily Shishkov dutifully tells the critic: "I want to forewarn you that I don't love your books . . . [but] you possess, in an almost physiological sense, a certain secret of the writing craft."

In the Vasily Shishkov incident we have an exact foreshadowing of the trap, this one anticipatory, that was slyly laid in Nabokov's *Onegin* translation and which caught Mr. Edmund Wilson in his essay directed against the translation. As one of his examples of archaic or obsolete usage Wilson cites the line *"worthy of old sapajous,"* thus giving Nabokov the opportunity to explain his word choice and at the same time demolish his critic's authority to offer serious commentary on matters pertaining to Pushkin. Nabokov's reply (*Encounter*, February, 1966) is worth quoting in full because I shall have occasion to refer back to it later in another connection:

True, *obez'yana* means any kind of monkey, but it so happens that neither "monkey" nor "ape" is good enough in the context. "Sapajou" (which technically is applied to two genera of neotropical monkeys) has in French a colloquial sense of "ruffian," "lecher," "ridiculous chap." Now, in lines 1–2 and 9–11 of Four: VII ("the less we love a woman, the easier 'tis to be liked by her . . . but that grand game is worthy of old sapajous of our forefathers' vaunted times") Pushkin echoes a moralistic passage in his own letter written in French from Kishinev to his young brother in Moscow in the autumn of 1822, that is seven months before beginning *Eugene Onegin* and two years before reaching Canto Four. The passage, well known to readers of Pushkin, goes: *Moins on aime une femme et plus on est sur de l'avoir . . . mais cette jouissance est digne d'un vieux sapajou du dix-huitième siècle.* Not only could I not resist the temptation of retranslating the *obez'yan* of the canto into the Anglo-French "sapajous" of the letter, but I was also looking forward to somebody's pouncing on that word and allowing me to retaliate with that wonderfully satisfying reference. Mr. Wilson obliged — and here it is.

The key words, of course, are "well known to readers of Pushkin." There is a diabolical humor at play behind sallies such as the Shishkov and sapajou incidents, to be sure, but they are not without their own charm and justification — mystification, purposeful or otherwise, being one of the basic components of Nabokov's artistic personality.

Vasily Shishkov is, in fact, only one of the names under which Nabokov's writings have appeared through the years. He has also been Valentin Nabokov, Cantab, F.G.-Ch., Vivian Calmbrood, and Vivian Darkbloom. But the most important of these pseudonyms, for it is the one under which his Russian works regularly appeared for a period of nearly twenty years, is Vladimir Sirin. The Sirin is a mythological Russian bird, and Sirin was also the name of the finest prerevolutionary Russian publishing house (among its authors were Andrei Bely, Fyodor Sologub, and Aleksandr Blok). Pseudonyms are a great deal more common in the Russian literary tradition than in most other European literatures, but in this particular instance there was a very practical reason to assume another name: Nabokov's father was then editing the leading Berlin Russian-language newspaper *Rul'* (*The Rudder*), and it was in the pages of this newspaper that most of the young Nabokov's poems and occasional pieces appeared in the early years of his writing career. Nabokov's prerevolutionary verse had appeared under his own name, and in his earliest émigré appearances in print, such as the journal *The Future Russia*, he signed his name V. V. Nabokov. But appearances in the same pages with his father, who frequently wrote on literary as well as political subjects, suggested that some clear differentiation was called for. Nabokov used the pseudonym Sirin until 1940 (he was never referred to in print as Nabokov, but his identity was in no way a secret to anyone, and the copyrights to many of the Sirin books were listed under V. Nabokoff), in spite of the fact that less than two years after he had become Sirin the name was no longer necessary: his father was assassinated by two Russian fascists on March 28, 1922.

Nabokov has written a short biographical sketch of his father which has been incorporated into the new *Speak, Memory*. His enormous affection for his father is a matter of record, and it is one of the few biographical "facts" which is of great import in the consideration of certain of his novels. V. D. Nabokov demands a book of his own; here it will have to suffice merely to add a stroke or two to Nabokov's own comments about him, which are, of course, written from a very special, filial perspective.

V. D. Nabokov, it has been said, was almost a dandy as a young man — a superb dancer, always impeccably dressed, and very much a ladies' man. He quickly discarded his frivolous interests, however, and plunged into political and social causes which were, on the surface, seemingly opposed to everything the Nabokov family stood for and benefited from (his father had been a staunch defender of Tsardom in general and Aleksandr II in particular). V. D. Nabokov was one of those young men who were spoken of as "the conscience of their class" and the "golden youth" of the Russian intelligentsia. Still, he remained very much of that class, as photographs of him in a straw hat with a close mustache clearly show, and it is probably true that, although Nabokov himself was entirely free of class snobbery, his very manner and station undoubtedly antagonized many in the lower and middle classes and thus were a distinct obstacle in his political career.

This was true, too, of many of the leading members of Nabokov's party, the Kadets, or Constitutional Democrats. The leadership of the party included many historians, lawyers, and intellectuals in the most serious sense of the term; a prominent historian once remarked to me that, in his opinion, the top fifty Kadets taken together would have constituted a university faculty which could not have been surpassed in brilliance and distinction by any of the great universities of modern times. V. D. Nabokov is generally counted by historians as one of the ten foremost Kadets.

The First Duma of 1906 may be criticized as having been more eloquent than pragmatic, but such a cavil is itself quite gratuitous, for what was a brief and hopeful moment of democracy was dissolved after its first year by the Tsar. We have a fascinating, if highly colored, portrait of Nabokov in the Duma by Ariadna Tyrkova-Williams, herself a prominent prerevolutionary political figure:

Nabokov was a sincere constitutionalist, an ardent defender of rule by law. He was happy to be able at last to express his political views in a high forum openly and in their entirety. And the approbation of the beautiful women in the gallery comforted him, too . . . Among the various spectacles of the Duma, one of the diversions was Nabokov's neckties. Nabokov appeared in a new suit almost every day, and every day he wore a new necktie, even more refined than the necktie of the preceding day. Suddenly someone's sharp eye noted that Alad'in [a political rival of Nabokov's] was also beginning to change his neckties frequently. As is well known, selecting and tying a necktie is a fine science. The pursuit of Vladimir Dmitrievich turned out to be beyond Alad'in's powers.

V. D. Nabokov's writings are marked by a finely distinct moral and political sensitivity, and he will sometimes insist on a point in the abstract (for example, that illegal sexual acts are equally illegal, even between consenting husband and wife) with no suggestion that there is any feasible legal applicability of the point. Even in the midst of a closely reasoned legalistic argument, one expects a literary analogy or reference to be made. When Nabokov puts forward a new word, *ravnopoly*, to replace the term homosexual, which is accepted in most European languages including Russian, it is on the grounds that the word homosexual has been impermissibly constructed from a combination of Greek and Latin roots, and in matters of this sort the close correspondence between father and son is self-evident. Nabokov wrote many literary articles, which are, on the whole, of not much importance as criticism, but they are intelligent and well-written appreciations, models of what the daily and occasional book review ought to be. He also wrote a study of Charles Dickens for Volume IV of the *Russian History of Western Literature* (1912), which is still the most outstanding Russian critique of that author.

In emigration V. D. Nabokov became the leader of the Kadet moderate faction, one of the two major ideological divisions of the party. Although this faction was committed to an extremely liberal policy, it differed with the Kadets led by Pavel Miliukov over the question of possible rapprochement with the Bolsheviks. Miliukov held the position, particularly in the early years after the Revolution, that a return to Russia and the establishment of some sort of *modus vivendi* with the Bolsheviks was the goal toward which liberal émigré politics should devote its energy. Nabokov, on the other hand, maintained that Bolshevism was intrinsically opposed to democratic principles and that, therefore, such a coalition was dangerous and foolish, even if it were possible.

The main organ of the Kadet moderates was *The Rudder*, founded in Berlin by Nabokov and several close, long-time associates from his St. Petersburg Duma days. At that time Berlin was the capital of the Russian emigration, and there were, if the smaller publications are counted, over forty Russian newspapers and journals in Berlin. Of these, *The Rudder* was by far the most important. Like most other modern Russian papers, both Soviet and émigré, *The Rudder*, a daily, usually was but four to six pages in length, and only occasionally (Sunday issues) ten pages long.

Although *The Rudder* was anti-Bolshevik, in reading it one is struck by the paper's moderate, factual tone; it has none of the vitriol by which "anti-Soviet" journals usually disconcertingly resemble their Soviet counterparts. Because the editors of *The Rudder* knew Bolshevism and, what is more, closely followed the Soviet press and received many reports from within Russia, it is startling to compare the paper with English and French newspapers of the same period. Western papers had much to learn over many years before they reached *The Rudder*'s level of sophistication about Russia and Soviet Communism. Also, in comparison with most Western newspapers, *The Rudder* devoted disproportionate space to cultural matters in its pages — besides Nabokov-Sirin, Bunin, Balmont, Zaitsev, Teffi, Remizov, and Korvin-Piotrovsky (an unjustly neglected poet and writer about whom Sirin wrote a most sympathetic essay) were some of the other notable émigré writers whose poetry and prose appeared frequently in *The Rudder*. Its regular book reviews were written by Yuly Aikhenvald — famous for his impressionistic three-volume *Silhouettes of Russian Writers* written before the Revolution — and, after Aikhenvald's death, by one of the finest of the emigration's literary critics, Alfred Bem, a professor of Russian literature in Prague. *The Rudder* was one of the two most significant Russian émigré newspapers. (The other was the Paris *Poslednie Novosti* [*Latest News*].) It ceased publication in 1931, by which time the tremors of incipient fascism (in September, 1931 a band of hooligans sacked its editorial offices) had caused the center of Russian emigration to move from Berlin to Paris.

The fullest account of the assassination of V. D. Nabokov is, for obvious reasons, to be found in the pages of *The Rudder*. It occurred at a political evening at the Berlin Philharmonic Hall. Nabokov was to introduce his Kadet adversary, Pavel Miliukov, and there was hope that the breach between them which had progressively widened since 1920 was to be healed on this evening, as, in a grim way, it was. Two right-wing extremists named Shabelsky and Taboritsky, living in Munich, read of the evening and traveled to Berlin with the express purpose of assassinating Miliukov, whom the monarchists held to be indirectly responsible for the murder of Nicholas II by the Bolsheviks. (Miliukov had publicly taken the position that monarchy was no longer necessary in Russia.) Shabelsky and Taboritsky rose from their seats in the second row, guns in hand, and headed straight for the dais. Amid great uproar and confusion, as Shabelsky aimed his gun at Miliukov, Nabokov lunged between them, deflecting the assassin's hand and receiving a bullet slightly below the heart. In the meantime, Taboritsky jumped onto the stage and began to wave his pistol and shout melodramatically until he was tackled, but not before he had had a chance to fire at Nabokov's prostrate body. In all, Nabokov was shot three times, and it was never made entirely clear which of the assassins had actually killed him. Nabokov's son, then a student at Cambridge, was in Berlin at that time, but he was not at the meeting and received the news at home by telephone and arrived at the hall some minutes later.

A certain air of mystery and confusion hangs over the entire crime, and reading the accounts of the interrogation and trial of the two killers (one of whom was to attain a position of some importance under Hitler in later years) one gets a glimmer of what might have happened had Lee Harvey Oswald lived. At first Shabelsky claimed full responsibility for the assassination and Taboritsky concurred in this ("one brave man was sufficient for this deed"). But when it was pointed out that two guns were used, Shabelsky changed his story and said, yes, he had had one gun in each hand. Although both men also disclaimed any organizational backing, it was never determined how they had even financed their trip to Berlin from Munich where they lived together in a shabby rented room. A convention of right-wing Russian monarchists happened to be meeting in Berlin at the time the killing took place.

Inquiries into their backgrounds revealed that Shabelsky had been shell-shocked in the war and suffered from a nervous disorder, and his fiancée had been killed by the Bolsheviks during their escape from Russia. He was described as distracted, but able to multiply two-digit numbers in his head and recite Cicero by heart. Taboritsky had a brother who had been tried for murder in the army, and he had formerly worked for the rightist papers *Ray of Light* and *Summons*.

V. D. Nabokov's eminence and especially the way in which he had lost his life (defending Miliukov as "an old friend under the mask of a political opponent") made his death an occasion of great sorrow for all segments of Russian society from the respectable right to the far left. The German government sent an official representative to his funeral. Messages of condolence and praise came from everywhere — from Olga Knipper of the Moscow Art Theater, Andrei Bely, Ivan Bunin ("no matter how long our acquaintanceship might have lasted, I am convinced I could never have been disenchanted with this man").

There was little Soviet commentary on the assassination, and what few articles did appear echoed the intellectual contortions of *Novy Mir* (not the magazine, which was founded three years later, but an earlier newspaper of the same name) which wrote: "The real monarchists are killing the quasi-monarchists and constitutional monarchists. Émigré White Guardism has reached the ultimate in its moral and political decline." For this very reason, perhaps the finest tribute paid to V. D. Nabokov after his death was a short article, signed only "Remarks of a Journalist," which appeared in the Soviet journal *Literary Annals* (May, 1922):

Pre-October Communists, among whom are to be found many good journalists who well knew Nabokov's political and literary activities, have chosen not to write about him. And this is more or less understandable: the tragic death of Nabokov does not predispose one to sharp criticism of his actions in recent years, and the Russian atmosphere is still not clear enough to be able to do without these sharp criticisms. . . . The judgment of history, which is not written today and especially not for today, and the sum of those characteristics which describe him as he was rather than those descriptions which describe only their authors, I am convinced, will converge to assure the recognition of Nabokov's social and cultural achievements.

A Sirin poem titled *Easter* appeared in *The Rudder* shortly after his father's assassination. It is a personal statement of religious faith which sounds in many of his poems of this period:

> *I see a radiant cloud, a brilliant*
> *roof in the distance like a mirror . . . I hear*
> *how the shadows breathe and the light drips down . . .*
> *Then how is it you are not? You've died, but today*
> *the damp world shows blue, the Lord's Spring draws near,*
> *grows, calls . . . You are not.*
>
> *But if all the streams are singing again of the miracle,*
> *and if the chiming and the gold of the thaw*
> *are not a blinding lie,*
> *but a quivering call, a most sweet "arise,"*
> *a great "bloom," — then in this song,*
> *   in this glitter, you do live! . . .*

One has only to recall how much Dostoevsky's critics and biographers have made of *his* father's violent death to realize that Nabokov's art can scarcely hope to escape the same fate. Certainly the assassination by mistake in *Pale Fire* recalls the circumstances in which Nabokov's father died, and one could fill several pages with a list of the violent deaths and appearances of guns in Nabokov's writing. But at the same time one should remember the serenity of this poem written by the twenty-three-year-old young man. Nabokov has said that he is certain that Shabelsky and Taboritsky have never entered his art, and perhaps this is so, if they are seen as merely another variation — and a particularly stupid one — on the violence that has been the lot of almost all Russians in this century. The Russian police state, Nabokov has acknowledged, is always at the back of his émigré mind.

Three

✺ ✺ ✺ ✺

THE Nabokov family moved to London during the summer of 1919. After a year, Nabokov's father went to Berlin to participate in the founding and publication of *The Rudder*. Nabokov and his brother Sergei remained behind and entered Cambridge University — Sergei in Christ College, Vladimir in Trinity. It was while he was in college that the Russian poems signed Cantab appeared, and it was also in this period of his life that he made his first appearance as an English writer with the following (according to his own later judgment) "wretched poem," written, he recalls, during the summer of 1919.

REMEMBRANCE
Like silent ships we two in darkness met,
*   And when some day the poet's careless fame*
*   Shall breathe to you a half-forgotten name —*
Soul of my song, I want you to regret.
For you had Love. Out of my life you tore
*   One shining page. I want, if we must part,*
*   Remembrance pale to quiver in your heart*
Like moonlit foam upon a windy shore.

Actually, this poem, which is not a translation but which closely echoes one of his Russian poems, is one of many English poems he wrote while at Cambridge, but the only one to find its way into print.

Nabokov's reaction to Cambridge in particular and England in general is somewhat surprising in view of the strong Anglophile background of the Nabokov family, and it is by his response to England that I would define Nabokov's true nationality as a writer.

Nabokov was apparently never able to think of himself as even "an Englishman of foreign birth." In the Russian version of his memoirs he tells how, in later years, it became clear to him that he had expected of England not a natural continuation of his life, but a realization of that portion of his childhood in which England and all things English had assumed an exotic fairy-tale air. The reality could hardly fail to keep Nabokov's attachment at a remove. And beyond this, there were the normal problems of youth (he refers to his four years at Cambridge as "a long series of awkwardnesses, mistakes, and every sort of failure and stupidity, including romantic") and of exile. He has written that his Cambridge surroundings assumed, if not a fantastic, then at least an "unreal" air, and his energies focused upon Russia and his own Russianness. In *Speak, Memory* Nabokov calls his college years "really the story of my trying to become a Russian writer," and in *Other Shores* — an emotional confession that he perhaps felt to be unnecessary for English readers who could not understand it anyway — he writes of the tears he shed thinking of the Russia he might have carried away "in the pockets of my soul" if he had only been able to foresee the separation.

In a 1921 article in the *The Rudder* — the sole instance in which Nabokov places his "contemporary impressions" in print — he wrote:

I sometimes sit in a corner and look about me at all these smooth faces, very attractive, one has to grant, but somehow always calling to mind advertisements for shaving cream, and suddenly it becomes so boring, so tedious that you almost want to whoop and smash some windows. . . .

We Russians and they have a certain glass wall between us; they have their own worlds, round and hard, like a painstakingly painted globe. Their souls do not know that whirlwind of inspiration, pulsation, radiance, that furious dance, that malevolence and tenderness, which transport us into God-only-knows-what heavens and abysses; we have moments when the clouds are about our shoulders and the sea about our knees — go free, my soul! For an Englishman this is incomprehensible, unheard of, yes, and alluring. If, having had a bit to drink, he does cause an uproar, that uproar is stereotyped and good-natured, and the guardians of order only smile as they watch him, knowing that he will not go beyond a certain point. Or, to put it another way, even the most furious drunkenness will not cause him to be deeply stirred, to bare his chest, to hurl his cap against the earth.

There is, according to the young Nabokov, no synthesis possible between these extremes of national personality type. The ancient university preserves and concentrates all the sobriety and propriety that is traditionally associated with the English, and the pressure to conform to this pattern of behavior is so strong, he feels, that a "wild foreigner" who insists on behaving in his own manner is first a source of wonder to the Englishman, and then someone to be avoided. "And that is why, at times, one's heart swells with grief, feeling that a true friend is not to be found here. And then every-thing seems dull — the spectacles of the sprightly little old lady from whom you rent your room, the room itself with its dirty red divan, gloomy fireplace, and ridiculous little vases on its ridiculous little shelves, and the sounds coming from the street, the cry of the paperboys: pai-pa! pai-pa!"

Cambridge's ancient history causes Nabokov to juxtapose its seemingly unbroken procession of generations with the turmoil and the upheavals of eight centuries of Russian history from the Tartars to Ivan the Terrible to Peter the Great, and the immutable Cambridge towers fall before his contemplations "about many things, about the caprices of fate, about my native land, and about how my best memories age with each day, and there is as yet nothing to take their place."

Nabokov has called himself "an American writer, born in Russia and educated in England where I studied French literature, before spending fifteen years in Germany." The particular quality of Nabokov's Americanism is captured by the thing he first admired about Americans when he arrived in the United States: the way they held their hands in their pockets. As American influences are more and more felt in England, the proposition which is about to be put forward is no longer precisely applicable in the 1960's and may become quite meaningless in subsequent years; but in the first half of the twentieth century an American was a person whose native language was English, but who could not (as could, say, the Indian) emulate the English manner either of speech or demeanor.

(The English poet from St. Louis is the exception to prove the rule.) And, carrying the definition a step farther, one may speak of Americanism as being a state of mind — and one which is by no means shared by all Americans — rather than an attribute of the inhabitants of specific geographical states. Vladimir Nabokov then is not, as he is usually called, a Russian-American author, but rather, he is an American-Russian writer, and was that long before he began to write in English, or had come to America.

Nabokov's very strong affection for the real America does not interfere with this perhaps overly elegant formulation of his true nationality. Nabokov has always been direct and eloquent in his statements about his adopted land — and especially so when he is not speaking to Americans. Thus, he told one French journalist who was seeking confirmation of *Lolita* as an attack on America: *"Mais j'adore l'Amérique, c'est mon pays,"* and to another he said: *"Quant à l'Amérique, elle m'a offert tout ce que la Russie n'a pas pu me donner."* The Philistine vulgarity which is described with such cheerful derision in *Lolita* is understood by Nabokov — he has said so in several different contexts — as a universal phenomenon which knows no particular nationality or social class. Beyond that, he has traveled all through the United States and knows the country too well to speak of it in generalities: "A little town in New England is so entirely different from a little town in Oregon. And a little town in one part of Oregon is so entirely different from a little town in another part."

Many criticists, particularly the European variety, have persisted in reading *Lolita* as a mockery of America: "Nabokov laughs at the smooth façade of American middle-class gentility . . . and debunks the big myths of a commercialized society of sellers, buyers, athletes, and entertainers." Nabokov has not concealed his distaste at this use of his fiction. "Whether or not critics think that in *Lolita* I am ridiculing human folly leaves me supremely indifferent," he told one interviewer. "But I am annoyed when the glad news is spread that I am ridiculing America." It is Nabokov's claim that he is trying to be an American writer and desires only those rights that other American writers have. A cursory glance through critical surveys of modern American fiction and poetry will show that Nabokov is frequently not discussed at all, or, if he is, it is as an afterthought (in the same way that Western surveys of Russian literature of the "from Gorky to Pasternak" type never discuss his Russian works). It is surely time that Nabokov be granted at least this basic American literary citizenship by literary historians and anthologists. Vladimir Nabokov *is* an American writer, and, as I have already said, in one sense he always has been.

If England herself failed to win the heart of Nabokov during the five years he lived there, English poetry did have a subtle but strong influence on the poetry of Vladimir Sirin. Of the poems produced during his Cambridge years Nabokov writes in *Speak, Memory:*

My fear of losing or corrupting, through alien influence, the only thing I had salvaged from Russia — her language — became positively morbid [and] it would have horrified me at the time to discover what I see so clearly now, the direct influence upon my Russian structures of various contemporaneous ("Georgian") English verse-patterns that were running about my room and all over me like tame mice.

Nabokov's particular favorite among the Georgians, although he outlived his youthful preference, was Rupert Brooke, and in 1922 he published a nineteen-page article in Russian on Brooke's poetry, including several hundred lines of his verse in poetic translation. The article is uncharacteristically impressionistic:

There is one uncommon and attractive feature in his art: an, as it were, radiant moisture — not for nothing was he in the Navy, and even his very name means "stream" in English. This Tiutchev-like love towards all that streams, murmurs, and is clear and cold is expressed so vividly, so convincingly in the majority of his poems that one wants not to read them, but to suck them through a straw, hold them close to one's face like damp flowers, to immerse oneself in them as in the freshness of a sky-blue lake.

In addition to his Brooke translations, Nabokov also published translations of some poems of the Irish poet Seumas O'Sullivan — the pseudonym of James Sullivan Starkey — but these were merely from an anthology that had pleased him, in addition to Keats' *La Belle Dame sans merci,* and Byron's *Sun of the Sleepless.* Although I have not been able to locate them, Nabokov recalls having published some Yeats translations. The influence of the prose of James

Joyce, which he first read when he was at Cambridge, is also most important for consideration of Nabokov's mature art. In a 1966 television interview Nabokov ranked Joyce even above Proust.

In his own English verse, and especially in the long poem *Pale Fire*, analogy to the whole canon of English poetry — Pope, Wordsworth, Shakespeare — is not only natural, but essential. It is difficult, however, for my perhaps insufficiently sensitive ear to separate and fix the individual Russian and English aspects in the Sirin poems, and this may well be due to the fact that, as indicated in the reference to the "Tiutchev-like" quality of Brooke's poetry, the Russian and English models are frequently too structurally similar in meter, imagery, and theme to be traced back in such a manner.

The poems of Vladimir Sirin appeared with great frequency in the early years of *The Rudder*, at times lapsing for a month or two, but often appearing several times a week. In 1923 he collected from these poems, excluding literally scores of the poorer ones, material for two books, *The Empyrean Path* (*Gorni put'*) and *The Cluster* (*Grozd'*). It would appear that even within this body of poems, there was another subdivision made by Nabokov, for the two books differ markedly in both length and quality.

The Empyrean Path was the first of the two to appear and is dedicated to the memory of his father. Its epigraph is taken from Pushkin's 1827 poem *Arion*:

> *Both the helmsman and the rower have perished!*
> *Only I, the mysterious singer,*
> *Have been hurled onto the shore by the storm.*
> *I sing the hymns of former times*
> *And my damp robe*
> *I dry in the sun, at the foot of the cliff.*

The epigraph refers primarily to the position of the artist in emigration, but a point that is more subtle and very appropriate to the early Sirin poems is Pushkin's line, "*I sing the hymns of former times.*" One of the first poems in the volume advises "*Without holding past visions in contempt,/ strive to create better ones.*" Another poem, *To the Poet*, cautions the poet against "*viscous swamps of sonorous absurdities,*" and the clear inference is that this refers to what we are wont to call "modern poetry."

The poems in *The Empyrean Path* have a measured elegiac and philosophical cast that brings to mind the poetic meditations of the great mid-nineteenth-century poet Fyodor Tiutchev. Compare, for example, the following stanza from Nabokov's *"O night, I'm yours! All evil is forgotten"*:

> *And I dream that across the night sky*
> *I shall sail far off in a phantasmal bark,*
> *And there is no end to the blue radiance;*
> *I am in it, it is in me.*

with the beginning of Tiutchev's 1836 poem *Dream at Sea*:

> *Both the sea and the storm rocked our bark;*
> *In my somnolence I was given over to every whim of the waves.*
> *Two infinities were within me,*
> *And they played with me in their own willful way.*

Such poetry, written in the 1920's, presents a difficulty for the reader that is easier to allow in the abstract than when presented with actual instances: to what degree is a poet obligated to be "of his time"? For Nabokov, who in later years was to declare that he does not believe in time but only an eternal present, the employment of classical diction and themes obviously was in no way unnatural. One may certainly agree that a beautiful poem is independent of its date of composition, and it is customary, in fact, to praise a poet for being "ahead of his time." The employment of older modes of artistic expression, however, except as an occasional diversion, rarely meets with approval. Each age has its own artistic forms and aesthetic currents, and the artist functions best, presumably, when he is responsive to them. There is a compelling logic in Nabokov's view of an art which is above the tyranny of fashion.

The Empyrean Path, however, was taken severely to task in nearly all the reviews of it which appeared. Typical of these was a notice in the short-lived but excellent journal *The New Russian Book*:

Sirin has everything one needs to be a poet: he has truly poetic perceptions, his poems are musical and are integral units, and, in spite of all this, the collection *The Empyrean Path*, with the exception of several poems which are really good, is a boring book. This is so not because the author wants talent, but because one cannot pass over all the achievements and gains of contemporary art, reject all currents and schools, and employ images which have long since faded and ceased to be symbols.

Independence, though it was expressed in a rather odd way, was present in Nabokov's art from the very beginning. The real problem posed by *The Empyrean Path* is not its air of antiquity so much as the extraordinary diversity of the components of that cultivated classicism. Consider, for example, poems written in the manner of both Pushkin and Tiutchev. There had long been a tradition in histories of Russian literature of the humbler sort that had Pushkin "passing on the torch of Russian poetry" to his successor Tiutchev; but, as a study by the brilliant Russian Formalist critic Yury Tynyanov conclusively demonstrated, this myth has absolutely no basis in fact. Tiutchev's first poems did appear in an almanac edited by Pushkin, but it is unlikely that Pushkin took any particular notice of them, and — much more important — the poetic styles of Pushkin and Tiutchev are antipodal. Beauty and lightness on the one hand; philosophical meditation on the other. Add to this the influence of a third poet, the Symbolist Aleksandr Blok, who is equally far removed from both Pushkin and Tiutchev, with certain English poets in the background, and it at once becomes clear that no single poet could produce poetry in so many diverse keys and yet still in his own voice. The majority of the poems in *The Empyrean Path* are best seen as poetic exercises, and, as the cited review shows, their technical mastery was granted even in hostile reviews of the book. In *Speak, Memory* Nabokov himself refers to these poems as "polished and rather sterile."

There are 127 poems in *The Empyrean Path* (more, if one counts separately groupings of short poems under a single title) as against only 36 in *The Cluster*, and it is worth the reader's while to be patient with the exercises of *The Empyrean Path*. There are enough successful poems in it to make a smallish book almost the size of *The Cluster*.

It is the longer poems in *The Empyrean Path* which are most successful, but this is to be true also of Nabokov's later mature poetry in both Russian and English. A poem entitled *The Crimea*, written in London, evokes the vivid impression made upon him by that exotic region, its flora, its butterflies, and of course its rich history and literary associations (among them Pushkin and Mickiewicz). *Two Ships* is a pleasing and quite original poem about two handsome ships which are docked near each other. They are treated as living *personae,* and when they set sail to different ports, each mourns for its "poor friend." After many storms and dangers they at last come together again and sit side by side murmuring to each other of the seas they have seen. The waves listen, but do not recognize the two old ships. And that is all — a theme which one would expect to carry a tedious cargo of symbolic or allegorical meaning becomes instead a whimsical and sparse sketch about space, time, and the graphic plotting of relationships. Another longer poem in which an object is similarly personified is *The Staircase.* The staircase in question is the one in the old Nabokov home, and it is depicted as straining to keep alive in its memory all the ascents and descents that were made on it. The poem is thus about memory summoning forth an object itself in the act of remembrance. Through a particularly skillful use of rustling *sh*'s and hard heel-like consonants, the staircase is most effectively recreated and the last descent of the poem is the poet's own exit from the house forever, *"free, hopeless."*

In a few poems the idiosyncrasy of the poet's vision completely effaces consciousness of their conventional form. *The Fairy's Daughter* is a poem that was originally written for *The Rainbow,* an anthology of children's verse edited by the prominent author of satirical and children's verse, Sasha Chyorny. Its subject is death and burial, and yet, in spite of this, *The Fairy's Daughter* remains a children's poem as well as a serious fantasy. The fairy's daughter has drowned in a dew drop while at play with her beloved little beetle. A butterfly (*"What is death to her?"*) gaily spreads the news as the funeral preparations are made. Two flowers with no sense of propriety gossip about how the fairy's daughter kissed the beetle just before she drowned. All the insects rush to the funeral, some in actual grief, others in their stupidity thinking they are going to a ball. A caterpillar, already wrapped in its cocoon, cannot stand it and crawls out again to attend. *"How pretty she is! This slender little curl,/ these little shoulders — who could describe this?"* Suddenly it is noticed that the little beetle is not there. The *"little black fiancé"* has gone off quietly by himself to pray to the setting sun. *The Fairy's Daughter* is one of my favorites among the early Sirin poems. It satisfies the requirement that is fulfilled by the best children's literature from *Alice in Wonderland* (which Nabokov translated into Russian in 1923) to *Huckleberry Finn* — namely, the ability to evoke the interest of adult readers.

A collection of seventeen eight-line poems under the collective title *Drops of Paint* includes some most interesting vignettes. One is a description of Napoleon in exile, but tragic significance is conspicuously lacking and he is merely *"pitiful in his wide-brimmed hat."* Another one devoted to Dostoevsky is even more impersonal, and offers a question rather than a statement:

> *Grieving in the world as though in Hell*
> *misshapen, convulsively inspired,*
> *in his prophetic delirium*
> *he outlined our disastrous century.*
> *Hearing his nightly wail,*
> *God thought: Could it really be*
> *that everything which was given by Me*
> *was so terrible and complicated?*

An effect similar to these poetic notations is achieved in literary allusions in which the terms or significance of the image are radically altered. Thus, in one poem, the image of Dante's Paolo and Francesca, doomed to fly forever in each other's arms, acquires a benign aspect as the poet sees himself flying through the heavens in the embrace of his beloved:

> *And there was no past, no purpose;*
> *the ecstasy of eternity united us;*
> *across the heavens we flew in embrace,*
> *blinded by the smiles of the heavenly bodies.*

In some of the better "Tiutchev poems" the philosophical theme is almost a gentle mockery of Tiutchev's own poetry. Thus, a *"boring god and a boring devil"* quarrel within the poet, or, instead of a troubled abyss, the poet's soul is as calm as a lake which accepts and reflects everything, but remains essentially untouched and calm.

Many of the poems in *The Cluster* are concerned with the

Russia that is portable: her culture. Beyond that there is the Russia of memory. But as regards the actual Russia, as early as 1919 Nabokov had declared calmly in one of his poems: *"We'll get on as we are — without Rus."* One poem that is dedicated to Ivan Bunin concludes with a promise *"not by thought or word to sin before your muse."* Exile is taken as the natural situation of the Russian poet: *"we are wisely homeless,/ and with us are the stars, the wind, God,"* and the muse is implored, after the manner of Pushkin, to be strict. A long poem, written on the occasion of the death of Aleksandr Blok in August 1921 has two parts. The first, in Blok's own poetic diction, evokes the figure of the famed poet and his cruel and mysterious Beautiful Lady who appeared to taunt him in shadows and mist; the second part enumerates the inhabitants of the Russian Parnassus:

> *Pushkin is a rainbow over all the land,*
> *Lermontov, the Milky Way above the mountains,*
> *Tiutchev, a spring flowing in the haze,*
> *Fet, a rubicund ray in a temple.*

They all converge and move *"at the appointed hour"* toward the soul of Aleksandr Blok, and

> *even we,*
> *in these years of sorrow and anger,*
> *perhaps shall hear from our prison*
> *the secret reverberation of their song.*

The other poems in the collection are love poems (not, however, addressed to Véra Slonim, whom he did not meet until May, 1923, and whom he married two years later) and poems devoted to the past. On the whole they surpass their counterparts in *The Empyrean Path.* A good representative of the modest but real merit of the poems in *The Cluster* is the following little eight-line poem, written in rhymed four-foot iambic meter except for the fourth line of each quatrain which is only three feet long:

> *There is freedom in solitude,*
> *and sweetness in noble fancies.*
> *A star, a snowflake, a drop of honey*
> *I fix in verse.*

And dying every night
I am glad to rise at the appointed hour,
and the new day is a dew-drop of paradise,
the past day, a diamond.

Probably the most balanced evaluation of these poems was given by Yuly Aikhenvald. "In general, the poems of Sirin," he wrote, "do not give as much as they promise." In spite of the fact that he had now published four volumes of poetry, Nabokov was, remember, only twenty-four. Such productivity is unusual even among Russian poets.

The influence of English literature upon Nabokov in this period of his life is much more evident in several short poetic dramas which he wrote between 1922 and 1924. The form itself is obviously an imitation of Pushkin's "little tragedies" — Nabokov translated one of them, *Mozart and Salieri*, into English (*The New Republic*, April, 1941) — but their subject matter is taken from English literature and life in three of the four little dramas. They are *Death*, *The Grandfather*, *The Pole*, and *The Wanderers*.

The most curious of these plays is *The Wanderers*, which appeared in the second (and last) number of the almanac *Facets*. It was not signed with his own name, but purported to be an English play written in 1768 by Vivian Calmbrood and translated by Vladimir Sirin. *The Wanderers* is Nabokov's first literary practical joke: Vivian Calmbrood is the anagram of "Vladimir Nabacov," which, it might be objected, is not playing quite fair, but in Cyrillic that "c" is a "k." At any rate, the trick worked, and the most suspicious comment was made by a reviewer who evidently had taken the trouble to check a history of English literature: "This writer does not know the 'Vivian Kalmbrud' whose tragedy, *The Wanderers*, Vladimir Sirin is translating from the English. One must take the translator's word that there is such an English writer and that what we have is actually a translation from his work. In any event, for the time being only the first act of the tragedy, done in a good poetic rendition, has been printed, and the question remains open."

Only the first act of this spurious romantic drama was written (Nabokov later referred to it as "an amelus"), which may have been due to the cessation of *Facets*, although it is quite possible that no more was intended. A good model with which to compare the play — although the young Nabokov was not familiar with the work — is *The Brothers*, the sentimental English drama by Richard Cumberland. Both the Sirin and the Cumberland play have the same date — 1768.

The Wanderers, like Cumberland's play, is about two brothers. They have both been away from their family home and have not seen each other for many years. They meet in the Tavern of the Purple Dog. One, Erik, has traveled in distant lands, but he has now returned to find his family home and, more important, his idealized past. The other brother, Robert, is a feared bandit and killer who has terrorized the owner of the tavern and fallen in love with his daughter Silvia, who is not indifferent to the bandit.

The confrontation and discovery of each other's identity by Erik and Robert release what appear to be the two primary dramatic springs of the play (of course, in the solitary act which was written one sees only the initial thrust) — the conflict and contrast between Erik and Robert and the tragic fate of the family, the Firenets. The romance between Silvia and Robert promises to be the countervailing force which will, according to the period formula of *The Brothers* and other such plays, divert *The Wanderers* from tragedy. As the first act ends, Silvia's entrance in a trance prevents Robert, in a fit of rash cynicism, from murdering her father. Robert is clearly the central figure in the play, and he vacillates between haughty fulfillment of his role as murderer and robber and despair at his lot. Robert describes his own soul as "*a goblet of rays of light and pus,/ a mixture of toad and swan.*" He taunts Erik by first telling him that the Firenet homestead is just as he left it and then mockingly suggesting that he was not telling him the truth, and Erik, stunned and confused by both his person and his words, sees Robert's shadow wavering on the ceiling "like a drunken Negro." If one wishes to look to the example of *The Brothers*, it may well be that, like the elder Belfield brother in Cumberland's play, Robert was responsible for whatever misfortune befell the Firenets, although, again, the genre demands a "happy" conclusion to the action.

The Wanderers is an "imitation" only in the broadest sense of that term, and one is struck most of all by precisely its superiority over model English melodramas of the period. Nabokov has made such literary expeditions to other centuries and literary climates on several other occasions throughout his career. In 1942 he even undertook to write a conclusion to Pushkin's unfinished poetic drama *The Water Nymph*. I think that there may be no more difficult type of literary exercise than this, and proper appreciation of such writing places greater demands upon the reader also. In a sense, even though its subject is "contemporary," this is the primary difficulty posed by the poem *Pale Fire*.

Death (1923) is a very short two-act play, written in unrhymed iambic pentameter and set at Cambridge University in 1806 — while Byron was a student there. It is a "Byronic play" (in which Byron himself appears briefly), and also the first youthful Nabokov work which may rightfully stand beside the mature writer's best minor works.

The play concerns a tutor named Gonvil who suspects that his beautiful young wife Stella has deceived him with a friend and disciple, Edmund. Beyond that, any plot summary of *Death* must be highly problematical, for it is by no means certain that death actually occurs in the play, and, if so, how many deaths there are. Gonvil sends a messenger to Edmund who at the time is with some friends — among them Byron, *"a handsome lame fellow"* — and the messenger tells him that Stella has suddenly dropped dead. Edmund goes to Gonvil and asks to be given some poison (Gonvil is a Master of Sciences), claiming that he has been living with a mounting fear of life for six months. Gonvil gives him a potion to drink.

The second act takes place several moments later in the same room. Edmund attempts to acclimate himself to death, and, when the spots have cleared from his eyes, he finds Gonvil still sitting in his armchair as before. Gonvil declares that he is but *"the echo of your mortal thoughts,"* and it develops that death is but the artistic re-use and exploitation of one's earthly life, and the richer one's life has been, the more satisfying and prolonged will death's dramatization of the past be. Sooner or later, however, the play must cease, and one's past memories will hurtle over the abyss into nothingness. Edmund and Gonvil begin a dialogue in which Gonvil attempts to draw out the circumstances of the relationship between Edmund and Stella. Edmund talks freely, and it develops that there was nothing more between him and Stella than a single intense glance that was exchanged once when Gonvil had left the room. His love for Stella was real, but he had managed to contain its storm within himself.

Then Gonvil declares that the potion he has given him was not really poison, and that even Stella has not really died. Edmund first bitterly sees the stratagem used by Gonvil to pry his secret out of him, but then — he has perhaps gone mad — he takes Gonvil at his first word and claims the entire discourse and Gonvil himself as his own invention: *"my thoughts, my vivid dream beyond the grave/ still lives and breathes, and creates."* As proof of what he says, Gonvil goes to the staircase and calls Stella, and Edmund, his inner thoughts bared and unsure of what reality he is in, begs him to close the door. The play ends before Stella appears.

The story "makes sense" if Gonvil's explanation is accepted, but the fictional "reality" of Edmund's fantasy, either as he is dying or after death, has an equally great claim to our credence. This same motif — death as a simulation of reality, and the simultaneous cofunctioning of two distinct worlds — is the subject of a 1931 story, *Terra Incognita*, about some Englishmen lost in the jungle, but the story is not as successful and interesting as the earlier closet drama. The two concurrent possibilities in *Death*, the dialogue between the two men, and its deft and mysterious conclusion make the play a model of its genre.

Nabokov's third "English" poetic drama, *The Pole*, is on a modern theme: Scott's fatal expedition to the South Pole in 1912 on which all five members perished, three of them when they were only a short distance from their camp. Nabokov himself had had the intention of going on an exploration of Asiatic Siberia after he finished at Cambridge, and the Scott expedition was, of course, one of the most courageous and dramatic in the annals of exploration. The specific inspiration for the drama was a visit to the British Museum where he saw Scott's journal under glass.

The Pole is an exploration not of the nature of death, but rather of the various means by which brave men can meet it. The play is the least interesting of the eight that Nabokov has written, probably because it remains a strictly historical treatment and offers no particular subtleties or elaborations.

The other outstanding "little drama," written in the same year as *Death*, is *The Grandfather*. It is set in France in 1816. A nobleman has returned to his native country for the first time since the bloody events of 1792. He stops at a peasant's house during a heavy rainfall and asks for shelter. In addition to the peasant couple and their daughter Juliet (who does not know who Romeo is), there is an old man living with the family. Although he is in fact no relation to the family, he is referred to as "grandfather." The old man had appeared in the village the previous spring, and to all questions that were put to him he would only smile timidly. He is evidently senile, for he talks to the flowers in the garden.

When the nobleman, de Merival, first arrives, the grandfather is asleep; de Merival tells the family about how he escaped execution at the time of the revolution. He was only twenty, and he cannot recall why he was sentenced to the guillotine — likely it was either his name or his powdered hair. He was to be decapitated at night in a torch-lit square and by a refined executioner who had raised his gruesome occupation to an art. As the youth ascended the platform he was unable to swallow, already anticipating the stroke of the blade on his neck, and his body and all his senses were trembling, although he remained outwardly calm. He escaped execution thanks to a fire which broke out at the last moment. He fled France, and in the course of the next twenty-four years he lived in England, Russia, Turkey, Greece, and Italy.

The peasants tell the grandfather about the tales that the stranger has been telling them of the Lyons executioner, and evidently de Merival and the old man recognize each other. When they are left alone, the old man excuses himself for a moment and returns gaily hopping from foot to foot. He is carrying an axe behind his back, and he tries to get de Merival to lie across a table for him. When Juliet returns she asks the stranger what has happened to the grandfather, and he tells her to stay out of the house. We must imagine the conclusion ourselves.

The grandfather is a perfectly logical character if insanity or senility is taken into account, but, beyond all considerations of verisimilitude, the character is memorable and impressive by that very contrast of bland mien and sinister character. He is a direct forebear of the lugubrious executioner Monsieur Pierre in *Invitation to a Beheading*.

After these little dramas, Nabokov wrote a five-act poetic drama in 1924, *The Tragedy of Mister Morn*. It is a further development of the death theme with which the previous shorter dramas are largely concerned. It is also the first time that Nabokov uses the theme of a king in exile. The play concerns a king in an imaginary country of some past age. The characters have names such as Midia, Edmin, Ganus, Tremens, Clian, and Dandilio; a "mysterious foreigner" from the twentieth century enters the play briefly and finds "an illusory semblance with my far-off native town, the semblance that occurs between the truth and an exalted invention." The king has compromised himself in a duel with his mistress' husband and, after a terrible period of wavering indecision, he decides to abdicate his throne. But his mistress deceives him, and his country is thrown into turmoil. In the end the king, who is living in hiding as Mister Morn, is found by the husband — we recall Pushkin's Silvio — and is wounded by his opponent's long overdue shot. With the duel now completed, the king feels that he has somehow regained his honor, and he decides to resume his throne. The kingdom is filled with a romantic aura of renewal, but too much has happened in the king's absence, and at a moment when he has apparently achieved happiness he commits suicide.

Every action throws its reflection upon another character and eventually everyone in the play is faced with death, each accepting it in his own way. Thus, although *The Tragedy of Mister Morn* is ostensibly an "historical" drama, its focus is not so much on the tragedy of a civilization in upheaval as on the tragedy of the individual caught in history's net and trying to extricate himself from it with dignity.

Mister Morn is a magnificent coward who wants his death only on the condition that it occurs in view of the whole world, so that he can meet it in ecstasy *"with an immortal exclamation."* His kingly achievement is the realization that the only real "other" is the *"thousand-eyed observer looking [at me]/ from suspicious mirrors."* Morn compares his impending death with falling toward his own reflection in a well, a metaphor that will occur to most of the protagonists of Nabokov's novels. The tragedy of Mister Morn is at the same time the triumph of the king he becomes for the first time.

There is one other unpublished poetic work of this period which is most intriguing and, in view of Nabokov's subsequent statements about his aversion to music, not a little surprising. This is a poetic accompaniment entitled *Agaspher* written for a staged dramatic pantomime (by Ivan Lukash) to accompany a symphony by the émigré composer V. F. Yakobson. This collaborative undertaking was performed once in Berlin.

Agaspher is one of the names attached to the legend of the Wandering Jew. Its first occurrence is in a seventeenth-century German chapbook, where it is given as the actual name of Buttadeus — the man who struck Christ on the way to the Cross and has, therefore, been doomed to wander until the Second Coming. In popular literature the name Agaspher acquired some amatory characteristics borrowed from another folklore character and became the Wandering Lover. The Sirin Agaspher is tormented by dreams of earthly beauty, and he claims that he would sell the heavens in order to sin with the object of his love — one aspect of which he recognizes in every century. He has inhabited Florence and also assumed the guises of Marat and Byron. *"I shall catch you/ catch you, Maria, my inexpressible dream,/ from age to age!"* he proclaims in the Prologue. In *The Tragedy of Mister Morn* and *Agaspher* we already have, by 1924, variants on the themes that were to become *Pale Fire* and *Lolita*.

If the poetic dramas are more engaging and, on the whole, have more lasting value than the large body of Nabokov's early poems, this merely foreshadows his gradual emergence as primarily a *narrative* poet. To be sure Nabokov continued to write odes, sonnets, and occasional verse. These shorter poems are addressed primarily to the themes of Russia and art, and, after about 1925, they are of a consistently higher quality. Nabokov's own estimate of his poetic maturation is rather more strict. He published only three more collections of his verse (1930, 1952, and — in English — 1959), all sparse and carefully chosen, and he attached an Author's Note to the 1952 book in which he said: "The poems selected for this edition were composed in Germany, France, and

America between 1929 and 1951. The first of them marks the end of the period of my youthful art."

The gradual shift from emphasis on the intimate to the narrative (even in poems which are personal statements rather than tales) may be seen not only in the poems themselves, but also in many of the book reviews which he wrote prior to 1930. In 1927, for example, he writes: ". . . in my view, the *fabula* is just as essential to a poem as to a novel." The poems on Russia and exile are now frequently presented in a fantastic, aerial mood somewhat reminiscent of Chagall — a bed floats back to Russia, a mirror loses its hold on the objects in a room, and in one poem the indignant citizens inform the poet: "*You have forgotten. It is forbidden to fly*" — and these, even if they are not, strictly speaking, "narrative" poems, are still closer to artistic *tableaux* than to philosophical meditative poems. There are many short poems which contain a complete narrative that might easily serve as the basis for a short story. In a poem entitled *The Boxer's Girlfriend* a woman sits among the spectators as her boyfriend is brutally defeated; remembering how she herself had been similarly struck by him in the face, she joins in the roar of approval for the victor. Another describes an old woman who goes to a carpenter to have some repairs done, but finds that he has gone off to Judea with his young wife. One poem is about an Egyptian lad who frolics on some damp bricks which are found three thousand years later by an archaeologist; another about the strangeness of seeing Leo Tolstoy, "*an uncomely old man of short stature,/ his beard disheveled by the wind*," captured on film and glaring his displeasure at the camera and the photographer; still another about Pushkin in exile at Mikhailovskoe, or how Pushkin might have reacted to the foreign exile of the twentieth century. And there is one — an exceptionally fine poem — about an old chess master who drinks and reminisces with friends about his glorious past, and, in the end, "*In delirious combinations, night and day / the maestro, a grey-haired old man hopped like a white knight.*"

In the twenty-four poems written between 1924 and 1928, which are included in the 1930 collection of short stories *The Return of Chorb*, there is one which is my own favorite among all of Nabokov's short poems. Entitled *In Paradise* it first appeared in

The Rudder in March, 1928 where it had another title, *To My Soul:*

> *My soul — after my death far-off*
> *your image appears to me like this:*
> *a provincial naturalist,*
> *an eccentric lost in paradise.*
>
> *There in a grove a wild angel slumbers —*
> *an almost peacock-like creature . . .*
> *You inquisitively poke*
> *at him with your green umbrella,*
>
> *imagining how at first*
> *you'll write an article about him,*
> *then . . . But it seems there is no journal,*
> *and there are no readers in paradise.*
>
> *And you stand, still not believing*
> *your mute woe . . .*
> *About this blue, somnolent beast*
> *Whom will you tell, whom?*
>
> *Where are the world and classified roses,*
> *the museum and stuffed birds?*
> *And you look and look through your tears*
> *at its nameless wings . . .*

My particular affection for this beautiful and wry little poem is probably based upon the fact that I take it as the very epigraph of Nabokov's artistic career.

Four

❈ ❈ ❈ ❈

NABOKOV has written eight major longer poems, although the number might be further increased by including some of his earliest, less significant poems already discussed. Five of them are in Russian; the remaining three, in English. They are *A University Poem* (1927), *The Night Journey* (1931), *Fame* (1942), *A Parisian Poem* (1943), *An Evening of Russian Poetry* (1945), *To Prince S. M. Kachurin* (1947), *The Ballad of Longwood Glen* (1957), and *Pale Fire* (1962).

A University Poem is a tale in sixty-three sonnet-stanzas about student life at Cambridge. This obvious adoption of the form of *Eugene Onegin* was in itself an act of boldness, if not impertinence, but the challenge was met. In no proper sense of the term an "imitation," *A University Poem* still cannot be far from what Pushkin himself would have written had he lived in twentieth-century England, which is praise of an order that may not be fully grasped by those who have not read *Eugene Onegin* in Russian.

Its plot, briefly, concerns an unnamed Russian university student in England, who is also the narrator, and his very circumspect romance with a girl named Violet. The narrator is puzzled by the intriguing and peculiarly English contradictions between Violet's conversation and her eyes. At a soccer game he gathers up the courage to touch her hand, which she casually withdraws, noting with amusement as she does so the awkwardness of one of the soccer players.

The romance with the amiably cold Violet progresses, through leisurely and delightful descriptions of Cambridge, university studies, lectures, exams, and boating excursions, to an embrace. But this greater intimacy only intensifies the undiminished distance between them. When the narrator meets a fellow student named Johnson whom he has not seen for some time, Johnson sadly tells him of an unhappy romance he has had, and later points the girl out on the street. It is Violet, and this discovery causes the narrator to lose himself in his studies, recalling Violet, with some surprise at his own behavior, only after he has completed his final examinations. They meet at the graduation ball, dance, and then part simply and — it would seem — casually. The "romance" is, as it were, an imagined dalliance between the poet-narrator of *Eugene Onegin* and the beautiful, sadly proud Tatyana of the end of Pushkin's novel-in-verse.

The distance imposed by Violet herself is matched by two other removes which are equally important in the poetic structure. The first of these is the cultural difference. He is a curiosity for her, the "first Russian" she has ever met; while he finds himself dreaming that he is talking to Violet in Russian and addressing her by the familiar form of speech. The second distance, and by far the most important one, is that between the student's "real acquaintances" and their transmutations in his poetry. For the narrator-protagonist is on the verge of accepting his calling as a poet, and art seems to him to preclude earthly pleasures: *"Don't let me, God, become a poet,/ foolishly let slip the earthly."* Violet herself becomes a figure in the narrator's poetic imagination, not merely as an object of devotion, but as someone who is refracted through time. The narrator muses on what the cleaning woman at the university was like as a young girl, and then Violet appears in his imagination as a similar of the cleaning lady, who, in her turn, is to see the narrator as another link in the continuing succession of students. When they are boating, the poet is already thinking of boat trips he will take with other girls and drifting back to a past love that the moment evokes. At her greatest remove, Violet seems separated from him by a file of mysterious centuries.

The essentially Pushkinesque quality of *A University Poem* is shown not only by its meter, rhyme, and sonnet form, but also in scores of casual turns of speech. *"To read, to write — what should I do?"* the poet muses to himself in boredom as he sits in his room in the dull little university town, and we recall the lines from *Eugene*

Onegin (Chapter Four, XLIII) which ruminate on the problem of living in the Russian countryside in the winter. And then, in the very next stanza, the poet is wearily reading the fourth volume of Dahl's monumental *Explanatory Dictionary of the Living Great Russian Language*, which he found along with some Pushkin in a Cambridge bookstall (in this at least *A University Poem* will not escape the biographer's smug smile, for the incident is mentioned in *Speak, Memory*), when he comes to the word *khándra*, and his recitations of the word's meanings — melancholy, depression, boredom, spleen, hypochondria — immediately recall an even more famous passage from *Eugene Onegin* (Chapter One, XXXVIII): *"similar to the English 'spleen' — / in short, the Russian 'chondria.'"* The difference is that in the Pushkin the English leads to the Russian word, while in the Sirin poem the verbal direction is reversed. Nabokov's description of Violet's eccentric aunt (*"one of those learned fools/ with which England is richly endowed"*), who reveres the ideal of culture, reads lectures to the working class, and thinks that Kharkov is a Russian general, stands comfortably by Pushkin's most charming portraits of country squires.

While *A University Poem* is not a stylization, there is, at least to my ear, a certain tension between subject and form, which might also be described as an amiable, familial disagreement between centuries. Some of the best stanzas are addressed directly to this theme:

> *Fashion does not control a living soul,*
> *but sometimes my freedom*
> *will by chance coincide with it:*
> *I'm pleased by the fox-trot, simple and tender . . .*
> *Some other mind inevitably will*
> *Symptoms of the age find in it —*
> *depravity accompanied by the music of bedlam;*
> *some lady who writes*
> *or ha'penny bard*
> *will bewail the disappearance of former dances;*
> *but for me, I'll tell you frankly,*
> *there is no special delight*
> *in a rude and unwashed*
> *marquis dancing a minuet.*

Inevitably, this portrait of the young man becoming an artist blends into a reconciliation between art and life, and the poet leaves Violet, the university, and England ready to sense and record *"the delicate gyrations/ of our slightly listing planet."* *A University Poem*, longer than the typical *Eugene Onegin* chapter by about a dozen stanzas, is complete in itself, and yet, so great is its poetic concordance with *Onegin* (the rhyme scheme of *A University Poem* uses the sonnet form of *Eugene Onegin* turned upside down), that the reader cannot help but be surprised by the absence of the anticipated "to be continued" at the end. Its more proper comparison is with but a single chapter of *Eugene Onegin*, and Nabokov himself may have felt a certain "incompleteness" in *A University Poem*, for some of its central narrative threads were to be extended and incorporated into one of the later Sirin novels.

The Night Journey, a rhymed iambic poem 133 lines long, appeared five years later in *The Rudder* in 1931 (in the meantime Nabokov had published three novels and a collection of short stories) and was his last contribution to his father's paper before it ceased publication. *The Night Journey* has no serious artistic pretensions, but it is a delightful tour de force which has a fascinating and involved story behind it. *The Night Journey* is the second appearance of "Vivian Calmbrood," and it appeared titled "From the Calmbrood long poem *Night Journey*." Although the title is evidently taken from a Rupert Brooke poem of the same name, the poem is set in England at an unspecified time, ascertainable, however, as not later than 1830. This is made clear through the identity of the second character in the poem, a writer traveling to London from the countryside with "Calmbrood" in an otherwise deserted coach. He tells Calmbrood that at his country seat, where he often goes strolling with his neighbor (a young man named Wordsworth), he has been at work on "a short drama from knightly times." The poem ends as Calmbrood, after listening to the stranger's long discourse, asks him who he is. The mysterious English writer turns out to be — as most Russians would have guessed by now — Chenston, the English author to whom Pushkin ascribed his little tragedy, *The Covetous Knight*, which he wrote between 1826 and 1830.

The Night Journey is, in fact, a programmatic statement about art and a sharp literary counterattack on Nabokov's part, and Pushkin's pseudonymous Chenston as the spokesman for his ideas serves as the poetic standard Nabokov grabs to carry into the fray. There are two specific targets in the poem: one is the critic Georgy Adamovich, the other the émigré poet and writer Georgy Ivanov.

Ivanov and Adamovich were two of the leading figures of the important coterie in Russian émigré literature centering around the Parisian almanac *Chisla* (*Numbers*), which began to appear in 1930 and in the next four years published eight thick issues (two of which were double numbers). In addition to the publication, which was edited by the poet, critic, and writer Nikolai Otsup, there were also regular *Numbers* literary salons and readings. The central figures in the *Numbers* grouping (and this was true of both Adamovich and Ivanov) had made their literary debuts prior to 1917. There were numerous talented younger writers and poets, too (Gaito Gazdanov, Boris Poplavsky, Anatoly Shteiger were the best of them), and this meeting of the older and younger literary generations in *Numbers* was notable if not exceptional — it was a frequent complaint among younger writers in the emigration that those writers with established reputations made no effort to encourage emerging writers or to cultivate a literary climate in which literature could grow and move forward. Equally notable in *Numbers* was the absence of many of the masters of émigré literature such as Mark Aldanov, Ivan Bunin, Vladislav Khodasevich, Aleksandr Kuprin, and Mikhail Osorgin.

It is quite possible that some of these absences may have been prompted at least in part — although certainly not entirely, for wherever Adamovich, Ivanov, and the Symbolist poet Zinaida Gippius congregated there was bound to be controversy and animosity, both literary and personal — by a vicious attack on Nabokov's writing which appeared in the very first issue of *Numbers*.

Actually, in certain respects, the declared intentions of *Numbers* were such that one would reasonably have expected Nabokov to appear in its pages. He did appear in that same first number in which he was attacked — a reply to a literary questionnaire on the influence of Proust — but never after that, although his cousin, Nikolai Nabokov, was the regular music critic of *Numbers*. The almanac's format — its high-quality paper and many art reproductions — set it off from most émigré publications and recalled the elegant journals of the prerevolutionary Silver Age of Russian literature such as *Apollo* and *The Scales*. Moreover, its credo stressed a European orientation of the sort that we associate with Nabokov's own attitude:

Twelve years of emigration constitute, if not in terms of history, then at least in terms of each separate individual's life, a sufficiently lengthy period. In this time we have seen much in the West, we have understood and experienced it differently than our forebears. We have seen and are seeing, as it were, from within, some of the most important developments in the Western world, for example, to speak only of literature, the growth of Proust's influence and the affirmation of his genius.

Further, *Numbers* declared itself to be above political questions (a position which Zinaida Gippius — whom Trotsky once described as "a lyrical Petrograd lady" turned "property-owning witch" by the Russian revolution — was to fulminate against in its pages); *Numbers* was to be devoted exclusively to matters of culture and art, whether Soviet, émigré, or foreign.

The *Numbers* attack on Nabokov was by the prominent "nihilistic" poet Georgy Ivanov (his most famous poem proclaims: *"It's good there is no Tsar./ It's good there is no Russia./ It's good there is no God."*); the motive behind his article requires an explanation in itself. Ivanov's wife was the poetess and writer Irina Odoevtseva. In 1929 her novel *Isolde* appeared and was reviewed by Nabokov in *The Rudder*. It was certainly not a favorable review, but it must be said that Nabokov was not "looking for a fight," since — as he told an interviewer many years later — Odoevtseva had herself sent him a copy of the novel inscribed in a coyly friendly fashion. What Ivanov wrote on Nabokov was not so much a devastating review as a *scandale* in the true Russian sense of the term. A significant segment of Russian intellectual society in Paris and Berlin held that the article had "soiled the pages" of the new publication, and a review of *Numbers* by Mikhail Osorgin in a leading Parisian newspaper did not deign to acknowledge the presence of the piece. Nabokov himself seems to have been quite unruffled by what Ivanov wrote, and he subsequently referred to the affair as "the amusing case of Georgy Ivanov, a good poet but a scurrilous critic."

The Ivanov article is a survey of the first three Sirin novels (*Mashenka; King, Queen, Knave; The Luzhin Defense*) and the collection of short stories and poems *The Return of Chorb*. The article does not pretend to be anything but a strong personal statement. But even Ivanov allows the talent and glitter (both of which, it is true, he implies are false) in Nabokov's writing and exempts *King, Queen, Knave* and *The Luzhin Defense* from discussion beyond repeating Georgy Adamovich's formulation that they are clever imitations of German and French models whose only virtue in Russian literature is their novelty. His attack is concentrated upon *Mashenka* and *The Return of Chorb. Mashenka* and the short stories are termed "vulgarity not without virtuosity," and the poems "simply vulgar." Here, according to Ivanov, may be found the true basis of Sirin's art which, stripped of its imitation of foreign models, is an "in-no-way complicated" counterfeit of the tradition to which he aspires to belong. Sirin, wrote Ivanov (and this sentence, at any rate, certainly is scurrilous), is "an imposter, a cook's son, a black sheep, a low scoundrel." Ivanov names some of the most insignificant poetasters in Russian literature as Nabokov's poetic mentors, and then adds that since he is a person of capability, he may yet surpass these teachers. The purity of the attack was unsullied by any specifics — two sentences by Nabokov are quoted as examples of his bad writing, but the article fails to refer to a single incident or character in any of the novels, and it does not bother to name, much less discuss, even one of the short stories in the *Chorb* collection.

All of this involved background information is essential to understand fully what *The Night Journey* is about. Neither Adamovich nor Ivanov is mentioned by name in Chenston's long discourse upon his art and his attitude toward literary critics, but there is certainly not the slightest doubt to whom his words refer. Chenston tells Calmbrood how "sinister gentlemen" follow his muse:

I incur the displeasure
of one critic because
I find amusing
his dolefulness
his delicate bestowal of favors,
the languour of his judgments, his effeminate style,
the ever-present resonance of offense,
and most of all, his poems.
Poor fellow! His bones squeak as he strums his tin lyre;
before the funereal pit he bows
his Adamic head.

From Adamovich, Chenston moves on to a cutting, perhaps somewhat heavy, mockery of the cultivated despair of Ivanov's poetry:

And in general poets are very much
concerned with death now; a wreath and faded toga
are what they usually wear.
Decline, sunset . . . A new Petronius,
a half-smile on his lips,
with the last turquoise rose
in his delicately folded fingers
settles in the bathtub. All is ready.
Close now is the hour of chosen death . . .
But wait! Instead of cutting one's vein,
would it not be better to take some soap
and wash for a change?

The clear reason that Nabokov could never be a member of the "*Numbers* group" is that, with an audacity more astonishing in the young Nabokov than in the older accomplished writer, he refused to make even the deferential gesture of tactful silence, and under no circumstances would allow himself to be conscripted into a "movement" or partake of "common inspiration in the back rooms of Parisian cafés." He was an émigré within émigré literature, and he accepted this as his natural and desired state.

Of far greater interest than the specific literary skirmishes in *The Night Journey*, though, are the generalized comments which Chenston makes upon the role of satire in his (that is, of course, Nabokov's) art:

> *There is a bloodthirsty streak*
> *in my gentle muse —*
> *she flails the prophets with a swish,*
> *she hides like a fiery tigress*
> *and leaps out suddenly with claw-like verse*
> *at the nape of human vulgarity . . .*
> *Long live satire! There is, however,*
> *no food for it in the dull*
> *world of journals where we bustle*
> *after our immortality.*
> *The days of Juvenal have passed.*
> *Should we really not celebrate then*
> *how, for a knavish article,*
> *they beat Johnson with a candlestick?*
> *There is no air in such a narrow world.*
> *I shall take my muse away.*
> *And how, you ask, does she live —*
> *untrammelled, gaily? Oh yes.*

This passage is surely as applicable to the later forays against Sartre and Wilson as to the encounters with Adamovich and Ivanov. It would be a mistake, however, to view this passage from *The Night Journey* as an emblem of Nabokov's attitude toward negative criticism. *The Gift,* for example, contains severe auto-criticism, and Nabokov had met more than a few unkind, but carefully considered and impersonal estimates of his art with equanimity. The "claws of his muse" are reserved for the criticist, and even then only for the criticist of a certain repute and flair. My own understanding of Nabokov's attitude toward literary controversy is taken from a remark made in the course of a book review. "It's my sin," he wrote, "that I love a polemic. (But only, of course, with honorable people.)"

Nabokov did not undertake any long poems during the next ten years, and he wrote very few short poems in this period, too. It was in the course of this decade that he wrote almost all of his most important Russian prose works. *Fame* was written in Russian (its Russian title is *Slava*) in 1942, that is, when Nabokov had come to the United States and "changed over" to English, a tempting and neat division which is clearly highly suspect.

Fame, like most of the fifteen poems in the 1952 book of Russian poems, is written in ternary meter — in this case, though, a slightly irregular meter. It is unique among Nabokov's poems in that it shares the sudden twists and turns of person, direction, and tone so characteristic of his novels. The poem is a serious dialogue with an absurd double. Its very first line, in which the interlocutor on little wheels or casters enters, is a cacophony of "k's" in Russian: *"I vót kak na kolyósikakh vkátyvaetsya ko mne nékto."* The "someone" (*nékto*) is lean, sinewy, and has soot in his red nostrils. The poet cannot make up his mind whether this is a person or garrulous corpse; as it turns out, he is something close to a combination of Ivan Karamazov's devil and Gogol's Akaky Akakievich (a reference to Akaky Akakievich in the twelfth line confirms the suspicion that this is the meaning of the play on "k's" in the poem's opening lines). The poet's guest is "like Adverb," the conglomeration of deceptive little verbal gestures from which Gogol forges a semblance of speech for Akaky Akakievich in *The Overcoat*. He is more a literary gesture than a clearly defined character or even double.

The poet's absurdity-on-casters does, all the same, have an air of intellectual and emotional substantiality working at cross-purposes to its appearance, and it is in this way that it resembles Ivan Karamazov's shabby devil. The apparition seems to the poet like "a sinister friend of childhood," "a master spy," "an executioner," and "a parody of conscience in a bad drama."

Fame's sentences, like so many of Pasternak's, are wildly fragmentary, really loose groupings of metaphors and images that refuse to submit to the autocratic yoke of grammatical meaning. *Fame* is not a mockery of or attack upon Pasternak in the way that another poem in the 1952 book, *About Heads of State* (1945), does specifically ridicule both the politics and the artistic style of Mayakovsky. (Nabokov pays respect to Pasternak the poet in a series of comments made in his poetry reviews in *The Rudder* throughout the Twenties. *Doctor Zhivago* is something else again, however, and Nabokov has said that on this subject he and Adamovich met symbolically for the first time as the only two émigré critics who recognized the sentimentality and vulgarity of the novel. Respect for Pasternak's poetic gift is accompanied by fascinated astonishment at how he disregards or overcomes the most elementary grammatical precepts of the Russian language. Once, Nabokov did allow his vexation to take the upper hand and wrote that "he has a rather poor knowledge of the Russian language" (*"plokhovato on znaet russky yazyk"*), but more typically he would speak of "the marvelous ungrammatical quality of the talented but murky Pasternak.") This Pasternakian manner of poetic speech does not dominate *Fame*, and should not be read (and was not intended) as a specific parody of Pasternak, but appears as an incidental motif, thus contributing to the air of strangeness produced by the "waxen guest":

> . . . *There are things, things*
> *which . . . even . . . (Akaky Akakievich*
> *loved, if you recall, "weedpatches of words,"*
> *and he is like an Adverb, my waxen guest),*
> *and the heart implores, and the heart palpitates,*
> *and I cannot . . .*

One should note in this disordered fragment how certain clear statements can be tentatively (but only tentatively) surmised by the attentive reader. The serious purpose behind the verbal jumble is suggested by the Hamletic beginning ("There are more things in heaven and earth, Horatio"), and the abrupt foreclosure of that beginning emphasizes the poet's inability to articulate the mysterious things he knows and uses to refute his garrulous adversary. The poem's concluding lines are: *"I saw, as in a mirror, the world and myself,/and more, and more, and more."* The very hesitation slides into consideration of Gogol's little clerk whose "conversation" is really an author's trick.

The discourse between the poet and the apparition is concerned in large part with the poet's relation to his native land and the endurance of his art. But the likely paths are not taken.

> . . . *It would've been fine*
> *if by this the joker had shown me*
> *that I had changed countries like counterfeit money,*
> *hurrying on and fearing to glance back,*

like a bifurcated spectre,
like a candle between mirrors sailing off to a sunset
. . . . .
But my word arches like an aerial bridge
across the world, and like a succession of spokelike shades
I pass ever along it incognito
to the fire-lit darkness of my native land.

The poet, "*a little idol . . . a sorcerer with a bird's head,*" blocks passage across that bridge by his interpreters and readers, and then neatly dismantles the bridge itself behind him:

. . . Reread
and ponder these lines.
apostrophizing the nonexistent: And by the way,
it's not a bridge, this rustling underfoot, but a
cloudrange . . .

The poet's attention wanders between his apparition and his reader. In another aside, the poet steps downstage to explain his poem for those of us who might not have caught the point:

In his long poem Fame *the writer*
is, so to say, occupied by the problem pursued
by the thought of contact with the reader's consciousness . . .

The point continually stressed by the apparition is that the writer's three hundred folios of *belles lettres* will scatter and be hopelessly lost in exile because, unlike real leaves (in Russian the term for folio is "leaf"), they have no ground to fall to. He conjures up a sentimental vision of provincial Russia and concludes: "*No, no one ever in that great expanse/ will mention even one page by you.*" The writing he has done in English is described slightingly as being "*not without brilliance in an entirely foreign language.*"

The apparition mocks the poet by another vision—the poet as an acknowledged master in his native land whom they dare not touch, a "European treasure." But this vision is discarded with a laugh almost as soon as it has been articulated, and the secret of his art and life remains untouched:

> *This is why I am so amused by the empty dream*
> *about the reader, the body, and fame.*
> *I matured without body, am alive without resonance,*
> *and my secret is ever with me.*
> *What is the perishing of my books, if even the break*
> *between me and my native land is but a detail?*
> *I'll grant that the night is well codified,*
> *but I have deciphered the stars*
> *and in myself have descried how to rise above myself,*
> *and I cannot say it more precisely than that.*

This same note is sounded in a most intriguing interview with Nabokov that appeared in January, 1964, in an American mass circulation magazine of randy inclination and lapses of seriousness. Asked whether he believes in God, Nabokov replied: "To be quite candid — and what I am going to say now is something I have never said before, and I hope it provokes a salutary little chill: I know more than I can express in words, and the little I can express would not have been expressed, had I not known more."

A Parisian Poem and *To Prince S. M. Kachurin* are not, by comparison with *Fame*, either especially complex or imposing, and yet both are successful poems and certainly can claim a place in Nabokov's *oeuvre*. The better of the two, *A Parisian Poem* concerns life in the "Russian émigré Parnassus" in Paris, where in a certain section and a very few cafés Russian émigré intellectual life centered for nearly two decades. There, in great poverty and an atmosphere of unreality, scores of poets created what came to be known as the "Parisian note" in émigré literature. A prominent example of the Parisian school (a better appellation that allows for the wide divergency between individual writers who shared a common atmosphere but did not sing in the same key) is the Georgy Ivanov poetry as satirized in *The Night Journey* — an ode to a rose on the sidewalk which the poet takes pleasure in discarding in a garbage pail. This atmosphere of soft despair and European twilight — in the best poems of Ivanov, the sad aphoristic poems of Anatoly Shteiger, the surrealistic bohemian poetry and prose of Boris Poplavsky, the Proustian stories and novels of Gaito Gazdanov — was not always a cultivated affectation; at its best, it may be said to be the most "genuine" literature of existentialism in modern writing.

Nabokov, of course, was a Berlin émigré writer who made infrequent trips to Paris, and he lived in France only from 1936 to 1940. *A Parisian Poem* is thus, in one sense, an outsider's view of Russian literary life in Paris, and it furnishes a most instructive measure and contrast with the main body of Parisian émigré writing. Given Nabokov's natural coldness to literary fashion and the fact that he was not really a Parisian émigré in the strictly geographical sense, there is then a double remove present in *A Parisian Poem*, although that is not one of the conscious functions of the poem.

The poem's central figure and protagonist is a poet, but the poetic exposition of the narrative is not given by a simple "I." The poet speaks from the first person and the third person (about himself *as* a poet), and it is extremely difficult to determine if and when the poetry becomes "a poem within a poem." Evidently the beginning of the poem (on the death of exile, real death, and the need for salvation) is a description of another poem or its conception, for *A Parisian Poem* breaks off abruptly at line 33, and begins again:

> But now we'll begin. There lived in Paris
> in number five rue Pierre Loti
> a certain Wolfe, a scrawny red-haired
> engineer of about fifty.
> And under him, my hero: that writer
> About whom I've written more than once,
> my friend, my employer.

The poet in his room is multiplied by himself many times as in a protracted photographic exposure, and he is seen simultaneously sitting, lying, and walking about his room. He wanders through the streets of Paris after having performed the *"manual labor of poetry,"* but there will be no poem since there is no audience for it (*nam nekuda s nim itti*).

But even as he reacts skeptically to the possibility of his own (émigré) art, he is aware that, for all he knows, his unfinished poem may have been a thing of great value, and he retrieves the crumpled piece of paper which he has discarded in the street.

The Paris cityscape is not given any symbolic function, but it is sharply and boldly etched by a poet's consciousness:

> . . . *the pissoirs*
> *gurgle behind their shields.*
> *There is Fate and an Alpine something*
> *in this desolate splashing.*

In the end the city does lead the poet to consciousness of his own mortality, which evokes the extraordinary isolation that is émigré literature, and this in turn reflects larger problems of creativity:

> *And the bridges — they are happiness forever,*
> *the happiness of black water. Look:*
> *like the display window of an incomparable pharmacy*
> *— and the orange lanterns.*
> *And overhead. It's not so good up there.*
> *Endlessly. Endlessly. Only mist.*
> *The dead moon in its slough glimmers.*
> *Shall I really die too? Forget it.*
> *Death is still far off (day after tomorrow I'll*
> *think it all through), but sometimes*
> *the heart needs an "Author, Author!"*
> *The author is not in the hall, gentlemen.*

A Parisian Poem has, however, none of the "Parisian" hopelessness that might logically be expected to follow from such poetic speculation. Its poetic program, given in the conclusion to the poem, is a call not even to summon up the past and Russia, the common desire, but rather to find correspondences between the Russian past and the Parisian present and, above all, to be able to know and appreciate the moment of the present. The poet's greatest happiness consists in being able to superimpose the present over the past as though folding a marvelous carpet — recalling a passage in *Speak, Memory* in which Nabokov wrote: "I confess I do not believe in time. I like to fold my magic carpet after use, in such a way as to superimpose one part of the pattern upon another."

To Prince S. M. Kachurin is Nabokov's longest poetic treatment of the theme, common to his poetry and predominant in émigré poetry, of return to his native land. With the exception of one 1920 poem, *Funeral Rites*, which proclaims faith in Russia even in face of the terror that has befallen her, the poems on Russia are not so much actual treatments of Russia or of a return to Russia in attainable time and space as they are metaphors of the geography of a poet's soul. Russia is the "other shore" of that soul, and the only mode of access is the imagination. This is the reason why these poems demand that either the land or the poet himself be invisible or transparent. He speaks in one poem of his "passportless soul," but the real boundaries it crosses are more temporal than political. In one of his best short poems on the subject, *An Apparition* (1924), the poet returns to his native land to see *"the mother of all birches,"* and someone is carrying a child's coffin toward it. It is his Russia which is in that coffin. In a poem entitled *To Russia* (1928) the wrinkles and veins on the poet's hand become "a strict cartographer's" map of Russia. And this is the sense behind the line, which continually recurs in variant forms throughout Nabokov's poetry: *"Oh, my native land, you are ever with me!"*

Those poems that describe or look forward to an actual return to Russia have about them a fairy-tale air of unreality, deriving primarily from their use of what is basically a folk motif: the cap of invisibility. One 1927 poem, *The Ticket*, takes a most specific and mundane subject, the ticket agent who will sell him the ticket for his return home, and thereby underscores the unreality of the dream. In other poems, such as *Ut pictura poesis* (1926), the journey is presented as a whimsical possibility achieved, as it were, by "stepping over there" in seven-league boots. In one of Nabokov's first works which treats of an imaginary land and language, *Uldaborg: A Translation from the Zoorlandian* (1930), the return is made, but not to St. Petersburg, and the poet's reaction is laughter, at Uldaborg perhaps, but more likely at the very possibility of "return."

To Prince S. M. Kachurin presents this same pattern of reality which is skeptical of itself at somewhat greater length. "Prince Kachurin" is an invented character. In *The Gift* there is a "General Kachurin," a writer of war novels who is a caricature of Pyotr Krasnov, "the White Sholokhov," but the Kachurin of the poem has no connection with him. It is Nabokov's wont to transfer the names of very minor characters from work to work, frequently radically transposing their personalities in the process. The Kachurin of the poem does not actually appear in it, but it is his advice that spurs the poet's return to Russia disguised as an American minister (the poem's first line is *"Kachurin, I've taken your advice"*). The Kachurins are an old princely family of Russia, and the Vengerov biographical dictionary does offer the mysterious citation: "S. Kachurin, belletrist, 1889."

Housed in a museum-like suite *"with a view on the Neva,"* the poet is made anxious by the cold and the thought of his faked passport. The Neva is, figuratively, but also quite literally, a picture-postcard view with the corner torn off for the (Soviet) stamp. This primary fantasy in turn gives rise to another journey, this time by train to the outskirts of St. Petersburg, and this trip involves "persuading" an official interpreter assigned to the disguised poet. The destination of the train he does not take is the explanation of the poet's entire life. But he asks himself how, really, he could board a *dacha*-train

> *in such a coat, with such glasses*
> *(and in essence completely transparent,*
> *with a Sirin novel in my hands).*

Finally the visitation proves terrifying, and the poet asks if he may return home and it is

> *to the prairies of my free youth,*
> *to the Texases I've found,*

which is a reference both to his childhood reading and painting and the real America where he now lives.

An amusing 1933 short story, *The Admiralty Needle*, concerns the Soviet present reaching out for the narrator's Russian past. The narrator's childhood sweetheart has seemingly told the story of their romance (but perhaps not, or perhaps she herself is the novelist) to a cheap two-penny novelist who uses it in a novel. The narrator writes an angry letter to his past, now resident in the Soviet Union:

Now, after your book, Katya, I am afraid of you. For God's sake it wasn't worth going through all that joy and torment that we did to have our past spat upon in a lady's novel. Now listen to me — don't write any more! Let this at least be a lesson. I say "at least" for I have the right to wish that you stop in terror at what you've done. But still, do you know what I am dreaming? Perhaps, perhaps (this is a very small and puny "perhaps," but, hoping it is so, I am not signing this letter), perhaps, Katya, all the same, in spite of everything, a rare coincidence has occurred, and it was not you who wrote this tripe, and your dubious but enchanting image has not been soiled. If this is so, I ask your forgiveness, dear colleague Solntsev.

One must now step back a few years to follow Nabokov's gradual emergence as an English poet. Of twelve poems written in the period between 1941 and 1947, eight are in English. The first of these, *The Softest of Tongues*, specifically announces his turn to English, but, as its very title indicates, it is also a poem to the Russian language. The poem is an enumeration of good-byes:

> *I've said the word that cheats*
> *the lips and leaves them parted (thus prash-chai*
> *which means "good-bye" — to furnished flats, to streets)*

with the final good-bye to his native tongue itself:

> *But now thou too must go; just here we part,*
> *softest of tongues, my true one, all my own . . .*
> *And I am left to grope for heart and art*
> *and start anew with clumsy tools of stone.*

Whether Nabokov's use of the English language was ever clumsy is doubtful, but the change of language does coincide with another noticeable change in his poetic manner. After 1941–42 his poems (continuing to be short or long narratives or vignettes) are, more often than not, humorous, in the manner of certain of his novels and stories, though far from what we call "light verse." These poems, most of them published in *The New Yorker* and then in his 1959 book of English poems, such as *The Refrigerator Awakes* (the workings and mortal torments of a refrigerator), *A Literary Dinner* (a gustatory presumption), and *Ode to a Model* (a speculation on the reality of fashion models) manage to be curiously awry and profound at the same time. They have no equivalents among Nabokov's Russian poems.

The Ballad of Longwood Glen, written in the summer of 1957, is the outstanding example of a longer poem in this vein. It is a humorous treatment of the traditional American ballad, done in such a way as to suggest a wildly improbable mixture of Longfellow and Charles Addams. In smooth rhymed couplets the poem relates the story of a florist named Art Longwood who visits a local glen with his wife, two sickly children, father, stepfather, and father-in-law. Asked by his wife to teach their crippled son Paul how to throw a ball, the florist throws it into a tree; it does not come down; he climbs the tree after it, and disappears. His wife, after Paul and Pauline die, remarries, and the site of the mysterious occurrence becomes a tourist attraction where the Deforests (her new married name) regularly go to eat lunch.

This little metaphysical jest is rife with shadows of the grotesque that tease and add sinister convolutions to the tale. The arboreal names, the mysterious convoy of various fathers, and the mis-shapen children ("*They were cute little rascals but could not run much*") are the most immediate grotesque effects in the poem; the most outrageous are the characters who gather at the scene

> *A drunken rogue with a rope and a gun*
> *Arrived on the scene to see justice done.*
> *Explorers, dendrologists — all were there;*
> *And a strange pale girl with gypsy hair.*

The environment is no less strange with its "*restrooms nestled in roses and vines.*" All of this is the frivolous or satirical surface of *The Ballad of Longwood Glen*, and the fullest enjoyment of it is to be had on the long-playing record *Lolita* (Spoken Arts 902) of Nabokov reading his own verse and prose, including this ballad, with histrionic gusto.

But the core of the ballad cannot be reduced to a joke and it is upon this that the whole spoof depends. This, of course, is the ascent into the oak. The tree is first introduced as an actor in the comedy ("*It stuck in a tree that was passing by*"), but by his ascent Art Longwood is involved in a metamorphosis, even though no one at the foot of the tree is aware of this:

What tiaras of gardens! What torrents of light!
How accessible ether! How easy flight!
His family circled the tree all day.
Pauline concluded: "Dad climbed away."

None saw the delirious celestial crowds
Greet the hero from earth in the snow of the clouds.

The flight has been foreshadowed by Art watching a bug climb a stalk and fly away, but in a certain sense the beginning of the journey — that is, departure from the other Longwoods — is of greater moment than the fact of flight or the celestial destination. Art Longwood's character is illustrated by only one detail: he has the ability to stare at a thing all day.

The poem is really about Art Longwood, whom we, like his family, scarcely see at all. He belongs to Nabokov's series of seemingly mediocre characters who harbor a secret and extravagant dream of escape or flight. The closest analogue to him among them is Paul Pilgram, the protagonist of the 1930 short story *Pilgram* (translated in English as *The Aurelian*). Pilgram owns a butterfly shop in Berlin, and it is his consuming dream to run away on a tropical expedition. By means of a fortuitous sale, which he conceals from his wife, of some especially rare specimens, Pilgram's dream seems about to come true, but the realization proves too much for him, and he dies of a stroke even as his mind is already deep in the tropics. And it may be just as well. Consider the fates of the other inspired mediocrities in Nabokov's fiction (the businessman Albinus Kretshmar in *Laughter in the Dark*, the chocolate manufacturer Hermann Karlovich in *Despair*) whose dreams do come literally true and in turn engender deadly nightmares. As for Art Longwood's intentions, we can only guess, not even being sure if he knew them himself. But there can be no doubt of what the poem is about: tearing a hole in reality and escaping to another realm, which, if it is death (and the poem can be so read), is so only incidentally. The more probable definition is the realm of art — the American nickname for Arthur could not fail to be used by Nabokov at some point — and the remove into which the florist vanishes is artistic inspiration. The major émigré poet and critic

Vladislav Khodasevich asserted that Nabokov really writes *only* about the creative artist, but that he does this under the guise of writing about salesmen, chess players, businessmen, and others pursuing similarly unlikely professions. Khodasevich was Nabokov's most perceptive Russian critic, and I think there is much to be said for this view that provides a universal key which "works" in almost all of Nabokov's fiction and his longer poems, including the comic *Ballad* with its inconsequential florist.

Nabokov's finest poem, written in English in 1945, twelve years before *Longwood Glen*, is *An Evening of Russian Poetry*. It also has the heavy quotient of levity that characterizes the majority of the English poems, but the delicate balance of the serious and the comic, the narrative and the intensely personal give it a central position in the broad spectrum of Nabokov's art. Yet the poem has for the more than twenty years since it first appeared in *The New Yorker* remained unanthologized and essentially unnoticed, with the single exception of F. W. Dupee who, to his credit, granted the designation of "great" to it in his article on Nabokov in *The King of the Cats*.

The "action" in *An Evening of Russian Poetry* is nothing more than the execution of another, more humble, literary genre, the lecture, and it would be possible to say that in the duality of its form the poem is distantly related to such artifices as the epistolary novel and to Nabokov's own novels. The "lecture" does not maintain even the flimsiest of epistolary appearances, however, and is, in fact, in no way a lecture. *An Evening of Russian Poetry* is a poem in the mimetic semblance of a lecture that has either already taken place or is yet to be delivered. A proper analogy to the organization and effect of the poem then would be an epistolary novel in which the letters indirectly but clearly smile at the pretense of an addressee and wander off into hermetic monologue. There are numerous unmistakable signs that this is so: the poem has as its epigraph an extract from what purports to be "a letter addressed to the visiting speaker," and yet the college girls who pose questions in the course of the poem are addressed familiarly by name: *"The birch tree, Cynthia, the fir tree, Joan."* Even more revealing is the abrupt conclusion in which the girls' coy compliments are answered by a macaronic stanza which strongly suggests that the "lecture" is a poet's nocturnal fantasy in which the form is just a pretext or convention:

> *"How would you say 'delightful talk' in Russian?"*
> *"How would you say 'good night?'"*
> *Oh, that would be:*
> Bezsónnitsa, tvoy vzór oonýl i stráshen;
> Lubóv moyá, otstóopnika prostée.
> *(Insomnia, your stare is dull and ashen,*
> *my love, forgive me this apostasy.)*

The shift into Russian and the sense of the lines — the English is a very good but not a precise translation of the Russian — point to the real subject of the poem: the poet who has carried his culture into another language — a fantastic "feat" and a source of very real personal pain. This is the "apostasy." "My love" refers, of course, to the Russian language. The poem is in the end an evening of *English* poetry.

An Evening of Russian Poetry has a deliberately disjointed progression. In the course of the panegyric on Russian poetry — only Pushkin and Nekrasov are mentioned, however, and that in passing — another *persona*, tenuously related to the "lecturer," repeatedly snatches away the discourse, only to give it back again. This figure is a stylized, almost cartoon-like monarch, an ironic representation of the poet and his lost kingdom of words:

> *Beyond the seas where I have lost a sceptre,*
> *I hear the neighing of my dappled nouns,*
> *soft participles coming down the steps,*
> *treading on leaves, trailing their rustling gowns . . .*
>
> . . . . .
>
> *My back is Argus-eyed. I live in danger.*
> *False shadows turn to track me as I pass*
> *and, wearing beards, disguised as secret agents,*
> *creep in to blot the freshly written page*
> *and read the blotter in the looking-glass.*

But this melodramatically described monarch-in-exile has an air of far greater seriousness than the visitant of *Fame*. He is not only the poet himself, but also the representative of the fate of all poets in Russian literature:

> . . . *Our roads were always fated*
> *to lead into the silence of exile.*
> *Had I more time tonight I would unfold*
> *the whole amazing story* — neighuklúzhe,
> nevynossímo — *but I have to go.*

These two Russian words, which remain untranslated for his "audience," are the center of *An Evening of Russian Poetry*. They are *"it's awkward, unbearable,"* and this too shows how the ostensible lecture topic is only secondarily and tangentially the subject of the poem. The speaker and the poet are each, in different ways, conjurors, and their tricks are distractions. The poet's feat is to make his muse ventriloquize so naturally that the imitation equals the original voice, which becomes the vital but secondary double or "blotter" page of his art. The speaker-as-conjuror is the public personality of the poet, and it is his trick to provide protective covering for the private self by means of distraction, indirection, and extravagant irony:

> *The conjuror collects his poor belongings* —
> *the colored handkerchief, the magic rope,*
> *the double-bottomed rhymes, the cage, the song.*
> *You tell him of the passes you detected.*
> *The mystery remains intact* . . .

Nabokov, who practiced conjuring as a child, has a deep fascination with the figure of the magician. The uses to which he puts the figure of a magician and the tricks he performs are far from simple. He is concerned not so much with the trick itself as with the involvement of the performer in his private life with his craft. In Nabokov's greatest short story, *The Potato Elf* (1929), there is a conjuror whose wife Nora has deceived him with the midget who assists him in his act. The deceit is short-lived, however, and the conjuror, Shock, learns of it. His revenge is a trick, a simulated stroke:

And suddenly Nora understood that she loved him more than anything on earth, and terror and tenderness made her head whirl. She circled around the room, poured water into a glass for some reason, put it on the wash-stand, and again dashed to her husband who had raised himself up and was pressing the edge of the bedsheet to his lips, shivering and moaning, and with his uncomprehending eyes, already tinged with death, bulging out. Then she threw her hands together, dashed to the next room where the telephone was, for a long time shook the lever for the operator, got the number wrong, then called again, moaning and banging her fist against the telephone table, and when at last the voice of the doctor came through, she shouted that her husband had poisoned himself and was dying, sobbed into the receiver, and, replacing it crookedly, dashed back to the bedroom.

In the bedroom Nora finds Shock standing coolly in front of a mirror, adjusting his necktie. The psychological situation in *The Potato Elf* is far more complicated than that in *An Evening of Russian Poetry*, but the function of the conjuror is the same in both works. The conjuring is not to be taken too literally in and of itself — Nabokov as conjuror has, with a nervous and excessive imitation of his prose, become the deadly cliché of the news-weeklies. What is really important is the tension between the performer and the performance. In *An Evening of Russian Poetry* the drama which in *The Potato Elf* occurs between Nora and Shock is played out, calmly and with no surfeit of emotion, within a single figure. The conjuror in Nabokov is not a direct symbol but a fine and deep metaphor. The 1939 Russian story which Nabokov never published and which became the novel *Lolita* was entitled *The Magician*.

None of the below-the-surface currents in *An Evening of Russian Poetry* disturb its steady glide and rich sheen. The lecturer's other *persona* speaks in quite a different manner, but the tone of voice remains the same throughout, the archness of the magician and monarch metaphors being balanced perfectly by the lecturer's sly humor:

> *My little helper at the magic lantern,*
> *insert that slide and let the colored beam*
> *project my name or any suchlike phantom*

> *in Slavic characters upon the screen.*
> *The other way, the other way. I thank you.*

The disquisition on the Russian language and Russian poetry constitutes a tour de force in which the *"long and serpentine"* English lines do seem somehow to reproduce a loose but perfect poetic "Russianness." Thus, while *An Evening of Russian Poetry* does not speak for its time or address itself to any universals, its simultaneous complexity and simplicity and its superb poetic diction fully justify Dupee's solitary commendation of the poem.

Pale Fire, published seventeen years later in 1962, is not as imposing a work as *An Evening of Russian Poetry*, but it is an important poem by Vladimir Nabokov (a very obvious point, but one which has been generally overlooked in treating the poem in the larger context of the novel) which deserves consideration by itself.

Its 999-line length makes *Pale Fire* Nabokov's longest English poem, although, if the poetic drama *The Tragedy of Mister Morn* is considered with his poetry, not his longest verse effort, and *A University Poem*, at 882 lines, is nearly as long. The poet-protagonist of *Pale Fire* is John Shade — he names himself in line 273 — a craggy Frostian campus poet. The poem itself, however, has nothing in common with Frost's poetry. (Nabokov has called the reference to Frost in line 426 merely "local color," claiming further that the only Frost poem he really knows is *Stopping by Woods on a Snowy Evening*.) The actual poetic forebears of "John Shade" are Wordsworth and, to a lesser degree, Pope ("a pinch of Pope"), which brings us back to consideration of the problem of art's obligation, or lack thereof, to employ "contemporary" forms.

Pale Fire provides a forceful case in favor of greater amplitude of artistic form; its heroic couplets notwithstanding, it is nothing if not "American" and "contemporary" to the core, and, if one is interested in such things as "the author's attitude towards and depiction of" America, it is here, rather than to *Lolita*, that one should turn. Shade's poem turns and shifts its focus to provide a collage of the essential coordinates in the poet's life. A remark made by Shade in quite a different connection applies also very well to the form his poem takes:

> *How ludicrous these efforts to translate*
> *Into one's private tongue a public fate:*
> *Instead of poetry divinely terse,*
> *Disjointed notes, Insomnia's mean verse!*

That public fate — note the inversion of the usual epithets — includes Shade's earliest childhood in which he was reared by an aunt after the death of his parents, his high school courtship of his future wife, Sybil, their everyday life together, his literary career, and — most important of all — the awkward life and suicide of their homely daughter Hazel.

Pale Fire is stubbornly matter-of-fact in the suburbanity of its matter, but its manner is still uncompromisingly poetic. When John and Sybil are at the senior class outing together she offers him *"a thimbleful of bright metallic tea,"* which is to say, a thermos cup. Shade's passionate love for Sybil is seen, as though by a third party, against the pattern of the typical American teenage romance:

> *Come and be worshipped, come and be caressed,*
> *My dark Vanessa, crimson-barred, my blest*
> *My Admirable butterfly! Explain*
> *How could you, in the gloam of Lilac Lane,*
> *Have let uncouth, hysterical John Shade*
> *Blubber your face, and ear, and shoulder blade?*

Their forty-year marriage is measured against the succession of free kitchen calendars, and the signs of his mature love for Sybil are tied to the necessary business of life in middle-class America

> *I love you when you're humming as you pack*
> *A suitcase or the farcical car sack*
> *With round-trip zipper . . .*

The most striking piece of Americana, however, both in itself and in the way it is employed, is the television set. Shade and Sybil sit watching for Hazel to come home from the "blind date" from which she will never return:

> . . . *You played*
> *Network roulette: the dial turned and trk'ed.*
> *Commercials were beheaded. Faces flicked.*
> *An open mouth in midsong was struck out.*

And as the set is switched off, the little light in the center of the screen which fades away *"in Black Infinity"* serves as a signal of Hazel's suicide which, we gather from the next lines, occurs at approximately that moment.

Hazel Shade's ungainly appearance and her morose, hyper-sensitive character do not require analogy with other literary characters, but there is perhaps a loose tie between Hazel's suicide on the thin ice of a neighboring lake and the (accidental) death of Lucy Gray in Wordsworth's poem of the same name. The poetic presence of Wordsworth in *Pale Fire* is necessary and useful to keep in mind (some of the reproaches leveled at Wordsworth for introducing "common" elements into serious poetry parallel criticisms of *Pale Fire* for departing from the canon of high modernism), but the emotional timbre of most of Wordsworth's poetry is not that of *Pale Fire*. Beyond the tenderness that one associates with Wordsworth's verse, *Pale Fire* is notable for its fixed attention to the problem of death; indeed, the poem is about death.

Hazel's death fulfills the most important narrative function in the poem, but it is merely one piece — the largest one — in the larger mosaic of death, time, and speculation on the hereafter. As a little girl:

> . . . *while children of her age*
> *Were cast as elves and fairies on the stage*
> *That she'd helped paint for the school pantomime,*
> *My gentle girl appeared as Mother Time,*
> *A bent charwoman with slop pail and broom,*
> *And like a fool I sobbed in the men's room.*

This role, as another critic has noted, neatly foreshadows her death close to a watchman, *"Father Time, all gray and bent,"* who comes along just too late to prevent the suicide. Hazel herself has a strange interest in the supernatural, and once she spends several nights investigating certain sounds in a byre.

Hazel's strangeness has its projection in past time in old Aunt Maude (rhymed with God) who lived till eighty, or in time *"to hear the next babe cry."* Her death is a painfully protracted guttering out that is perhaps not unrelated to Hazel's *"murmuring dreadful words in monotone"* in childhood. Maude's death causes Shade to speculate skeptically on the standard notions of death and afterlife. He effaces the precise boundary between life and death for Aunt Maude, and later he muses cynically on the inevitable complications of immortality: the widower who has remarried and must deal with both jealous wives throughout eternity. Life is a most ludicrous show staged in a "most artistic cage," but that very fact presents the possibility of a kind of immortality in art.

Shade's parents died when he was still an infant. Because of the efforts he has made to evoke them from certain chance words and attributes he has retained, he now has "a thousand parents." In the initial portion of *Pale Fire* the poet plays with reflected (for which we should read: artistic) realities. His room is hung above the grass or snow — a common optical illusion at night — and he possesses the Wordsworthian ability to take photographs with his eyes:

> *Whatever in my field of vision dwelt —*
>
> *. . . . .*
>
> *Was printed on my eyelids' nether side.*

The root equality of the illusion with the reality in Shade's mind is shown by his remarks (lines 41–48) on a view of the lake, which could just be made out from the house, but can no longer be seen, evidently because

> *some quirk in space*
> *Has caused a fold or furrow to displace*
> *the fragile vista . . .*

(a demonstration of *An Evening of Russian Poetry's* pronouncement that *"space is collapsible"*).

The well-known opening lines of *Pale Fire*

> *I was the shadow of the waxwing slain*
> *By the false azure in the windowpane*

contain the two themes of death and illusion-reality; but almost never commented on, yet equally important, is the conclusion of that same sentence:

> *. . . — and I*
> *Lived on, flew on, in the reflected sky.*

Hazel Shade lives in a fixed pattern or cage —

> *a tryptych or a three-act play*
> *In which portrayed events forever stay.*

a permanence toward which the entire poem pulls. It ends on line 999, indicating Shade's death, but the first line provides that last line, and thus the circle is closed on the theme of death (as in *The Circle* and the Chernyshevsky biography in *The Gift*).

Canto Three of the poem — Hazel's suicide ends Canto Two — returns to Hazel's childhood, but death is present here, too. Shade is invited to lecture on death at an Institute of Preparation for the Hereafter and the treatment of death in this Canto is largely a spoof as Shade relates the utilitarian philosophy of the school:

> *How to keep sane in spiral types of space*
> *Precautions to be taken in the case*
> *Of freak reincarnation . . .*

But even here the intent is serious, and it teaches Shade what to avoid in his consideration of the problem.

Shade dies in Canto Three — and comes to life again. After giving a club talk (*Why Poetry Is Meaningful to Us*), he suffers a stroke just as a peevish questioner in the audience stands up and points his pipe at him — a metaphysical "assassination" which Shade, on later reflection, decides was unrelated to his stroke. In that instant of death Shade has a vision of a tall white fountain. His vision is mocked, however, by a similar account in a magazine story which turns out to have been a misprint ("fountain" for "mountain"). But like the Institute of Preparation for the Hereafter and the Canto as a whole, this incident also serves an important function for Shade — it convinces him even more of the ascendancy of pattern over meaning:

> *Life Everlasting — based on a misprint!*
> *I mused as I drove homeward: take the hint,*
> *And stop investigating my abyss?*
> *But all at once it dawned on me that this*
> *Was the real point, the contrapuntal theme;*
> *Just this: not text, but texture; not the dream*
> *But topsy-turvical coincidence,*
> *Not flimsy nonsense, but a web of sense.*

When he returns home he has been firmly convinced that he can grope his way *"to some — to some — 'Yes, dear?' Faint hope."*

Has John Shade also committed suicide? No, but his literary suicide is presupposed by the ending of the poem. The common fate of the writer and his child is hinted at in Canto Three, lines 661–664:

> *"And now what shall I do? My knight is pinned."*
> *Who rides so late in the night and the wind?*
> *It is the writer's grief. It is the wild*
> *March wind. It is the father with his child.*

In the concluding Canto Shade writes that man's life is ". . . commentary to abstruse/Unfinished poem. . . ." and he appends to this: *"Note for further use."* The fact that the first line of *Pale Fire* does supply the necessary thousandth line to complete the poem does strongly suggest that the poet's end is a conscious one, as does the constantly recurring theme of death in the course of the entire work. The most compelling clue in favor of this understanding is the poet's apparently artlessly simple declaration at the conclusion of Canto Four, lines 975–981:

> *And if my private universe scans right,*
> *So does the verse of galaxies divine*
> *Which I suspect is an iambic line.*
> *I'm reasonably sure that we survive*
> *And that my darling somewhere is alive,*
> *As I am reasonably sure that I*
> *Shall wake at six tomorrow, on July*
> *The twenty-second, nineteen fifty-nine,*

This, I submit, can only be the guileful note left by the artist before passing through the windowpane to give his poem its necessary annular completeness: his own death.

Wordsworth's masterpiece, *The Prelude*, is an autobiographical poem, and its central concern is the conveyance of an essential metaphysical "secret" that Wordsworth felt he had discovered. The role of nature in *The Prelude* is very much akin to that of art in *Pale Fire*, and, what is most important, *The Prelude* was a posthumously published poem, since Wordsworth felt that it might somehow still be "incomplete" and he never could make the decision to submit it to print. This tenuous and distant, but very real affinity — and such, after all, is the only kind of "influence" one should seek in an artist like Nabokov — between two outwardly dissimilar works is of much greater import than formal, metrical similarities with Wordsworth's verse in understanding what *Pale Fire* is all about.

John Shade does share many views with Nabokov, although there is certainly no basis for supposing autobiographical parallels. These views are stated for the most part in the last Canto during the period in which Shade — and we recall Buck Mulligan and the opening scene of *Ulysses* — is shaving:

> . . . *I loathe such things as jazz;*
> *The white-hosed moron torturing a black*
> *Bull, rayed with red; abstractist bric-a-brac;*
> *Primitivist folk-masks; progressive schools;*
> *Music in supermarkets; swimming pools;*
>
> . . . . .
>
> *Brutes, bores, class-conscious Philistines, Freud, Marx,*
> *Fake thinkers, puffed-up poets, frauds and sharks.*

The important question, however, concerns the very sanity of the poet. I have posed the question but do not feel obligated to answer it. We do know, though, that Shade had a fit of madness or a stroke when he was only eleven (lines 140–156), and at the beginning of Canto Two he refers to his "demented youth," when he felt that his ignorance of death was the result of a great conspiracy of all other people to keep the truth from him. Lastly, he ponders whether his stroke after the lecture might not have been *"one of my old fits."*

That is all — but this question is one of the essential determinants that can be used to plot the relationship between *Pale Fire* the poem and the novel *Pale Fire* of which the poem is but a part. Discussion of this matter should properly wait until a later chapter when certain precedents in Nabokov's fiction — not yet discussed — may make the resolution of the question easier.

Five

❋ ❋ ❋ ❋

BETWEEN 1924 and 1932 Nabokov wrote seven novels, or slightly less than one a year, and some twenty-two short stories, in addition, of course, to occasional poetry, criticism, and two plays, one of which was staged in Berlin in 1927. These years comprise the most intensively productive period in Nabokov's artistic career.

One cannot characterize this period in any single way, as some of the best and poorest writing was done by Nabokov during this time. Probably the worst thing ever written by him, excepting his juvenilia, is a piece of dubious genre – a long prose poem or short poetic essay – *The Russian River*, that appeared in the Berlin Sunday supplement *Our World* in September, 1924. It is a painfully sentimental and highly emotional, though not badly written evocation of the beauty of Russian rivers and their soul-like individuality. I would hazard the guess that it will in some distant future be among the first Nabokov works to be published in the Soviet Union. Among the short stories written from 1924 to 1926 there are, on the other hand, several that cannot hope to be so blessed.

The Razor is a cleverly serious adaptation of Gogol's *The Nose* (Adamovich once declared: "Granted, Russian literature came out of *The Overcoat*, but Sirin came out of Gogol's *Nose*") put to a political use. The story concerns a Captain Ivanov, who is nicknamed "the Razor" by his army comrades, and this name turns out to be prophetic when, after the defeat of the White army, Ivanov actually becomes a barber in Berlin. One day, when his two fellow barbers are not in the shop and the owner has taken the scrawny but compliant manicurist to a back room, Ivanov finds himself shaving a Red officer who had interrogated him in Kharkov six years before. All his fierce hatred for the Red regime is concentrated upon this personal enemy who now sits powerless beneath his razor. When he recovers from the shock of recognition — the officer has not recognized him — he speaks to him in Russian: "My respects, Comrade. Have you been abroad long? No, please don't move, otherwise I can slice your throat right now." Ivanov plays with his victim for a long time, recounting in detail the entire story of what the Red officer did to him, and the man is reduced to nervous protoplasm. His only defense is to close his eyes and wait for the end. But Ivanov does not kill him (it must be said that this conclusion, while wholly in keeping with Nabokov's own views, is scarcely justified by Ivanov's character as presented in the story), and the officer staggers out of the shop — the best touch in the story — "with the eyes of a Greek statue."

The story *Letter to Russia* (1925) is a serene and undramatic tale — as its title indicates, it is literally an artistic letter, addressed to a woman living in the Soviet Union, or perhaps to Russia herself — but its very serenity makes it as objectionable to official Communist dogma as anything Nabokov has ever written. It is a "given" for the Soviet press that the emigration is a sterile and bitter purgatory, and when émigré writers have been published in the USSR, a careful selection is made from their writings to "substantiate" this dogma. *Letter to Russia* is a declaration of the writer's complete happiness in life and his independence from the restraints of time and place imposed by history. The writer of the letter even professes to see a "childish smile" in death.

Ages will gallop past — school children will grow bored over the history of the staggering events we lived through — everything will pass, everything, but my happiness, dear friend, my happiness will remain — in the damp reflection of a streetlight, in the gradual circular movement of stone steps leading down to the black waters of a canal, in the smile of a dancing couple, in everything with which God has so lavishly surrounded our human loneliness.

Letter to Russia was announced as a chapter from a novel with the rather un-Nabokovian title *Happiness*, which was never written, and it may well be that the very sureness of the letter writer was intended, in the larger context of the novel, to be symptomatic of a strident and unbalanced character, as is the case with Smurov in the 1930 novella *The Eye*.

A 1932 story, *The Meeting*, concerns the reunion of a Berlin émigré with his Soviet brother who is traveling on assignment through Berlin. The meeting, both as imagined beforehand and as it actually occurs, is a Chekhovian study in noncommunication. The two men have too much to talk about to be able to say anything, and they can only grope to remember the name of a pet dog (there is a similar episode in *Speak, Memory*) which they have forgotten, and which the émigré remembers only after his Soviet brother has left. This particular story is probably Nabokov's most "realistic" attempt, without ideology or politics, to convey what the division of 1917 really means in terms of an individual's relation to his past. Although the Marxist reader will inevitably bring the political background of works such as *The Razor, Letter to Russia*, and *The Meeting* to the fore, they are primarily character studies, and the characters scarcely concur with each other in their political views, much less with any broader émigré way of thinking.

It is a fact, though, that in these early years, when the political situation was still rather fluid and it was by no means certain that the Bolsheviks would persevere, the Soviet Union (as differentiated from Russia which, as we have seen, is the theme of memory) does figure frequently in Nabokov's writing, either as a central theme or in the political convictions of individual characters. It could hardly be otherwise, except where Nabokov goes beyond the emigration — which he first did in 1928 — to find subjects for his art.

Nabokov's first non-poetic drama, written in 1926 and staged in 1927, was called *The Man from the USSR*. It is a political drama in five acts about a double agent, but it cannot really be commented on here since only the first act of the play — in which the characters are introduced in the setting of a Berlin Russian café but little actually happens — ever appeared in print, in *The Rudder* (January 1, 1927).

There are two prose works, one a novel and the other a short story, on the theme of actual return to Russia. In the novel *The Exploit* (1931), the protagonist's Russia is a need that has no rational concern or connection with political reality. It is closer to a neurotic and irrational despair. *The Exploit* is in some respects the least exciting of Nabokov's fifteen novels. (That figure includes one novella and one incomplete novel.) In the first place, while *The Exploit* is certainly not an autobiographical novel, the particulars of its setting and a great many minor details retrace Nabokov's own experience. The novel's protagonist, Martin Edelweis, is a Russian of foreign extraction and inclination (his first language was English) who emigrates from Russia by ship from the Crimea at the time of the Revolution, then studies at Cambridge, and later goes to Berlin. Certain scenes of *The Exploit* also take place in Greece (some of the poems in *The Empyrean Path* were written in Greece where the Nabokov family stopped briefly before traveling on to England) and in France and Switzerland (where Nabokov vacationed while he was a student), thereby making *The Exploit* the most truly international novel Nabokov has written. The character of Martin Edelweis is a pure Nabokov invention, but it is also true that there is no other Nabokov work which repeats so frequently and precisely incidents from *Speak, Memory* and *Other Shores*.

In *Speak, Memory* there is a beautiful poetic description of the manner in which Nabokov used to deal with the cold Cambridge nights:

So I would heap on more coals and help revive the flames by spreading a sheet of the London *Times* over the smoking black jaws of the fire-place, thus screening completely its open recess. A humming noise would start behind the taut paper, which would acquire the smoothness of drum-skin and the beauty of luminous parchment. Presently, as the hum turned into a roar, an orange-colored spot would appear in the middle of the sheet, and whatever patch of print happened to be there . . . stood out with ominous clarity — until suddenly the orange spot burst. Then the flaming sheet, with the whirr of a liberated phoenix, would fly up the chimney to join the stars. It cost one a fine of twelve shillings if that firebird was observed.

And here is Martin Edelweis, also in his university room on a cold night:

Having covered the jaws of the fire-place with a spread-out sheet of *The Times*, he adjusted the draft: the taut sheet acquired a warm lucidity, and the lines of print on it, blending with the lines on the lower side which had been made visible, seemed like the strange and wonderful characters of some gibberish language. Then, when the roar and conflagration grew stronger an orange, darkening stain appeared on the sheet of paper and, suddenly it burst, the whole sheet blazed up, the draft instantaneously sucked it in, it flew away up the chimney — and a late passer-by, a master in his black cloak, saw through the dim light of the gothic night a fiery-haired witch tearing out of the chimney into the heavens, and on the next day Martin had to pay a fine.

There are literally scores of such parallel passages — always with the same artistic autonomy as is found in these two passages, never simple repetitions. Even more arresting, however, are the comments made in passing in *Speak, Memory* that seem to have acquired extensive fictional substance in *The Exploit*. Thus a return to Cambridge many years later prompts Nabokov to note: "Different too were the garish uniforms worn by the waitresses, of whom none was as pretty as the particular one I remembered so clearly"; in *The Exploit* Martin has a brief but passionate dalliance with "Rosa the goddess of the sweet-shop," and is only saved from having to marry her by the timely and wise interference of a friend who correctly guesses that Rosa is imaginative rather than pregnant.

The fact that Martin Edelweis is a fictional character walking over but not in the footsteps of Nabokov's own youth may be one factor which serves to inhibit the author's imagination, for *The Exploit* is the longest Sirin work which does not challenge the reader with subtle multiplicity of meaning.

Another factor whch may contribute to the uncomplicated manner in which the narrative unfolds is the apparent kinship which *The Exploit* has with *A University Poem*. It is a geometric congruity of situation rather than a similarity between the characters. *Speak, Memory*, *A University Poem*, and *The Exploit* come together in the reader's mind to form a triptych of sorts, and the very variation upon obviously related incidents in the three panels forcefully reminds us how futile it is to seek to fix Nabokov in his own novels.

The Exploit is most centrally about the inability of Martin Edelweis to form any sort of lasting relationship, and this finally leads to the seemingly mad, but for him logical, decision to undertake a daring "exploit" — a short foray into Soviet Russia. Nabokov writes in *Speak, Memory* that he was tempted for a time to join Denikin's army, primarily to see if he could locate his girlfriend somewhere in the Ukraine, but Martin is outspokenly apolitical and unreceptive to even the most refined feelings of nationalism to a degree that Nabokov never was. Martin has no real reason within Russia to return there, which in the end is the reason he goes.

The roots of Martin's isolation are most likely to be found in his resemblance to his dead father. His parents were divorced, and Martin's remembrance of his father, about whom he does not like to hear others speak, is of a man whose emotions were all but wholly concealed from view. Martin's character is convincingly drawn in a series of repeatedly similar encounters, but apart from the clue provided by his father, there is no detailed information tendered to "explain" Martin.

He has a love affair in Athens with an older woman, a minor St. Petersburg erotic poetess named Alla Chernosvitov, for whom he is merely a young lad to seduce (she comes to his room). Not only is she married, but Martin actually has to share a room with her husband (a not particularly sympathetic chap whose conversation consists largely of the entreaty: "Young man, I ask you only not to spoil the air"); Martin is in constant dread that he will talk in his sleep. Alla repeatedly tells Martin that he will always remember and cherish their lovemaking, but his feeling for her is quickly dampened when Alla and her husband become involved in a conversation about their personal affairs while Martin is in the room, and he suddenly realizes that she has completely forgotten he is there.

Martin is émigré literature's most vivid contribution to the century-old Russian theme (Griboedov, Lermontov, Turgenev) of the "superfluous man." The way in which Martin is different from all the previous superfluous men is that romance is not an end in itself but a compensatory quest for him. When he was in the Crimea, he was almost shot (by a man he later meets in emigration), and the actual incident lingers as a sweet and fantastic episode in his imagination. He goes mountain climbing in the Swiss

Alps and, openly testing himself, nearly loses his life. The trip to the Soviet Union is simply another even more dangerous test, for which he does not bother to assume any melodramatic ardor. Somehow the exploits themselves are even more superfluous than Martin.

A corollary to the theme of the daring exploit for Martin is the fascination of travel, especially by train. At one point he reflects on his perpetually changing life, and "it seemed to him that he had never left the Express but simply loafed away his time in one car after another, and in one were young Englishmen, Darwin triumphantly hanging on to the brake handle, in another Alla with her husband, or his friends from the Crimea, or his snoring Uncle Heinrich, or the Zilanovs, Mikhail Platonovich with a newspaper, Sonya staring out the window with a dreary look."

Martin's metaphor is applicable for most of the major characters who appear in the novel, but they either manage to establish satisfactory relationships on their journey or, like Sonya and Darwin, they adjust to their chosen or imposed solitude. Martin, however, allows consciousness of his rootlessness — he repeatedly reflects that he is "necessary to no one and loved by no one" — to lead to virtual self-effacement. He sometimes stands off and watches himself as though from the side. His failure to win Sonya's love — and in the process of trying he compromises his friendship with Darwin — is an example of the way in which he is emotionally accident prone and always a superfluous quantity. While Martin is staying at the Zilanovs' house shortly after the death of Sonya's sister Nellie, Sonya comes to him at night and lies down on the bed with him; but she is simply attempting in her grief to simulate the talks till dawn that she used to have with Nellie. One feels that Martin could have won her by playing the role of Nellie, but instead he humiliates himself by trying to make love to her. His relationships seem to be only of two sorts: a childish, almost intentional tactlessness, followed by a stubborn passivity (his father's model) that places the entire burden of action — or love — upon the other person. Thus there is an implicit invitation in the rejections he suffers, the cruelest of which is Sonya's measurement of him against a writer she plans to (but doesn't) marry: "He at least has talent, while you're nothing but a traveling young nobleman." When Martin goes to a whorehouse, his wallet is stolen.

Equal in importance to the rejection by Sonya is his mother's marriage to her brother-in-law, his Uncle Heinrich, a wealthy Swiss, who in his self-satisfied blandness is the very antithesis of both his brother and his nephew. Martin doesn't even learn of the marriage until after it has taken place, and from his uncle rather than from his mother. Against this pattern of small and large, intentional and chance failures, the thought of Russia occupies his thoughts more and more.

His first "feeling" for Russia — and it is not so much that as a vague sense of offense — is prompted by yet another of his broken relationships, this time with his college instructor in Russian literature, Archibald Moon, who, he learns from Darwin, is a homosexual. Moon, while not disallowing the possibility of culture at some future time in Russia, sees Russian civilization as a closed book: "The civil war seemed to him to be stupid: the one side fought for the ghost of the past, the other for the ghost of the future — and in the meanwhile Archibald Moon had stealthily spirited Russia away and locked her up in his study." Martin is also made conscious of Russia by various facsimiles — certain parts of Switzerland duplicate the atmosphere of Russia, and later in Berlin — where Martin, like the young Nabokov, lives by giving tennis lessons — he is engulfed by the sound of Russian being spoken at every street corner.

The first clear sign of Martin's intention is a Tolstoyan excursion to live and work in a French workers' community. But Martin does not speak about Russia or his intention to go there. Instead, in jesting exchanges with Sonya, he invents an imaginary Zoorlandia, and this Zoorlandian motif is the sole customary Nabokovian complexity in *The Exploit*. (It will be recalled that Nabokov published a short poem as "A Translation from the Zoorlandian" in the same year that the novel appeared. The theme of an imaginary land and/or language is used, casually or centrally, five more times by Nabokov before reaching its major expression in *Pale Fire*'s Zembla.) Martin's Zoorlandia is not an ironic metaphor expressing the loss of Russia, nor is it a madman's magnificent lost Zembla. It is a recognition by Martin that he will not be able to live in Russia, which has become "the merciless Zoorlandian night." Zoorlandia is a metaphor of death, even though Martin does protest to himself at one point that, of course, he will return.

A detailed picture of Zoorlandia is given in a 1936 story. *The Annihilation of Tyrants*. The narrator is a provincial drawing teacher in a terrible dictatorship, and his principle concern is to kill the tyrant "who struck one with his giftlessness as others strike one with their talent"; to his great regret, he knew the dictator when he was young and cannot forgive himself for not having foreseen the banality and evil in him. The narrator's simple formulation is that "first, a real man is a poet, and second, that he, our ruler, is the incarnate negation of a poet."

The Annihilation of Tyrants is not a fantasy of political intrigue. For one thing the narrator, like Martin Edelweis, is disinclined to accept customary notions of politics and patriotism: "I have nothing of the civic hero who perishes for his nation in me. I shall perish only for myself, for my own good and truth, for that good and that truth which are now distorted and held in contempt in me and around me, and if they are equally dear to someone else, so much the better; but if not, and if my native land requires people of a different sort than I, I shall gladly accept my uselessness, but will all the same do what I have to do." The decision to kill the tyrant on moral and aesthetic grounds falters with the narrator's realization that his means will be as vulgar as his goal is noble. This leads him to consider suicide as a means to eliminate the tyrant, annihilating by his own death the tyrant and his profane political order that has debased everything the narrator holds dear. He is saved from his intention by his discovery, in rereading his notes, that he has effectively slain the tyrant with ridicule, and he imagines that his little tract will serve mankind at some future time "on the eve of new unpleasantnesses, no less amusing than those we have now," for with it every man has the power to destroy tyranny.

There are ample indications that Martin Edelweis' Zoorlandia is the same land as that in *The Annihilation of Tyrants*, but Zoorlandia — or Russia, or death — lies outside the limits of *The Exploit*. The novel ends as Martin has bid good-bye to Sonya and gone off to accomplish his exploit. Zoorlandia had been a link between Martin and Sonya, but she tells the writer who has been courting her about it, and he uses it in a newspaper feuilleton. The betrayal is likely the real reason (the apparent one is a conversation on a train with a French *paterfamilias*) for the decision to undertake the dangerous exploit. As he leaves the Zilanovs, Irina Zilanova, who was raped by soldiers while escaping from Russia and left in a permanent state of shock or idiocy, hurls herself hysterically at Martin and clutches at him. This, he is told, happens frequently.

The Exploit's abrupt and inconclusive ending has been a source of bewilderment to all of the novel's Russian critics. Martin has departed for the Soviet Union, and Sonya, when she finds out shortly after he leaves what his intentions are, becomes greatly distraught and sobs uncontrollably. Darwin, who was in Berlin and also saw Martin just before his departure, is given the task of going to Switzerland to inform Martin's mother of what he has apparently done. And there the novel ends. Has Martin, by the very fact of his absence, at last won Sonya's heart? Is it likely, as the critic Mikhail Kantor suggested, that Martin, like the hero of a previous Sirin novel, will realize the futility (spiritual not practical) of attempting to bring his quixotic fantasy to fruition and turn back at the border?

I venture to suggest that the unwritten conclusion to *The Exploit* is carefully prefigured in the novel. Martin's return to Russia is on its surface an attempt to force his way back into a past which no longer exists, but in practical terms it is a return to the scene, a reenactment of his father's lonely death. Thus seen, *The Exploit* is Martin Edelweis' unconscious imposition of a congruent pattern upon the past. But this, of course, is simply speculation.

The other Nabokov work dealing with a return to Russia is a 1938 fantastic short story, *A Visit to a Museum*. It has been and is still frequently said that Nabokov's 1935 novel *Invitation to a Beheading* was written under the influence of Kafka — in fact, however, Nabokov did not at that time know Kafka's work — but it is *A Visit to a Museum* which has the clearest formal affinity to Kafka, although the story is at the same time very much within the thematic context of previous Sirin works. The narrator of the story is asked by a friend to stop in at a provincial French museum where the friend thinks there is a portrait of his grandfather that through a complicated chain of events made its way to the little museum. Letters of inquiry have produced no response, and the friend wishes the narrator to see if the portrait is really there and, if it is, to arrange to purchase it.

Although it is the narrator's intention to think up some excuse for not having performed the errand, he finds himself by chance on the museum steps during a heavy autumn rainfall, and so he does go in to look for the picture. The portrait is in the museum and the narrator goes to see the director who has a face "very similar to a white borzoi, and more than that, he had his tongue out in a quite canine manner licking a stamp to go on an envelope when I entered his smallish but richly appointed room." His name is Monsieur Godard. The director asks what he can do for him, and at the same time he throws the freshly sealed and stamped envelope into the wastebasket. The mystery grows when Monsieur Godard claims that the picture he has just seen is not in the museum. They agree to go there together, on the understanding that if it is there it may be purchased, but if it is not the narrator must pay the museum the same sum. Strangely, although M. Godard makes him write out the understanding "with a red, red pencil," no actual sum is named.

The picture is there, and a huge crowd of people, too. Godard grants that he is right — and here there is probably a little Poe in reverse — but he tears up their contract, throwing the pieces into a large spittoon. As the narrator tries to talk with Godard about a price for the picture — the director hedges and says that everything depends on the mayor, but he has just died and a new one has not yet been chosen, and besides, he does not think the law will allow it — he is shoved along with the crowd into other halls. The tiny museum turns out to extend backward in an extraordinary manner. But when the narrator tries to leave he discovers that Godard has disappeared, and he is unable to work his way out of the museum; he just keeps moving further and further backward into it.

After working his way through a chamber of fountains and one of darkness the narrator at last comes to one that appears to be real rather than a museum exhibit. Snow is falling and there is some-

thing vaguely familiar about the surroundings. After a short time
he recognizes that he is in Russia, but he also sees that it is not *his*
Russia, but one that is "hopelessly enslaved and hopelessly dear." It
is a dream about a repeated dream that has suddenly come true. He
tries to do away with everything that suggests his émigré origins,
which means "to be left ideally naked, and, although I was trembling from grief and cold, I did what I could." At this point *A
Visit to a Museum* breaks off with a five-line "précis" of what
happened after that — arrest, further adventures, and, after great
effort, a return abroad with the firm resolution never again "to run
the errand of someone else's madness." If this story is taken to be a
Kafkaesque expression of Nabokov's personal conception of a
return to Russia — and it does have a certain resonance with the
later *To Prince S. M. Kachurin* — then one should note that in this
important respect, too, Martin Edelweis is antithetical to his
creator.

In *Mashenka*, the first novel written by Nabokov, in 1925, the
central concern is the expected arrival in Berlin of a girl named
Mashenka who has been allowed to leave the Soviet Union. This is
simply a variation on the themes of memory and return, with the
difference that in *Mashenka* the past is traveling to Berlin. The
epigraph to the novel is from Chapter One of *Eugene Onegin:*
"*Remembering romances of former years,/remembering former
love.*"

The novel is built on the simple and time-honored principle of
the Grand Hotel grouping: a number of people living in a single
hotel, rooming-house, or dormitory and the — always — complex
web of relationships that develops between them. The hero of the
novel is named Lev Ganin, and the mainspring of the action is
introduced on the very first page when Ganin meets another
boarder for the first time while they are both caught together in
the dark returning to their *pension.*

"I didn't inquire about your name out of idleness," continued the
voice in an unperturbed fashion. "In my opinion every name . . ."
"How about if I press that button again," interrupted Ganin.
"Press it. I'm afraid it won't help. As I was saying: every name is
indicative. Lev and Gleb is a complicated and rare combination. It
demands dryness, firmness, and originality from you. My name is a bit

more modest; and my wife has a wholly simple name: Maria. By the way, allow me to introduce myself: Aleksei Ivanovich Alferov. Excuse me, I think I stepped on your foot . . ."

Alferov suggests that there is something "symbolic" in their meeting in the dark, and to Ganin's annoyed request to explain what he has in mind, Alferov replies: "Well, there's the halt, the motionlessness, this darkness. And the waiting. Today at dinner that — what's his name . . . the old writer . . . yes, Podtyagin . . . was arguing with me about the meaning of our émigré life, our great wait." There is indeed something symbolic about their meeting, although the assertively insignificant Alferov will never learn what it is — his wife Maria, whom he has not seen for four years and who is expected to arrive in Berlin in just six days is the same Mashenka (a diminutive form of Maria) with whom Ganin was passionately in love shortly before the Revolution, and still is for that matter. But Ganin himself does not learn who Alferov's wife is until nearly halfway through the book (the novel is deceptively simple and terse — we do not learn, for example, that the opening scene with Alferov takes place in a stalled lift until several chapters later), by which time all the inhabitants of the *pension* have been introduced and several secondary plots set in motion.

Ganin is having an affair with a girl named Ludmila toward whom he has a mounting feeling of revulsion, and in fact it is his intention to break off his relationship with her and to move away from the *pension* that Saturday. There is another, somewhat bovine but goodhearted girl, Klara, who lives at the *pension* and is a casual friend of Ludmila's, and is hopelessly in love with Ganin too. One evening he goes to the movies with both Klara and Ludmila; it is a movie in which he has been an extra, and the combination of Ludmila's prattling to Klara and seeing his "double" on the screen (this, by the way, is the first place we get a description of Ganin) causes Ganin to feel "not only shame, but also the rapid current, the unrepeatability of human life." Later, back at the *pension*, he reflects on how his shade will go from city to city, screen to screen, and this in turn causes him to think of the dreary houseful of "seven lost Russian shades" where he lives.

The other roomers besides Ganin, Alferov, and Klara — the

house is owned by the Russian widow of a German businessman, — are the old poet Podtyagin and a pair of ballet dancers named Kolin and Gornotsvetov. These last two are Nabokov's first portrayal of homosexuality in his fiction. Actually, the two dancers are the only people in the *pension* who are satisfied with their lot and are not reaching for some other person or time or place. Alferov, of course, is happy, especially with Mashenka coming, but then one feels he would be happy anywhere, even in the Soviet Union, which he despises. The landlady, Lydia Nikolaevna, is so timorous that when she comes to clean, she seems to the tenants to be simply a little, grayish, snub-nosed old woman who has wandered into someone else's apartment. Podtyagin has been struggling with bureaucratic red tape to get an exit visa to go to Paris, but the move seems as purposeless as it is spiritually necessary to the old man. Podtyagin is a "positive hero" in the mellow, early nineteenth-century sense of the term, and he evokes the confidence and sympathy of the other boarders. It is only with the kind help of Ganin that the old poet is at last able to get the necessary papers to leave Germany; and as they are riding back after having successfully completed the passport formalities, Ganin tells Podtyagin that he has two passports — his real Russian one, and a false Polish one which is the passport he uses. His actual name isn't even Ganin.

In a similar manner Klara feels no need of pretense in Podtyagin's presence.

"If we were in Russia, Klarochka, a district doctor would be courting you or some reputable architect. Do you, well, love Russia?"

"Very much."

"That's precisely it. One must love Russia. Without our émigré love, there's nothing left for Russia. No one there loves her."

"I'm already twenty-six years old," said Klara. "I bang away on my typewriter all morning and five times a week I work till six. I'm very weary. I'm completely alone in Berlin. What do you think, Anton Sergeevich, will it continue like this for a long time?"

Each roomer's attitude toward Russia is a faithful reflection of his soul. Alferov despises the new Russia; Ganin, on the other hand, expresses a deep and unequivocal love for Russia, and his lack of political qualification is slightly mysterious since, judging from what he tells Podtyagin, Ganin has fought as an anti-Communist partisan. With the hindsight afforded by *The Exploit*, one may reasonably speculate upon Ganin's likely eventual destination. His immediate goal, significantly, is to work his way to France *using no visas*.

Mashenka, however, challenges all of Ganin's former plans, for, as Maria (or Mary or Mother Russia) she may be understood as a portable living metaphor of Russia — or at least she was so interpreted by a number of critics. Mashenka is by no means an abstraction, though, except in one important respect: she does not appear in the novel. In the course of the three days from the time he learns the identity of Alferov's wife, Ganin, in a Proustian act of recreation, relives in his memory his entire romance with Mashenka, and he lays elaborate plans to beat Alferov to the railroad station early Saturday morning and take Mashenka away with him.

Although everything proceeds according to plan, Ganin does not meet Mashenka. He realizes that his romance with her in Russia has been completely exhausted by his four-day consecration of memory in Berlin. The Mashenka who has been touched by Alferov is not the same woman he knew, and he sees that it is best that she remain a shadow superimposed upon the *pension* of shadows that has itself become a memory. He waits until the train actually draws into the station — Alferov has been plied with liquor at a party given by the homosexual dancers in honor of all the imminent changes at the *pension* and put to bed with his alarm clock set several hours too late — and then he hails a cab and goes off to another station.

Although the progression of the action in *Mashenka* is rather rapid — there are several extremely dramatic secondary episodes such as Podtyagin's death and Klara's discovery of Ganin in Alferov's room searching for the photographs of Mashenka — the narrative at the same time conveys the impression of being a series of hundreds of very carefully chiseled cameos or bas-relief scenes. Here, for example, is the description of Ganin pondering the fate of his romance with Ludmila:

He did not know what jolt from without had to occur in order to give him the strength to break off his three-month affair with Ludmila, just as he didn't know precisely what must happen so that he could arise from his chair. His real attraction to her had lasted but a very short time: that state of his soul in which Ludmila had appeared to him in a seductive daze, the state of searching, lofty, almost unearthly excitement, which is like music playing just when we are doing something quite ordinary – we go from our table to the counter to pay the bill – and turning this simple movement of ours into some sort of internal dance, into a significant and immortal gesture.

And because of this carefully measured and conveyed sense of tempo, *Mashenka* may be profitably compared with Hemingway's first short novel *The Sun Also Rises* – which also was published in 1926 – particularly in its scenes of quiet stress and oblique intercourse. One Russian critic spoke of the clearly discernible stylistic influence of Bunin, which is, up to a point, true, and one may note as well a certain similarity to Chekhov (the dramatist, not the short-story writer). But such imaginary echoes are merely the analogies inevitably suggested by a work of art that speaks in its own distinct voice, and their application to the novel is in the end the best confirmation of *Mashenka*'s originality. Although it is no more a "slice of life" than is *The Sun Also Rises*, *Mashenka* is one of the best portraits of Russian émigré life in Berlin in the 1920's. The sole estimate of *Mashenka* as a major work of art at the time of its appearance, however, was made by the critic A. S. Izgoev, who wrote: "This is a page not only in the biography of a young author, but also in the history of Russian literature, and not merely its émigré branch. *Mashenka* has about it something of the national self-awareness of the Russian intelligentsia." Unfortunately, Izgoev spoils the prophetic thrill of early recognition by going on to discuss the novel in relation to two of Nabokov's favorite authors: Chernyshevsky and Turgenev.

The Nabokov work which most readily pairs itself with *Mashenka* – and this has been also noted before me by one of Nabokov's discerning Russian critics, Nina Berberova – is his 1957 novella *Pnin*. It, too, contains an extremely accurate portrayal of the life of intellectual Russians in America (not to the same extent that *Mashenka* reflects Berlin émigré life though, for the simple reason that *Pnin* centers on a single character to a much greater degree than does *Mashenka*), and this serves as the background for a highly stylized and yet wholly "realistic" story. And just as the deftness with which "personalities" are sketched it constitutes one of the principal virtues of *Mashenka* (not present to anywhere near the same degree in any of the later Russian novels), so the success of *Pnin* resides almost entirely in the delightful person of Prof. Timofey Pnin.

Unlike Lev Ganin, Timofey Pnin, who teaches Russian in America at Waindell College (and so is in his second emigration), does meet his lost love, a Parisian poetess named Liza Wind, who left him many years before and remains unchanged in appearance and manner from what she was then — vulgar, infantile, tempestuous, cruel, and absolutely necessary to him. Liza Bogolepov, a twenty-year-old medical student, had first met Pnin in 1925, when he was a young scholar with a part-time job in a Russian bookstore. The marriage was simply another of the unrestrained poetess' impulses, on the advice of analyst friends who foresaw a beneficial effect in marriage and a child. There is no child, there are several lovers, and then Liza leaves Pnin almost as suddenly as she married him — to live with a Dr. Eric Wind. Two years later she returns pregnant, to be his "faithful and lawful wife," but this turns out to be only a ruse to gain transatlantic passage (Dr. Wind is on the boat with them), and she leaves Pnin again at Ellis Island. She comes to him a third time at Waindell, on her way back from the elegant prep school her son is attending, and as Pnin waits for her "a flood of happiness foamed and rose behind the invisible barrier that was to burst open any moment now." She will, of course, leave him again, this time in just a few hours; the only purpose of her visit is to ask Pnin to assume some financial responsibility for Wind's child, Victor. When Liza first arrives, "he helped her into a taxi, her bright diaphanous scarf caught on something, and Pnin slipped on the pavement, and the taximan said 'Easy,' and took her bag, and everything had happened before in this exact sequence." Pnin's past comes sailing back to him all too easily, and *his* misfortune is that he cannot get away from it.

Pnin is the most gently and sadly comic of all of Nabokov's books, and Timofey Pnin is the most winning of all his eccentric characters. This is, in large part, a formal matter. In Nabokov's other novels the humor — and Nabokov has never written a novel that is not in some degree funny — derives from the highly developed self-irony of the narrator (Humbert Humbert is the best instance of this, and, in quite a different way, John Shade is another) or else its source is a radical disparity of norms in which either the character (the chess master Luzhin in *The Defense*) or the society (*Invitation to a Beheading*) must be adjudged "mad." In *Pnin* the humor is not a vital function of Timofey Pnin's personal misfortunes (that is, the humor is not a *device* of the novel; one can rather easily mentally transpose the dour personality of Luzhin into the narrative in place of Pnin, and it would remain essentially the same novel, but Pnin could never play the part of Luzhin). Neither madness nor self-irony play any role in *Pnin*. Pnin does have a delightful donnish sense of humor, but his conscious wit is minor indeed in comparison to the hilarious eccentricity of which he is quite unaware and which has made him an academic legend and source of cocktail-party hilarity at Waindell. The humor in *Pnin* comes to us directly (or, as seen from a different vantage point, indirectly) from a discreetly omniscient narrator. In this, the novels closest to *Pnin* are *Mashenka* and *The Gift*, but neither of these novels allows humor anywhere near the scope and prominence that it has in *Pnin*.

The narrator of *Pnin* is unnamed, but, unlike almost all other novels told by an omniscient third person, he does figure in the action; yet if one is not alert, he may appear and disappear again without being noticed. There are ties both apparent and unseen that connect the narrator with his hero. Liza Bogolepov's marriage to Pnin had its initiation in the depression she was in "because of a rather silly affair with a littérateur who is now — but no matter." This aborted sentence is fully explicated in the very last pages of the book, where it is revealed (strongly implied) that the narrator seduced Liza while devastating her poetic efforts: "I suggested she let me see those poems again in some quieter place. She did. I told her they struck me as being even worse than they had seemed at the first reading. She lived in the cheapest room of a decadent little hotel." Liza's suicide attempt was made very shortly thereafter "in the course of events, the narration of which would be of no public interest whatsoever"; and then she received Pnin's offer of marriage by letter, which she gives our narrator, telling him that if she does not hear from him by midnight, she will accept the offer. She not only marries Pnin, but she also tells Timofey everything, and although the narrator meets Pnin at various social occasions in Europe and America through the years and at one point refers to him as "my good friend," it is evident that the hero has not forgiven his narrator, for Pnin refuses his "most cordial" offer of academic protection when the narrator receives a professorship at Waindell and adds that, to his great regret, he will be leaving Waindell two or three days before the narrator is to give a public lecture there. At some point in the distant past they would seem to have been close friends though; the narrator relates an incident, some half dozen years after Liza and Pnin married, when one evening at a small party and *à propos* of nothing at all Pnin blurts out across the room: "Now don't believe a word he says, Georgiy Aramovich. He makes up everything. He once invented that we were schoolmates in Russia and cribbed at examinations. He is a dreadful inventor."

Insofar as Pnin himself is concerned then, the narrator is a spiritual relative of the repulsively effusive Dr. Wind, chasing him from country to country and forcing his way into the most intimate corners of his life. Indeed, the narrator, by the very fact of the novel he has written, is finally a greater intruder than Wind. Pnin's comment to an academic friend on Dr. Wind's theory of group psychotherapy might also serve as the expression of his deepest conviction about life: "Why not leave their private sorrows to people? Is sorrow not, one asks, the only thing in the world people really possess?"; and as Pnin's sedan glides away from the narrator's "roar of greeting" on the last page, one thinks of Pnin's anguished entreaty when he encounters Dr. Wind on the transatlantic voyage: " '*Lasse mich, lasse mich,*' wailed Pnin, trying to beat off the limp fawning hand." The narrative movement of *Pnin* is the flight of a character from his author, and, like Gogol's Akaky Akakievich, Pnin finally succeeds in escaping, with the help, of course, of the author.

There are compelling reasons why the omniscient narrator, unlike the advice we give children, should be heard but not seen. His actual presence in the narrative at once drastically curtails his divine power of observation since, as soon as the novel involves more than two characters, there must be scenes and conversations that the narrator cannot observe without himself becoming a major character (in which case omniscience plays no role). There are — and I take my examples from Russian literature — two ways in which this compositional problem may be solved. The first is by means of documents and personal accounts which have come to the narrator — thus the narrator of Lermontov's *Hero of Our Time* sees the novel's protagonist, Pechorin, only fleetingly, but he hears the tales of Pechorin's old companion, Maksim Maksimich, and receives essential "documents" from him, among them Pechorin's diary; the second and lower way is by means of the narrator who is merely a pretext on the part of the author and is only remembered from time to time by him — Dostoevsky's narrator in *The Possessed*, "Mr. G-v," who is completely forgotten for vast stretches of the novel, is the best example of this. *Pnin*, needless to say, follows the pattern of Lermontov's novel, and from a purely technical point of view the novel is a virtuoso performance.

Prof. Pnin is the outstanding Waindell campus curio, and so the narrator quite naturally hears tales and imitations of his antic exploits, which plausibly accounts for a major portion of the anecdotes. There is one member of the faculty, at whose house the narrator spends the night when he arrives at the campus, who has devoted the better part of ten years to cultivating imitations of Pnin until it has become a "fatal obsession which substitutes its own victim for that of the initial ridicule." The narrator's task is simply to note down and order the lore collected from such amateur raconteurs, and descriptions of Pnin's performance in the lecture room would of necessity be gleaned from students by the narrator, who presumably takes over Pnin's courses and students. Consider the narrator's personal acquaintanceship with Pnin (which, whether intentionally or unconsciously, is presented rather ambiguously: ample evidence, already cited, indicating a marked distaste on Pnin's part is combined with odd little bits and pieces such as a letter-to-the-editor drafted "with the help of" the narrator that contradict this impression); his relationship with Liza, from whom he gets Pnin's letter declaring his love for her; and, finally, his meeting with Dr. Wind, from whom he learns of their transatlantic voyage. All of these encounters provide the narrator with the material necessary to him for his story, and in almost every instance the source and method by which the information was acquired are subtly mentioned at some later point in the story.

It is, however, axiomatic that fiction which strives to present itself in the light of strict verisimilitude must present slips and incongruencies in direct proportion to the refinement of the attempt. There are both obvious and exceedingly clever narrative "slips" in *Pnin*, and one has reason to suspect that the latter are the narrator's mockery of the convention he has used so brilliantly. In his delightful description of Pnin on the wrong train, the narrator suddenly stops himself to add: "Thus he might have appeared to a fellow passenger; but except for a soldier at one end and two women absorbed in a baby at the other, Pnin had the coach to himself." The narrator does much the same thing again when, after a description of four people going to sleep, he slyly finishes the passage off by saying: "Presently all were asleep again. It was a pity nobody saw the display in the empty street, where the auroral breeze wrinkled a large luminous puddle, making of the telephone wires reflected in it illegible lines of black zigzags." The technical mechanics of literature are at one point the subject of a conversation between Pnin and a Russian friend who debate whether *Anna Karenina* begins on a Thursday or a Friday, and later Pnin picks up the conversation again to make an observation on the differences in time in the novel. The most interesting example of the way in which the narrator makes his novel inform upon itself are the two versions of the same incident which frame the novel. In the first version — the narrator's — Pnin takes the wrong train to Cremona where he is to address the Cremona Women's Club. But, as if to gain our confidence, the narrator confides that, although he too is disappointed ("Some people — and I am one of them — hate happy ends"), there is nothing to be done:

Had I been reading about this mild old man, instead of writing about him, I would have preferred him to discover, upon his arrival to Cremona, that his lecture was not this Friday but the next. Actually, however, he not only arrived safely but in time for dinner . . . And soon afterwards, surfeited with sweets, wearing his black suit, and juggling three papers, all of which he had stuffed into his coat so as to have the one he wanted among the rest (thus thwarting mischance by mathematical necessity), he sat on a chair near the lectern.

In the concluding vignette of the novel, Cockerell, Pnin's best imitator, prepares to tell the narrator "the story of Pnin rising to address the Cremona Women's Club and discovering he had brought the wrong lecture." Which of the two stories is the correct one? Has the narrator re-ordered Cockerell's story (as he certainly had to transpose what Dr. Wind told him about the ocean crossing in order to arrive at a version so unflattering to Wind) so that the humorous incident would be less banal, or is Cockerell merely repeating a second-hand, garbled account (wrong lecture instead of wrong train)? Since neither the narrator nor Cockerell is exactly a close friend of Pnin's, is there any surety within the context of the novel that either version represents what "really" happened? Both versions, at any rate, are set down by the narrator who can be trusted when, as in this instance, he indicates that he is not to be trusted. In the last chapter the narrator gives us his childhood recollections of Pnin. His description of Pnin's black gymnasium uniform, together with his comment that he himself attended "a more liberal school where we wore what we liked," directly contradicts his assertion that he had been a schoolmate of Pnin's and had cheated on examinations with him. The reader with taste for such details may catalog a score of contradictions. The narrator is, to vary slightly Pnin's own judgment of him, a dreadfully clever inventor.

The artistic function of the narrator who cannot be believed is obviously not the most essential part and purpose of *Pnin*, since the untrustworthy narrator is only a *diabolus ex machina* in regard to Timofey Pnin, and his actual relations with Pnin are never more than tangential. The narrator (and a reference to an Anglo-Russian novelist who is coming to teach at Waindell and to an entomologist whose name and patronymic are Vladimir Vladimirovich strongly suggest that he is Nabokov) uses the technique of the questionable account not merely for the sake of its own aesthetic charm and fictional veracity, but, even more, as a device to separate Pnin as a serious character from Pnin the campus "character." The narrator has two distinct voices, and only one of them is serious. The first, and frivolous, voice is the one from which Pnin flees and the one that relates all the hilarious misadventures of the insecure little "assistant professor *emeritus*"; the second narrative voice, under cover of the other's jocosity and meticulous source-accounting, creates and describes a real and finely drawn character calmly utilizing the novelist's license to the utmost. The same split in narrative voice may be found in Gogol's *The Overcoat*, but it is curious that although Gogol's second, serious voice is all but buried beneath the brilliant verbal and narrative façades of the comic first voice, readers of *The Overcoat*, under the tutelage of Russia's nineteenth-century criticists, have for the most part heard only the "compassionate," "humane" (and largely non-existent) second narrative voice. The title of Gogol's tale is particularly indicative because the overcoat is indeed considerably more substantial than Akaky Akakievich. But whereas Nabokov's character, like Akaky Akakievich, also has a joke instead of a name ("a preposterous explosion"), the second voice in Pnin is strong and central to the story. There is a very real person in the overcoat into which Pnin, with such Slavic artfulness, struggles — despite the fact that almost all of the novel's critics have perceived him only in the voice of the novel's first narrator. And insofar as he gives himself up to enjoyment of Pnin's zany speech and ways, the reader is also drawn into the circle of those characters in the novel who are the audience for those who mock and taunt him, as indeed Pnin's own broken language mocks him. "I haf nofing," wailed Pnin between loud, damp sniffs, "I haf nofing left, nofing, nofing!"

Timofey Pnin's overcoat is his language, and it is well to remember that there are not only two narrative voices, but also two Pninian voices — the one his natural Russian voice, which corresponds most closely to his thought (this is best shown in the literary comments he makes at The Pines, a New England summering place for Russian émigrés), and the other, his grotesque semblance of English. Seen in another way then, the narrator's two voices are a necessary stratagem to deal with the "two Pnins" (and they are the inner and the outer, rather than simply the American and the Russian Pnin); what seems to be the narrator's fitful conscience is actually the voice closest to Nabokov's own, controlling and directing its humorous narrative twin. A key passage in the novel is the description of Pnin's first heart attack. The narrator's first voice lightly assumes the guise of a physician in attendance ("Was his seizure a heart attack? I doubt it. For the nonce I am his physician, and let me repeat, I doubt it"), while the second voice, ostensibly speculating on the nature of death, makes a statement which is at the same time applicable to Pnin as a character (and, I might add, rather close in spirit to several statements made by Pnin himself): "I do not know if it has ever been noted before that one of the main characteristics of life is discreteness. Unless a film of flesh envelops us, we die. Man exists only insofar as he is separated from his surroundings. The cranium is a space-traveler's helmet. Stay inside or you perish." The narrator's second voice respects Pnin's human sorrow and human integrity by ignoring all that is surface and extrinsic. This voice addresses itself not to the Pnin who is a source of amusement, even to the kind Joan Clements, but to the one who has suffered heart attacks — and the statement is its own authority — "on August 10, 1942, and February 15 (his birthday), 1937, and May 18, 1929, and July 4, 1920." Pnin has three such attacks within the approximately four-year time span of the novel. Two of them are in rapid succession (and one of these, occurring while he is on the lectern just before he gives his Cremona talk, parallels John Shade's attack), while the third comes upon him at The Pines. As he looks out at the audience from the lectern, Pnin sees the people of his past, among them his parents, many old friends, and a youthful sweetheart. The spasm that he suffers at The Pines happens to take place just as a chatty old woman refers to her cousin Mira Belochkin, who was that youthful sweetheart:

Only in the detachment of an incurable complaint, in the sanity of near-death, could one cope with this for a moment. In order to exist rationally, Pnin had taught himself, during the last ten years, never to remember Mira Belochkin . . . because one could not live with the thought that this graceful, fragile, tender young woman with those eyes, that smile, those gardens and snows in the background, had been brought in a cattle car to an extermination camp.

This remembrance brings together the only two things Pnin "has" — his past (which for various reasons such as this is largely unusable) and his death, which is the safest and most negative possession of all.

Pnin does, in fact, have one person who needs him and who is in many respects in the same position as he is. This is Liza's fourteen-year-old son Victor, whose father, in a cruel parody of his own belief, is disdainful of his son for not evidencing the proper Freudian hatred of him. (Victor views Dr. Wind as "a cranky refugee doctor," does not much like him, and almost never sees him.) Liza's trip to see Pnin, moreover, was not an idle whim, for shortly after she speaks with him about assuming some financial responsibility for Victor, she leaves Wind and is "about to be married in Buffalo to a man named Church." From what we know of Liza Bogolepov there is every reason to assume that, for all practical purposes, Victor has been orphaned.

The portions of *Pnin* that concern Victor are those most obviously and uniformly written in the second narrative voice. Victor lulls himself to sleep each night with a fantasy that is largely Russian émigré in character: the King, who, faced with revolution, chooses exile over abdication and waits on a beach alone (*solus rex*) to be rescued by a powerful motorboat. "The King's" beautiful wife is dead, but Victor's imaginary monarch is not really Dr. Wind; he is an image of himself "as that underformer imagined he would look at forty himself." Victor's dream, although it is little more for him than a utilitarian means of getting to sleep, may be seen as a radical change of the major roles in the novel. The child Victor is the king who, in chess terms is the *solus rex* awaiting rescue, and his rescue by water (Liza refers to Timofey as the boy's "water father") may be by Timofey Pnin — "a cheerful American adventurer" — whose erratic course has a knight-like angularity. When Pnin plays chess with Eric Wind he comments on the play in his own special brand of German: "*Wenn Sie so, dann ich so, und Pferd fliegt.*" Nabokov has affirmed that none of his novels are plotted chess games ("One of EW's screwless turns"), but some such vague solution seems best suited to account for Victor's presence in the novel and Pnin's bold exit in his little sedan to "where there was simply no saying what miracle might happen." The open-ended narrative is, along with the circular, one of Nabokov's most teasing literary forms, and, because it is far less obvious, *Pnin* evinces an even more sophisticated usage of this form than *The Exploit*.

For Victor, Pnin is "the great Timofey Pnin, scholar and gentleman, teaching a practically dead language at the famous Waindell College" (certain of the particulars need to be changed, but scarcely any reader of *Pnin* could challenge the overall justice of that estimate), and Victor's magnificent present, a crystal punch bowl — the value of which Timofey is at first not aware — is the sole thing in Pnin's life that remains unbroken after the disastrous "housewarming" party at which he learns he has lost his job. If Victor's gift is a royal favor — and the amount he evidently paid for it strongly suggests it has some subconscious meaning for him — Pnin for his part seems ready to partake in the game's new pattern. There has been a marked tendency on his part — quite correctly — to pair his friends and his opponents (in the end the two are the same), as when his "benefactor" Hagen, whose departure from Waindell will mean the loss of Pnin's job, is seen before the fact as a "double" of Eric Wind: "Whom does he remind me of? thought Pnin suddenly. Eric Wind? Why? They are quite different physically." This again suggests the pairing of all secondary chess pieces. But Timofey Pnin could not be abandoned to the further cruel caprices of fate, and we are warmed and relieved to learn in *Pale Fire* that he has a new job and is, in fact, a departmental chairman.

Before leaving *Pnin* I should like to note two striking peculiarities of this particular novel. More than any other of his English novels, *Pnin* seethes with private Russian jokes, some of them esoteric enough to be understood by only a very select circle of Russians. They are mostly after the pattern of — to take an instance of an open joke — "Dr. Rosetta Stone." The most important of these is Pnin's very name, which is taken from the name of the eighteenth-century Russian poet Ivan Pnin. This real Pnin was the illegitimate son of Prince Repnin — at that time such truncated names were quite common for the bastard offspring of noblemen — and his most famous work, *The Wail of Innocence*, is a passionate protest against his position as "half a person" in the eyes of society. In his frequent moments of great emotional stress, Pnin almost always "wails," and Pnin's one constant characteristic is certainly his innocence, which he defends against every effort of the elements and people to pierce it: "Yes — sonic disturbance," said Pnin. "I hear every, every sound from downstairs, but now it is not the place to discuss it, I think." Paired with this cruel and funny name taken from the eighteenth century, the name of Pnin's former wife is also a semi-serious joke: Liza is the heroine of Karamzin's famous eighteenth-century sentimental tale, *Poor Liza*, and so when the narrator exclaims, "Poor Liza!" he is indulging in a joke at the expense of his English readers. But such details are in no way central to understanding the novel, any more than are the references to real people and places that occur in *Pnin* more than in any other Nabokov work in Russian or English. I have been told of the Russian teachers in America from whom little bits were taken for the formation of Pnin's character, and I have even had the extraordinary experience of hearing one delightful and very plausibly Pninian Russian tell me how one particular conversation he had with Nabokov found its way into the novel. The Pines and the Russians who vacation there are a fictional re-creation of several little colonies of Russian intellectuals (principally in Vermont) where Nabokov used to summer and astound the natives by painting the tree trunks in the nearby woods with molasses every evening. And, of course, Waindell College bears a certain resemblance, verbal and otherwise, to the school in upstate New York where Nabokov was teaching when *Pnin* was written. On one occasion I wrote Nabokov about someone in quite a different connection and was told, "Look him up in *Pnin*," where, sure enough, he was. But it would be a thankless task to attempt to fix upon all the real people who are present in whole or in part in *Pnin*. Besides, such considerations distract our attention from what is a self-contained work of art.

From what has been said of the two works, I hope it is clear that the natural affinity between *Mashenka* and *Pnin* also serves to contrast the differences, as well as show the similarities, between the young writer and the mature artist. In the intervening years, in addition to *The Exploit*, Nabokov continued to practice, in many of his short stories, a more conventionally realistic art at the same time he was writing his ever more unconventional novels, so that one is not really able to speak of a movement "from-to" in his prose. It is a question, rather, of following the development of a major and a minor line.

The simpler short stories are only rarely "vignettes" or "scenes."

The first story he ever wrote, *Well-Being* — which appeared in *The Rudder* in April, 1924 — is more or less that. It is a soliloquy addressed to a lover with whom the narrator has quarreled; the story leaves something to be desired since a great deal of what is said in the narrator's "mental letter" to his lover is obviously "background information" unnecessary to anyone but the reader. After their quarrel he calls her, and they arrange to meet by the Brandenburg Gate, but, as the narrator foresaw, she does not come. The substance of *Well-Being* is a fervent description — perhaps too fervent (one wonders whether this story was, like *Letter to Russia*, to have been part of the abandoned novel *Happiness*) — of the people he sees by the gate and of nature, and the realization he proclaims that "the happiness which I sought in you is not only hidden in you but is breathing everywhere around me." Another, more successful story of a purely descriptive sort is *Guidebook to Berlin* (1925). The narrator of the story goes to a bar with "my ever-present co-drinker," and there he tells his friend "about sewer pipes, trolleycars, and other important things." Again we have an instance in *Guidebook to Berlin* of fiction that in places comes extremely close to the form of the prose poem. The eight-page story is divided into five little numbered sketches: "Sewer Pipes," "The Tram," "Jobs," "Eden," "The Tavern," the shortest of them only twenty lines long. The narrator describes some sewer pipes lying on the street where he lives, how children at first played on them but now have left them alone, the thin stripe of snow that appears on them one morning, and the reflection of a passing tram. The second sketch deals with the tram as a symbol of the Berlin that is already passing, for in about twenty years, the narrator predicts, the tram will have vanished just like the horsecar. His wandering reflections lead him to imagine how the tram and contemporary Berlin will be written about in the twenty-first century, but this is finally only a pretext to define and justify his own conception of the writer's role:

I think that the meaning of the writer's art lies in this: to portray ordinary things as they will be reflected in the flattering mirrors of future times, to find in them that fragrant tenderness which our descendants will feel in those far-off days when every trifle of our daily life will become in itself beautiful and festive, in those days when a person who has put on the very plainest sort of jacket that we wear today will be at once attired for a courtly masquerade.

The only one of the sketches that in any way conforms to the proclaimed "guidebook" pattern is the fourth one, "Eden," which is a description of the Berlin zoo in winter, "an earthly paradise created by man." The image of the zoo and the cage, both figurative and real, is one that is to be recurrent in Nabokov's prose and poetry. The actual description of the zoo is not as fascinating as the narrator's perversely anti-romantic admiration of the zoo, which he sees as being as close to a model of heaven as man is capable of creating: "It's just a pity that this is an artificial paradise, all in bars, but it's true that, were there no barriers, the lion would devour the doe." Nabokov understands the cage in much the same way as the poet Blok understood it — as the dual metaphor of artistic form and human fate.

The concluding sketch in *Guidebook to Berlin*, the best of the five, has some of the air of the carefully arranged "careless sketch" used by Turgenev in his first and best book, *A Sportsman's Sketches*. For the first time the "ever-present co-drinker" speaks: "This is a very bad guidebook . . . Who cares about knowing how you rode in a tram, how you went to the Berlin aquarium? . . . In a word, it's dull. A dull, alien city. And it's expensive to live here." But the narrator is already describing the tavern itself, and his attention is drawn to a little boy sitting in a back room. He describes the boy's field of vision, which, of course, includes himself, and the thought occurs to him that no matter what happens to that little boy later in life, he will always remember the view he sees every day from that back room. " 'I don't understand what you see there,' said my companion, again turning to me. And how could I make him understand that I had caught a glimpse of someone's future remembrance?" *Guidebook to Berlin* is a guidebook written with a very restricted type of tourist in mind; it is a guidebook for artists.

The Fight, another story written in 1925, also takes place in a tavern, and it, too, suggests comparison with *A Sportsman's Sketches*, or with some of Bunin's more lyrical short stories. *The Fight* is a most successful exercise because of the skillful way in which Nabokov superimposes the poetic stillness, so characteristic of his early prose, upon an extremely melodramatic subject. The narrator of the story goes sunbathing every day, and every day "exactly at nine" there appears another sunbather, a middle-aged German who spreads himself out under a black umbrella, so that its shade covers just his face, and reads the paper. The narrator comes to feel a certain kinship with his fellow sunbather and would like to share some of his solar thoughts with him, but he knows too little German. And so, without ever speaking to him, he begins to speculate about who he is.

By chance the narrator discovers that the German is a bartender named Krause, and while he is in the bar, a violent argument takes place between Krause and his daughter's lover. Krause tells the man to pay for his drink, and they go outside and stand shouting at each other (because of his poor German the narrator does not really understand what they are saying) until, in the end, the boyfriend beats the father up and leaves. The narrator goes back into the tavern to get his hat, and before he goes, he strokes the distraught daughter's hair and kisses her lightly. The conclusion of the story strongly suggests that everything that happened may be nothing more than the sunbathing poet's far-ranging imagination: "I don't know and don't want to know who was guilty and who was right in this little *histoire* . . . And it may be that the matter does not concern human sufferings and joys but the play of shadows and light on a living body, the harmony of little details brought together just today, right now, in a singular and unrepeatable fashion."

A later story, *Recruitment (Nabor)*, written in 1935, is an open experiment in the composition of a complete story about a chance passerby while he is still in the presence of the storyteller. The imagined character is an old Russian who has lost everything and everyone in his life; his past, his thoughts about death, and a return from a funeral are described with Chekhovian pathos. In reality, however, the man, sitting on a park bench with the storyteller, is not even a Russian, but an old German who has been thus appropriated "with dizzying speed because it was absolutely necessary for me to have just someone like him for an episode in the novel with which I have been struggling for three years." The trick is held until the end of the story when the "real" old man is described. The narrator speaks of himself as "a gentleman with a Russian newspaper [*whom*] it is difficult for me to describe, and besides there is no point — an auto-portrait is rarely successful, since the expression of the eyes is almost always strained: the hypnosis of the mirror which one can't avoid." But there is a second shock in the final lines of *Recruitment* when the narrator himself turns out to be only a facsimile of the real writer — "my representative." That designation, as we are shown by a later story, is for man when he has finished with his work as artist. As is the case with *Mashenka* and *Pnin*, the similarities and differences between the 1925 and the 1935 story are most instructive.

In the stories in which there are no complexities of exposition, the narrative, as often as not, leads to a single striking poetic image or situation. In *Port* (1924) a Russian named Nikitin has come to a seaport in the south of France from Constantinople where he found life unbearable. Here it is the character himself who, in a manner wholly in keeping with his aimless way of life, confuses dream and reality, past and present. After a visit to a little Russian restaurant, where "of course, there is no France on the other side of the door," Nikitin goes strolling the streets; in a café he sees a woman whom he is sure he knows, and he follows her out onto the street. The woman is a French prostitute, but Nikitin cannot believe he is mistaken. " 'Listen,' he said simply and quietly in Russian. 'We've known each other a long time now, so let's speak in our native language.' " The only responses from the prostitute are her standard questions for foreign clientele — "Ewe speak Inglish? . . . *T'es polonais, alors?*" With a laugh he impulsively thrusts the last money he has into her hand and walks away. He hears hurried footsteps and the rustle of a dress behind him, but when he turns around there is no one there. *Port* ends with Nikitin, who has no clear past, present, or future, sitting on a wharf and looking up at the sky through which at that moment a shooting star is falling.

As is the case in his novels, many Nabokov short stories are devoted to a character's fixation upon his past, often prompted by a recent death, and the protagonist, when it is not the narrator himself, is almost always a plausible understudy for the artist

(Nikitin is the necessary exception). One of the early stories dealing with the past moves toward a single striking *pointe* which is not the character's attainment of the sought past, but a beautifully poetic transubstantiation of the past into another present. The 1925 story *Christmas* concerns a man whose young son has recently died, and in his grief he has gone to their summer house in the midst of winter, where he rummages in his son's things and papers and tries to understand the fact of his death. When his grief has become such that, on the eve of Christmas, the father is sure he will now die, too, there is suddenly a slight sound in the room. The son had been a lepidopterist, and the sudden presence of heat in the summer house has caused an Indian cocoon to hatch. *Christmas* ends with a lyrical description of the emergence of the damp insect and its gradual unfolding of its wings. Resplendent as they are in nature, Nabokov's passion for butterflies sometimes appears as an annoying stylistic mannerism in his novels. There is an amusing article which, in fact, attempts to reduce *Lolita* to a butterfly chase. In *Christmas,* as in *The Aurelian,* however, the image of the butterfly is both natural and essential to the narrative fabric which probably is the reason why I find these stories in no way cloying. One oddity in *Christmas* is that the summer house is slightly outside St. Petersburg, and while no specific time of action is indicated, it seems clear that the story is set in prerevolutionary Russia. Certain émigré writers, generally of minor stature, are notable for the way they steadfastly avoided descriptions of life in emigration in their art, setting their stories in a kind of timeless Russia which is oblivious of history. This is the only instance, though, in which Nabokov employs this sort of setting.

Two of Nabokov's best early treatments in his shorter fiction of tragic confrontation with the past are *The Return of Chorb* — written in 1925 and used as the title story for his 1930 collection of stories and poems — and *The Doorbell,* which appeared for the first time in that collection and is undated. In *The Doorbell* a son has been parted from his mother for seven years during which time he has fought in the White army, wandered all over Russia and then, in emigration, to Africa, Italy, and the Canary Islands. For periods he had thought of her often; for a long time he had completely forgotten her; and lately he had taken to remembering her more and more often; he never concerned himself with her well-being since her deceased second husband had owned property in Berlin, and he therefore assumes that she "is not living in poverty." In all, Galatov has lost a finger, acquired two new languages, and nothing about him has remained the same except his laugh.

When he finally does come to Berlin to search his mother out, it is a Sunday, and the Russian newspaper offices and the registry of addresses are closed. Galatov chances to see the sign of their family's old St. Petersburg dentist, and, though it turns out not to be the same dentist, it happens that his mother is his patient. Amazed and delighted, Galatov sets off straightaway to see her, and to his further astonishment she seems little changed from his remembrance of her. But the son has come at the most inopportune moment: a visitor, probably his mother's lover, is expected any moment, and he sees an unlit birthday cake with twenty-five candles. Galatov himself is twenty-eight. His mother is happy to see him but stunned and distracted by the imminent disastrous meeting; when he has fully grasped the situation, Galatov sees that there is nothing for him to do but exit as quickly as he returned, and he hurriedly and awkwardly excuses himself saying that he will be passing through Berlin again in a year or so. No confrontation between Galatov and his mother's lover actually occurs, but then none is necessary, for the mother and son clearly see that their pasts and presents are mutually exclusive.

The Return of Chorb is about a reunion which is even more grotesque than that of *The Doorbell* because it is not real but, rather, the expression of pathetic and uncontrollable grief. Chorb, a poor émigré man of letters, has married a half-Russian, half-German girl from a fairly well-off family, and on their honeymoon in Italy she is accidentally killed. Chorb is too shocked to tell her parents, and, more than that, his grief is so pure that he does not even want to share it with anyone. And so, with no word to anyone, Chorb allows his wife to be buried in Italy and sets out to retrace their footsteps in an attempt to fix the memory of their few days firmly in his mind and assuage his bitter grief. By the time he has returned to the shabby German hotel where they spent their honeymoon, Chorb finally realizes that he cannot postpone telling her parents indefinitely; but instead of telling them the truth he sends word that she is "ill."

The parents, who have not heard from their daughter for a full month and are anyway more than a little suspicious of their son-in-law, come to the hotel slightly earlier than Chorb had expected them. That evening Chorb is unable to go to sleep, and he roams the strange town to find a prostitute; when he does, he takes her back to the hotel, where she has frequently worked before and where the sound of squeaking beds in use can be heard as one walks down its halls. He merely wants her to sleep in the same bed with him and promises that he will give her still more money in the morning. Although the prostitute is convinced he must have some special demand, Chorb falls soundly asleep, and, after roaming the room for a while and gingerly peeking at Chorb's suitcase with his wife's clothes still in it, she does, too. Chorb awakes during the night and, seeing his wife in bed beside him, screams out at full voice, sending the poor prostitute vaulting out of bed in fright. When, after a few moments, he has come to himself and recognizes the woman, Chorb feels that he has at last conquered his grief. But at that moment his wife's parents come down the hallway with a frightened lackey plaintively repeating: "But he's with a woman . . ." The prostitute leaves the room when she sees the porter gesticulating to her behind the old couple, and she and the porter stand in the hall together perplexed and listening to the quiet room where "it seemed unbelievable that there were three people there on the other side of the door." The abruptly penultimate conclusion of *The Return of Chorb* makes it another instance of Nabokov's usage of the "open form," but in the case of this story the reader is as powerless as Chorb himself to imagine what will "happen next." One Russian critic termed *The Return of Chorb* a masterpiece; I would prefer to reserve that designation for *The Potato Elf* and will say merely that *The Return of Chorb* is one of Nabokov's finest short stories.

Another excellent story of a re-encounter that does not really take place is *Music* (1932). Although the tale is straightforward enough, its conclusion does depend on a little literary jest, but one which the attentive reader will have guessed long before it is actually made. An invited guest arrives somewhat late at a piano concert being given in a private home. There are about thirty people present, and, after quietly taking a seat, he begins to glance around to see who is there. Music which he does not know well — the piece being played is new to him — is like a rapid conversation in some strange foreign tongue as far as he is concerned. Then he sees his former wife in the audience. During the rest of the piece he relives all the essential details of their marriage and ugly separation, and all the defenses which he has built up during the two years of separation are swept away. After the piece is over he sees that his former wife, who must have seen him as he entered late, has swiftly gone to the door and, in spite of her hostess's attempts to hold her, is leaving. "And Viktor Ivanovich understood that the music, which at first had seemed to him a constricting prison where they were both held by sounds and had to sit opposite one another at a distance of six to eight meters, was in reality unbelievable happiness, a magical glass bubble which had formed over and enclosed him and her, giving him the opportunity to breathe as one with her." The whimsical jest at the story's end is the name of the composition played.

Two parallel stories, one Russian and one English, are *Spring in Fialta* (1938) and "*That in Aleppo Once* . . ." (1943). *Spring in Fialta* is a story without a plot, or, at least, it does not much require the one it has; its strength and beauty are combined in the person of the story's heroine, one of Nabokov's most charming creations. The narrator of the story tells of his many chance meetings and dalliances with a married woman named Nina. Her character remains as unfathomable as she herself is attractive to him, and, when she is killed in an auto crash, the narrator learns with surprise that she "turned out to be mortal after all." Nina's reality for the reader depends upon the conveyed emotion of the narrator. Not only in his descriptions of Nina, but in almost every line one feels a rich and tactile prose that perfectly transmits his feeling; "the sorry-go-round" (in Russian, *v zastyvshei karuseli*); "waves too sluggish to break into foam" (*nikak ne mogut vspenit'sya nepovorotlivye volny*); and — when the narrator, who is also married, tells Nina he might love her — "something like a bat passed swiftly across her face, a quick, queer, almost ugly expression, and she, who would utter coarse words with perfect simplicity, became embarrassed" (*chto-to, kak letuchaya mysh', mel'knulo po eyo litsu, bystroe, strannoe, pochti nekrasivoe vyrazhenie, i ona, kotoraya zaprosto, kak v raiu, proiznosila nepristoinye slovechki, smutilas'*). *Spring in Fialta* is, both in Russian and in English (Nabokov was its co-translator), a verbal sunshower, and in the course of it one only occasionally hears the inadequacy and sorrow in the teller's voice. At the time of its appearance a prominent émigré poet referred to this story as "necessary to no one"; in 1960 a French translation of it was included in the collection *Les Vingt Meilleures Nouvelles russes.*

A critic once noted that Nabokov's unsympathetic female characters are all foreigners, chiefly Germans and Americans, while Russian women are almost always shown in a sympathetic and soft light by him. This, of course, is an inaccurate generalization — we have already seen Liza Bogolepov in *Pnin* — but one must grant a certain warmth and investment of creative emotion in most of his Russian heroines, and this — to paraphrase Nabokov — is probably his strongest link with classical nineteenth-century Russian literature. Another of his infrequent "negative" Russian women is the former wife of the narrator in the English story "*That in Aleppo Once . . . .*" The story is written in the form of a letter to a literary friend by a former poet ("But just now I am not a poet. I come to you like that gushing lady in Chekhov who was dying to be described"), and it concerns his relations with his wife and their parting. Unlike Nina in *Spring In Fialta*, however, the narrator's wife seems to act with a morbid and sadistic self-consciousness. She and her husband are parted when the train they are traveling on pulls away while he is out to buy something at the station, and they are not reunited for about a week. She at first tells him a rather ordinary tale of where she went and what happened to her, but later she says: "I've been lying to you, dear . . . *Ya lgunya.* I stayed for several nights in Montpellier with a brute of a man I met on the train. I did not want it at all. He sold hair lotions." And then, just as suddenly, she swears that she didn't, that she was just trying to test his love. The way in which they come together and part, always unsure of the reality of each other's actions and thoughts, makes them phantoms. "She placed one hand on my shoulder, staring down at me as if I were a reflection in a pool, which she had noticed for the first time"; and it is the narrator's final conclusion that "I suddenly knew for certain that she had never existed at all." The narrator of *Spring in Fialta*, who does not question Nina's existence, indeed her immortality, is in a certain sense like the hair lotions salesman — reality, it must be, decreases in direct proportion to length and proximity of contact. Or there is another possibility, which the narrator himself is aware of: *"Yet the pity of it*. Curse your art, I am hideously unhappy. She keeps on walking to and fro where the brown nets are spread to dry on the hot stone slabs and the dappled light of the water plays on the side of a moored fishing boat. Somewhere, somehow, I have made some fatal mistake . . . It may all end in *Aleppo* if I am not careful. Spare me, V.: you would load your dice with an unbearable implication if you took that for a title." The line "That in Aleppo once . . ." is from *Othello*, and the implication is that it is our mistakes which make our phantoms, our losses, and, in the end, madness, and even more that the narrator will commit suicide as Othello does after the Aleppo speech.

The sum total of what I have chosen to call the "minor line" in Nabokov's art consists of *Mashenka, The Exploit, Pnin*, two plays, and approximately two full-sized volumes of short stories, most of them written in Russian. Certainly the theme of reality and fantasy is present in these works just as much as in Nabokov's more complex writing, with the primary difference in the explicitness and functional simplicity of the motif's application to the story, or, where there is a complex theme present, as in the use of ciphers in the delightful short story, *The Vane Sisters* (1959), it is applied in a similarly limited fashion, usually as the attribute of a single character rather than the entire narrative. It has been the habit of some English and American critics basically hostile to Nabokov's art to single out *Pnin* for praise as the best and, sometimes, lone novel of importance by Nabokov. Undoubtedly *Mashenka* and *The Exploit* will be greeted with approbation and an ill-concealed sigh of relief by these same critics. The one Sirin novel which was granted something near genuine approbation by Georgy Adamovich was *The Exploit*, and one recalls how crafty old Tolstoy, asked what his favorite Dostoevsky work was, named *Notes from the House of the Dead*. Within the more narrow limits of their intentions *Mashenka* and *Pnin* and many of the short stories discussed in this chapter are minor but unquestionably original and striking works of art; *The Exploit* is merely a very good novel. If he had written only these things, Nabokov would deserve a place in the history of literature similar to that of the still unappreciated émigré Gaito Gazdanov or, say, Flannery O'Connor or Isaac Babel. It is, though, a shame when these works are used to belittle or launch an attack against the imposing row of Nabokov masterpieces in whose shadow they stand.

Six

❋ ❋ ❋ ❋

NABOKOV'S first novel written in a highly mannered form is *King, Queen, Knave* (1928). One can hardly speak, as is usually done, of the young writer's difficulty with his second novel, for *King, Queen, Knave* is a wholly new departure that has almost nothing in common with *Mashenka*. Even more shocking to many émigré critics than the stylization of the novel was the fact that *King, Queen, Knave* is not about Russia or Russians. The characters in the novel are Germans, and it was undoubtedly this coincidence of strange manner and "foreign" subject in this second novel that gave rise to the empty formula "at times like a translation from ———" that was to travel from review to review through the years.

As its title suggests, *King, Queen, Knave* is a stark and very plain triangle. A young lad named Franz comes to Berlin from the country and gets a job in the department store owned by his uncle who is named Dreyer. At the same time he becomes the lover of Dreyer's wife, his Aunt Marta. Together, but really at the cold and insistent command of Marta, they plan Dreyer's murder, and after considering various possible methods they settle on drowning him (Dreyer does not swim, Franz and Marta do) while out for a row. When they are actually in the boat and ready to begin, Dreyer remarks on an enormous business deal he is on the verge of concluding, thus causing Marta to delay the murder several days. But in that time Marta comes down with a high fever and dies, to the great grief of Dreyer and the equally great relief of Franz, who has felt ensnared and powerless before the aunt whom he had once desired so greatly.

The source of the novel's title is a posthumously published tale of Hans Christian Andersen with the same title. Andersen's *King, Queen, Knave* was written in 1868, but certain of his friends thought it too revolutionary and persuaded him not to publish it. It appeared in a Russian translation in *The Rudder* in February, 1927; Nabokov began to write his novel in July of that same year and finished it in June, 1928. The plot of the Andersen fable — it is a tale of palace revolution — has no bearing on the novel. What obviously caught Nabokov's attention was the manner in which the tale is told: all of its characters are paper figures living in a house of cards, and *King, Queen, Knave* is a novel of substantial length done in just this "two-dimensional" fashion.

In a sense then, *King, Queen, Knave* is an extraordinary tour de force. It is no easy task to adapt the means peculiarly suited to the fable to a full-length work of fiction, and Nabokov has succeeded by engaging the reader's interest fully while never letting him forget that he is involved with cardboard figures. Consciousness of the fact that literature is an artificial convention is stretched to its farthest limits and used to create a radically different style of writing. An analogy to what Nabokov has done in *King, Queen, Knave* may be seen in the early monodramas of Meyerhold, in which actors performed on a narrow catwalk with highly angular and deliberate body and facial movements. This method of staging exploited artificiality to the fullest by abstracting the actions of the characters from anything resembling a natural environment. The novel's artificiality is so deft and its mechanism so cunning that *King, Queen, Knave* is, far more than *Pale Fire* or any other of Nabokov's novels, a work in which one sees and feels the artist in the very act of manipulating his subject and characters.

Franz first encounters Dreyer and Marta on the train to Berlin, before he knows who they are. Dreyer casually glances at the young provincial and notes the probable cost of his clothing. Marta (who is thirty-four) sits scarcely even blinking, almost as though she has some fixed goal she cannot let out of her sight. The sunlight in the car gives her unmoving eyes "the appearance of life." Meanwhile Franz, who has sneaked into the second-class car and regards this as a passage from hell to heaven (the Dreyers are slumming by not traveling first class), "was living as though he were *outside of* himself in the chance movements and chance words of his traveling companions." He lowers his paper and stares almost boldly at the woman, and then he idly considers how many days of his life he would give to possess the woman. As it turns out, very many indeed, and almost his entire life. He begins to day-dream about the woman, and then, in his dream, he puts the head of a peasant girl he knew on her shoulders as though Marta were nothing but an elegant mannequin. When Franz slumbers off while thus dreaming, Dreyer notices the pattern of three holes, two glistening (the lenses of his eyeglasses) and one black (his open mouth), that the provincial's face assumes as he sleeps. Marta, too, thinks indifferently that he is like "a corpse with glasses" and expects him to tumble off his seat onto the floor.

Only Dreyer at times gives some indication of a secret life. The train stops at a station and Dreyer gets out to stroll and buy a paper: "As he went he thought about how good it would be to stroll under the arches of a strange railway station somewhere on the way to Andalusia, Baghdad, Nizhny Novgorod . . . One could set off today: the globe is huge and round, and there was enough money for five, perhaps even more, complete round trips. Marta, of course, wouldn't go for anything." But this is only an idle fancy for Dreyer, and it never threatens to gain control of his life in the way that it engulfs Paul Pilgram's. He almost misses the train, and when he finally works his way back to their car, Marta, who seemed to have been dozing, opens her eyes and says calmly: "Demented idiot." Dreyer's expression of dissatisfaction with the deadness and mechanical quality of the life he is leading is his absorption in the making of a new kind of extremely natural movable mannequin for the display windows of his department store and production for sale to other stores. His escape thus is merely a duplication of what he is ostensibly escaping from.

Franz breaks his glasses on his first night in Berlin, and since he is practically blind without them, does not recognize Marta when he goes to see Dreyer. Marta observes the awkward, almost sightless lad and thinks to herself: "Here's warm and pliant wax out of which one can make anything one wants." Marta's flirtation and subsequent affair with her nephew would seem at first glance to run counter to her earlier thought that "life must go according to plan, directly and strictly, without any original turns." But Dreyer himself has threatened that strict order with his barely perceptible evidences of life and independence — he reads a leather-bound book on the train, and Marta thinks that a man who calls himself a businessman cannot, must not do this. It is only a minute deviation, but it clearly bespeaks other differences; in a completely automated scheme the smallest cog is capable of completely changing the mechanism.

When Franz, Marta, and Dreyer are not thinking of each other as objects, they make objects of themselves. Franz is sitting in the Dreyer living room when he suddenly feels that his feet are getting out of control and that his body is becoming simply a head which will go sailing around the room. Dreyer's fatal fault in Marta's eyes is no more, but just as serious as his leather-bound book or Karenin's ears: " 'He dances poorly,' thought Marta. 'He will always dance poorly. He doesn't like to dance. He doesn't understand how fashionable it is now. How fashionable and essential this is.' " It does not occur to her that she is "unhappily married," however. She accepts her marriage to Dreyer as "normal" in every respect, and she thinks of an "unhappy marriage" as one in which the husband is poor, or goes to prison, or wastes money on the support of his mistresses. For Marta the famous opening line of *Anna Karenina* could be changed to read: All happy families are like one another, all unhappy families are, too.

The cardboard stylization enables us to see Marta, Franz, and Dreyer as both actors and objects, to observe the internal urge and the external force at the same time. It would not be going too far to say that *King, Queen, Knave* anticipates in many ways the object-centered "objectivity" of the French *nouveau roman* of the 1950's. Franz imagines how he will boldly kiss Marta, but things (which don't like him) seem to conspire against him: he trips on a rug, she isn't in the room anyway, and on the spot he is overcome with his usual fearful timidity. But he will kiss her anyway, since "Marta decided that today he would kiss her for the first time." We are at a loss to explain the true starting point in the action. Marta dominates Franz, but she herself seems as subservient to a higher manipulator as he is to her, and it is true, of course, that the narrative leads inexorably to her destruction (death would not be

the proper word). Dreyer is passive and never shows any awareness of what is happening to him, although throughout the novel it
seems that he is *about* to show us that he does see.

In the department store Dreyer is showing Franz how to be a
salesman, and he tells Franz that he will play the salesman, while
he, Dreyer, will be "an inexperienced young man, indecisive, easily
seduced," but, although it is a precise definition of Franz, the talk
only concerns neckties, and Dreyer shows no signs of putting the
two things together to draw the logical conclusion. We are reminded of a generalized tendency in people that Nabokov has
frequently spoken of in his fiction. In *Lolita*, for example, Humbert
Humbert is greatly surprised by the tone of a letter he receives
from Farlow, the former family friend and legal executor of the
Haze estate, and he remarks:

I have often noticed that we are inclined to endow our friends with the
stability of type that literary characters acquire in the reader's mind
. . . Thus X will never compose the immortal music that would clash
with the second-rate symphonies he has accustomed us to. Y will never
commit murder. Under no circumstances can Z ever betray us . . .
Any deviation in the fates we have ordained would strike us as not
only anomalous but unethical. We would prefer not to have known at
all our neighbor, the retired hot-dog stand operator, if it turns out he
has just produced the greatest book of poetry his age has seen.

In different ways we apply this static pattern both to strangers and
intimates. Dreyer goes to a museum of crime exhibits, and afterward he amuses himself by playing detective and seeing a criminal
in every passerby. But as he approaches his home and sees Marta
and Franz sitting together in the garden: "He felt a pleasant sense
of lightness when he saw at last two completely human, completely
familiar faces." E. M. Forster's famous division of literary characters into "flat" and "round" in which the flat character is basically
humorous and can be reduced to a single sentence ("I never will
desert Mr. Micawber") simply doesn't apply to *King, Queen,
Knave*, a novel of flat but very complicated characters and circumstances.

The plot is amply furnished with cardboard dangers. Dreyer
returns home unexpectedly on purpose to see if Marta will be glad

to see him, and the lovers narrowly avert being discovered together. On another occasion Dreyer walks Franz back to his rented room for the first time, and Marta is there waiting for Franz. She desperately tries to hold the door shut, and they are saved when all seems lost because Dreyer suddenly understands that Franz "has a mistress" and chuckling to himself goes away without entering the room. The rowboat trip is another instance of a catastrophe that doesn't come to pass. The most fascinating of them all, however, is Franz's mysterious landlord, who, it seems, must play a key role in the novel. Returning to his room at night Franz tiptoes past his landlord's room, and glancing in through the partially open door sees the old man in his underpants down on his hands and knees looking at himself in a mirror through his legs. But the landlord never fulfills his potential for the novel: he might have been a blackmailer or unsprung the plot in some other way, but turns out instead to be nothing more than a harmlessly mad magician who pretends that he is various animals and people at night; he is a digression with absolutely no significance in the context of the novel's plot, unless we count the fact that he is the only truly "live" character in it.

Both Franz and Dreyer do have a suggestion of real lives in the past: Franz, in his native village; Dreyer, in an old love affair. It is only when he meets his former lover that we at last learn Dreyer's first name is Kurt. Dreyer regrets that he met "Erika number two" and so spoiled his memory of the original Erika, thus indicating that he does have some secret feelings about their affair, but Erika tells him that she long ago sensed his superficiality, and she correctly remarks to him that his wife must have a lover. The first time Marta calls her husband by his given name in the novel is when she tells him that she wants to go for a row.

Marta is by far the most purely mechanical of the three. She has no past that we know of, and she treats Franz and Dreyer in essentially the same way. She is a threat to both of them, and it is clear that the novel's strict geometry requires either that she perish or that Dreyer and Franz be sacrificed. Marta's sole spark of life is reminiscent of Odette's cattleya in *Swann's Way*: before making love Franz always offers her his gift, a pair of slippers, but she is able quite easily to ignore this when something more important, the planned murder, occupies her thoughts. Franz comes to life at the very end, in madness, a machine run amuck.

The fact that the characters of *King, Queen, Knave* are not Russians is an essential artistic device to establish the novel's abstraction and "distance" from the lives of its (Russian) readers. But the novel is clearly not "about" Berliners, nor does it contain, as many reviewers thought, "Berlin as seen through Russian eyes by a writer familiar with the St. Petersburg of Dostoevsky and Bunin." The real influence upon Nabokov's novel was that of Andrei Bely, specifically, Bely's innovatory use of distance and the geometric figures formed by various relationships as a means of conveying the emotional value and reality of those relationships. Nabokov's characters are posited "in an unseen geometric figure, and they were two points moving along it, and the relation between these two points could be felt and calculated at any given moment—and although it seemed that they moved freely, they were however strictly bound by the unseen, merciless lines of that figure." This is a statement which equally applies to the writing of Bely. The novel is, in a way, a realistic portrayal of the Russian émigré's way of *not* seeing the natives of the countries into which he had happened to fall (Nabokov has written about this in *Speak, Memory*) except as celluloid or cardboard figures, but this again does not really concern Berlin or Germans in particular. Nor do the opinions holding that *King, Queen, Knave* is a "merciless satire of contemporary German bourgeois life" evidence any real understanding of what the novel is about. Not only the nationality but also the given social class of the characters could be easily transposed. The novel is an *eternal* story, and, when its movement has once been traced, any other set of characters could be led over Nabokov's carefully placed chalk marks. Different as their "personalities" are, Marta Dreyer (who almost drowns her husband) and Charlotte Haze (who is almost drowned *by* her husband) join hands across borders and decades.

After an interval of four years and two novels (*The Luzhin Defense* and *The Exploit*), Nabokov again wrote a completely "non-Russian" novel, *Camera obscura*. Its protagonists are also Germans, and, to give the cliché life, *Camera obscura* may be profitably thought of as an adaptation or free translation from the

Russian of *King, Queen, Knave*. The fatal pattern remains, but this time it is the "king" who is sacrificed, and "real" Germans stand in place of the other novel's pasteboard figures. There is a moment on the train ride in *King, Queen, Knave* when Franz's memory "became a waxworks exhibit, and he knew, knew that somewhere in the back there was a chamber of horrors" (*kamera uzhasov*). The hero of *Camera obscura*, Albinus Kretschmar, enters this *camera obscura* or room of terrors, and it is the more terrible because the "room" is one that is well known to him, but which he sees for the first time only when he has been blinded. It is as though Kurt Dreyer were suddenly to have seen clearly the plot against him but had no defense against its steady progression to his death. The tragedy in *Camera obscura* begins to unfold when a letter from Kretschmar's mistress is intercepted by his wife, and among the other opened letters Kretschmar finds scattered on his desk when he returns is an invitation from the Dreyers.

Vladislav Khodasevich keenly saw that the entire plot of *Camera obscura* is simply a literal application of the time honored dictum "love is blind," a phrase which does occur in the novel. Kretschmar, according to Khodasevich (writing in the Parisian newspaper *Renaissance*, for which he was the regular literary critic, May 3, 1934), is punished with physical blindness in retribution for his moral blindness. Insight can only come with loss of sight, and understanding is the greatest terror of all. The fable-like quality of the novel is fixed from its opening lines: "Once upon a time there lived in Berlin, Germany, a man called Albinus. He was rich, respectable, happy; one day he abandoned his wife for the sake of a youthful mistress; he loved; was not loved; and his life ended in disaster." The fable acquires its modicum of reality because the action is played out in terms of the cinema, so that it is a story involving real people realistically presented, but in an unreal, two-dimensional projection. Khodasevich is again right when he points out that the novel is not cinema-ized by Nabokov but by the characters themselves: Kretschmar, an art critic by profession, is a movie buff; he meets his future mistress, Margot, in a darkened movie theater where she is an usherette; Margot's dream is to become a movie actress; and the "knave" of the tale is brought into the action when Kretschmar decides to produce a motion picture of his own.

Camera obscura was published in an English translation in England in 1936, but when it was published in the United States in 1938 Nabokov changed the title to *Laughter in the Dark* and substantially altered the novel. Textual comparison of the differences between the two versions should properly be reserved for a scholarly monograph. This problem of alterations also arises for Nabokov's 1934 novel *Despair*, but whereas the later version of *Despair* "cancels out" or replaces the first one, the differences between *Camera obscura* and *Laughter in the Dark* are a great deal more far-ranging, and there are many passages from the original novel which were not carried over into *Laughter in the Dark*. They should be viewed not as separate novels, of course, but as fraternal twins, and it is the critic's job to focus the double image into a single novel.

Two essential differences stand out above all. First, the names of the characters are not the same in the two versions. Kretschmar remains — in the 1966 version of *Speak, Memory* Nabokov reveals that the name is his gleeful revenge upon a German lepidopterist of that name who had previously made a discovery Nabokov himself thought he had made first. But Margot was originally Magda (later she adopts the name Margot), and the Robert Gorn of *Camera obscura* becomes Axel Rex, a play upon his role as the jack who usurps the king's role as lover. Secondly, *Camera obscura* stresses cinematic analogies much more than does *Laughter in the Dark*. The artist Gorn in *Camera obscura* is the inventor of a Disney-esque comic strip which becomes very popular, is made into movie cartoons, and makes him both wealthy and famous. *Camera obscura* opens with this cartoon character (the opening of *Laughter in the Dark* is the better one), and it figures throughout the novel:

Around 1925 there spread around the world an endearing, amusing creature, a creature now almost entirely forgotten, but in its own time, that is, in the course of three or four years, it was ubiquitous — from Alaska to Patagonia, from Manchuria to New Zealand, from Lapland to the Cape of Good Hope, in a word, everywhere where colored postcards could go — and this creature had the attractive name Cheapy.

Cheapy is a guinea pig. The idea, as originally given to Gorn by a young medical researcher was for a cartoon character to evoke support for anti-vivisection sentiment. Cheapy was to be a long-suffering little beast, but becomes instead a symbol of Gorn's superficiality, and perhaps also of the deadly superficiality of all the characters. Cheapy has been deleted from *Laughter in the Dark* — Nabokov does not remember precisely why. While many of the omissions do tighten and improve the novel this particular frivolous symbol seems to me to be a good counterweight to the harsh and cheerless story of Albinus Kretschmar. On the other hand, there are many little ways in which the later version is somewhat softened: Margot is merely taught to bathe daily and keep her fingernails clean by Kretschmar, whereas Magda also must be taught to shave her armpits, and cuts herself badly doing it the first time. Axel Rex is quite as unattractive as Robert Gorn, although the specific details of their nastiness vary somewhat.

In *Camera obscura* Kretschmar is given a history of many affairs prior to his marriage, and all of his lovers have some particularly unpleasant trait: one suffers from some unsavory woman's disease, another has very attractive teeth which turn out to be false. Kretschmar has also had literally hundreds of affairs in his imagination. For all her coarseness the sixteen-year-old usherette is overwhelmingly attractive in comparison with Kretschmar's staid and not very pretty wife, Annelise (later Elisabeth). He goes to Magda like a moth to a flame, in spite of his clear awareness from the first moment he touches her arm that he is doomed. Kretschmar does love Magda passionately, a Magda who is like the movie star she dreams of becoming, but when Magda actually does get a small part in a movie with Kretschmar's aid she appears on the screen "awkward and ugly, with a swollen, strangely altered leech-black mouth, misplaced brows and unexpected creases in her dress." She realizes as she watches herself in horror that she is "like her mother, the porter's wife, in her wedding photograph."

Axel Rex also feels if not love, then at least real affection for Margot, who was his mistress before she became involved with Kretschmar. Rex values the quality of the cool caricaturist in himself, and his "art" depends upon his ability to cultivate cruelty and see the humor inherent in it: "And if, in real life, Rex looked on without stirring a finger while a blind beggar, his stick tapping happily, was about to sit down on a freshly painted bench, he was only deriving inspiration for his next little picture." But all this did not apply to the feelings which Margot had aroused in him: "In her case, even in the artistic sense, the painter in Rex triumphed over the humorist. He felt a little annoyed at being so pleased to find her again." By picking up his old tie with Margot, Rex is presented with a rare chance to allow himself scope for affection while at the same time enjoying the spectacle of Kretschmar caught on the wrong end of a triangle.

Margot's chief concern is the financial security that Kretschmar provides, enabling her to live "like in a first-class film." But she does remember Rex with a bitter sorrow: "She was crying because he had left her that time; because he had concealed his name and reputation from her; because she might all this time have been happy with him if he had stayed; and because she would then have escaped the two Japanese, the old man and Albinus." But the allure of having her attractive past lover and Kretschmar's money (Rex is no longer wealthy when he returns to Berlin) is greater than her apprehension, and an additional inducement is the feeling as she sits between them at dinner that she is "the chief actress in a mysterious and passionate film-drama." When Kretschmar has lost his sight, the character of the drama changes. He has learned of the affair between Margot and Rex — it was his emotional state that caused the auto accident in which he was blinded. But he has allowed himself to be convinced it is not so.

The cuckoldry now becomes a wild parody in the hands of Rex who moves in with Margot and Kretschmar without the blind man's knowledge: "Rex, meanwhile, leaned out of the window and made droll gestures of greeting to Margot; he pressed his hand to his heart and flung out his arms jerkily — it was a capital imitation of Punch — all this, of course, in dumb show, though he could have squeaked remarkably in more favorable circumstances." This mummery, although Rex cannot know it, repeats many previous window scenes, such as the one in which Kretschmar returns to see an old acquaintance he has just left and receives confirmation of Margot's infidelity in a conversation held through a window. When Albinus' brother-in-law arrives and announces Rex's presence to Kretschmar, the two drive away together, while Rex, who has been beaten up and is stark naked, looks out the window at them.

Even more important is the function of doors in the novel. Actual doorways stand for the spiritual doorway of the *camera obscura* that is the novel: " 'Margot, Margot!' he shouted, rattling the handle (and quite unconscious of the queer part doors played in his and her life)." Framed in doorways, Kretschmar will twice almost murder Margot (and two other times, at the very beginning of their affair, he considers it). The first threat is when he has been told of her affair and interrogates her at pistol point in their hotel room: "('If I were to rush to the door' she thought, 'I might just manage to run out. Then I'd scream, and people would come running up. But then everything would be spoiled — everything . . .')." In the concluding scene the blind Albinus really does try to shoot Margot, but she escapes through the open door which he has been trying to guard with his body, having been unable to find a key for it ("doors were always against him"). In the scuffle as Margot tries to escape, Albinus is shot by Margot with his own gun. The punishment is the just and necessary one, but the agent has no awareness of this, for his moral blindness remains undisturbed through everything. A question occurs: which is the more repulsive character in the Punch and Judy show, Kretschmar or Rex?

If the three central characters are judged by one Nabokovian standard, *Camera obscura* (far the better title, though the book is obtainable now only as *Laughter in the Dark*) is a novel about three failed artists. Only one of them, Axel Rex, has any talent at all, though it has been completely perverted and corrupted. Margot is the most innocuous. She is merely a very bad actress, but when she is not acting she has a charm and natural beauty that is not without an art of its own (the way, for example, that she tosses her undergarments on a chair as she undresses for a bath). Kretschmar is a bad artist (the scenario which he starts and which Rex takes over and improves by making it worse); and worse yet, he is a bad critic. He first writes to Rex because he has had the idea, which is not even his own, of making an animated cartoon out of some well-known picture by a Dutch master. The painting (by, say, Breughel) was to be brought to life and then gradually to work its way back to its original form at the conclusion. Because he is a bad critic Albinus does not notice or remember later that the movie at whose tail end he entered the theater when he first saw Margot is that initial picture which will match his own end: "He had come in at the end of a film: a girl was receding among tumbled furniture before a masked man with a gun. There was no interest whatever in watching happenings which he could not understand since he had not yet seen their beginning." Kretschmar is the author of a biography of Sebastiano del Piombo (another obscure Sebastian, the sixteenth-century Portuguese king after whose death many "false Sebastians" appeared, will provide one of the meanings of Sebastian Knight's name), and Rex compliments him on the book, although he regrets that Kretschmar avoided citing his extremely bad sonnets (the brief conversation is a monologue in the first version). Kretschmar is predisposed toward the "beautiful" and the "happy ending," and as a critic he equates beauty with simplicity: Sebastiano is known for the marked characterization and vivid coloring of his art. How bad a critic Kretschmar really is, is demonstrated by the fact that he has a forged painting (done by Rex eight years previously when he had worked as a professional forger of pictures) hanging in his own home and doesn't realize it. Kretschmar can claim only one discovery, Margot, and he never understands her even though her nature is monochromatic and constantly before his eyes.

The emotional relief for the reader in *Camera obscura* is provided — and again we think of how contrary to Forster's formula of flatness and roundness this is — by the minor characters who evidence the moral depth and complexity that Kretschmar, Margot, and Rex lack. Elisabeth's brother Paul is mentally compared by Kretschmar with Margot's brutish and greedy brother, but it is Paul who, in spite of his contempt for Albinus, feels pity for his "being so utterly helpless in the wicked world that he had let grow up around him." And it is Paul who rescues Kretschmar at the urging of Elisabeth who proves to have resources and sensitivity that Kretschmar never suspected. But the most fascinating member of *Camera obscura*'s "secondary triangle" is the writer Udo Conrad whose art and opinions directly contradict those of

Axel Rex and coincide with those of Nabokov. Conrad, who shares control of the narrative with Rex (it is his idea of the animated masterpiece that causes Kretschmar to write to Rex, and it is from him that Kretschmar receives confirmation of Margot's love affair), is a German writer living in exile in France. Conrad tells Kretschmar:

It'll be a long time — a solid century, perhaps — till I am appreciated at my worth. That is, if the art of writing and reading is not quite forgotten by then; and I am afraid it is being rather thoroughly forgotten this last half century, in Germany . . . When a literature subsists almost exclusively on Life and Lives, it means it is dying. And I don't think much of Freudian novels about the quiet countryside. You may argue that it is not literature in the mass that matters, but the two or three real writers who stand aloof, unnoticed by their grave, pompous contemporaries. All the same it is rather trying sometimes. It makes me wild to see the books that are being taken seriously . . . It is a queer thing: the more I think of it, the more I feel certain that there comes a time in an artist's life when he stops needing his fatherland.

It is curious that, because it is all pattern and structure, *King, Queen, Knave* does not have an oppressive effect upon the reader, whereas *Camera obscura*, in spite of the islands of light provided by Conrad, Paul, and Elisabeth, is a novel which we must admire but cannot really "like" (significantly, Udo Conrad is quite cool toward Kretschmar) unless we very consciously subordinate the "real" protagonists to the surprisingly complex and ingenuous narrative pattern in which they function. Nabokov's fiction from this point on will be largely an ever more successful coordination of craft and pattern for its own sake with the less important but still essential elements of "realism." I think that the writer Mikhail Osorgin was in essence correct when he wrote in *Contemporary Annals* that *Camera obscura* should be seen as marking the point at which Sirin emerged from the ranks of the "promising" and became an "accomplished" artist of certain stature.

Two of the earlier Sirin works on which that accomplishment rests are *The Luzhin Defense* (translated into English as *The Defense*) and *The Eye* (this English rendition of *Soglyadatai* is a bit free: the Russian word's meaning lies somewhere between the chance "observer" and the professional "spy"). *The Eye*, which was written in 1930, a year after *The Defense*, is the slighter work in most respects including length. It is really a short novella which served as the title story for a 1938 collection of short stories and was only promoted to the rank of a separate novel in its 1965 English translation, but in certain ways it is more interesting.

As its very title shows, *The Eye* is, like *Camera obscura*, concerned with problems of vision and appearance. *The Eye* also has a "break" in its narrative progression that is even sharper and more extraordinary than Kretschmar's sudden descent into blindness. Before *The Eye* has progressed past the one-quarter mark, its narrator-hero Smurov does the one thing that a narrator must never do until the last page—he shoots himself. Smurov's attempt on his own life doesn't succeed; after some time in a hospital he recovers from the shot, but the narrative proceeds as though he actually had killed himself. Its voice switches from first person to an impersonal third person "he." The trick of this amazing transition is that Smurov does not identify himself by name when he is speaking in the first person, and then a certain Smurov enters the story "comparatively a newcomer, although he hardly looks it." A long and winding sentence at the point of juncture contains several clues that can be noticed by the careful reader, and the excessively flattering description is more than a little suspicious: "His manners were excellent. A quiet, somewhat melancholy smile lingered on his lips. He spoke little, but everything he said was intelligent and appropriate." But there is really no trick at all, since the "I" rambles on for fully three pages (after he has shot himself) about how "after death human thought lives on by momentum . . . I assumed that the posthumous momentum of my thought would soon play itself out, but apparently, while I was still alive, my imagination had been so fertile that enough of it remained for a long time." And these comments, borrowed with certain elaborations from Nabokov's 1923 verse drama *Death*, should prepare the reader for the practical application of the narrator's declaration: "In respect to myself I was now an onlooker."

The change in the narrative is, whether one catches it early or later, unusual, but it is fully justified both psychologically and formally. I would compare it to one of the exceptional rules in chess such as the convention that allows a pawn to be taken by an opposing pawn that lands beside it as a result of utilizing its first move option to move ahead two squares instead of one: the pawn does not actually "take" the other one by moving into its square, but rather, it moves diagonally into its row and the pawn that had been beside it is removed *en passant* (the name of the move). In the taking of a pawn *en passant* the question of timing is not left to the discretion of the player, because the move may only be made at the proper moment, that is, in the move immediately after the opposing pawn has made its two-square move forward. In *The Eye* two entirely distinct, but actually closely connected occurrences — a suicide attempt and a change in the narrative — are made simultaneously, as in the *en passant* chess move. From a psychological point of view, the change to the impersonal mode after the suicide attempt simply reflects the complete dissociation of personality and lack of relatedness that led to the suicide attempt in the first place.

The subject of suicide became a favorite theme among certain Parisian émigré poets, and many prose works besides *The Eye* (the excellent short story *The Yid* by the poet Anatoly Shteiger, to take but one example) are concerned with this too frequent fact of émigré life. There are, of course, questions as to the degree that different cultures report suicides and especially the openness or lack thereof with which self-caused death is alluded to in newspaper obituaries, but the general assumption of a high suicide rate among Russian émigrés seems to be logically warranted on the basis of the enormous wrench in their lives, involving not only change of station in life and great material want but also separation from close members of one's family and lack of empathy with one's foster country.

Sergei Yablonovsky, a critic who wrote at some length about *The Eye*, reported that he had himself on two occasions heard exclamations of surprise expressed impersonally by people he knew who had tried unsuccessfully to shoot themselves ("How can this be? I shot myself, and yet I still see, hear, and feel things?"). And this alone, one realizes, disproves the generally accepted notion that suicide, like death in general, is a severely limited and terminal theme for a writer — one which may be vividly and convincingly presented (Luzhin hurling himself from a window at the end of *The Defense*), but not extended and examined from within. I cannot think of any more convincing description of the psychology of suicide than that contained in *The Eye*.

It has been said that because Smurov is such a "hospital type," *The Eye* is the Nabokov work most clearly showing the influence of Dostoevsky. (In 1930 Nabokov had not yet expressed his opinion on Dostoevsky in print, apart from the two short poems, and because the two writers treat many similar psychological problems, critics would quite often make the careless assumption that Sirin was under the influence of Dostoevsky.) In general terms there are certain broad similarities between Smurov and Dostoevsky's underground man or Kirillov from *The Possessed*, but when the philosophic uses to which Dostoevsky subjects his disturbed characters are compared with the way Nabokov subjects his to the dictates of his craft, the similarity becomes far more apparent than real. That is to say, Dostoevsky (for all his other virtues) is an impetuous and uncontrolled writer; Nabokov is a consummate craftsman. One might as well speak of Herman Melville as being a "disciple" of the author of *Two Years Before the Mast*.

Considering its brevity, one cannot help but note that *The Eye* contains more major characters — ten — than do some two or three of Nabokov's full length novels taken together. Like *Mashenka*, *The Eye* is a group portrait of émigré life, but the characters in this novella are all reasonably well settled in terms of having jobs and close personal ties. It is the narrator Smurov who stands apart from all of them. In his English Foreword to *The Eye* Nabokov writes: "The people in the book are the favorite characters of my literary youth," and he then proceeds to supply excellent thumbnail sketches of them with some further biographical speculation:

The expatriates in the Berlin of the book range from paupers to successful businessmen. Examples of the latter are Kashmarin, Matilda's cauchemaresque husband (who evidently escaped from Russia by the southern route, via Constantinople) and the father of Evgenia and Vania, an elderly gentleman (who judiciously directs the London branch of a German firm, and keeps a dancing girl). Kashmarin is probably what the English call "middleclass," but the two young ladies at 5, Peacock Street obviously belong to the Russian nobility, titled or untitled, which does not prevent them from having Philistine reading tastes. Evgenia's fat-faced husband, whose name [*Khrushchov*] sounds rather comic today, works in a Berlin bank. Colonel Mukhin, a nasty prig, fought in 1919 under Denikin, and in 1920 under Wrangel, speaks four languages, affects a cool, worldly air, and will probably do very well in the soft job into which his future father-in-law is steering him. Good Roman Bogdanovich is a Balt imbued with German, rather than Russian culture. The eccentric Jew Weinstock, the pacifist woman doctor Marianna Nikolaevna, and the classless narrator himself are representatives of the many-faceted Russian intelligentsia.

All of these characters, except Matilda, who is Smurov's mistress while he is still speaking in the first person, are seen only insofar as they reflect a Smurov who, he says when he switches back to the first person at the conclusion, does not really exist: "There exist but the thousands of mirrors that reflect me." Smurov is seen by us in a half dozen quite contradictory ways, but the other characters, who are merely Smurov's mirrors, have only two images — the first incorrect one (Smurov is a very poor judge of mirrors) and the later images which come to us through the characters' own actions. The only character who, Smurov allows, is not a mirror is Vanya, whom he loves. But she is engaged to Mukhin, a character whom Smurov had scarcely taken note of. When Smurov blurts out to Vanya that she does not really know him and that he is always hidden behind a mask, she retorts: "Come, come . . . I know you very well indeed, and I see everything, and understand everything. You are a good, intelligent person." She is just putting him off as nicely as she can. Smurov sets out to find "the real Smurov," and the reader's task is no less. It is, indeed, perhaps more difficult, but it may well be that the secondary mirror characters do indeed have a unified and reasonably accurate vision of Smurov that he and consequently we the readers are incapable of seeing. Or it may be that Smurov deliberately withholds the "true" image.

The most outstanding mirror image of himself — Smurov literally steals it — is a portion of a diary kept by Roman Bogdanovich "for posterity" and sent to a friend in Tallin. Smurov grabs the envelope saying he will mail it for him, but he keeps the letter to read himself. Previously he had searched Vanya's room while the family was out at the theater — he lives in the same apartment building as Vanya and her sister — to see if he could find any references to himself in letters. This intrusion into Vanya's room is quite different from the search Ganin made in Alferov's room in *Mashenka* — while reading the portion of Roman Bogdanovich's diary he has stolen, Smurov finds a description of himself as a kleptomaniac. And Roman Bogdanovich has an equally remarkable theory about Smurov's sexual nature:

Smurov belongs to that curious class of people I once called "sexual lefties." Smurov's entire appearance, his frailness, his decadence, his mincing gestures, his fondness for Eau de Cologne, and, in particular, those furtive, passionate glances that he constantly directs toward your humble servant — all this has long since confirmed this conjecture of mine. It is remarkable that these sexually unfortunate individuals, while yearning physically for some handsome specimen of mature virility, often choose for the object of their (perfectly platonic) admiration — a woman — a woman they know well, slightly, or not at all. And so Smurov, notwithstanding his perversion, has chosen Varvara as his ideal. This comely but rather stupid lass is engaged to a certain M. M. Mukhin, one of the youngest colonels in the White Army, so Smurov has full assurance that he will not be compelled to perform that which he is neither capable nor desirous of performing with any lady, even if she were Cleopatra herself.

Smurov is greatly concerned that he not be thought to be a thief, but he makes no comment at all on the remarks about his being a homosexual. In addition to plump Matilda, Smurov has had another mistress exactly like her in Russia — and there is Khrushchov's maid whom he visits in her room. Weinstock, the owner of the bookstore where Smurov works, calls him a Don Juan and Casanova, but that may just be a reflection of Smurov's boasting and fabrication. He has been caught in a purposeless lie once by Mukhin. But if Smurov does indeed arrange, move, and control the other characters (and this is the one statement he makes that can be accepted without reservation), the corollary of that must be that Smurov himself, controlling the mirrors, also effectively controls the confusing picture of himself that emerges from them, and the most unflattering views then belong to him fully as much as do the naïvely flattering ones.

When psychological problems are seen as problems of composition, *The Eye* becomes a novel about the artistic process. The

Smurov who speaks to us in the first person is the "easy" portrayal of the narrator-hero, and the many Smurovs which emerge when the narrative becomes impersonal are aspects of the whole that the artist must seek to fuse. A casual remark by Evgenia Khrushchov toward the end of the narrative tells us that Smurov is a poet, or at least *says* that he is. Certain minute details seem to suggest compositional clues: when Smurov prowls through the Khrushchovs' living quarters he sees a copy of a French novel, *Ariane, jeune fille russe*, and we recall that at the very beginning of the novella Matilda had tried to persuade Smurov to read *Ariane, jeune fille russe*. It was on the pretext of giving him that book, in fact, that she first lured him into her apartment, while her husband was away, and seduced him. Smurov is beyond any doubt seen as a neurotic, but it is a question very much open to debate as to whether *The Eye* is a study of a writer who cannot separate himself from his creativity and so fails as an artist, or whether it is a diabolically cunning illusion performed by a first-rate artist: success in the guise of failure. Smurov's closing speech is an eloquent and somewhat pathetic panegyric justifying the artist's involvement with self:

What does it matter that I am a bit cheap, a bit foul, and that no one appreciates all the remarkable things about me — my fantasy, my erudition, my literary gift . . . I am happy that I can gaze at myself, for any man is absorbing — yes, really absorbing! The world, try as it may, cannot insult me. I am invulnerable. And what do I care if she marries another? Every other night I dream of her dresses and things on an endless clothesline of bliss, in a ceaseless wind of possession, and her husband shall never learn what I do to the silks and fleece of the dancing witch . . . Oh, to shout it so that all of you believe me at last, you cruel, smug people.

Nabokov has explained that, all signs and opinions of other characters to the contrary, Smurov is *not* actually a homosexual, but without the author's word, of course, the reader is free — indeed bound — to make as many mistakes as Weinstock, the Khrushchovs, and the others. Perhaps we are following a false path when we search for the "real" Smurov in *The Eye*. The point of the novella may be precisely the creation of a multiplicity and disparity of impressions and images, each of which becomes a "little Smurov" with an artistic life of its own.

In the period immediately preceding the writing of *The Eye*, Nabokov wrote two excellent short stories — *A Christmas Story* (1928) and *Lips to Lips* (1929) — which concern unsuccessful writers. *A Christmas Story* is about an older Soviet writer named Novgorodtsev whose collected works have even been published in a six-volume set but who is all the same little read or spoken of. A literary critic of his acquaintance has brought a young writer named Anton Goly (Anton the Naked) to Novgorodtsev to read a short story Goly has written. Novgorodtsev had written the critic a short time before to say that, although the twenty-fifth anniversary of his writing career was approaching, he would prefer no celebration be arranged "in view of the fact that my years of intensive work in behalf of the Soviet Union still continue." The critic simply accedes to his preference, and Novgorodtsev reflects that this Anton Goly has probably been brought to him for his judgment in secret compensation for the celebration that he didn't receive.

As Novgorodtsev listens to Goly reading his story, he suddenly realizes that he is listening to a continuation of the novella he had published with great hope in the previous year, but which had gone unnoticed by the critics. Rather than say anything himself, Novgorodtsev waits to hear the critic remark on this — but the critic evidently has not read Novgorodtsev's novella, for he says nothing. Novgorodtsev then begins to make gentle criticisms of the story without saying anything about his own work: "And suddenly Novgorodtsev became so sad — not offended, but simply sad — that he stopped short and began to wipe off the lenses of his glasses with his handkerchief, and he had very kind eyes." The critic and Anton Goly get up to leave, and as they are going they talk briefly about the sort of Christmas tale that used to be written when the winter was as deep and beautiful as it is now. The critic talks about a completely new sort of Christmas tale that could be written "depicting the struggle of two worlds on the snow." After they have gone Novgorodtsev thinks bitterly that the critic undoubtedly considers that he has no more originality left in him.

Novgorodtsev sits down to write a Christmas tale and settles on precisely the theme of "a struggle of two worlds" so that "later he himself will remember it in print: I dropped in on him once and in passing I happened to say, 'It would be a good idea, Dmitri Dmitrievich, if you were to depict the struggle of the old and the new against the background, so to say, of the Christmastime snow. That would complete the line you began so remarkably in *The Border* — remember the dream of Tumanov?' Well, that was the line . . . And during that night there was born the work which . . . "

After some hesitation — he can't imagine writing about the scrawny Soviet New Year's trees — the theme comes to him, at first in the form of a tale of émigrés weeping around their Christmas tree, but he can't see the émigrés whom he personally knew in Russia doing this. Then suddenly he enthusiastically begins to describe a beautiful and sumptuous tree in a store window in some European city with well-dressed and well-fed people passing by and a starving worker, the "victim of a lock-out," staring at it harshly and seriously. Novgorodtsev's theme is banal, not really his own, and, in spite of the starving worker, one knows (but Nabokov does not say) that he can never even print such a fantasy description of European affluence.

Lips to Lips is an even sadder tale, about an émigré widower named Ilya Borisovich who writes an unspeakably wretched novel (entitled *Lips to Lips*) and is maneuvered into underwriting the continuance of an almanac called *Arion* which promises to print it. Ilya Borisovich, whose previous literary production consists of two prose poems, a necrologue (prerevolutionary and in a newspaper) and an étude called *Travelers by Land and Sea* (in a modest little émigré newspaper in Chicago). Ilya Borisovich's naïveté about literature is both hilarious and touching. *Travelers by Land and Sea* is the title of a novel by Mikhail Kuzmin, and the pseudonym he chooses for *Lips to Lips* is I. Annensky, the name of one of the foremost prerevolutionary poets. When it is suggested that he use Ilya Annensky instead, he writes the editor (who has been recommended to him as "the Russian Joyce"): "You're completely right. I simply didn't know that there is a litterateur writing under this name" (Annensky has been dead for twenty years). Ilya Borisovich knows Pushkin mainly by Chaikovsky's operas, and can recite by heart only two poems. He is familiar with some of the more popular decadent writers and, though he feels they are corrupting youth, his own novel is strangely like their writing in all but its moral purity: "Take me, my chastity, my suffering . . . I am yours. Your loneliness is my loneliness, and no matter how long or short a time you love me I am ready for all, for around us Spring calls to humaneness and good, for the earth and the heavens glitter with divine beauty, for I love you."

When *Arion* does appear, it first seems that they have not even printed *Lips to Lips*, but it turns out that they have printed about three pages under the title *Prologue to a Novel* and with the pseudonym A. Ilin. The editor of *Arion* visits Berlin, and he is to meet with Ilya Borisovich, but quite by chance the old man over-hears a conversation in a theater lobby. A lady is telling a young man: "Pardon me, but I think that if you print him only because he gives you money . . ." They are talking about him. His illusions of authorship shattered, he runs out of the theater when the editor is introduced to him. The old man's exclamations and the editor's lame attempt to explain himself as they both struggle with Ilya Borisovich's coat constitute a masterly scene that contrasts sharply with the opening scene in the story — Ilya Borisovich trying to get his ecstatic hero and heroine out of a theater into the spring night and worrying about how to deal with the awkward necessity to stop at the coatcheck room without breaking the romantic spell. The last paragraph is not at all funny, and it casts its shadow back on the story: "He thought about how old and alone he was, how few joys he had, and how old people must pay for their joys . . . He knew that it was necessary to forgive everything or else there would be no continuation."

As it happens *Lips to Lips* is yet another chapter in that most interesting and lively disagreement that developed between Nabo-kov and the Paris *Numbers*. The almanac *Arion* is *Numbers*, and the pathetic Ilya Borisovich is in reality a certain Aleksandr Burov who was being courted and milked by the *Numbers* clique and whose quite incredibly bad novel *There Was a Land* did appear in *Numbers*. The plot of *Lips to Lips* is based upon an actual incident, and *There Was a Land* appeared initially, as in the story, in just a three-page fragment (subsequently, however, *Numbers* did print the entire work).

One other story, written a year after *The Eye*, concerns an unsuccessful writer. But the hero of *A Busy Man*, a newspaper feuilletonist who writes under the name Graf Ite, is not primarily concerned with his art. He is a "transcendental coward" with no special sins or principles, and he occupies himself primarily with thoughts of his own death. He is thirty-two and because of a dream, he feels that he will die at Christ's age, but the dream is just an idle fancy and his life will continue as before. Graf Ite feels all the stupidity of his morbid fear of elevators, drafts, and traffic, but he is not able to overcome it. After he has passed the fatal time limit he set himself, it appears, as the story ends, that he will no longer have this stupid fear, but neither does his "new life" imply any understanding or fear of the stupidity of the old one: " 'What does your daughter do?' 'She's a sadist.' 'What do you mean?' 'She sings sad songs.' " And such jokes, with which he fills his news-paper columns, are the sad sum of his life.

The Defense is also a novel about failure, but failure at the very threshold of genius and triumph. Its protagonist is not a writer but a professional chess master. Chess is, of course, an art form in itself and thus a particularly close metaphor for the writer of near genius reaching beyond his grasp. Luzhin is a Pnin-figure (his fiancée at one point calls him "absent-minded like an old professor") in whom comedy has been made the handmaiden of tragedy. He is a former *Wunderkind* who has never mastered those little gestures whose sum is society. A chess strategist, he sees only the more significant gestures or patterns through which the real course of life is played out. And in *Speak, Memory* it is interesting to note how Nabokov uses an impersonal chess analogy when speaking of his own childhood and the death of his father: "But no shadow was cast by that future event upon the bright stairs of our St. Peters-burg house, and the large, cool hand resting on my head did not quaver, and several lines of play in a difficult chess composition were not blended yet on the board." These patterns, as Nabokov has already shown in *King, Queen, Knave*, have a fascination which is quite independent of the people (or figures) who participate in them. Nabokov has always had a marked predilection for the view

from above, and there is his own description of the "subliminal coordinates" by which a novel is "plotted."

Luzhin's defenselessness before life's manners occasions an endless succession of comic scenes in which he either misunderstands
or understands too precisely. When asked a polite question: "How
long have you played chess?", he at first says nothing and then,
suddenly, replies: "Eighteen years, three months, and four days."
If his courtship *à rebours* in which he succeeds by making all the
wrong moves is a literary Chapliniad (his future fiancée runs after
him to return the filthy handkerchief he has dropped), the scene in
which the dazed Luzhin becomes involved with a group of tipsy
Berliners is pure Keystone comedy. But the comedy is the beginning of Luzhin's madness (the title of the 1934 French translation is *The Course of a Madman*, the French word for madman
also signifying the chess bishop). Indeed, Luzhin's chess promoter
Valentinov, a ubiquitous knave who has his counterparts in other
novels, eventually tries to involve him in the filming of an actual
movie. By this time Luzhin understands chess so well that life has
become the abstraction for him, and he can scarcely resolve the
problem (the theme of doors again) of how to leave a room.

The Defense is a chess novel, and yet it is in some respects the
simplest of Nabokov's patterned novels. There are no fantastically
complex moves to fool the reader, and we do not have to play chess
ourselves while reading it. There is a continuing use of windows,
tiles, linoleum squares, and the like, but these are only thematic
reflections and not "clues." True, there is a swift move in which
sixteen years pass in the course of a single paragraph, and the shift
of focus and time between Chapters Four and Six is not without
intricacy. But Nabokov has graciously detailed these matters in his
English Foreword to the novel. For the rest, there is an important
semblance of a chess move (first noted by John Updike) when
Luzhin marries. His manager Valentinov "kept him at a distance
from women and rejoiced over his chaste moroseness" so that his
unreleased sexual energy should be diverted to chess; thus the
marriage is a defensive castling. The last move, Luzhin's leap from
a window toward "dark and pale squares," is a desperate suicide
mate. In *The Defense* Luzhin plays thirteen games (in the expanded version of his original *New Republic* essay appearing in his
1965 book *Assorted Prose*, John Updike lists them neatly in

order), but they are not important *as games;* their true significance
lies in the personal encounters they represent. The critical game is
the thirteenth, with the Italian master Turati, in which Luzhin's
mastery is not as spectacular as before (it is not revealed, however,
who was closer to winning that last game). In chess as in art, only
victory is adequate consolation. Luzhin's suicide mate is a desperate
move devised to avoid arriving at the position of his partner in the
sixth chess game in the novel: "A senile chess genius who had been
victorious in all the cities of the world but now lived in idleness and
poverty, purblind, with a sick heart, having lost forever his fire, his
grip, his luck."

The character of Luzhin is based in part, Nabokov has acknowledged, on that of the chess master Rubenstein and of another, lesser
known master. But, as in the case of Pnin, who is also made up of
recognizable bits of actual people, the entire fictive structure is
more than the sum of its real "pieces." In the pitiful and charming
chess master Nabokov conveys the extreme, unpierceable isolation
of the individual, and the tragic consequences resulting when that
individual is an artist whose ability is not equal to his demands
upon himself: "And in the middle of this bleak disorder sat the
most unfathomable of men, a man who occupied himself with a
spectral art, and she tried to stop, to grasp at all his failings and
peculiarities, to tell herself once for all that this man was not the
right one for her — and at the same time she was quite distinctly
worried about how he would behave in church and how he would
look in tails." Chess is intimately connected in Luzhin's mind with
his parents' unhappy marriage, and it is his unexpected involvement
"in life" again that will unbalance his strategy. Luzhin was first
taught how to play chess by his father's mistress, and the melodies
and combinations of chess serve as a surrogate for life, which is
"not entirely comprehensible" to him. His choice of complete
immersion in this surrogate is an anti-Platonic one, in which the
illusion — chess — is consciously chosen over the unpleasant reality
of life. As if in confirmation of Luzhin's unconscious inversion of
Plato's cave allegory, shadows of people and objects in the novel
do in fact give rise to chess combinations in Luzhin's mind. It
would not be too much to suggest that all of Nabokov's novels are,
to a degree, ironic, anti-Platonic propositions.

There is a vital connection between the shadows of chess and the events in Luzhin's life, and we can frequently see a move made in life by watching carefully and remembering the circumstances of the earlier chess games. When young Luzhin would play chess with his "aunt" (his father's mistress) her "pieces would conglomerate in an unseemly jumble, out of which there would suddenly dash an exposed helpless King," which is precisely, in chess terms, how Luzhin meets his death. When life intrudes too much upon chess and destroys his control of his game, Luzhin is put on the defensive and ends in flight from both sun and shadow. The expression of his tenuous position between the two realities is his acrophobia: Luzhin is terrified of heights — the third dimension which takes him beyond the chessboard. In the final scene Luzhin barricades himself in a room and hurls himself downward, imagining in that moment that eternity is a chessboard toward which he is falling. "The door was broken down. 'Aleksandr Ivanovich, Aleksandr Ivanovich!' screamed several voices. But there was no Aleksandr Ivanovich." In one sense there never was an Aleksandr Ivanovich, for this is the first time that the reader learns Luzhin's given name. Luzhin's wife, too, remains only "she" throughout the novel, the point being, I take it, that the "individual" is wholly subordinate to the larger pattern of the game. In the case of Luzhin the absence of a name also serves to point past itself to that "clear madness" — the phrase is from one of Nabokov's Russian poems — which in various forms possesses so many of his artist-heroes.

The Defense, when it first appeared, was scarcely attacked at all — indeed, it was generally recognized as his first major achievement. When the Soviet writer Evgeny Zamyatin, author of the anti-utopian novel *We,* was allowed to go into emigration, he singled Sirin out as "an interesting and brilliant writer" whose *Luzhin Defense* was the most important émigré novel he had read. Isaac Babel is reported to have had a similarly high opinion of it. In 1934 Khodasevich in an article on *Despair,* which had just been serialized in *Contemporary Annals,* wrote that "*The Luzhin Defense* is the best thing written by Sirin, and *Despair* is not inferior to it." There are still readers who prefer *The Defense* even to *Lolita* and *Pale Fire,* and it is most curious that *The Defense* is the first Nabokov novel to have been nominated for a National Book Award in the United States. In part at least this popularity is due to the novel's simplicity, but even more it is due to the inexplicable charm and warmth of Luzhin himself that, in Nabokov's words, "transcends both the coarsensss of his gray flesh and the sterility of his recondite genius." Nabokov himself, however, does not include *The Defense* in the first rank of his fiction. The novel is an ornament and perhaps even a cornerstone to Nabokov's art, but one does not feel a need or compulsion to read it more than twice.

A very similar and equally charming 1924 short story, *Bachmann*, concerns an eccentric and partially demented pianist. The story of Bachmann is told by the musician's former manager, Zak, to the narrator who in turn relates it to the reader. Bachmann has the ability to enter a party in his honor and sit down to read a newspaper, not out of any conscious desire to be coarse or rude, but simply because it seems to him to be a perfectly natural thing to do. He is a brilliant musician and a hopeless alcoholic, and Zak frequently must search him out in taverns and "wind him up" so that he can perform his concerts. Like Luzhin, Bachmann meets a woman in whom he shows no interest whatsoever (in fact, when they first meet, the woman — her name is Perova — happens to touch his fingers which causes Bachmann to break into tears as though he had been caused great pain). But Perova is fascinated by him and perseveres in her efforts to establish a tie with him. There are many other ways, however, in which Perova is quite different from Luzhin's wife. She is, to begin with, married to another man, she is much older and a far more forceful character. She is so forceful, in fact, that she emerges as more important to Bachmann than his art. Zak retrieves Bachmann only when there is a concert to be played, but Perova takes a constant interest in him, and sometimes he will appear at her door downcast and disheveled. Perova begins to travel around on Bachmann's tours, always sitting in the first row when he plays, and sometimes she even appears with her husband, who is quite aware of her strange passion but doesn't interfere and lives his own life.

Perova is lame, and she is attractive only because of a certain look of failed beauty in her features. Their tie is a constant torment for her. Zak tells the narrator how Bachmann once fastened onto her with his teeth like a monkey when she simply reached out to adjust his necktie. But Bachmann's love for her, however abnormally it is expressed, is unquestionably real. When Perova is sick and does not appear at a concert, Bachmann refuses to play until she comes. They sleep together that night, evidently for the first time, and afterward the sick Perova loses consciousness and dies the same day. Bachmann did not understand that Perova was ill, or perhaps he understood her illness in his own way. The narrator tells us: "I think that this was the sole happy night in the whole of Perova's life. I think that these two, a semi-demented musician and a dying woman, discovered during this night words which the greatest poets of the world have not dreamt of."

Perova was evidently able to accomplish what Luzhin's wife could not do. Her love for Bachmann brings him back to life, and his art is forgotten. Bachmann vanishes immediately after her funeral, and Zak loses track of him for several years until by chance he sees him at a railway station playing a jukebox and sobbing. When *Bachmann* is placed side by side with *The Defense*, we realize that the "warmth" of Luzhin's strange personality and life affords him little or no human heat, and his affecting story is perhaps really no less chilling and dark than that of Albinus Kretschmar.

Madness and art are always in each other's presence in Nabokov's prose. The varying shades and expressions of madness in his art compel us to abandon any notion of dementia as either a simple or an indescribable phenomenon. In *Signs and Symbols* (1948) a young man, whose cousin — perhaps Luzhin — was a famous chess player, is confined in an institution, suffering from referential mania: "Clouds in the staring sky transmit to one another, by means of slow signs, incredibly detailed information regarding him. His inmost thoughts are discussed at nightfall, in manual alphabet, by darkly gesticulating trees. Pebbles or stains or sun flecks form patterns representing in some awful way messages which he must intercept. Everything is a cipher and of everything he is the theme." His desire (he has attempted to commit suicide several times already) is "to tear a hole in his world and escape"; the real artist can *draw* a hole in the world and return unharmed and exhilarated.

Seven

❈ ❈ ❈ ❈

N ABOKOV once said his "second favorite fact" about himself is that: "Since my youth — I was nineteen when I left Russia — my political outlook has remained as bleak and changeless as an old gray rock. It is classical to the point of triteness. Freedom of speech, freedom of thought, freedom of art. The social or economic structure of the ideal state is of little concern to me. My desires are modest. Portraits of the head of the government should not exceed a postage stamp in size. No torture and no executions . . . With the passing of years I grew less and less interested in Russia and more and more indifferent to the once-harrowing thought that my books would remain banned there as long as my contempt for the police state and political oppression prevented me from entertaining the vaguest thought of return."

That statement is forthright and comprehensive enough. In the 1966 *Speak, Memory* Nabokov tells how, while he was at Cambridge, he spoke against Bolshevism at a Union debate in 1920 (he lost to an apologist for the Soviet regime from the *Manchester Guardian*), and how this was the last political speech he ever made. Apart from his treatment in his early stories of characters who hold strong political views — which is quite a different thing from a "political story" — and the general theme of return to Russia — which is a theme of memory deeply felt — there is a period of slightly over a decade, roughly from 1935 to 1947, in which Nabokov frequently utilized *seemingly* political themes in his art. But, as in all of his works, the apparent theme is most frequently the least important one, and even taken as political tales these works are equally applicable to (and thus equally independent of) fascism, communism, or any other form of oppression, including democratic tyranny.

Seven years after his loss at the Union debate, however, the young Nabokov did return to politics once more in an article entitled "An Anniversary," which appeared in *The Rudder* on the tenth anniversary of the 1917 revolution (November 18, 1927). It is an eloquent and stirring émigré *profession de foi*. The article clearly belongs to Nabokov's youth, but it has great interest both because it is a solitary instance of Nabokov's use of rhetorical discourse and because it presents a statement that spells out in detail and in a more positivistic light the terse political statements — such as the one just cited — which Nabokov has in recent years frequently made in reply to questions put to him by reporters and interviewers. The essay begins harshly:

In these days when the putrid odor of anniversary wafts to us from over there, why should we not celebrate our anniversary, too? Ten years of contempt, ten years of fidelity, ten years of freedom — isn't this worth at least one anniversary speech? One must know how to have contempt. We have studied the science of contempt to perfection. We are so satiated with it that sometimes we grow lazy in our contempt. A slight palpitation of the nostrils, eyes squinting for a moment, and silence. But today let us speak out.

Ten years of contempt . . . I hold in contempt not a person, not Sidorov the worker, an honorable member of some Kom-pom-pom, but that ugly and stupid little nostrum which turns Russian simpletons into Communist ninnies, which makes ants out of people, a new species called *Formica marxi var. lenini.* And I find unbearable the sham aura smacking of middle-class Philistinism that is in everything Bolshevik. Philistine boredom wafts from the gray pages of *Pravda,* the political harangue of the Bolshevik has the sound of Philistine fury, his poor little head has grown swollen with Philistine nonsense.

Nabokov goes on to say that he regards communism's ideal of the lowest level of equality as a boring page in the festive history of mankind and a negation of all that is beautiful. It should be said that this critique of communism on grounds primarily of moral quality rather than of ideology is a very model of understatement in comparison with Communist fulminations against the "émigré

White Guardists," and it is restrained, too, in comparison with statements made by other émigré writers such as Ivan Bunin, Boris Zaitsev, and Mark Aldanov. (Aldanov — a fine historical novelist known, if at all, to English readers chiefly by a brief 1944 essay by Edmund Wilson in which he is praised at the expense of Soviet novelist Leonid Leonov — wrote, for example, of the "total political amorality" of Lenin and the "terrible, incalculable, unredeemable evil" he brought to Russia.) If the beginning of "An Anniversary" does at moments sound somewhat strident, the argument soon takes a direction that lifts it quite above ordinary political rhetoric:

The strength of my contempt lies in the fact that, expressing my contempt, I do not allow myself to think about bloodshed. And there is also strength in the fact that I do not bemoan, in bourgeois despair, the loss of an estate, a house, a gold ingot which was insufficiently cleverly concealed in the workings of a toilet.

And finally Nabokov addresses himself to the émigré experience itself:

We are the wave of Russia which has left her shores — we are spread over the entire world, but our wanderings are not always in depression, and our courageous longing for our fatherland does not always prevent us from enjoying a strange country, refined solitude in a foreign electric night, on a bridge, in a square, at a railway station . . . We have, for one thing, ten years of freedom to celebrate. Such freedom as we know, perhaps, has not been known by any nation. In that particular Russia which invisibly surrounds, quickens, and supports us, nourishes our souls, adorns our dreams, there is not a single law except the law of love for her, and there is no power except that of our own conscience. We may say everything about her, write everything, for we have nothing to hide, and there is no censorship to limit us — we are free citizens of our dreams. Our far-flung state, our nomadic empire has its strength in this freedom, and someday we shall be grateful to the blind Clio for the way in which she allowed us to taste this freedom and in emigration to understand thoroughly and develop a deep feeling for our native land.

In these days when a gray USSR [*séry, eseséséry*] anniversary is being celebrated, we are celebrating ten years of contempt, fidelity, and freedom. Let us not curse exile. Let us repeat in these days

the words of that ancient warrior about whom Plutarch wrote: "During the night, in desolate fields far from Rome, I would pitch my tent, and my tent was Rome to me."

(Amusingly, the "Plutarch citation" is Nabokov's own invention.) "An Anniversary" is an important document in the history of Russian émigré culture, and, I think, it will at some unforeseeable future date have a place in the intellectual history of Russia in the twentieth century.

The next time that Nabokov sounded this note was in a little Russian poem written in 1944. The occasion was evidently Hitler's protracted siege upon the Soviet Union which by 1943 caused Stalin to relax certain aspects of his dictatorship — the churches, for example, were allowed to reopen — in order to rally greater patriotic fervor among the Russian people. The poem is aimed at émigrés whom Russian victories led to forget and forgive Soviet iniquities. Nabokov's poem says simply that he will never make peace with "tinsel Soviet Rus" no matter what its battle situation and no matter how full of pity his heart is for the fate Russia is suffering. His separation from Soviet Russia is seen by him as an affirmation of the fact that he is still a poet: "... *No, No, I shout,/ My spirit is still quick, still exile-hungry./ I'm still a poet, count me out!*" Most frequently though, Nabokov's usage of political themes is primarily playful and humorous. Nabokov, with the early Ilya Ehrenburg (a weird and momentary contiguity), is one of the very few Russian writers who was able to laugh at the Russian revolution. A typical instance is a little piece of light verse entitled *Leningrad* which appeared in *Our World* in 1924. It is based on a pun involving the names Lenin and Helen (in Russian the name is *Elena*, its possessive adjective is *elenin*, and its diminutives are *Lena, lenin*):

> *At times great*
> *changes occur* . . .
> *But, my fiery gentlemen,*
> *what is the meaning of this fantasy?*
> *It was Petrograd — which was worse*
> *than Petersburg, I'll not conceal it —*
> *but it has no resemblance —*
> *do what you will — to Troy:*

Why then did you christen it —
and in such a familiar fashion —
in honor of Helen?

It is true that one cannot find a "sympathetic character" in Nabo-kov's fiction who is also a Communist — the Soviet brother in the short story *A Meeting* and the writer Novgorodtsev are about the closest to it — but it is also true that one will not find a Communist character who is used to "prove a point."

It was perhaps inevitable, given the number of remarkable alle-gorical professions and situations employed by Nabokov to explore and demonstrate artistic problems, that he would finally use a "political" theme in such a way. He first did this in his major 1935 novel *Invitation to a Beheading*, a novel which gave rise to more controversy and commentary than any other of his Russian works. *Invitation to a Beheading* is a fantasy, but rather than a fantastic description of the real world Nabokov has insisted that the novel is a real description of a fantastic world. Cincinnatus C. has been condemned to death for the crime of being opaque in a transparent world. He is in prison where he is attended by a grotesque and treacly corps, the most hideous of which, M'sieur Pierre, tries to become his true friend and confidant and turns out to be his appointed executioner. The family of Cincinnatus is no less lugu-brious and sinister. When his wife Marthe arrives to see him, she brings their entire family with her, and all their furniture as well. Marthe comes in her best black dress (that is, already in mourning attire) and casually holding a hand mirror. "Meanwhile, furniture, household utensils, even individual sections of walls continued to arrive. There came a mirrored wardrobe, bringing with it its own private reflection (namely, a corner of the connubial bedroom with a stripe of sunlight across the floor, a dropped glove, and an open door in the distance)." Everything in that description is both very real and, in its presentation, fantastic. The children are "lame Diomedon and obese little Pauline" (recalling *The Ballad of Long-wood Glen*), and Marthe brings in addition her father, her al-most identical twin brothers, her maternal grandparents, and "a very proper young man with a flawless profile" who is constantly at her side. The father-in-law attacks Cincinnatus with a vindictiveness that recalls the hero's family in Kafka's *Metamorphosis* after he has been indiscreet enough to turn into a dungbeetle: "Silence, insolent fellow . . . I am entitled to expect from you — if only today, when you stand at death's door — a little respect. How you managed to get yourself on the block . . . I want an explanation from you — how could you . . . how you dared . . ." When the interview is over, two of Cincinnatus' guardians "looking each other in the eye, grasped the couch on which Marthe was reclining, grunted, picked it up and carried it toward the door. 'Good-by, good-by,' Marthe called childishly, swaying in time with the step of the porters, but suddenly she closed her eyes and covered her face."

This gesture is the only sign of sympathy or concern (and we cannot be sure it is that) evinced by his wife. She has been untrue to him many times. In a political sense Cincinnatus is as much a victim of a totalitarian culture as of a totalitarian "regime": his crime ("gnostical turpitude") is individuality and thus requires his complete alienation (in the French sense of the term, with its implication of mental derangement). A simple dictatorship would presuppose the secret resentment of at least a significant portion of the population, but the crime of Cincinnatus is "rare and unutterable," and the society in which he lives is truly monolithic, not merely oppressed.

Although he understands his situation, Cincinnatus still feels a desire to return to his society: "Even though in reality everything in this city was always quite dead and awful by comparison with the secret life of Cincinnatus and his guilty flame, even though he knew this perfectly well and knew also that there was no hope, yet at this moment he still longed to be on those bright familiar streets . . . but then the clock finished ringing, the imaginary sky grew overcast, and the jail was back in force." Cincinnatus had told himself that in spite of everything he still loved Marthe, and it is his hope that ". . . one day we shall have a real all-embracing explanation, and then perhaps we shall somehow fit together, you and I, and turn ourselves in such a way that we form one pattern, and solve the puzzle." But Marthe remains aloof and promiscuous, and Cincinnatus' sole hope is the twelve-year-old daughter of his jailer. If there is anyone else in the novel besides Cincinnatus who is "alive" it is little Emmie, but her very immaturity prevents any communication between them: "When she came rushing in today — only a child, with certain loopholes for my thoughts — I wondered, to the rhythm of an ancient poem — could she not give the guards a drugged potion, could she not rescue me? If she only would remain the child she is, but at the same time mature and understand: her burning cheeks, a black windy night, salvation, salvation."

Perhaps wild little Emmie is the craftiest trap of all — she herself suggests that they will run away together and marry, and then she goes into a rapid pirouette which is suspiciously like the antics of M'sieur Pierre. Sex, even illicit sex, is one of the most potent means by which Cincinnatus could be bound to his society. In her final visit Marthe offers to copulate in much the same way one offers a cigarette or coin to a beggar: "If you need it badly, Cin-Cin, go ahead, only do it quickly." He accepts neither Marthe nor Emmie however. Sex is a function, something one *does*, and which can (and will) be done quite as well by any other practiced member of society. Even before the execution, Marthe cheerfully informs him she has received an offer of marriage. In M'sieur Pierre's eloquent definition, love is "a systematic and persistent extraction of pleasure buried in the very bowels of the belabored creature," and viewed with such frankness sex is merely a variant form of defecation — "The bliss of relieving oneself, which some hold to be on a par with the pleasure of love." (M'sieur Pierre approves of sex as an exercise, Cincinnatus does not, but one should note that, after Marthe tries to give herself to impotent Pierre to obtain an interview with Cincinnatus, Pierre refers to her as "a disgusting whore.")

Cincinnatus has a choice of two fates, both of which, in different ways, are death. Cincinnatus may execute the wishes of the commune, or he may himself be executed. The choice is quite in his own hands at all times ("If he were now honestly to admit that he is fond of the same things as you and I . . ."), and more than that, the choice is in his own mind, for in spite of his irrational fear, Cincinnatus "knows perfectly well that the entire masquerade is staged in his own brain." And since this is so, it follows that M'sieur

Pierre is really nothing but the baser portion of Cincinnatus himself. Pyotr Bitsilli, one of the five or six best émigré literary critics, wrote two pieces on *Invitation to a Beheading*, both of which appeared in *Contemporary Annals*, and in one of them he makes just this point:

Cincinnatus and M'sieur Pierre are two aspects of "man in general," the *everyman* of the old English outdoor mystery dramas. There is a potential "M'sieur Pierre" in every man insofar as he lives, that is, insofar as he remains in that condition of a "bad dream," of *death*, that we call life. For "Cincinnatus" to die means to extract from himself the "M'sieur Pierre."

Bitsilli's judgment, though it is somewhat loosely formulated (rather, M'sieur Pierre is the everyman which controls and obscures the individual in each of us), is confirmed by the novel's conclusion, in which Cincinnatus walks away from the scene of the scheduled execution, and it is Pierre who is dispatched: "Little was left of the square. The platform had long since collapsed in a cloud of reddish dust. The last to rush past was a woman in a black shawl, carrying the tiny executioner like a larva in her arms." The highlight of the "festivities" on the eve of the execution is a special effect for the banquet guests — a "nocturnal landscape with a grandiose monogram of 'P' and 'C' which, however, had not quite come off." In Russian the significance of the initial letters of the two names is quite evident, for the Cyrillic *Ts* (in Russian the name is *Tsintsinnat*) and *P* are almost, but not quite, perfect inversions of each other: Ц and П.

Both Pierre and Cincinnatus are also doubles in their own right. Their full names are Cincinnatus C and (he is called this only once) Pyotr Petrovich. M'sieur Pierre's other self is no more than the exaggeration of his natural perversity, as when little Emmie is engaged in eating a large piece of melon at her father's house, and M'sieur Pierre, sipping a cup of tea with his right hand, "inconspicuously reached under the table with his left hand. 'Eek!' cried Emmie as she gave a ticklish start, without, however, taking her mouth from the melon." Like his hand under the table, we do not *see* M'sieur Pierre's other, "real" self, but it can be smelled: " 'Why do you smell like that?' asked Cincinnatus with a sigh. M'sieur

Pierre's plump face twisted into a forced smile. 'It runs in the family,' he explained with dignity. 'Feet sweat a little. I've tried alums, but nothing works. I must say that, although I have been afflicted with this since childhood, and although any suffering is customarily regarded with respect, no one has ever yet been so tactless . . .' 'I can't breathe,' said Cincinnatus." This smell that only Cincinnatus takes note of is Pierre's real essence and perhaps also the reality behind Marthe, Emmie, and all the other cardboard characters. In his discussion of the unique Russian word *poshlost'*, which signifies a kind of subtle or "beautiful" (but no less repulsive or corny) vulgarity, in his 1944 book on Gogol, Nabokov writes of the hero of *Dead Souls:* "The chink in Chichikov's armor, that rusty chink emitting a faint but dreadful smell (a punctured can of conserved lobster tampered with and forgotten by some meddling fool in the pantry) is the organic aperture in the devil's armor."

The duality of Cincinnatus is a gradation, too, but of an entirely different sort. Cincinnatus is an individual, but, as we have already seen, he sometimes has an almost overpowering urge to comply and return: " 'Oh well,' said Cincinnatus, 'as you wish, as you wish . . . I am powerless anyway.' (The other Cincinnatus . . . a little smaller, was crying, all curled up in a ball.)" Later, the false Cincinnatus runs headlong into the wall of his cell trying to smash his head (that is to say, the "real" or corporeal Cincinnatus is the false one), while "the real Cincinnatus, however, remained sitting at the table, staring at the wall." The real Cincinnatus has no contact at all with anyone else, and after the other one has done something, we are told: "Cincinnatus did not do this." The execution marks the total dominance of the inner Cincinnatus. As he walks to the platform, Cincinnatus painfully jumps back from anyone who attempts to touch him, and as M'sieur Pierre starts to swing his axe: "One Cincinnatus was counting, but the other Cincinnatus had already stopped heeding the sound of the unnecessary count which was fading away in the distance . . . Why am I here? Why am I lying like this? And having asked himself these simple questions, he answered them by getting up and looking around." Cincinnatus has not been killed, but rather he has been liberated. The world of M'sieur Pierre has committed suicide.

If Bitsilli was able to see *Invitation to a Beheading* as the morality play that it essentially is (with characteristics rather than characters and, like the fifteenth-century English plays, leading always to death), many of the novel's Russian critics could see the novel only as an egoist's grotesque caricature and rejection of the real world. A representative review showing how the novel was misread as a direct allegory of life is the one by a Harbin critic, Natalya Reznikova, which appeared in the Manchurian Russian journal *Border*.

The first and most sincere reaction after reading through *Invitation to a Beheading* is perplexity. What is this? Why was this book written? Perplexity and bitterness come over the reader. It's clear that Sirin is seeking new paths. But it is no less clear that he has wandered into a blind alley . . . Describing Cincinnatus, a citizen of an unspecified country who has been sentenced to death for a mysterious crime, was the author not really saying that we are all condemned to die although we do not know who our executioner will be and for what we shall die? After all, like the hero of Sirin's novel, we too do not know the time of our death, and we are terrified of it, feel that it is inevitable, and ask fate: when will it be? . . . Cincinnatus is not surrounded by people but by ghosts; Cincinnatus is a pitiful helpless little fellow clinging to life and surrounded by traitors . . . There is nothing on this Earth — love is only an animal urge, friendship is treachery, man is alone and helpless. Even the mother of Cincinnatus isn't a mother but an awful parody. There is nothing. A complete void . . . Contemporary man has no mother, no wife, no friend — he is alone and unfree, and the sole human feeling he has is that of fear . . . An inexorable book, a terrifying and tormented book. Of course only a unique talent such as Sirin's could have created it, but one is truly sorry that he wastes his talent on such fatalistic delirium and presents the reader with a black pit of terror in which there does not fall even a pale stellar ray of hope.

Such a reading of the novel, and it was quite common, is not altogether in accord with what the narrative says — the crime of Cincinnatus is not mysterious, and far from being a "little fellow" he is extremely strong-willed and obdurate, and in the end (it is far from certain that the end is death) it is the other characters who become "little fellows" while the giant Cincinnatus strides away toward "where, to judge by the voices, stood beings akin to him."

By far the more serious misreading of the novel, however, is the notion that *Invitation to a Beheading* is a "terrifying and tormented book." It is, I would say, the most hilarious of Nabokov's Russian novels and inferior in this respect only to *Lolita, Pale Fire*, and *Pnin*. Nabokov's souls in *Invitation to a Beheading* are indeed, as several critics pointed out, "more dead" than Gogol's dead souls, but they are also no less amusing. M'sieur Pierre in particular is a more perfectly Gogolian character that any created by Gogol himself: he is, like Gogol's Khlestakov, fond of eating — apparently whole — watermelon (a fruit that has even more complex historical class connotations in Russia than in America); one of his nipples has two green leaves tattooed around it so that it looks like a rose (obvious but sublime *poshlost'*); and he performs secret and shameful dances, but unlike Chichikov, performs them in public:

In one leap M'sieur Pierre hopped up on the table, stood on his hands, and grasped the back of the chair in his teeth. The music paused breathlessly. M'sieur Pierre was lifting the chair, clenched firmly between his teeth; his tensed muscles were quivering; his jaw was creaking . . . Something gave, and M'sieur Pierre, releasing the chair from his mouth, turned a somersault and was again standing on the floor. Apparently, however, not everything was well. He at once covered his mouth with his handkerchief, glanced quickly under the table, then inspected the chair . . . His hinged denture . . . was embedded there. Magnificently displaying all its teeth, it held on with a bulldog grip. Whereupon, without losing his head, M'sieur Pierre embraced the chair and departed with it.

Beyond these rather obvious Gogolian motifs, there are many finer details (first pointed out by Bitsilli), such as the peculiarly Gogolian manner of "listing" characteristics in a seemingly matter-of-fact, but actually absurd manner: "His wig was glossy as new, the rich dough of his chin seemed to be powdered with flour, while in his buttonhole there was a pink waxy flower with a speckled mouth."

One enormous difference between Gogol and Nabokov, however, is the manner in which the basic unreality of the characters in *Invitation to a Beheading* is constantly spelled out for the reader ("Yes, that's fine. I thank you, rag doll, coachman, painted swine."). Gogol believed that his fantastic creations were real people, and in the face of all evidence to the contrary, many readers accepted him as a comic realist, but a realist all the same. And the critic Vladimir Varshavsky, in his book *The Unnoticed Generation* (1956), commented that "if Cincinnatus himself had not continually underscored the fact that he is surrounded by grotesque apparitions rather than people, most likely many readers whose tastes were formed on 'healthy realism' would not even have noticed how these personages, so credible and speaking just as in life, differ from real people." *Invitation to a Beheading* is about consciousness, and it also in a sense concerns the resolution of the problem that Gogol could not solve — that of turning shadows into substance. Gogolian grotesques cannot, by the very nature of their being, Nabokov shows, be turned into "real" people; but a real person may exist in their midst.

By "Gogolian" art one should understand not only a particular artistic style, but also a particular sort of "primitive consciousness" which accompanies the artist's genius. As Nabokov put it: "Gogol, being Gogol and living in a looking-glass world, had a knack of thoroughly planning his works *after* he had written and published them." The "Gogolian tradition" in Russian literature — one of its two most important currents — is thus really only partially Gogolian: writers such as Dostoevsky, Sukhovo-Kobylin, Saltykov-Shchedrin, Sologub, Bely, Savich, Nabokov, and Tertz-Sinyavsky do more or less *deliberately* what Gogol did in spite of himself. The important Gogolian writers, such as the ones named above, are those who have found a unique and personal voice and viewpoint to accompany (and, in the end, form) some new variant of Gogol's manner. The artist who merely follows after and tries to "play at Gogol" — the Italian writer Tommaso Landolfi very often does this — produces only a strained and exaggerated imitation. The influence of Gogol is most fruitful when it plays a clearly secondary role, and Nabokov's own cautionary words on the subject apply equally well to many other of the finest "Gogolian" writers: "Desperate Russian critics, trying hard to find an Influence and to pigeonhole my own novels, have once or twice linked me up with Gogol, but when they looked again I had untied the knots and the box was empty."

The more interesting critical juxtaposition, precisely because there is usually no question of "influence," is between two writers in the Gogolian tradition, and Pyotr Bitsilli paired Nabokov and Mikhail Saltykov-Shchedrin for just such a comparison in his longer article "The Rebirth of Allegory," in *Contemporary Annals* (No. 61, 1936). It would seem at first glance that the nineteenth-century satirical realist Saltykov-Shchedrin — best known for his relentless and depressing satirical novel *The Golovlyovs* — and Nabokov have nothing in common, but Bitsilli ingeniously juxtaposes passages, works, and devices in such a way as to produce a rather striking similarity. Concentrating primarily on *Invitation to a Beheading*, Bitsilli compares it in general and in some specifics to the delirium and fantasy of Saltykov-Shchedrin's *Tangled Affair* and *Diary of a Provincial in St. Petersburg*. Just one of the citations introduced by Bitsilli will give some idea of the affinity that can be found between Saltykov-Shchedrin's works and *Invitation to a Beheading:* "Now, after the two farces I've been in, I can't sit down without thinking: well, what if this chair suddenly should collapse under me! I can't step on a floorboard without being disturbed by the thought: what if this floorboard isn't a floorboard at all, but just the appearance of one? . . . Do I exist or don't I? Am I living in an apartment or not in an apartment? Am I surrounded by walls or some kind of pretense of walls?" Bitsilli's fourteen-page article was harshly criticized by several émigré pedants for the wildness of the comparison, but the important thing is that Bitsilli himself repeatedly stated in the article that he was not speaking of influence in the usual sense of the term. Precisely because of the distance between Nabokov and Saltykov-Shchedrin and the care with which Bitsilli posits his points of comparison, the analogy is most helpful for the unusual light it throws on both writers. (Toward the end of his article Bitsilli makes another, somewhat less impressive comparison between *Invitation to a Beheading* and Céline's *Voyage to the End of Night*.) Bitsilli's comparison of Nabokov with Saltykov-Shchedrin, however, serves to place Nabokov's novel in its proper tradition and to temper greatly one's natural inclination to relate the novel to "contemporary life" or to, say, the political novels of Orwell or Huxley.

In the same way that *Camera obscura* is the artistic execution of a common saying ("love is blind"), *Invitation to a Beheading* is an enactment of the aphorism "life is a dream." Nabokov has a great fondness for aphoristic bases in his art — the 1939 story *Lik*, for example, appropriates the saying "I'd like to be in your shoes": a character with a weak heart seems about to collapse and die, but when he returns to the apartment of an unpleasant old schoolmate — whom he has just met after many years — to get a box of new shoes he forgot there, the schoolmate has in those few minutes shot himself and is wearing the new shoes. Besides life as a dream, there is a related aphorism in *Invitation to a Beheading* — "the world as a prison": "I am here through an error — not in this prison, specifically — but in this whole terrible, striped world," Cincinnatus says at one point, and in another place he comments that his rib cage showing prominently in his thin body is "a triumph of cryptic coloration inasmuch as it expressed the barred nature of his surroundings, of his jail." The jail and the dream are, in a sense, one. Vladislav Khodasevich in writing on *Invitation to a Beheading* follows through his repeatedly used notion of Sirin as a novelist who writes only about art and artists. The novel is, according to Khodasevich:

. . . only the play of decorator-elves, the play of devices and images which fill the creative consciousness or, to put it in a better way, the creative delirium of Cincinnatus. When their play breaks off, the novel comes to an end. Cincinnatus is not executed and not un-executed because in the course of the entire novel we see him in an imagined world where no real events are possible. In the concluding lines the two-dimensional, pained world of Cincinnatus comes apart, and "amidst the flapping scenery, Cincinnatus made his way in that direction where, to judge by the voices, stood beings akin to him." This, of course, represents the return of the artist from his art to reality. If one wants to see it in this way, at this moment an execution occurs, but it is not the one or in the same sense that the hero and the reader expected: with his return to the world of "beings akin to him" the life of Cincinnatus-as-artist is cut off.

If *Invitation to a Beheading* is read in this way the novel is essentially about the distance and incompatibility between art and life. An interesting question, similar to the one we have already had to pose about Smurov in *The Eye*, is whether Cincinnatus is a real or a flawed artist.

Varshavsky, not willing to accept Khodasevich's proposition

without reservation, preferred to see a different sort of artistic demonstration in the novel — the contrast between literary characters and language which possess the secret of life (as in Tolstoy) and characters and language which are dead (socialist realist fiction). Although Varshavsky does not see this, his reading, which returns the novel somewhat to the sphere of politics, is still consonant with Khodasevich's understanding, and it conveniently presents a solution to what kind of artist Cincinnatus should be seen as. For Cincinnatus then becomes a real artist who has temporarily allowed himself to be imprisoned by a dead, ready-made art. He returns not to life, but rather to the realm of true art. The artistic provenance of *Invitation to a Beheading* is underscored by the very title which, Nabokov has acknowledged, refers to Baudelaire's *Invitation au voyage*. The hero's name seems to refer not to Lucius Quinctius Cincinnatus, who is generally the model of the simple and virtuous statesman, but rather to the statesman's son (the mother of Cincinnatus at one point tells him that, although it was not generally known, his father had also been opaque), who was censored in 461 B.C. for his extraordinary oratory and excessive pride by a Tribune of the People and forced to go into exile. This then is the real "politics" of *Invitation to a Beheading*: the inevitable and natural exile that is the fate of all culture — especially in Russia — a theme reminiscent of *An Evening of Russian Poetry*, in which the narrator tells us:

> But to unneeded symbols consecrated,
> escorted by a vaguely infantile
> path for bare feet, our roads were always fated
> to lead into the silence of exile.

Although it is true that the tale is complex and cannot be reduced to any simple *pointe*, *Invitation to a Beheading* is all the same the most patently fable-like of Nabokov's novels. If the novel has a weakness it is the disparity between the air of fable and the story's rather protracted length (for a fable). The fable and moralistic fairy tale in most European literatures — Andersen, the brothers Grimm, Krylov, La Fontaine — may vary considerably in many respects, but brevity is a constant. A good case in point in modern literature are the fable-stories of D. H. Lawrence such as

The Man Who Loved Islands. The three exceptions I can think of are Orwell's *Animal Farm,* where the fable form is used to tell a long, detailed, and real political story; the novels of Golding, which are not without interest but whose permanence seems highly improbable; and — what to me is the greatest "fable-novel" ever written — Kafka's *The Castle.* But in Kafka's novel, delay and protractedness are an essential function of the narrative. This is true, only to a much lesser degree, ot *Invitation to a Beheading.* The matter may be put in another way: imagine, if you will, Gogol's Chichikov not traveling from estate to estate but, with the help of a few other of the "dead souls," closeted up in one place where a "live" person is being held by them. The absence of movement from one place to another and the comparatively restricted number of characters requires that the narrative contain, in compensation, a number of "busy" set pieces. A good instance of this in *Invitation to a Beheading* is the tunnel which is dug toward the cell of Cincinnatus, not, it turns out, by someone who is trying to free him, but by M'sieur Pierre. The "set pieces" of *Invitation to a Beheading* are brilliant in themselves, but to this reader at least, even in subsequent rereadings of the novel, an involuntary impatience with the hilarious antics of M'sieur Pierre and Co. begins to gain control. This, of course, does place one in much the same frame of mind as Cincinnatus and so may be a very conscious function of the novel after all. However that may be, the tale's potential for reduction is noted by Nabokov himself on the second page of the novel: "So we are nearing the end. The right-hand, still untasted part of the novel, which during our delectable reading, we would lightly feel, mechanically testing whether there were still plenty left (and our fingers were always gladdened by the placid, faithful thickness) has suddenly, for no reason at all, become quite meager: a few minutes of quick reading, already downhill, and — O horrible!"

An interesting contrast to *Invitation to a Beheading* is provided by the 1937 short story *Cloud, Lake, Tower* — translated into English as *Cloud, Castle, Lake* — which Khodasevich referred to as an "afterword" to the novel, and indeed even the phrase "invitation to a beheading" occurs in the story. *Cloud, Castle, Lake,* however, is written in a totally different manner. It is a "realistic" tale about a Russian émigré who wins a pleasure trip that he really doesn't want to take; but finding that he is unable to cash in his ticket, he goes. There is a certain air of indefiniteness in the beginning of the tale: the hero is one of the narrator's "representatives," and yet the narrator cannot exactly remember his name — "I think it was Vasili Ivanovich." It starts quietly enough as the tour group — a leader and four men and four women, besides "Vasili Ivanovich" — meet at a Berlin railroad station and set out together — the destination is never mentioned — in an obviously third-class car. Vasili Ivanovich settles down by himself with a volume of Tiutchev, but he is forced to join the group. The other tourists are all rather chunky Germans, and one of them — a young man with a "vague velvety vileness" about him — turns out to be a sort of agent provocateur from the "Bureau of Pleasantrips." Vasili Ivanovich is the odd man out, and when he does join the group, they begin to play with him maliciously. Then, unexpectedly, the tour group and the tormented Vasili Ivanovich come upon a lake scene "so unique, and so familiar, and so long-promised" that he decides to remain there forever. But the tour leader will not let him leave the group, telling him "I am responsible for each of you, and shall bring back each of you, alive or dead." So Vasili Ivanovich is forced to return, and in the train the other tour members amuse themselves by torturing Vasili Ivanovich. At his urgent request, the narrator lets his "representative" go, and though one assumes he will go back to the perfect and dream-like lake, Nabokov has explained to me: "He will never find it again. If I let him go, it is in the hope that he might find a less dangerous job than that of my agent."

Cloud, Castle, Lake is quite indisputably a fable or allegory stressing the primacy of memory and individuality over social coercion: Vasili Ivanovich's plea to the narrator is that "he had not the strength to belong to mankind any longer." On the other hand, one has no firm basis upon which to decide whether *Cloud, Castle, Lake* is truly meant to be an "afterword" or "commentary" to *Invitation to a Beheading* or whether it is meant to be an independent and quite different variant. Comparison of the two works does help by example to justify the length of *Invitation to a Beheading* — the novel is one of Nabokov's major works (he himself considers it his fourth best novel), while the tale is too sketchy to be counted in the first rank of Nabokov's short stories.

Nabokov's second English novel, *Bend Sinister* (written in 1945–46 and published in 1947), has strong and obvious ties, which Nabokov himself has acknowledged, to *Invitation to a Beheading*. *Bend Sinister* is about a dictatorship in an imaginary country, and the harassment of that country's leading thinker, the philosopher Adam Krug. While *Bend Sinister* also cannot be adequately, or even approximately, described as a "political novel," it does contain more specifically identifiable political referents than does *Invitation to a Beheading:* there are in *Bend Sinister* bits of Lenin's speeches, echoes of fascist efficiency, and even a small portion of the Soviet constitution. Like the figures that surround Cincinnatus, the citizenry and political functionaries that surround Krug belong to another, lower reality. He, too, lives in a dream world. "Surely, this is a dream, thought Krug, this silence, the deep ridicule of late autumn, miles away from home. Why are we here of all places?" The extreme but logical extension of the communal instinct is first standardization and then interchangeability. In *Invitation to a Beheading* the secondary figures are in constant danger of losing their shadowy selves altogether — " 'Nerves, nerves, a regular little woman,' said the prison director — alias Rodrig Ivanovich — with a smile." The director of the prison dissolves effortlessly into the jailer Rodion, and this change cancels them both out, for, according to Cincinnatus' axiom, that which does not have a name does not exist. Even Cincinnatus himself, in the early stages of his imprisonment, comes apart easily: "He took off the linen trousers and shirt. He took off his head like a toupee."

In the concluding scene of *Bend Sinister* much the same thing happens. Adam Krug has been brought to a courtyard where his friends and colleagues are gathered together. The scene itself is not presented, but rather a "colored photograph" of it which has become animated ("You may move again") is described. The place of one character has been taken by "an extremely gifted impersonator." The courtyard is the same one in which Krug used to play in childhood, and the adults, including the dictator Paduk whom Krug knew when they were fellow students, turn into children. The lives of everyone depend upon Krug's willingness to submit to Paduk, but Krug turns the execution scene into a reenactment of the schoolday attacks upon the repulsive and inferior Paduk who was called the Toad. There is, however, a "logical" explanation for all this: Adam Krug has gone mad. Nabokov has "felt a pang of pity for Adam and slid towards him along an inclined beam of pale light — causing instantaneous madness, but at least saving him from the senseless agony of his logical fate." His very name is a partial anagram of his fate — mad Adam, which is what the Toad calls him. Words themselves reflect the unreality of the world in which Krug lives.

In his Introduction to the 1964 edition of *Bend Sinister* (perhaps the most interesting and informative of all his introductions to his own novels), Nabokov explains this connection in the following manner: "Paranomasia is a kind of verbal plague, a contagious sickness in the world of words; no wonder they are monstrously and ineptly distorted in Padukgrad, where everybody is merely an anagram of everybody else." (These remarks on the role of language in *Bend Sinister* apply even more to the verbal intricacies of *Pale Fire*.) Krug's linguistic perspicacity enables him to part and reshuffle words and see behind them. His colleague Ember enters into the game, finding that Ophelia's name is "quite possibly an anagram of Alpheios, with the 's' lost in the damp grass — Alpheus the rivergod, who pursued a long-legged nymph until Artemis changed her into a stream, which of course suited his liquidity to a tee (cf. Winnipeg Lake, ripple 585, Vico Press edition)." (That last, by the way, is a literary allusion.) Krug also suggests that Telemachos — meaning fighting from afar ("which again was Hamlet's idea of warfare") — may be pruned of all its unnecessary letters, which are simply secondary additions, to obtain "Telmah": "Now read it backwards. Thus does a fanciful pen elope with a lewd idea and Hamlet in reverse gear becomes the son of Ulysses slaying his mother's lovers. *Worte, worte, worte.* Warts, warts, warts."

The title of the novel is itself a linguistic definition of human and/or social aberration. It is — to quote again Nabokov's Introduction to the novel — "an attempt to suggest an outline broken by refraction, a distortion in the mirror of being, a wrong turn taken by life, a sinistral and sinister world." The Toad also has

Krug's ability to scramble names and words, but he does not use this to see into and through words, but only to justify and reflect his own preconceived notions. As a child he referred to all his fellow pupils anagramatically, and he explains that "all men consist of the same twenty-five letters variously mixed." (The language spoken in the state in which Krug lives is an invented one composed of Germanic and Slavic elements, but it often lapses into pure Russian, which, however, has thirty-two letters; if the number is taken to refer to the English twenty-six-letter alphabet, the letter which the Toad does not count must obviously be "I.") When he grows up the Toad will head the Party of the Average Man, based on a debasement of a scholar's theory of balance as a basis for universal bliss which is called "Ekwilism." The scholar, a well-meaning but bumbling socialist, dies, and the Toad literally becomes a sartorial imitation of an "Everyman" cartoon strip that had ridiculed the scholar's theory.

There are numerous moments at which the action in *Bend Sinister* slips into Pierre-esque absurdity. When Krug is finally taken to see Paduk, two masked men come into the waiting room and search him: "Then one of them retired behind the screen while the other produced a small vial marked H_2SO_4, which he proceeded to conceal under Krug's left armpit. Having had Krug assume a 'natural position,' he called his companion, who approached with an eager smile and immediately found the object: upon which he was accused of having peeped." When Krug's son David vanishes, Krug imagines himself ". . . turning this way and that like the baffled buffeted seeker in a game of blindman's buff; battering with imaginary fists a cardboard police station to pulp; running through nightmare tunnels." Closest of all to Cincinnatus is the manner in which Krug doubles in moments of great emotional stress: " 'I want my little boy,' said Krug (another Krug, horribly handicapped by a spasm in the throat and a pounding heart)."

In Russian *krug* means "circle," and so Krug is, like Cincinnatus, a world unto himself. But Krug's world has its moon — his little boy — and David is the only means by which the dictatorship could have gained control of Krug had the Toad been smart enough to realize it. Instead, David has been inadvertently killed by the bungling police state. This is what initiates Krug's madness, with the help of which the pain of his loss will be alleviated and the unreality of everything around him will be revealed. The death of Krug's wife occurred simultaneously with the national revolution, which has no significance beside this real loss. The revolution in fact becomes simply a "fatuous hoax." If he will submit to the Party of the Average Man, Krug is promised that "his works would be republished in new editions, revised in the light of political events. There might be bonuses, sabbatical years, lottery tickets, a cow — lots of things." The state, which condones murder but not official inefficiency, is prepared, among other things, to have the six main culprits responsible for David's death executed in Krug's presence by an inexperienced headsman.

In Paduk's palace Krug is shown a room where doctors sit and listen to a machine that goes thump, a-thump, following the dictator's heartbeat as he sits in his office fifty feet away. But the machine, one suspects, *is* the heartbeat of the Toad, the only one he really has. The mechanized heartbeat of the Toad is meant to contrast sharply with the real heartbeat of Krug. "The main theme of *Bend Sinister*," Nabokov has written, "is the beating of Krug's loving heart, the torture an intense tenderness is subjected to — and it is for the sake of the pages about David and his father that the book was written and should be read." The two other important themes in the book, according to Nabokov, are the innate stupidity of totalitarian regimes and Krug's sudden understanding, in his madness, that he and everybody else are merely the whims of Nabokov.

Bend Sinister goes beyond *Invitation to a Beheading* in that after the execution, the narrative continues, and we are given a glimpse of the creator (lower case) amidst the "chaos of written and re-written pages." His novel is finished, and his attention is drawn to a moth which has been attracted to the window screen and is clinging there. The moth, of course, represents the author's hero on the other side of the glass that separates art and life. The novel ends with the author's view of the special spatulate puddle that appears on the pavement near his apartment (which, at the time this book was written, was on Craigie Circle in Cambridge, Massachusetts) after every rainstorm. The novel began with this same puddle as perceived by Krug, thus closing another circle to match his name. This pool is echoed and repeated throughout the book in various ways (they are listed by Nabokov in his introduction) — an inkblot, spilled milk — and this image is important "not only because he had contemplated the inset sunset from her death-bedside, but also because this little puddle vaguely evokes in him my link with him: a rent in his world leading to another world of tenderness, brightness and beauty."

The reader may sense the author as a real participant throughout the novel. The narrative manipulations in *Bend Sinister* are, in fact, very much in the (subdued) spirit and manner of Laurence Sterne. Frank Kermode has detailed the echoes of *Tristram Shandy* in this novel in his 1962 book *Puzzles and Epiphanies*. Kermode sees "Sterne's ubiquitous Latin and the invented Slavonic language which erupts all over Nabokov's text as a farcical acknowledgment of the need for verisimilitude, though it is also an indulgence of superior linguistic powers." Other Sterne mannerisms noted by Kermode include notes to himself by the author ("Describe the bedroom . . . Last chance of describing the bedroom") and digressions used to indicate emotional evasion or stress on the part of the hero. If Kermode had extended the comparison still further he would have found many passages in *Bend Sinister* that are not merely vaguely reminiscent of *Tristram Shandy*, but clearly ape specific moments of that playful book: "I think I want to have the whole scene repeated. Yes, from the beginning. As you came up the stone steps of the porch, your eyes never left your cupped hands, the pink chink between the two thumbs. Oh, what were you carrying? Come on now . . . I think I shall have you go through your act a third time, but in reverse — carrying that hawk moth back into the orchard where you found it." This, quite obviously, is Sterne's Uncle Toby going up and down the stairs in *Tristram Shandy*, and Nabokov, while casually denigrating several other prominent eighteenth-century English writers, has acknowledged his special affection and respect for Sterne ("A Conversation with Vladimir Nabokov" in *Twentieth Century*, London, 1959).

There is a passage in the second from last chapter of *Bend Sinister* that is a counterpoint to the emotionally terse opening of *Laughter in the Dark*. Krug, recently widowed, is being tempted by his maid:

It is not clear why he indulged in all this ascetic self-restraint business when he might have ridden himself so deliciously of his quite natural tension and discomfort with the assistance of that keen *puella* (for whose lively little abdomen younger Romans than he would have paid the Syrian slavers 20,000 dinarii or more). Perhaps he was held back by certain subtle supermatrimonial scruples or by the dismal sadness of the whole thing . . . He was a big heavy man of the hairy sort with a somewhat Beethovenlike face. He had lost his wife in November. He had taught philosophy. He was exceedingly virile. His name was Adam Krug.

Krug thinks to himself that, if his heart could be heard like Paduk's, its beating would waken the dead. He is actually about to accept little Mariette's invitation ("This is going to be a beastly explosion, and you might get badly hurt. I warn you. I am nearly three times your age and a great big sad hog of a man. And I don't love you."), but he is saved from it by the Toad's police who come to arrest him at that very moment, just as he is later saved from submission to the police state by knowledge that David has been killed. The cost of his integrity — in the root meaning of the word — is tragic. A Dutch critic wrote that the primary theme of *Bend Sinister* is fear, but, far from it, the novel is about courage, courage and pain. Humbert Humbert and Albinus Kretschmar are grotesque distortions of man's proper image, and the best portrait of that true image, and its cost, in Nabokov's fiction is Adam Krug. When Cincinnatus walks away from *his* execution and police state toward those "beings akin to him," he is walking toward Adam Krug. Both characters, for all the differences between them, are variants on a theme that may be referred to as "Prospero bound and freed."

Bend Sinister was written during the most "political" period of modern history since World War I and the Russian Revolution. Two short stories, one written about a year and a half before *Bend Sinister* and the other during the course of his work on it, are concerned with politics in a specific and limited fashion. Both stories, *The Assistant Producer* and *Double Talk* (its original title was *Conversation Piece, 1945*), are interesting period pieces, and one — which will perhaps be a surprise for those accustomed to Nabokov's ill-concealed disdain for "facts" and "real life" in art —

is based upon an actual historical incident. *Double Talk* is a story about an invitation which is accepted by mistake. The narrator has been followed across Europe by a disreputable and reactionary namesake whom he has never met. The first awareness that he had of his namesake's existence was a request that he received while living in Prague to return his copy of the *Protocols of the Wise Men of Zion* to a little White Army library. The narrator receives many such misdirected letters and telegrams over the years, but being settled in Boston the narrator assumes he has finally left his namesake behind for good. He accepts the invitation not intended for him because of another doubling — the woman who issues the invitation says that she is a close friend of Mrs. Sharp, and the narrator also happens to know a Mrs. Sharp. The meeting to which he goes in a private apartment turns out to be a gathering of apologists for Nazi Germany. The speaker of the evening, a Dr. Shoe (not his "actual" name, which the narrator somehow missed), remarks on the subject of Hitler's madness: "*Naturally* he was mad! Look, only a madman could have messed up the war the way he did. And I certainly hope, as you do, that before long, if he should turn out to be alive, he will be safely interred in a sanatorium somewhere in a neutral country." A little old lady in a corner feeds Dr. Shoe leading questions which he fields deftly:

Dr. Shoe smiled a tired smile. "I was expecting that question," he said with a touch of sadness in his voice. "Unfortunately, propaganda, exaggeration, faked photographs, and so on are the tools of modern war. I should not be surprised if the Germans themselves had made up stories about the cruelty of the American troops to innocent civilians. Just think of all the nonsense which was invented about the so-called German atrocities in the first World War — those horrible legends about Belgian women being seduced, and so on . . . Well, they did not find one scintilla of evidence to prove that Germans had not acted like soldiers and gentlemen."

The narrator sits there listening and "trying to convince myself that these were real people and not a Punch-and-Judy show." Finally, when Dr. Shoe sits down at the piano to play The Star-Spangled Banner, he can stand no more and bolts out of the apartment, stammering to the hostess: "You are either murderers or fools, or both, and that man is a filthy German agent." But he has taken Dr. Shoe's hat by mistake, and so the sinister farce has yet another act when Dr. Shoe comes to retrieve it. The result of all this is that the narrator at last enters into communication with his namesake, who writes him an aggrieved letter: "You have been pursuing me all my life. Good friends of mine, after reading your books, have turned away from me thinking that I was the author of those depraved decadent writings." He ends with a demand for money.

Knavery knows no nationality for Nabokov — in *Double Talk*, for example, the narrator's namesake and one of the guests at the meeting are Russians. But it is a reasonable deduction that Vladimir Nabokov cannot be counted among the most fervent admirers of German civilization and culture (there are, though, at least two exceptions: Heine and Kafka). Timofey Pnin's youthful sweetheart was cremated at Buchenwald:

. . . in the beautifully wooded Grosser Ettersburg, as the region is resoundingly called. It is an hour's stroll from Weimar, where walked Goethe, Herder, Schiller, Wieland, the inimitable Kotzebue and others. "*Aber warum* — but why —" Dr. Hagen, the gentlest of souls alive would wail, "why had one to put that horrid camp so near!" for indeed it was near — only five miles from the cultural heart of Germany — "that nation of universities" . . .

In the Gogol book Germany is in the forefront of all nations for its highly developed *poshlost'*:

Among the nations with which we came into contact, Germany had always seemed to us a country where *poshlust* instead of being mocked, was one of the essential parts of the national spirit, habits, traditions and general atmosphere, although at the same time well-meaning Russian intellectuals of a more romantic type readily, too readily, adopted the legend of the greatness of German philosophy and literature; for it takes a super-Russian to admit that there is a dreadful streak of *poshlust* running through Goethe's *Faust*.

The very term *poshlost'* is a "fat brute of a word" whose "first 'o' is as big as the plop of an elephant falling into a muddy pond and as round as the bosom of a bathing beauty on a German picture postcard." The narrator of *"That in Aleppo Once . . ."* asserts that "with all her many black sins, Germany [is] still bound to remain forever and ever the laughing stock of the world." These views are, to be sure, strong — Nabokov's devoted German translator has written an article, *Germany in the Work of Nabokov*, accepting the justice of everything Nabokov has written about Germany but expressing bewilderment and pain that Nabokov has never acknowledged the existence of "another Germany, a country consisting of art, culture, and humanism." And if it were not for the events of this century, Nabokov's attitude toward things German might be regarded as whimsically as Dr. Johnson's attitude toward Scotsmen.

The "true" political story is *The Assistant Producer*, written in English in 1943. It concerns the case of General E. K. Miller, and an account of the main circumstances, which are more or less exactly as portrayed in the story, may be found in the Paris Russian paper *Renaissance* for 1938 (No. 4108). The title *The Assistant Producer* is a concealed affirmation of the story's relation to the actual event, but it is also an indication of the intended subordination of the actual abduction of Nabokov's art ("Meaning? Well, because sometimes life is merely that — an Assistant Producer. Tonight we shall go to the movies"). In one of his introductions Nabokov has written about how the tremendous outflow of Russian intellectuals at the time of the Bolshevik Revolution "remained unknown to American intellectuals (who, bewitched by Communist propaganda, saw us merely as villainous generals, oil magnates, and gaunt ladies with lorgnettes)." *The Assistant Producer* is a lighthanded and fascinating treatment of those "villainous generals" and "Russian émigrés whose only hope and profession was their past," a treatment that gives the subject reality. Aldanov was the only other émigré writer who succeeded in doing this. At the same time, by presenting the story as though a cheap movie scenario were being described, Nabokov imparts to it a strange and insubstantial air. The story opens with a quick flashback and fill-in on the life of a popular singer called "La Slavska," (the real one's name was Plevitskaya, and she was eventually sentenced to twenty years in prison where she died). In her career "La Slavska" has sung for the Tsar and Comrade Lunacharsky and is now the wife of a former White Army general named Golub-kov, who has long schemed to become the head of a reactionary émigré organization called The White Warriors Union. "Why the vision of presiding over an organization that was but a sunset behind a cemetery happened to be so dear to him is a conundrum only for those who have no hobbies or passions." Actually a large percentage of the membership of the White Warriors consists of German and Soviet agents, and the talented Golubkov himself is a triple agent. Two presidents of the organization have lost their lives under mysterious circumstances, and it is expected that an older man, General Fedchenko, who is in line for the post, will step aside in favor of Golubkov. But Fedchenko takes the post. The conspiracy in the story is a plot by Golubkov, using a Soviet agent who also belongs to the White Warriors, to abduct and dispose of Fedchenko. (The actual abduction took place on September 23, 1938.) The plot fails when it develops that Fedchenko was suspicious of the meeting which Golubkov had arranged and so left a note behind in the event that anything happened to him. But Golubkov succeeds in slipping away and leaves La Slavska to take the punishment:

She was arrested early on the following morning. Never once during the inquest did she depart from her attitude of grief-stricken inno-cence. The French police displayed a queer listlessness in dealing with possible clues, as if it assumed that the disappearance of Russian generals was a kind of curious local custom, an Oriental phenomenon, a dissolving process which perhaps ought not to occur but which could not be prevented . . . Newspapers abroad treated the whole matter in a good-natured but bantering and slightly bored manner. On the whole, L'affaire Slavska did not make good headlines — Russian émigrés were decidedly out of focus.

The attraction of the subject for Nabokov was probably not the plot itself so much as the personalities of the conspirators. The story is narrated by a former priest who claims, through having heard the confession of a very horrible criminal, that he under-stands the relationship between Golubkov and his wife, a deep shame that keeps them from discussing "whether perhaps in her heart of hearts she despised him or whether she secretly wondered if perhaps in his heart of hearts he despised her."

The details surrounding the fictional abduction seem even more mysterious than they actually were. The abduction occurs on Rue Pierre Labime, and the narrator tells us: "The old man was never seen again. The quiet foreigners who had rented a certain quiet house for one quiet month had been innocent Dutchmen or Danes. It was but an optical trick. There is no green door, but only a gray one, which no human strength can burst open. I have vainly searched through admirable encyclopedias: there is no philosopher called Pierre Labime." Even La Slavska's death in prison shortly after the outbreak of World War II is described as only "possibly" the truth.

In the year of the Plevitskaya affair Nabokov wrote two full-length plays, one of which was staged while the other was being prepared for the stage when the war broke off its production. The plays, *The Waltz Invention* and *The Event*, both appeared in the short-lived but excellent journal *Russian Annals* (1937–39) which was in a way a sister to the much older *Contemporary Annals*. (Its contributors included, besides Nabokov, who also printed three of his short stories there, Pavel Miliukov, Aleksei Remizov, Aldanov, Bitsilli, Osorgin, and Marina Tsvetaeva.) This journal was especially notable for the attempt which it made to unite the diaspora of Russian culture abroad. It was published simultaneously in Paris and Shanghai, and in its early numbers devoted unprecedented space to Far Eastern Russian literature (in addition to the important Russian émigré center at Harbin, there were enough Russians living in Shanghai at one time to support a daily newspaper which came out in morning and evening editions). Only one of the two plays, *The Waltz Invention*, is "political"; both, however, are Gogolian, although the nature of their Gogolian character contrasts sharply.

The Waltz Invention is a fantasy play in three acts about a madman named Salvator Waltz (in Russian the name, Sal'vator Val's, seems to be an overlapping partial anagram) who dreams that he has invented a machine which will allow him to become dictator of the world. The entire play takes place in Waltz's mind as he sits in the waiting room of the Minister of War of an imaginary country. The time of the action is about 1935. Whereas "in reality" the interview with the Minister takes place only in the last scene of the play, in Waltz's dream he demonstrates his invention (which slices off the top of the capital city's beautiful neighboring mountain), becomes dictator of the country, and then, when he is well on the way to becoming dictator of the world, loses all his power after one of his generals refuses to hand his beautiful daughter over to him. After his dispute with the general, Waltz's factotum — a woman named Trance dressed as a man — expresses disappointment in him and reveals "one little truth" to Waltz: he has no machine. Then the real interview takes place, and, sputtering threats of destruction, Waltz is carried out of the Minister's office as a madman.

In its English version *The Waltz Invention* has been changed in several interesting and necessary ways which are detailed in Nabokov's introduction to the translation; only one of the changes, "an increased femininity in the Trance character," is of major import. But of even greater interest is the curious listing of the *dramatis personae* which was not given when the play appeared in *Russian Annals*. Salvator Waltz is described as "a haggard inventor; a fellow author." In the play itself, when Trance, a newspaper reporter, appears suddenly out of a closet and calls Waltz "dear colleague," he answers: "Here's my hand. Only why did you call me your colleague? I have never written for the newspapers, and I have burned the poems I wrote in my youth." And in the last act, when Trance is displaying a harem for Waltz to choose from and a corpulent and dreadful woman begins to sing a sad prison ballad, Waltz suddenly muses: "Strange song! Sad song! Good God . . . A wide, desolate Siberian river . . . I'm beginning to remember something . . . Yes, I know those words . . . Yes, of course! . . . *I* wrote that poem!" Trance is at one point described as "a figment of my imagination," and at the beginning of Act Three an impudent Colonel tells Waltz: "It's useless to speak with you. We are all only participants in your delirium, and everything that is taking place is the ringing and throbbing inside your sick brain." But none of these things constitutes the real meaning or Nabokov's labeling of Waltz as "fellow author." I understand him to mean that not only is the story the invention of Waltz's delirium, but the very delirium itself is an invention of Waltz's. This is how one may understand the slightly strange title: the "invention of Waltz" is not the deadly Telemort machine, but the play. We have already seen an instance of the narrative in which it is unclear whether the narrator is an uncontrolled neurotic or a fantastically clever artist *pretending* to be that neurotic — Smurov in *The Eye*. Other major works in which this ambiguity also occurs are *Despair, Lolita,* and (in its clearest form) *Pale Fire*.

If the play is viewed as a literary waltz, it is the story of an artist who has put his gift at the bidding of a false and fatal ideal, political power. Homosexuality is an analogue of this false ideal (as it is, for that matter, in *The Eye, Despair,* and *Pale Fire*). Viola Trance is described in the list of characters as "a smart woman of 30 in black masculine dress Shakespearean-masquerade style." As in *The Real Life of Sebastian Knight*, Viola Trance's name refers to Shakespeare's *Twelfth Night*. In *Twelfth Night* Viola, separated from her twin brother Sebastian after a shipwreck, assumes the guise of a boy. Viola's disguise occasions several impossible romantic desires (for example, Olivia falls in love with Cesario, who is really Viola). In *The Waltz Invention* it is quite clear, in spite of her masculine dress, that Viola Trance is a woman. That is the reason why Waltz will not take Trance as a lover, though she begs him to, but keeps her constantly at his side, always referring to her as a man. *Twelfth Night* is a play about mistaken identity; *The Waltz Invention* is a play about mistaken intention, political and sexual. The potential brides chosen for Waltz by Trance are all repulsive. The one he chooses for himself is the one he cannot possibly get even though he threatens to blow up the entire world with his machine. Before Waltz passes inspection upon the girls Trance has chosen for him, he asks her to get him a mask to wear. The one he selects from among those she brings him is not described, but from Trance's comments we gather that it must be either a repulsive man's face ("It's a little scary. Brrr!") or perhaps even a woman's face ("How odd that you should receive ladies in that get-up"). It is, at any rate, a mask which repels, and in concealing reveals his true intention.

The play of names in *The Waltz Invention* is very similar to that in *Twelfth Night*. In Shakespeare's play many of the characters have names that are partial anagrams or are in some other way related to each other: Viola, Olivia, Malvolio, Cesario, Antonio. In

The Waltz Invention the secondary characters are a series of verbal jumping beans: in the Russian the *dramatis personae* are listed as Berg, Breg, Brig, Brug, Gerb, Grab, Grib, Gorb, and Grob; they have been transmuted into English as: Plump, Gump, Bump, Dump, Hump, Lump, Mump, (Intersexual) Rump, and Stump. (Grob, who becomes Mump in English, is the doctor who comes to treat Waltz after an unsuccessful attempt has been made on his life and who drives Waltz into a frenzy of fear. In Russian *grob* means "coffin.") Many of these characters play several roles. Lump, for example, is an official, a general, and a dentist. This extension of the casual device of *Twelfth Night* to such lengths moves *The Waltz Invention* from the realm of Shakespeare into that of Gogol. There is a paradox here. For while the secondary characters of the play look like "dead souls," they are frequently very much alive, in particular General Gump who replies to Waltz's attempt to intimidate him: "I never understood the noble dilemmas of tragic heroes. All questions are unicorns to me. Blast away, my friend." And in the end, of course, it is they who turn back into "real people" (quite a different ending than either *Invitation to a Beheading* or *Bend Sinister*), and it is the delirious Waltz who is carried off. Waltz's opposite number from *Twelfth Night* is Malvolio, the malevolent puritan who haughtily declares: "You are idle shallow things: I am not of your element." It is Malvolio who, through his strange manner and coolness, stands apart from all the others. Mark Van Doren has written astutely of *Twelfth Night*: "Even Viola, much as we like her, stands a little to one side of the center. The center is Malvolio. The drama is between his mind and the music of old manners." With the addition of a modifying phrase, so that the sentence reads "perversely poetic mind," I think that the statement stands equally for *The Waltz Invention*.

Nabokov has commented that any production of the play should "take into account the poetry and the pathos underlying the bright demented dream" and employ scenery "as rich and verisimilar as a Dutch painting." Absurd action within an apparently perfectly realistic setting is the most fundamental characteristic of Gogol's art. The particular Gogol work with which I would compare this play is not *The Inspector General* but *The Nose*. Like that story, *The Waltz Invention* contains numerous themes and possible interpretations, but no one of them is fully revealed and developed to the point where it can represent the play as a whole. There is certainly an assumption about the nature and fatal danger of tyranny, and the island Palmora to which Waltz wishes to retreat might be an allusion to Palmyra (St. Petersburg), but there are no other specific details to support that assumption, and the Colonel declares bluntly that there is no such island. The sexuality of the play, though it can scarcely be questioned, is equally indefinite. In his introduction to the play Nabokov writes with tongue in cheek: "Why is he such a tragic figure: What upsets him so atrociously when he sees a toy on a table: Does it bring back his own childhood? Some bitter phase of that childhood? Not *his* childhood perhaps, but that of a child he has lost? What misfortunes, besides banal poverty, has he endured? What is the macabre and mysterious memory linked with Siberia, which a convict's dirge sung by a whore so strangely evokes? Who am I to propose such questions?"

The other play of this period, *The Event*, is a remarkable reversal of the pattern of *The Inspector General*. Whereas the real inspector comes only at the end of Gogol's play — causing general consternation among the officials who took Khlestakov to be the inspector — *The Event* is permeated with fear from the beginning — an old enemy has just been released from prison prematurely and the protagonist is sure he is coming to kill him. In *The Event*, however, the danger and hence the fear prove unreal in the end. Vladislav Khodasevich wrote one of his longer and most interesting articles on the art of Sirin about the 1938 production of the play by the Russian Theater in Paris (*Contemporary Annals*, 1938). Khodasevich described the relationship between *The Inspector General* and *The Event* in the following manner:

Troshcheikin awaits Barbashin, the ultimate judge of his life, with just as much terror as the mayor awaits the inspector. The fact that Gogol's comedy ends with the terrible news about the arrival of the inspector, while in Sirin, on the contrary, Troshcheikin learns that Barbashin has gone abroad forever, should be interpreted, it seems to me, as a sign of Sirin's deep pessimism: everything in the world is vulgar and soiled, and that's how it will remain — the inspector won't come, and one need not be afraid of him; "Barbashin isn't so terrifying anymore." The point, however, isn't the difference, but the similarity — or the *inverse* similarity: having taken Khlestakov for the inspector, Gogol's mayor achieves not only peace of mind, but also a certain illusory happiness; the unmasking of Khlestakov and the news of the arrival of the real inspector brings him to a state of terror before an inexorable catastrophe, on which the author lowers the final curtain. Sirin's Troshcheikin, however, calms down before the final curtain, when he has learned that Barbashin will not appear; but during the course of the entire play he is in that state of terror which overwhelms Gogol's mayor only at the end. And it would seem that the fear which possesses both of them has a common effect: under its influence, reality grows both more obscure and more apparent for Troshcheikin and his wife, just as it does for the mayor: more obscure because in their eyes people lose their real aspect, and more apparent because that very reality turns out to be transitory, from behind which another still more real, more authentic reality begins to flash . . . And when Troshcheikin says that the "friends and relatives" who have gathered around are in essence ugly mugs painted by his imagination (by his fear), this moment corresponds precisely to the wail of the mayor who has either been struck blind or has seen through everything: "I don't see anything: there are some sort of swine's snouts instead of faces, and nothing else at all."

Nabokov wrote very much the same thing about Waltz and *The Waltz Invention:* "As his waiting room dream unfolds, broken by intermissions of oblivion between the acts of his fancy, there occurs now and then a sudden thinning of the texture, a rubbed spot in the bright fabric, allowing the nether life to glimmer through." But it is obvious that the "ordinary" reality of *The Event* — Troshcheikin is an artist who lives in an apartment with a very real family, and, Nabokov has acknowledged, there is even an amiable parody-portrait of Ivan Bunin in the person of the "important writer" who visits the Troshcheikins — makes the "Gogolian effect" far more difficult to carry off. There is, too, the enormous problem of maintaining over a long period of time the tension that is but a single moment in *The Inspector General.*

For reasons that were largely, but not entirely, financial, drama was the weakest of all the literary arts in the emigration. Other good plays intended for the stage were written by such writers as Aldanov and Teffi (a kind of "émigré Chekhov" who deserves to become known), but the far more frequent occurrence was for the émigré writer to compose closet or poetic dramas. (As we have seen, Nabokov wrote four such plays, and, to take another example, the poetess Marina Tsvetaeva wrote eight short plays, none of which ever reached the stage.) It is difficult enough in any circumstances to get a play produced, and it was doubly so for the émigré writer. *The Event* was perhaps the most successful play presented in the emigration. The production at the Russian Theater by Petrunkin (who for some reason did not attach his name to the production) played to full houses, and its meaning and whether or not the play was a success were the subject of sharp debate both in print and in conversation. Khodasevich saw *The Event* as an affirmation of the fact that there was, after all, an audience for émigré drama:

One cannot say that *The Event* was met with universal acclaim. No, there were critical voices (from among which, let me add, one should not take into consideration those which were clearly prejudiced). But it is an interesting and pleasantly indicative fact that the play called forth a very lively, sometimes emotional exchange of opinions, and that, when it was being presented, the theater was filled with people who had clearly not come to kill time. That means that there is, even among our audiences, a need for a theater the repertory of which is on a serious artistic level. Even if such spectators do not comprise a majority, all the same it means that there is a certain fairly perspicacious contingent among them, and this in itself is warming. Of course one can put the question: why then did this contingent not support Mikhail Chekhov, why was it absent from the performance of Pushkin's little tragedies [in 1927 by Roshchina-Insarova]? The answer is that, evidently, it was because the level of the productions in these cases was too out of accord with the level and very style of the repertory. The cultured spectator became partially convinced, and partially had been able to foresee, how unbearable it is to see Shakespeare and Pushkin staged in the conditions of material and artistic want of our theater. But as soon as he was presented with a play which did not demand too excessive means to stage and at the same time was artistically on a high level, spectators appeared in sufficient numbers and evidenced an interest in the performance which, even allowing for differences of opinion as to its quality, signifies the clear success of the play and the production.

That is true, but it is also true that even the most enthusiastic critics of the play were vaguely uneasy about something they couldn't quite put their fingers on. Khodasevich seemed to feel that the problem was essentially that Petrunkin had understood the play *too* well and had made overly obvious displays of the play's inner grotesqueness. Only the Troshcheikins were portrayed as real people while all the secondary characters were presented in so extreme a manner as to seem only the figments of Troshcheikin's imagination. Khodasevich held that the actors performed on a uniformly high level, but he asked:

Was it really necessary to introduce this grotesque? Has not the director acted just as though a director were to attire Gogol's characters in swine masks? It seems to us that this is what he has done, that is, he has shown too much, completely bared that which should not have been shown in such a way. It would have been artistically more satisfying to simplify the production and have all the actors appear more realistic, to force the spectator to guess and feel how the world around them changes and becomes grotesque in the profoundly disturbed consciousness of the Troshcheikins.

On the other hand, another critic complained that the direction had tried but been unable to attain a sufficient level of grotesqueness, as a result of which the Russian Theater had "blown (*profukal*) an interesting play." Khodasevich himself was evidently extremely uncertain in his own mind just where the problem lay, for writing about *The Event* in *Renaissance* he expressed an opinion quite at variance from what he says in *Contemporary Annals*. "My love for Sirin has been evidenced so many times," he wrote, "that I have the right to be very demanding of him, and it seems to me that Sirin has not succeeded in finding a balance between the very gloomy subject of the play and its underlying comic style." Khodasevich decided that the final act was too static, and most critics seem to have agreed that there was some difficulty arising from holding a note of tension for so long in the play.

There is, I think, an extraordinarily difficult director's problem in the play, one which I am unable to resolve satisfactorily in my own mind. In the hands of a brilliant and subtle director — say, an Alan Schneider — *The Event* could be enormously successful, but it is a play meant to be acted rather than read. Perhaps the answer is to be found in some sort of free flow back and forth between the grotesque and the realistic. For in addition to the dominant theme of fear, there are in the play numerous important sub-themes which ought not in any way to be grotesque: the unhappy marriage of Liubov and Troshcheikin, their dead child, the sadness of Liubov's sister over their unretrievable past, the past family melodrama with Barbashin, Troshcheikin as both an unsuccessful provincial artist and someone disliked by everyone without realizing it. The patently grotesque minor characters such as the curious harpy of a neighbor who speaks only in rhyme or Troshcheikin's mother-in-law, a foolish and untalented poetess, should not be allowed to dominate these themes.

The duality of the real and the grotesque is indicated by Troshcheikin's description in the first scene of the manner in which he paints the good provincial citizenry of their town:

This is our sixth year of moping around in this particularly provincial little town, where it seems sometimes that I've ground out pictures of all the family patriarchs, all their loose-living wives, all the dentists, all the gynecologists. My position becomes paradoxical if not downright obscene. By the way, you know, several days ago I again used my method of double portraiture. It's devilishly amusing. I surreptitiously painted Baumgarten two ways at once — as a respected elder the way he wanted it done, while on another canvas the way I wanted it.

The "play-like" nature of everything that has happened is frequently remarked on by the major characters, and thus in a sense it is naturalized. When Antonina Pavlovna, Liubov's poetess-mother, begins to remark that everything that is happening would make a good play, Liubov cynically cuts her off by saying: "In a word: Gentlemen, the Inspector has arrived in the town." But Liubov is curious to know how her mother thinks the melodrama will end, and Antonina Pavlovna suggests that perhaps Barbashin will commit suicide at her daughter's feet. Troshcheikin himself has a much better understanding of what will happen — but then why is he so afraid? — when he puns on Chekhov and says that a gun which is hanging on the wall in the first act must misfire in the last. He has already been through the melodrama with Barbashin, who wounded both him and his wife before he was stopped, and the second performance is the "real" drama.

There are two moments in the play when reality is made explicitly unreal. The first is at the end of the second act when Antonina Pavlovna is reading from her work. The stage instructions say:

She reads with a bright face, but she has seemingly receded with her armchair so that her voice ceases to be audible, although her lips are moving and her hands are turning pages. Those listening around her also seem to have severed all connection with the front-stage area, and they sit in frozen semi-somnolent poses: Ryovshin has frozen with a bottle of champagne between his knees. The writer has covered his eyes with his hand. There should be a transparent cloth or secondary curtain which drops down and on which the entire grouping is painted precisely repeating their poses. Troshcheikin and Liubov move quickly downstage.

And this, needless to say, is simply a variant of the conclusion to *The Inspector General,* with the essential difference that Nabokov's scene is a purposefully placid tableau which does not represent fear or any other emotion, only itself.

The other grotesque moment — an entire scene — is at the end of the third and last act. A detective named Barboshin arrives and talks and behaves in an exceedingly strange manner. He assures the Troshcheikins that they have nothing to fear because he will protect them and even promises them a happy life. When Troshcheikin shows Barboshin his studio and says that he fears that the room, where Barbashin tried to kill them, will draw him back again, Barboshin answers: "Child! Oh, what charming Philistine naïveté! No, the scene of the crime attracted criminals only until this fact became the property of the broad public. When a wild nook turns into a resort, the eagles fly off. (*Again he bows deeply to Liubov.*) Once again I bow to taciturn pensive wives . . . I bow to the feminine riddle." One suspects that Barboshin is the agent of Barbashin, and that Barbashin, who never comes onstage, is the author of the play. Its course of development and the state of mind of the Troshcheikins depend entirely upon his will. His revenge is *not* to appear so that, with no more reason to be afraid, the

Troshcheikins will, we assume, continue to live their "real lives" but will also have an awareness of the flat stageboard reality their lives really are. At the end of the second act Troshcheikin and Liubov move out from the tableau, but as the play closes, they themselves have become the tableau. It is a case of *dramatic* murder, and the weapon is the absence of fear. Or so it seems to me. To me *The Event* is one of the most intriguing and perplexing works Nabokov has written, and the difficulties already inherent in the play are further increased by the fact that much of the dialogue is a diabolical pastiche of quotations from famous Russian authors.

Fear is, when one thinks of it, the basic emotion of all politics: fear that property or ideology will be threatened, fear that reform will not be made in time, fear that traditions are not being properly preserved, and so on. Nabokov over and over again, in both his poetry and his prose, scoffs at fear, and for this apparent disregard for the "vital burning issues of contemporary politics" he has been called, among other things (I choose one of the more amusing charges from the German press): "a true disciple of the great Oscar," who can resist anything except the temptation to shock. But it is well to remember that Nabokov's life has been more than infrequently impinged upon by politics. If only for that reason one should not hastily dismiss his hauteur before political questions as a mere affectation intended to *épater les engagés* (although, granted, there must be some of that, too). It was frequently said of Sirin in the emigration that had he lived in the nineteenth century, he would probably have been a philosopher or a philosopher-novelist. In a way he is both of these things, and it is helpful to place his ultimate political statement against the background of thinkers such as Thoreau and Chaadaev rather than Wilde. This statement, when taken seriously in such a context, becomes not at all shocking or irresponsible and far from simple:

I have never been interested in what is called the literature of social comment (in journalistic and commercial parlance: "great books"). I am not "sincere," I am not "provocative," I am not "satirical." I am neither a didacticist nor an allegorizer. Politics and economics, atomic bombs, primitive and abstract art forms, the entire Orient, symptoms of "thaw" in Soviet Russia, the Future of Mankind, and so on, leave me supremely indifferent.

Eight

✻ ✻ ✻ ✻

FOR a writer whose claim is that he recognizes but one number – One – and only the individual ("Only the individual reader is important to me. I don't give a damn for the group, the community, the masses, and so forth"), the incidence and importance of the *doppelgänger* motif in Nabokov's art may seem rather incongruous. In fact, Nabokov is not only the foremost living practitioner of the *doppelgänger* theme, but also its most subtle and imaginative manipulator in the history of literature. There are few Nabokov works in which the "double" motif does not at least poke its way into the narrative fabric, and there are many in which it constitutes the narrative axis.

Historically, the "double" motif may be traced back to primitive belief. (I am indebted for much of the following information to an excellent monograph on the subject by Ralph Tymms, *Doubles in Literary Psychology*, Oxford, 1949.) The number Two was frequently regarded as a sacred cipher. Early appearances of the double in folklore include tales of werewolves, vampires, wizards, truant spirits, and guardian angels. The double may be found in Roman literature, and it is very much in evidence in what is usually regarded as the first novel, the sixteenth-century *Monkey* by the Chinese writer Wu Ch'êng-ên. The *doppelgänger* is primarily associated, however – as the very term, coined by Jean Paul Richter, indicates – with German literature. It was used in a simple form by Goethe, at great length by Richter, plays an important role in the writing of Tieck, and is one of the primary themes for which E. T. A. Hoffmann is famous. The *doppelgänger* was for the German Romantics an adaptation of a primitive but highly dramatic idea to express and explore psychic mysteries and sophisticated formulations inherent in German philosophy. The "double" motif is best known in Russian literature in Dostoevsky's short story *The Double*, but it figures very prominently in the works of many other Russian writers, especially during the 1830's in the Romantic prose of such minor figures as Antony Pogorelsky (*The Double, or My Evenings in Little Russia*) and V. F. Odoevsky (*The Tale of the Body of Unclear Ownership*). Its most brilliant, albeit oblique, expression in the nineteenth century was in the work of Nikolai Gogol (*The Nose*). To this list may be added certain non-Russian writers: the poet Heine, since Nabokov printed an early fragment of his novel *Despair* as a short story entitled *Still ist die Nacht*, taken from Heine's *Die Heimkehr* in which the "double" motif figures, and perhaps most important of all, Edgar Allan Poe. Today the theme has very few advocates in literature (Aldous Huxley and Andrei Tertz-Sinyavsky are two that come to mind) and is generally regarded, with some justice, as a quaint and curious historic chestnut of the Romantic era in literature.

What is new in Nabokov's use of the "double" theme is that it is presented in a markedly ironic, anti-Romantic way. In comparison with Nabokov's doubles, those of Hoffmann, Dostoevsky, de Musset, and Poe appear as crudely constructed as the earliest Duryea and Panhard self-propelled vehicles. Gogol comes closest, but his doubles are by and large too lighthandedly and frivolously used. Nabokov makes fun of the double, even as he uses it to examine and portray not only psychological but also aesthetic and formal artistic problems, such as the relationship of the author to what he is writing. The doubles may stand in for author or character, and — which is, after all, only fitting — in so doing they become "double" agents. Nabokov uses and refers to them, now whimsically, now seriously, in a myriad of ways, ranging from the simple and forthright — "one of my literary impersonators" — to the dizzying "elusive, double, triple, self-reflecting magic Proteus of a phantom." Nabokov's doubles are reflections, refigurations, and refractions, and their whimsical deployment in a palpable fictional context constitutes a new and wonderfully malleable variant of realism.

The 1950 short story *Scenes from the Life of a Double Monster* concerns the childhood of Siamese twins, and so its subject is the only thoroughgoing "doublehood" there is in life. Oddly, the story is written by only one of the twins, and there is no indication that the other is present at all, nor do we know anything of the narrator as the story is being told, except that he is twenty years older, since the story breaks off at the point where the twins are stolen by their unscrupulous uncle Novus to be exhibited as freaks. This most disturbing of stories is told without any embellishment, nor is any needed. Floyd describes how they were exhibited and had to perform:

They derived quite a kick from having us match wits at checkers or *muzla*. I suppose had we happened to be opposite-sex twins they would have made us commit incest in their presence. But since mutual games were no more customary with us than conversation, we suffered subtle torments when obliged to go through the cramped motions of bandying a ball somewhere between our breastbones or making believe to wrest a stick from each other. We drew wild applause by running around the yard with our arms around each other's shoulders. We could jump and whirl.

When Lloyd and Floyd sleep together they revert to a foetal position with their faces pressing against each other which disgusts them both. Floyd dreams of himself "fleeing from my grandfather and carrying away with me a toy, or a kitten, or a little crab pressed to my left side. I saw myself meeting poor Lloyd, who appeared to me in my dream hobbling along, hopelessly joined to a hobbling twin while I was free to dance around them and slap them on their humble backs." Conjoined Siamese twins do exist, even marry and get on quite well (as did Chang and Eng, the original twins from whom the term derives), and the effective evocation of this most peculiar state of being is no small artistic feat. All the same, *Scenes from the Life of a Double Monster* is not one of the most successful Nabokov stories, perhaps because the published story is merely the first part of what was originally intended to be a much longer tragic tale: in the second part the Siamese twins were to marry two normal girls — sisters — and in the conclusion they were to be separated by surgery, but only the narrator was to survive the separation, and he too would die after finishing his story.

Lloyd and Floyd each strive to keep their "secret selves," so that even though they are conjoined identical twins who share certain thoughts, they are not truly doubles, and, as the individual conjures up another self in his fantasy or his sleep, so the dream of Floyd is singularity. Doubling does occur, but it is not necessarily to be found in physical resemblance. In a 1933 short story *The Kinglet* two brothers senselessly set about to torment a taciturn new neighbor. The story is unrealistic, and its opening and closing portions are descriptions of the setting and removal of the "scenery" against which the story takes place. (In this it somewhat foreshadows *Invitation to a Beheading*, written two years later.) The persecuted neighbor Romantovsky, however, only *seems* to be a Cincinnatus or Krug figure. When the brothers have stabbed him to death, it turns out that Romantovsky was a forger (or, in Russian slang, a "kinglet") just released from prison, and the narrator adds sadly: "My poor Romantovsky! Why I thought, just like they did, that you really were special. I'll confess that I thought you were an outstanding poet who was forced by poverty to live in that poor area. Judging by various signs, I thought that every night, polishing your verse or nursing your growing thought along, you celebrated a personal triumph over the brothers." It is the brothers, Gustav and Anton, who present the greatest mystery in the story and their only justification for existing, for being the way they are, seems to be their duality: they lend each other a kind of surrealistic truth ("And then the brothers began to swell, to grow, they filled the whole room, the entire house, and then they grew beyond it"). The doubling serves in this instance as a sign not of individual irrationality, but rather of the mindlessness of the "generalized other" that we call society. And, of course, at the time the story was written Nazi Germany must have been especially in the author's mind.

In the same way that two minus quantities can produce the effect of substantiality, a person's conscious dissociation from himself may lead to a complete loss of self. Nabokov's 1927 short story

Terror is about a mentally unstable person who loses all contact with the face he sees in the mirror:

And the more fixedly I examined my own face — the unfamiliar, un-blinking eyes, the glimmer of little hairs on my jaw, the shadow along my nose — the more firmly I said to myself: this is who I am, said my name aloud — the more incomprehensible it became why ex-actly this was I, and the more difficult it became for me to identify this face with some sort of incomprehensible "I" reflected in the mirror. When I would speak of this I would be told with some justice that this could lead to seeing things.

It does lead to a state in which the narrator is terrified of being in the same room with someone else and even of the very notion of someone else existing. At its height his psychic terror leads him to think that he is "not a man, but naked vision, an incorporeal look moving in a meaningless world. The sight of a human face made me want to scream." The narrator of the story is saved from madness only by his grief at the death of his lover: "There were two people standing in front of her — I myself whom she did not see, and my double which was invisible to me. And then I remained alone — my double died together with her."

It is, to say the least, an unfounded oversimplification to say that in ignoring "the masses," Nabokov champions the individual as some sort of Nietzschean ideal in and of itself. Nearly all of Nabokov's most appealing heroes (Godunov-Cherdyntsev in *The Gift*, Adam Krug in *Bend Sinister*, and John Shade in *Pale Fire* are three good examples) have intimate and strong personal ties to other characters; the alienation of Cincinnatus, as we have seen, is simply a consequence of his being a real literary character sur-rounded by flat ones. Particularly in the early 1930's Nabokov's art explores many instances of alienation that slides off into mad-ness. Besides *The Defense*, *The Exploit*, and *The Eye*, the two short stories *In Memory of L. I. Shigaev* (1934) and *Heavy Smoke* (1935) are about characters who have become separated from their own selves. The separation, however, has quite a different signifi-cance in each of the stories. In *Heavy Smoke* nothing in particular happens — a young man is asked by his sister to get some cigarettes from their father with whom she has just had an argument —

except that the protagonist is described as being in the process of becoming an artist. As he goes to get the cigarettes:

At some indefinite point in his somnambulic course he again got into that region of mist, and this time the renewed impulses in his soul were so imperious and, above all, so much more alive than any exterior impressions that he did not completely and at once recognize as himself, as his own boundary and image, the stoop-shouldered young man with the pale unshaven cheek and red ear who soundlessly floated past in the mirror. When he had overtaken himself, he entered the living room.

The duality of the narrator is, just as in *The Eye*, expressed in terms of speech from a single character in two persons. The change in *Heavy Smoke* is from the third person singular to the first person. The young man Grigory, the cigarettes obtained, lies down on the sofa again, and thoughts of his father and of his dead mother begin to turn into the shadow of poetry "as on the wall when you walk upstairs with a candle." The concluding sentence of *Heavy Smoke* (". . . and I know that this happiness is the best there is on earth"), echoes a portion of the last paragraph of *The Eye* ("I swear, I swear I am happy"), but it does not share the neuroticism of Smurov and thereby demonstrates the closeness and the distance between the artistic personality and the neurotic one.

In Memory of L. I. Shigaev is a story, told in the first person, about a young man named Viktor who is saved from a mental breakdown by a kindly neighbor named Shigaev. But Shigaev eventually moves away to accept a teaching position in Prague, and the narrator tumbles back into solitude, bitterness, and drunkenness. He recalls the rented room in which he used to live and thinks:

And it still seems to me that even now after ten years there sits before that ripply mirror that same pale black-bearded young man with a glossy forehead, dressed in just a shredded shirt, and he swills alcohol, touching glasses with his reflection. Ah, what a time that was! Not only was I unnecessary to anyone in the world, but I was unable even to imagine the circumstances in which someone might have need of me. By prolonged, determined, solitary drinking I drove myself to the tritest of visions, that is, the most Russian of hallucinations: I began to see demons.

When Shigaev leaves, Viktor falls back into "the darkness howling with thousands of voices," and as the story closes he defines his life as "a continual parting from objects and people, who often pay no attention to my bitter, mad, and fleeting greeting."

The most neurotic of all the major characters in Nabokov's Russian fiction is Hermann Karlovich, the protagonist of *Despair*, a novel written in 1932, published serially in 1934, and as a book in 1936. *Despair* is the "simplest" of Nabokov's major novels, but in spite of its narrative simplicity, it continually flits out of our grasp, a fact of which the author genially forewarns us in his 1966 Introduction: "Plain readers . . . will welcome its plain structure and pleasing plot — which, however, is not quite as familiar as [one character] assumes it to be."

For the reader of the 1966 English translation of *Despair* there is a certain intrusive echo from *Lolita*, though it is really a retrospective echo. It is present most of all, perhaps, in the rhetorical flourishes and sinister jollity of Hermann Karlovich which at times reproduces even the verbal meter of *Lolita*'s Humbert. Thus, in *Lolita:* "All of a sudden I noticed that he had noticed that I did not seem to have noticed . . ."; and, in *Despair:* "He listened, that was certain. I listened to his listening. He listened to my listening to his listening." But Hermann and Humbert are only as alike as any two mad murderers, or, in Nabokov's own words: "Hermann and Humbert are alike only in the sense that two dragons painted by the same artist at different periods of his life resemble each other. Both are neurotic scoundrels, yet there is a green lane in Paradise where Humbert is permitted to wander at dusk once a year; but Hell shall never parole Hermann." There is no direct correspondence between *Lolita* and *Despair*. The two novels are comets moving in opposite directions, and we may do no more than appropriate a line from Byron to mark their nexus in the literary firmament — "The nympholepsy of some fond despair." All the same, the reader who grasps the full, multi-faceted meaning of Hermann's carefully plotted assault on his double, Felix, in this simple Nabokov novel will most likely find himself thinking back to Humbert and Quilty and wondering if perchance he missed something in *Lolita*.

A German chocolate manufacturer of Russian parentage is on

the verge of bankruptcy. He goes on a business trip to Prague, where by chance he meets a tramp who is his perfect double, and, not too unpredictably, he proceeds to murder and change places with the tramp ("I've just been reading a story like that. Oh, do please stop," Hermann's bovine wife entreats him).

If the reader acquiesces in Hermann's train of exposition, trustfully lowering his critical faculties, *Despair* rolls steadily and evenly along its narrative tracks. But when the shot has been fired and Hermann has fled abroad (as "Felix, 'the happy one.' What his surname was, gentle reader, is no business of yours"), a switch is thrown in the tracks that turns the excursion into a mad roller-coaster descent. The shock is one of re-cognition: for the densely bearded Felix learns from a newspaper story that the murdered Felix, although he was found wearing Hermann's clothes, in no way resembled him. And this detail, of course, at once turns the entire narrative, in all its "simplicity," into something else, with strange and sinister convolutions.

The theme of the double is in one sense eliminated as surely as poor Felix, but it is providentially replaced by many other pairings, both psychological and artistic. Hermann and Felix may be taken together, with Felix playing the role not of Hermann's "secret self" but merely that of the necessary and complementary mirror without which Hermann cannot be seen in proper focus. Hermann is righthanded, Felix lefthanded, and, significantly, after he has murdered Felix and assumed his place, Hermann cannot bear to look into a mirror and hides behind a luxuriant growth of beard. In a key sentence added to the original text (the 1966 English translation is also a substantial revision of the novel), the relationship is neatly stated as "Narcissus fooling Nemesis by helping his image out of the brook." In Greek mythology Nemesis is the personification of divine retribution for violation of sacred law. Hermann's murder of Felix, in other words, is not the primal violation.

Hermann's despair is (not exclusively by any means, but predominantly) sexual. In the original version of the novel this could find only peripheral documentation in various asides by Hermann, but the 1966 *Despair* has "an important passage which had been stupidly omitted in more timid times." This scene is Hermann's description of intercourse with his wife Lydia:

She was plump, short, rather formless, but then pudgy women alone rouse me. I simply have no use for the long young lady, the scrawny flapper, the proud smart whore who struts up and down Tauentzien-strasse in her shiny tight-laced boots. Not only had I always been eminently satisfied with my meek bedmate and her cherubic charms, but I had noticed lately, with gratitude to nature and a thrill of surprise, that the violence and the sweetness of my nightly joys were being raised to an exquisite vertex owing to a certain aberration which, I understand, is not as uncommon as I thought at first among high-strung men in their middle thirties. I am referring to a well-known kind of "dissociation." With me it started in fragmentary fashion a few months before my trip to Prague. For example, I would be in bed with Lydia, winding up the brief series of preparatory caresses she was supposed to be entitled to, when all at once I would become aware that imp Split had taken over. My face was buried in the folds of her neck, her legs had started to clamp me, the ashtray toppled off the bed table, the universe followed — but at the same time, incomprehensibly and delightfully, I was standing naked in the middle of the room, one hand resting on the back of the chair where she had left her stockings and panties.

As the aberration progresses, Hermann tries to move farther and farther away from the scene of action. From half a dozen paces "in the laboratorial light of a strong bed-lamp" he coolly watches various colors play off her body as it shows beneath his own panting torso. Eventually he leaves the room altogether and ob-serves from the parlor; but even this is not enough, and he dreams of being able to watch the "small but distinct and very active couple" through "optical instruments of yet unknown power that would grow larger in proportion to my increasing rapture."

This revelation also serves to explicate a "very singular and very nasty dream" in which Hermann opens a door to a perfectly empty, newly whitewashed room. Thirty-four years later Nabo-kov has allowed Hermann to add that there was a chair in that room "as though somebody had brought it to climb upon it and fix a bit of drapery, and since I knew *whom* I would find there next time stretching up with a hammer and a mouthful of nails, I spat them out and never opened that door again." Hermann's Felix is thus an intimate, long-time acquaintance, and, properly under-stood, he is more of a threat than a victim.

Hermann's assault upon Felix is really an assault on the "refuse particles" of his own past. Hermann tells us that it is not he but his memory that is the author of his tale, and as he waits for Felix in a dingy hotel room "Christina Forsmann, whom I had known carnally in 1915, fingered the Tartar's carpet, and sand flew, and I could not discover what the kernel was, around which all those things were formed, and where exactly the germ, the fount — suddenly I glanced at the decanter of dead water and it said 'warm' — as in that game when you hide objects; and very possibly I should have finally found the trifle, which, unconsciously noticed by me, had at once set going the engine of memory."

Apart from this one moment of Proustian sublimity, however, Hermann's past seems singularly devoid of love (the necessary catalyst), and there is nothing worthy of being *retrouvé*. The gun that may become the murder weapon — another weapon appears later, or it may just be another story about the same one — was won by Hermann as the result of an unspecified "sordid bet" with a "wenching upperformer." At the age of sixteen Hermann has "sampled" all seven girls at a "pleasantly informal bawdy house" and settles on "roly-poly Polymnia," who prefigures his wife whom he never kisses on the mouth. "I loathe the slush of lip kisses," he tells us, and adds a bit of gratuitous embroidery: "It is said the ancient Slavs [*"the Japanese" in the original Russian*], too — even in moments of sexual excitement never kissed their women — found it queerish, perhaps even a little repulsive, to bring into contact one's own naked lips with another's epithelium." Hermann's "twin" (invented to involve Lydia in the crime), on the other hand, "loved to smell my pocket handkerchief, to put on my shirt when still warm from my body, to clean his teeth with my brush. At first we shared a bed with a pillow at each end until it was discovered he could not go to sleep without sucking my big toe."

The centripetal nature of Hermann's personality is clear enough, and yet Nabokov, especially when he plays the psychological novelist (Hermann has entrusted his diary to an émigré writer, "a well-known author of psychological novels . . . very artificial, though not badly constructed"), can always be counted on to leave the Freudians in despair. Hermann leers at the "rat-faced, sly little expert" who will discover a sure sign of psychic abnormality in his tale, and some of the embellishments are surely intended to be at the expense of his first reader (the psychological novelist) and the secondary readers — ourselves. The careful reader of *Despair* must always bear in mind two attributes which, by his own admission, govern Hermann's personality: his "gift of penetrating life's devices" and his "light-hearted, inspired lying." And anyway, Nabokov might remind us (in another novel he has, in fact) that, interesting as sexual matters are, "the breaking of a wave cannot explain the whole sea."

The "real" story of the novel can only be guessed at from the infrequent *lapses* in Hermann's commentary. Thus Lydia leaves a note for him one evening saying she has gone to the movies. Left alone at home, Hermann finds his own company "intolerable, since it excited me too much and to no purpose" and on impulse goes to visit Lydia's cousin Ardalion ("a mountebank of a man, red-blooded and despicable"), where he finds his wife lying half-dressed on Ardalion's bed. Hermann, however, assures us many times that he has complete faith in his wife's fidelity and love, and it is only the taciturn and "stupid" Felix who seems to give any thought to such possibilities when he tells Hermann: "I'd like to have a real friend. I'd serve with him as a gardener, and then after-wards his garden would become mine, and I'd always remember my dead comrade with grateful tears. We'd fiddle together, or, say, he'd play the flute and I the mandolin. But women . . . now, really, could you name a single one who did not deceive her husband?"

The possibility, indeed probability, that Lydia's affair with Ardalion is the "real" story of the novel leads to some most interesting further thoughts. For the "meek" Lydia plays a key role in Hermann's crime, and, if she is not in fact the submissive and loyal wife Hermann portrays her to be, there emerges the strong chance that the entire story is a madman's fantasy. This view is corroborated by a technical detail at the end of the novel, for Hermann is writing a description of what he is doing *at the very moment* he is supposedly doing it.

To pay attention exclusively to such hints and details is to see Hermann only as a "case" and neglect the extraordinary story he thinks he is telling. Hermann offers his own explanation of the tale's significance, and, surprisingly, it is a political one. For he is a convinced Communist, and it is his fondest hope that his story will be published in the USSR. "It even seems to me sometimes that my basic theme, the resemblance between two persons, has a profound allegorical meaning . . . In fancy, I visualize a new world, where all men will resemble one another as Hermann and Felix; a world of Helixes and Fermanns; a world where the worker fallen dead at the feet of his machine will be at once replaced by his perfect double smiling the serene smile of perfect socialism." Hermann's ideal world, needless to say, is not a round, but a square one.

Hermann's comment as a possible interpretation of *Despair* is perhaps only a whimsical bit of byplay on Nabokov's part — there is even less politics than sex in the novel — and not nearly as intriguing as yet another interpretation, also courtesy of Hermann, that the reader may anticipate. In his first paragraph Hermann compares himself to a poet. If one wishes to follow this curious analogy, the murder becomes the artist's assault upon his creation, and Hermann's failure then is a matter of interpretation. "Any remorse on my part," he says, "is absolutely out of the question: an artist feels no remorse, even when his work is not understood, not accepted." Hermann is striving to achieve not merely a perfect crime, but rather the "pride, deliverance, bliss" of artistic triumph. His inability to fashion himself out of his chosen image (in the manner he intends to, that is) is an allegory of the absurd pretension of realistic, "representational" art. There are but two truths in *Despair*. One is stated by Hermann: "Every work of art is a deception," and Nabokov gives the other to Lydia's cousin Ardalion who, significantly, is an unsuccessful artist: "Every face is unique."

So, too, one might add, is every literary style, and Hermann's is a composite of "twenty-five different handwritings." The virtuosity with which he changes his narrative voice and the thrust and hilarity of his literary parodies constitute a semi-autonomous work of art within the novel. If there is anything held in common between Hermann and his creator, it is their mutual contempt for the great Fyodor Mikhailovich who ends as the second, unnoticed corpse of the novel:

Did it actually go on like this? Am I faithfully following the lead of my memory, or has perchance my pen mixed the steps and wantonly danced away? There is something a shade too literary about that talk of ours, smacking of thumb-screw conversations in those stage taverns where Dostoevsky is at home; a little more of it and we should hear that sibilant whisper of false humility, that catch in the breath, those repetitions of incantatory adverbs — and then all the rest of it would come, the mystical trimming dear to that famous writer of Russian thrillers.

Hermann also speculates mockingly on a Dostoevskian conclusion to his story "according to a classic recipe. Something is told about every character in the book to wind up the tale; and in doing so, the dribble of their existence is made to remain correctly, though summarily, in keeping with what has been previously shown of their respective ways." English offers some splendid opportunities for further fun — another rejected title for Hermann's book is *Crime and Pun* (in another place it becomes *Crime and Slime*), Hermann confesses "a grotesque resemblance to Rascalnikov," and Dostoevsky is familiarly reduced to "Dusty."

Even without benefit of the later emendations, one would have thought that the *contra* Dostoevsky animus of *Despair* was not open to misunderstanding. But precisely such a misreading does occur in a 1939 article by Jean-Paul Sartre, a short essay on the Gallimard edition of *Despair* (*La méprise*) translated in that year from Nabokov's own English translation (John Long, 1937). Sartre's essay on Nabokov is perhaps the most intellectually careless thing ever written by him, and it is worth quoting at some length both because Sartre subsequently deemed it worth reprinting and because it serves as a splendidly low watermark in the critical literature on Nabokov and on Russian émigré writing in general.

It was a question perhaps of a "mistake," one of those phantom relationships that grip us on days we are fatigued, that we see in the face of a passer-by. Thus, the crime destroys him, and the novel as well.

It seems to me that this desperate eagerness to attack and destroy himself is quite characteristic of the manner of M. Nabokov. This author has a great deal of talent, but it is of the old school. I am thinking of his spiritual mentors, particularly [*! ! !*] Dostoevsky; for the hero of this strange, abortive novel resembles, more than he does his double Felix, the characters of *The Raw Youth, The Eternal Husband, Notes from the underground* . . . But Dostoevsky believed in his characters. M. Nabokov no longer believes in his, nor even in the art of the novel. He does not conceal borrowing Dostoevsky's artistic method, even as he ridicules it . . .

Here, one thinks in closing the book, is a lot of noise for nothing . . . I fear that M. Nabokov, like his hero, has read too much. But I see still another resemblance between the author and his character. Both are victims of the war and emigration . . . There now exists a curious literature of Russian émigrés and others who are *rootless*. The root-lessness of Nabokov, like that of Hermann Karlovich, is total. He does not concern himself with any society, even to revolt against it, because he is not of any society. Karlovich [*through ignorance Sartre elevates Hermann Karlovich's name to the form of patronymic address used only for Lenin!*] has nothing to do but write about unnecessary things in English.

Ten years later Nabokov won the decisive advantage in a review of Sartre's *La Nausée* (New York *Times* Book Review, April 24, 1949):

Nausea belongs to that tense-looking but really very loose type of writing, which has been popularized by many second-raters — Barbusse, Céline, and so forth. Somewhere behind looms Dostoevsky at his worst, and still farther back there is old Eugene Sue, to whom the melodramatic Russian owed so much . . . Great importance is attached to an American song on the café phonograph. Roquentin would like to be as crisply alive as this song, which "saved the Jew [who wrote it] and the Negress [who sang it] . . ." I have taken the trouble to ascertain that in reality the song is a Sophie Tucker one written by the Canadian Shelton Brooks . . . When an author inflicts his idle and arbitrary philosophic fancy on a helpless person whom he has invented for that purpose, a lot of talent is needed to have the trick work. One has no special quarrel with Roquentin when he decides that the world exists. But the task to make the world exist as a work of art was beyond Sartre's powers.

The most charitable possible comment on the Sartre essay is that, in his chagrin at the novel's lack of "social commitment," Sartre failed to see that, far from being "rootless," *Despair* rests on a remarkably widespread and strong network of literary and cultural roots. In another of his handwritings, for example, this one far removed from the Dostoevskian cursive, Hermann evokes Pushkin and thus raises — if only for a moment — his despair to a more universal level. (Hermann's very name, it should be pointed out, may hark back to Pushkin's *Queen of Spades*.) The lines of a short but well-known 1834 Pushkin poem (*Pora, moy drug, pora! pokoya serdtse prosit —*) are woven by Hermann into a banal conversation with Lydia. In the English Foreword the poem has been presented whole in a poetic translation:

> *'Tis time, my dear, 'tis time. The heart demands repose.*
> *Day after day flits by, and with each hour there goes*
> *A little bit of life; but meanwhile you and I*
> *Together plan to dwell . . . yet lo! 'tis then we die.*
> *There is no bliss on earth: there's peace and freedom, though.*
> *An enviable lot I long have yearned to know:*
> *Long have I, weary slave, been contemplating flight*
> *To a remote abode of work and pure delight.*

Hermann thus implies that his impulse is far more ambitious than a simple flight abroad to enjoy ill-gotten insurance money, and so he may claim distant kinship with the band of more sympathetic Nabokov heroes each of whom strives to "tear a hole in his world and escape."

The title word, despair (*otchayanie*), occurs — in the Russian text but, inexplicably, not the English — in a little snatch of Hermann's youthful poetry which, we are told — in the English text but not the Russian! — is a parody of Swinburne. The poem in English pleasantly reproduces the melodious alliteration that constitutes both the chief charm and defect of Swinburne:

> *Bold and scoffing but inwardly tortured*
> *(O, my soul, will your torch not ignite?),*
> *From the porch of your God and His orchard*
> *Why take off for the Earth and the night?*

The Russian poem is quite different in many particulars, though not in its general "sense," and is not merely a simple parody but an imitation of Swinburne's *own* self-parodies, because in addition to *ch*, it plays upon the phonetically and literally contiguous *ot* from the Russian title word: "ot *luchei*, ot otch*ay*an'*ya* otch*ego*, / otche-go *ty* otch*alila v noch*'?"

Frolicsome orchestration of this sort is not too easily found even in Swinburne (no one, of course, can excel Swinburne at his willful worst: *"Villon, our sad bad glad mad brother's name!"*), yet one is struck by the "Nabokovian" elements in Swinburne's more serious art. The parody of Swinburne may have a certain importance, since it has a reverse-image similarity to the Pushkin poem. Both poems concern an anticipated "flight" that is clearly more spiritual than temporal — in the Pushkin poem the flight is an ideal; in Hermann's parody, a return from divine madness. For Swinburne, despair was "twin-born of devotion" (*Dolores*), and one surmises that Hermann does not receive Humbert's one day respite from Hell because his devotion has as its object that most dubious of beauties, oneself.

The concluding chapter — which is one more than Hermann intended — is written at "a slightly higher altitude" where "the hurricane wind which had been raging lately was stilled." That wind, to which reference has been made earlier, is the wind of madness, and Hermann has at last moved — taken sanctuary — into the very eye of that storm. Hermann himself alludes to Gogol's phantasmagoric tale *Memoirs of a Madman* (he is able to recall, however, only the first part of the title), and as the novel ends he lapses into disjointed, diary-like entries similar to those of Gogol's protagonist. The last one is dated April 1st. But the similarity ends there. Hermann has the confidence of his madness and does not lapse into Gogolian simpering ("No, I have no strength left. I can't stand any more! My God! What are they doing to me!"), and his calmness stands in marked contrast to Luzhin's impulsive leap. Alone among Nabokov's major villainous characters, Hermann is allowed to dismiss the world with a sweep of his hand: "This is a rehearsal. Hold those policemen. A famous film actor [*Hermann had first described himself to Felix as a famous actor in need of a double*] will presently come running out of this house. He is an arch criminal but he must escape . . . *Attention!* I want a clean getaway. That's all. Thank you. I'm coming out now." This magisterial gesture to "lift the curtain" does not convince — on the contrary, the curtain is fast *falling* on Hermann — but his exorcism of "reality" is close to that which occurs in the next novel Nabokov wrote — *Invitation to a Beheading*.

Despair is, measured against the outstanding fiction of this century, a major novel — the first one Nabokov wrote — but it has been its poor fortune to be overshadowed by some four or five other later Nabokov novels. When it first appeared Vladimir Weidle (another of the emigration's good literary critics) wrote in the almanac *Circle:* "Really, there is no point in writing reviews about *Despair*. Everyone who has not yet lost interest in Russian literature has read this novel or will read it. Everyone who has not yet lost his sensitivity to literary innovation and freshness in Russian prose will acknowledge the enormous giftedness of its author." Weidle will yet, I believe, be numbered among the prophets, and, since Nabokov himself has been so patient in regard to literary acknowledgment, there is no need to be impatient with the still limited response accorded *Despair*. It should properly be compared not with *Lolita*, *The Gift*, and *Pale Fire*, but with the best works of Fitzgerald, Waugh, Anderson, Faulkner, and Hemingway (choose any two).

Weidle's reading of *Despair* in particular and Nabokov's art in general is very close to Khodasevich's interpretation:

The theme of Sirin's art is art itself; this is the first thing that must be said about him . . . The urge to transfer himself into his double, to turn the reality surrounding the narrator inside out, to achieve something like a frustrated suicide by means of murder, and finally the failure of the whole plan, the detection behind all the fictions and apparitions, behind the crumbling reality and the destroyed dream of the bare, trembling spiritual protoplasm which is condemned to death — does not all of this bespeak an intricate allegory behind which is concealed not the despair of a murderer scheming for money, but the despair of an artist incapable of believing in the object of his art? *This* despair constitutes the basic motif of the best things created by Sirin. It puts him on a level with the most significant [*artists*] in contemporary European literature, and moreover gives him a place occupied by no one else in Russian literature.

As partial as I am to this interpretation of Nabokov — especially the views of Weidle and Khodasevich on *Despair*, it does not take into account one other important artistic intention, which makes its first appearance in this novel and will be developed to a much greater degree in *Invitation to a Beheading*, *Bend Sinister*, and *Pale Fire*. That theme is the literary character's awareness (or ignorance) of the fact that he *is* a literary character. Adam Krug goes mad when he glimpses the face of his creator through the mirror of a puddle. Hermann Karlovich, like Charles Kinbote, struggles against the control of his creator, striving to become his own master, and we can never be really sure just how much Hermann Karlovich does understand. This theme is, in essence, a theological joke, and it is in this context that we may read Hermann's impassioned protest:

If I am not master of my life, not sultan of my own being, then no man's logic and no man's ecstatic fits may force me to find less silly my impossibly silly position: that of God's slave; no, not a slave even, but just a match which is aimlessly struck and then blown out by some inquisitive child, the terror of his toys. There are, however, no grounds for anxiety: God does not exist, as neither does our hereafter, that second bogey being as easily disposed of as the first. Indeed, imagine yourself just dead — and suddenly wide awake in Paradise where, wreathed in smiles, your dear dead welcome you. Now tell me, please, what guarantee do you possess that those beloved ghosts are genuine; that it is really your dear dead mother and not some petty demon mystifying you, masked as your mother and impersonating her with consummate art and naturalness? There is the rub [*Hamlet*], there is the horror; the more so as the acting will go on and on, endlessly; never, never, never, never, never [*King Lear*] will your soul in that other world be quite sure that the sweet gentle spirits crowding about it are not fiends in disguise, and forever, and forever, and forever [*Macbeth*] shall your soul remain in doubt, expecting every moment some awful change, some diabolical sneer to disfigure the dear face bending over you.

This argument is over authorship, and Hermann is striving to establish himself as the primary author of everyone and everything around him while at the same time freeing himself from any possible similar control. The true explanation of the abrupt "movie rehearsal" conclusion to *Despair* may thus be an insanely impetuous last effort on the part of Hermann to snatch the story away from his creator, Sirin, who smiles gently from behind the mask which is Hermann.

I myself believe that, all his protests to the contrary, Hermann does understand that he is Nabokov's character, but he can no more accept that than the fallibility of his own art: ". . . The pale blotting paper upon which I leaned my elbow was all crisscrossed with the imprints of unreadable lines. Those irrational characters, preceded as it were by a minus, remind me always of mirrors: minus × minus = plus. It struck me that Felix too was a minus I, and that was a line of thought of quite astounding importance, which I did wrong, oh, very wrong, not to have thoroughly investigated." Indeed, as Stanley Edgar Hyman has noted, *Despair* is, no less than *Pale Fire*, a novel about mirror reflections. Khodasevich even went so far as to include Nabokov himself as a spectral character in the novel, with Hermann corresponding roughly to Salieri, the artist tormented by his own inadequacies and the genius of his contemporary, Mozart.

The 1928 short story *An Affair of Honor* (in Russian, *The Scoundrel*) is also a fantasy about murder, but in this story it is the protagonist who is the intended victim. A Russian named Anton Petrovich returns home earlier than he had told his wife he would (recalling *King, Queen, Knave*), and he finds a business acquaintance named Berg in his apartment getting dressed while his wife Tanya is singing in the bathtub (recalling *Camera obscura*, as does the scene in which Anton Pavlovich returns to his empty apartment after Tanya has left). Anton Petrovich is, if you will, a sympathetic Kretschmar; his only fault is that he is a craven coward, and, although he does not lose his life, he does lose his wife, his public honor, and his private self-respect. At the end of the story he has fled to a cheap hotel room where he greedily munches on a sandwich like a hungry animal.

When he comes upon Berg in his apartment, Anton Petrovich automatically hurls a glove at him challenging him to duel. But Berg is a former White Army man who boasts of having single-handedly killed over five hundred Reds, and Anton Petrovich knows nothing about guns. Shortly before the duel he imagines what it will be like, and his fantasy is an absurd burlesque of cardboard figures in an amusement-park setting. When he actually sets out with his seconds on a train for the duel which is to be on the outskirts of Berlin "he was seized by a feeling such as happens in sleep when speeding along in the train of a light nightmare, you suddenly notice that you have set out in only your underpants." Anton Petrovich asks his seconds to stop for a brief drink at a bar before they go to the duel, and, ostensibly getting up to go to the toilet, he flees out a back door and returns to Berlin alone. His fantasy after the duel that didn't take place is far more artful. Anton Petrovich returns home where he finds his seconds and wife waiting for him:

Mitiushin and Gnushke rushed to him and began speaking at once, interrupting each other: "Well, you've been lucky, Anton Petrovich! Just imagine — Mister Berg also proved to be a coward. No, not also was a coward, but simply, was a coward. While we were waiting for you in the tavern, his seconds came in and informed us that he had changed his mind. Those broad-shouldered impudent fellows always turn out to be cowards. Gentlemen, we ask you to pardon us for having agreed to be the seconds to such a scoundrel. So you see how lucky you've been, Anton Petrovich! That means that everything has been kept nice and quiet. And you have emerged with honor, while he has been shamed forevermore. But the main thing is that your wife, when she learned it, at once left Berg and has returned to you. And you must forgive her."

But Anton Petrovich cannot believe in his own fiction, and he confesses to himself that "such things don't happen in life." In the gallery of Nabokov's characters Anton Petrovich is superior to Albinus Kretschmar, but he is inferior to the exceedingly un- pleasant Hermann because he can order neither his life nor his fantasy. And that is the basic duality that Nabokov recognizes in all his characters. The truly superior characters are those who can move freely between the two spheres. Next come those characters who willfully or in madness cross through into the realm of artful insanity. The unfortunate ones are those who can believe only in life, which we, as the readers of the novels in which they appear, know is only an illusion.

The natural complex duality of all things (object and shadow, idea and image, reality and art) is expressed most forcefully in the presentation of abnormal characters — all of Nabokov's major heroes, in one sense or the other of the term, are abnormal — and extraordinary situations and states. Stories of death provide perhaps the most perfect refinement and interpenetration of the two realities of any given proposition. There are, in fact, only three Nabokov novels in which death is not a paramount force, and there is none in which death is absent entirely.

Three short stories show death as it is experienced, intimately perceived, and gradually comprehended. *The Catastrophe* (1927) is a story about an unprepossessing young German named Mark Standfuss who is on a trolley going to see his fiancée Klara. Mark, who is slightly tipsy, misses his stop. He attempts to jump from the moving trolley, and in so doing he is killed. The utter triviality of the young German (he is described at one point as a "demi-god") is given substance — pity might be another way to put it — only by death, which allows Mark the momentary ability to stand off and view himself as the narrator and the reader see him: "He glanced around. Away off he saw his own figure, the thin back of Mark Standfuss, who, as though nothing at all had happened, was walking obliquely across the street. With a feeling of surprise he overtook himself with one quick movement, and then he himself walked to the sidewalk filled with a fading ringing sound . . ." There follows a visit to Klara, described in detail, but it is all in the mind of Mark lying on the pavement. Then he realizes what has happened:

He felt tired, wanted to sleep. He embraced Klara around the neck, pulled her to him and fell back. And then the pain again seared through him, and everything became clear . . . And what pain . . . God, his heart seemed about to hit his ribs and burst any moment . . . God, now . . . How stupid this is. Why isn't Klara here . . . The doctor frowned and clicked his tongue. And Mark was no longer breathing, Mark had departed — into what dreams we know not.

In the 1932 story *Perfection* an émigré has charge of supervising a small boy at the seashore, and through the boy's frivolity the tutor has a heart attack and drowns. Before that happens he is daydreaming about his own unborn son. He had loved only one woman in his life, someone else's wife, who became pregnant by him but did not bear the child. Had his son been born, thinks

Ivanov, he would now be just about David's age. Ivanov's attention strays back over his whole life, which he confesses to himself has not been very good:

The even, dull mist suddenly broke, it blossomed exquisitely, various sounds rang out — the noise of the waves, the clapping of the wind, human cries — and David stood with the bright water up to his ankles, and he did not know what to do and was shaking with fear and dared not explain that he had only pretended to flounder in jest, while, farther out, people were diving, exploring the water to the bottom, and then they looked at each other bug-eyed, and dived again, but they came up empty-handed, and others were shouting to them from the shore, advising them to search more to the left, and a man with a Red Cross band on his sleeve came running, and three men in jerseys were launching a screeching boat into the water, and the distraught David was led away by a stout woman wearing a pince-nez, the wife of a veterinarian who had been supposed to come on Friday but had been detained, and the Baltic Sea sparkled from end to end, and across the green road in the thinned-out forest lay felled aspens, still breathing, and a youth black from soot was washing up at a kitchen sink and gradually becoming white, and over the eternal snow of the New Zealand mountains black parakeets fluttered, and squinting from the sun a fisherman solemnly declared that the waves return a body only on the ninth day.

This magnificently sinuous sentence is a worthy descendent of the famed ending of Chekhov's *Gusev* (a description of a body sinking deep into the sea after a sea burial and of the clouds and sun overhead), while at the same time it bears the distinct stamp of Nabokov's art, demonstrating in a single sentence the unsure line between art and reality and life and death. Ivanov had formulated the maxim to himself that the child is the most perfect form of man. And that, as the title shows, will be the determinant and sole justification of a larger pattern over which Ivanov has no power.

In the 1936 story *Notification* a son, who lived in another city, has died while his mother is out doing some routine shopping. The death is announced in the opening sentence of the story, and the story concerns the slow and painful process by which friends who converge on her apartment gradually make her understand what has happened, not so much by words (she is rather deaf) as by intuition. Thus — and this is very much the way it is when a death in the family occurs — the numbing fact of death throws its shadow back upon the very ordinary shopping day with its petty cares about credit and minuscule triumphs such as finding truly marvelous bananas. *Notification*, one of Nabokov's less successful short stories, shares this theme with an important segment of Nabokov's greatest and longest Russian novel, *The Gift* (written between 1934 and 1937).

The Gift is like Lermontov's *Hero of Our Time* (although its structural originality is far bolder of course) in that it is a novel of tenuously connected short stories. In addition to the biography of Chernyshevsky and the life of Fyodor Godunov-Cherdyntsev's father (which have already been discussed), the other most significant "autonomous stories" within the novel are Fyodor's romance with Zina Mertz, the vignettes of émigré literary life in Berlin, the imaginary discourses on Russian literature, and the strange death of Yasha Chernyshevsky. The story of Yasha Chernyshevsky — it was, in fact, printed as a separate short story entitled *Triangle in a Circle* in *The New Yorker* — is told to Godunov-Cherdyntsev by Yasha's mother, a "forty-five-year-old, plain, indolent woman, who two years ago had lost her only son [*and*] suddenly come alive: mourning had given her wings and tears had rejuvenated her." As Evgeniya Isakovna in *Notification* will remember her day, so Mme. Chernyshevsky gives all sorts of shades and premonitions to the period preceding Yasha's suicide, although in fact she had sensed nothing. The father, Aleksandr Yakovlevich, becomes mentally deranged as a result of his son's suicide, while Mme. Chernyshevsky begins to act as though she were pregnant with Yasha's ghost, and she orders her life according to Yasha's tastes, or what she imagines them to be.

Yasha wrote juvenile verse, and so Aleksandra Yakovlevna begins to sponsor literary gatherings. It is here that she meets Fyodor, whose first book of poems has just appeared, and it is Fyodor's poor fortune to bear a close physical resemblance to the dead Yasha. Aleksandra Yakovlevna plies him with tales of Yasha and how he died, and it soon becomes clear that Fyodor is being placed under an obligation to write a story about Yasha Chernyshevsky. It was Aleksandr Yakovlevich who suggested that Godunov-

Cherdyntsev undertake the biography of their famous namesake Nikolai Chernyshevsky. Fyodor *says* that he was able to resist the pressure: "Fortunately I did not fulfill the order — I am not sure what saved me: for one thing, I kept putting it off too long; for another, certain blessed intervals occurred between our meetings; and then perhaps Mme. Chernyshevsky herself grew a little bored with me as a listener; be that as it may, the story remained unused by the writer — a story that was in fact very simple and sad." But following immediately after that statement is the "triangle within a circle" story of Yasha Chernyshevsky. This stratagem is the same one which was employed in telling the biography of Fyodor's father which was "never written." *The Gift* as a whole is intended to be a "not-yet-written" novel. As it ends Fyodor has "finally found a certain thread, a hidden spirit, a chess idea for his as yet hardly planned novel . . ."; at the beginning of the novel we read: "Some day, he thought, I must use such a scene to start a good, thick, old-fashioned novel." Ironically, it is the free-wheeling biography of Chernyshevsky, together with Fyodor's childhood poems, that stand as "finished."

Yasha and Fyodor had attended Berlin University at the same time, but they did not know each other. Yasha becomes involved in a complex triangle of affection in which he is in love with a fellow student named Rudolf Baumann. In Yasha's diary the love is expressed in a fervently idealistic way ("My blood throbs, my hands grow icy like a schoolgirl's when I remain alone with him, and he knows this and I become repulsive to him and he does not conceal his disgust. I am fiercely in love with his soul — and this is just as fruitless as falling in love with the moon"), but Godunov-Cherdyntsev coolly speculates that, while Yasha's devotion to Rudolf might be taken at his own evaluation of it if Rudolf had had some trace of nobility or charisma, Rudolf's patent typicality suggests the matter may have been more complex. For his part, Rudolf is in love with a Russian girl named Olya who, of course, is in love with Yasha. Yasha defines their relationship as a triangle inscribed in a circle, with the circle representing their normal feelings of friendship. Fyodor has glimpsed Olya only once, and he has never seen Rudolf. Thus his (tentative) description of them is professedly artistic: "I use a different method to study each of the three individuals, which affects both their substance and their coloration, until, at the last minute, the rays of a sun that is my own and yet is incomprehensible to me, strikes them and equalizes them in the same burst of light." The story is held within the — again — apparent bounds of reportage, but there are many signs of artistic ordering. ("Yasha had, as it were, broken the alliance and had initiated his separation from them, so that when he rejoined them on the platform he was, though as much unaware of it as they were, already on his own and the invisible crack . . . continued irresistibly to creep and widen.") This intention is subtly stressed by a page-long chronicle of "news events" taking place at the same time and shortly after Yasha shoots himself (Rudolf and Olya abandon their intention to commit suicide): "In Russia one observed the spread of abortions and the revival of summer houses; in England there were strikes of some kind or other; Lenin met a sloppy end; Duse, Puccini, and Anatole France died." The list concludes with a miniature "news" story about some lower-class Germans who go on a drunken spree in the country, as a result of which one of their little children is shot to death. (I have not checked German newspapers for 1924, but judging by the frequent use of actual newspaper stories in *Lolita*, I would guess that it is an actual event.) The story of Yasha Chernyshevsky, as we have it, is just such a tale — a piece of raw material for a novelist.

Fyodor Godunov-Cherdyntsev himself appears in the novel as a character midway between an author's "I" and a more removed "he." This interchange of person, although distantly related to that of *The Eye*, does not represent any psychological change within Fyodor, but merely the intermittent way in which, as an artist, he at times stands off from himself and uses himself as a literary character. The first paragraph of *The Gift* is interspersed with first person remarks in parentheses: — "(in *my* suitcase there are more manuscripts than shirts)," but by the second paragraph the voice has already shifted into the impersonal mode: "Someday, he thought, I must use such a scene . . ." The duality is given one possible explanation in the novel as being the presence within Godunov-Cherdyntsev of someone who "on his behalf, independently from him, had absorbed all this, recorded it, and filed it away."

Fyodor Godunov-Cherdyntsev's appearance is a matter of style and form — matters which are, in *The Gift*, still to be resolved in a future novel. The minor characters, however, are more easily presented, and we see Fyodor in the process of translating them from life into art as he sits and observes at the Chernyshevsky home during one of their evenings. This procedure is essentially a kind of spiritual masquerade: "His soul would fit snugly into the other's soul — and then the lighting of the world would suddenly change and for a minute he would actually become Aleksandr Chernyshevsky, or Lyubov Markovna, or Vasiliev." In this manner even the dead Yasha can appear briefly in the guise of Fyodor, and Fyodor then exists — or so he thinks to himself — "only because of a vague congruity with the deceased." The uncertainty surrounding each of the characters, including Fyodor, is very much like that in *The Real Life of Sebastian Knight*. Godunov-Cherdyntsev has a *little* bit of Nabokov (there are certain details repeated from *Speak, Memory*), but he cannot be called an autobiographic character. Similarly, the rival poet Koncheyev is *in part* Vladislav Khodasevich, but, Nabokov has acknowledged, Koncheyev is also partly "one of my literary impersonators," which accounts for the compatibility between Godunov-Cherdyntsev and Koncheyev in their (imaginary) conversations, as well as that between them and the very minor character Vladimirov, who is Nabokov. Most of the literary characters in *The Gift* are collated and completely reformed from bits and pieces so that only "here and there history shows through artistry." Besides Vladimirov, according to Nabokov, the only other "real" person in *The Gift* is Goryainov, an official of the Berlin committee of émigré writers, "who could recite marvelously *Woe from Wit* as well as Ivan the Terrible's dialogue with the Lithuanian ambassador (when he used to do a splendid imitation of a Polish accent)"; Goryainov portrays a certain Plaksin who was active in various émigré organizations.

The book is most centrally about Russian literature — that is to say, the greater number of its subordinate thematic units concern different aspects of Russian literature. The "biography" of Chernyshevsky covers the utilitarian aspect, and also neatly sets it aside from the rest of the novel. Nabokov's contention that "Chapter Two is a surge toward Pushkin" is an accurate description (there is a great deal of Pushkiniana in the chapter), but the statement that "Chapter Three shifts to Gogol" is to be taken figuratively. The dialogues between Fyodor and Koncheyev are a brilliant and irreverent causerie on nineteenth-century Russian literature. Fyodor declares that he either loves a writer fervently or completely rejects him, while Koncheyev takes the position that Russian literature is confined to a single century, and they begin a little debate over specific writers. Goncharov is ridiculed, and that leads to Pisemsky, who fares only a little better; Leskov is also treated roughly, if somewhat vaguely. Pushkin, Gogol, Tolstoy, and Chekhov are wholly accepted. With reservations, Lermontov, Tiutchev, Fet, and Blok are admitted to the Russian Parnassus too. Turgenev and Dostoevsky are treated without ceremony. Various additions to the proper canon of Russian literature are scattered throughout the book: when Yasha Chernyshevsky commits suicide, copies of Annensky's *Cypress Chest* and Khodasevich's *Heavy Lyre* are found lying on his bed at home.

The first clue that the dialogue between Godunov-Cherdyntsev and Koncheyev is imaginary is an exchange of comments over Fyodor's tight shoes, and then Koncheyev makes some tentative efforts toward composing a poem based on Fyodor's unspoken thoughts as he looked at his feet through a fluoroscope while buying shoes. There is a second dialogue between Fyodor and Koncheyev, and — perhaps a greater surprise than the first time — it, too, is imaginary. The conversation takes place in the forest near the spot where Yasha Chernyshevsky shot himself. Fyodor has gone there to sunbathe, and in the sun's direct rays his inner self that records and files away impressions becomes his dominant self: "The scrawny, chilly, hiemal Fyodor Godunov-Cherdyntsev was now as remote from me as if I had exiled him to the Yakutsk province. He was a pallid copy of me." Another clue to the loosened reality of the scene is the brief swim Fyodor takes in which time is both magnified and mocked: "He swam for a long time, half an hour, five hours, twenty-four, a week, another. Finally, on the twenty-eighth of June around three P.M. he came out on the other shore."

The conversation with Koncheyev this time is a critique of

Fyodor's Chernyshevsky book (and, by implication, of Nabokov's art). The ploy that leads one to think that this conversation may be real is Fyodor's remark that "once, about three years ago, I imagined most vividly a conversation with you on these subjects." But it develops that there is only a "Koncheyevoid German sitting on the same bench: (Perhaps a poet? After all, there must be poets in Germany. Puny ones, local ones — but all the same not butchers. Or only a garnish for the meat?)." On this occasion Koncheyev's views differ markedly in certain respects from Fyodor's and are quite close to Khodasevich's: "You and I differ in many things, I have different tastes, different habits; your Fet, for instance, I can't stand, and on the other hand I am an ardent admirer of the author of *The Double* and *The Possessed*, whom you are disposed to slight . . . There is much about you I don't like — your St. Petersburg style, your Gallic taint, your neo-Voltaireanism and weakness for Flaubert." Koncheyev's derisive comments on émigré fame ("Two thousand out of three million refugees! That's provincial success, but not fame") are very close in spirit to the many moving essays that Khodasevich wrote on the situation of the émigré writer. And what were the actual relations between Khodasevich and Nabokov? As we have seen, Khodasevich wrote rather frequently on Sirin and, although most of his articles are short ones, he has a strong claim to being Nabokov's most appreciative Russian reader. Nabokov for his part wrote two articles about Khodasevich, both of which give a very high estimate of his talent, one in 1927 (the imaginary dialogue in *The Gift* takes place about 1928 or 1929) and the other a necrologue. But the two men met very rarely, and Nabokov has said of these encounters: "My conversations with Khodasevich, with whom I was not in accord in many literary appreciations, consisted mainly of unkind gossip about Adamovich and his group and various homely matters of purely personal and private interest." In *The Gift* Koncheyev says to Fyodor: "And the historian will dryly tell him that we never took a walk together, that we were hardly acquainted and that if we did meet we only talked about routine trifles."

But in a work of art anything is possible, and doubly so when the protagonist himself is an artist. In the world of Fyodor's mind even death does not exist, and his biography of his father has been written:

His father said something, but so quietly that it was impossible to make anything out, although one somehow knew it to be connected with his return, unharmed, whole, human, and real . . . then he spoke again — and this again meant that everything was all right and simple, that this was the true resurrection, that it could not be otherwise, and also: that he was pleased — pleased with his captures, his return, his son's book about him — and then at last everything grew easy, a light broke through, and his father with confident joy spread out his arms . . . But something in his [*Fyodor's*] brain turned, his thoughts settled and hastened to paint over the truth — and he realized that he was looking at the curtain of a half-open window, at a table in front of the window: such is the treaty with reason — the theater of earthly habit, the livery of temporary substance.

Zina, the daughter of Fyodor's landlord and the poet's future sweetheart, is also at least part invention in Godunov-Cherdyntsev's mind: "In dark Berlin, it is so strange to me to roam, oh, my half-fantasy, with you." When he first meets Zina, he has the feeling that he already knows a great deal about her. His love for her is signaled by the fact that his image of her pales before her actual beauty.

The Gift is plotted according to intricate analogy and coincidence. The misfortune of the Chernyshevsky family serves as a parallel in Fyodor's mind to the loss of his father. The ridiculous parodic reviews counterpoint the serious literary discussions. Fyodor's meeting with Zina occurs after a long series of unsuccessful tries on the part of fate to bring them together. The couple Fyodor watches moving into his rooming-house in the first pages of the novel are one unused means, a rejected opportunity to help with some translations into German is another, and when fate decides "to take no chances," Fyodor is moved into the same house with her. After talking with Zina's rather coarse stepfather, Fyodor almost decides not to take the room, but he changes his mind when he sees a bluish ball dress draped across a chair; the dress, it turns out, does not even belong to Zina.

Fyodor suggests their romance as the theme for a novel: "What a theme! But it must be built up, curtained, surrounded by dense life — my life, my professional passions and cares." Zina's objection ("Yes, but that will result in an autobiography with mass executions of good acquaintances") is laid to rest by Fyodor's assurance that in his novel, which he will be a long time in writing, autobiography will be shuffled, mixed, and twisted to the point where nothing recognizable remains of it. This conversation about the novel Fyodor will write is also a description of the novel Nabokov has written. *The Gift* has an open ending ("nor does this terminate the phrase"), and we can foresee that Fyodor and Zina will be married, Fyodor will emerge as a major artist, and, in the more immediate future, they will be unable to get back into their house since they have both forgotten their keys. The childhood poems and the somewhat excessive parody of Chernyshevsky each serve a definite and carefully calculated function. The blandness of the poems contrasts sharply with the biography, which indicates a necessary step forward in Godunov-Cherdyntsev's artistic maturation. The faults in the biography point toward the next necessary phase in his art, and Fyodor tells both Koncheyev and Zina that these faults will not be present in his next work. Nabokov's goal, in other words, is to present a major writer *before* he has attained complete mastery of his art, but in such a way that the question of his emergence as an important writer is never in question. This, I take it, is the explanation behind the Sirin poems which, beginning in 1934, occasionally appeared in the Paris *Latest News* with the notation "from F.G.Ch." but were not used in the novel. One, for example, is about a woman and her seducer, and its language strongly conveys an understated bitterness:

> *Hurrying this life's finale,*
> *loving nothing on earth,*
> *I keep gazing at the white mask*
> *of your face in death.*

Such poetry, both in theme and mastery, belongs to a fully mature poet, and thus it more closely resembles the later verse of Nabokov or Khodasevich than the poetry of Godunov-Cherdyntsev. It would demonstrate too abruptly the gift that is meant only to be promised in the novel.

In his review of *The Gift* which appeared before the novel's serialization had been completed, Khodasevich laid stress on the "natural slowness" of the novel's development. *The Gift* does indeed proceed at a deliberate, almost regal pace (we remember the "good, thick old-fashioned novel" Fyodor visualized at the beginning of *The Gift*), and this pace is both necessary and natural to the novel. If *Invitation to a Beheading* calls forth a certain uneasiness in regard to its tempo and extent, *The Gift* neither needs nor permits any change in its scope or movement. It is written on the plan of a mighty river serenely picking up its already subdued tributaries and, in the process, gradually but unmistakably expanding its shores. *The Gift* has been rather carelessly called the "key" to Nabokov's art. It is true that its form does in a vague way look forward to *Pale Fire*, and much of its substance looks backward to the early sources of Nabokov's art, but the particular tone and manner of *The Gift* are unique, and so it is better to say that *The Gift* occupies a singular place in Nabokov's art. It is the greatest novel Russian literature has yet produced in this century.

The counterpart to *The Gift*, which it resembles only in the perfection of its art, is the 1929 short story *The Potato Elf*, a story that stands on a par with Bunin's *The Gentleman from San Francisco* and the best of Chekhov, Babel, and Olesha. (*The Potato Elf* appeared in an English translation in *Esquire* in 1939, but has not been reprinted since then.)

As a literary form, the short story is, as Norman Friedman put it in an excellent discussion of the subject some years ago, "tainted by commercialism and damned by condescension" and generally held to be "a poor fourth to poetry, drama, and novel-length fiction" ("What Makes a Short Story Short?" in *Modern Fiction Studies*, Summer, 1958). At its best though, the short story is an independent and sophisticated art form which is no less "complex" or worthy of respect than the novel. The reasons for the "shortness" of the short story, as Friedman notes, can neither be firmly fixed nor fully justified, but there are certain discernible tactical justifications that can be seen in particular short stories. Friedman takes Tolstoy's *Death of Ivan Ilyich* as a good instance of the "large" story that has to be told in compressed form because, although Ivan Ilyich's life must be shown, it is important only for the culmination of death that is the story's main point and purpose. A short story, according to Friedman (and this statement is not as simple as it may appear at first glance), "may be short because its action is intrinsically small; or because its action, being large, is reduced in length by means of the devices of selection, scale, and/or point of view [and] because much of its action is best shown on a contracted scale."

The Potato Elf is a classic instance of a brilliantly executed short story whose compressed action is an essential function of its success. Although the plot is full both in the number of characters and the time span it covers, there is no way in which the narrative could be extended and filled out without substantially damaging and weakening it. The story, in brief, concerns a dwarf named Frederick Dobson, the assistant to a stage magician named Shock; the sobriquet "potato elf" refers to Dobson's bulbous nose. Shock brings Dobson home in his arms, like the child he and Nora do not have, and when the magician leaves them alone, Nora and Dobson become lovers. Rather, they make love once, and that is merely a confused and perhaps not even understood impulse on Nora's part connected with her non-existent son. For Fred Dobson, however, the brief affair with Nora Shock is a turning-point in his life. He at first thinks she will leave Shock and go away with him, but when this does not come to pass, Dobson quits the stage and London and goes to live in the little town of Drowsieton, where he hides himself from the view of the townspeople.

After many years and on a day when Fred's servant woman Anna is off, he opens the door, thinking that it must be the doctor (the only other person in the town who knows he is a dwarf), and sees instead a woman dressed in black. He flees in terror and tries to hide himself before she can see that he is a dwarf. But the woman comes into the house and calls out: "Fred, why are you so afraid of me?" It is Nora Shock. Nora has come to tell him that she had a child by him, and also — the reason for her attire — that his son has just died. But when she sees the radiant expression on the dwarf's face upon learning that he has a son, she cannot bear to tell him and leaves the house as abruptly as she came. Fred joyfully puts on his best clothes and runs to overtake Nora:

And at once, God knows where they came from, there appeared other little boys who, open-mouthed, began to chase after the dwarf admiringly. He walked ever more quickly, glancing at his gold watch and all full of joy and excitement. He was slightly giddy from the sun. Meanwhile the crowd of boys was constantly growing, and the infrequent passers-by halted in surprise, somewhere bell carillons poured forth sonorously, the sleepy little town came to life, and suddenly burst into irrepressible, long hidden laughter. Unable to curb his impatience, the Potato Elf broke into a run. One of the boys slipped forward and looked into his face; another screamed something in a coarse, guttural voice. Fred, knitting his face against the dust, ran on — and suddenly it seemed to him that the boys following after him in a crowd were all his sons, gay, ruddy, slender — and he smiled with embarrassment, and continued running, grunting and trying to forget his heart tearing at his chest like a fiery wedge.

The dwarf does overtake Nora, but he collapses and dies at her feet. Fred does not live to see the cruelest stroke of all those he has endured: Nora steps away from him, telling the people gathered around them that she knows nothing about the dwarf.

The dwarf functions in the story as a fine metaphor of emotional perspective. He is Nora Shock's unborn child, and he gives her a child who, although he was normal, Fred can only visualize as a dwarf like himself. The affair with Nora began with Fred sitting at her feet, and it is there he dies. Most of all, Fred Dobson's size corresponds exactly to the small share of life he is given — when he learns he has a son, he thinks he understands the whole purpose of his life and his long grief; the form of the story precisely matches his life, which in essence has only two moments, and it is at both these moments that he feels he is no longer a dwarf. Fred Dobson, in spite of his size and his nose, is not a grotesque dwarf of the Pär Lagerkvist type: "Fred was excellently proportioned, and, if it were not for the wrinkles on his round forehead and around his screwed-up eyes and the general sinister air of compression as though he was making an effort not to grow, the dwarf would have quite resembled a quiet, eight-year-old boy." But when Nora visits Fred, even though he has aged greatly and has been caught without his wig on, it is she who is repulsive to the dwarf: "Could I have once . . . She's all yellow. And she has a moustache." The extraordinary power of *The Potato Elf* derives primarily from its use of strangeness, not to exemplify feeling but to provide a background and contrast to it. Shock, behind his compulsive practice of his art in life, is a sorrowful and even tragic figure. Dobson beyond any doubt possesses a full measure of human grief, and in reading the story it is, in fact, hard to accept and visualize him as "small." The grotesque counterpoint to Nora's misfortunes are Shock and Dobson themselves. In a sense the one criticism that could be made of this short story in which every detail and proportion are perfect (follow, for example, the references to gloves) is that it has perhaps been inadequately titled: Dobson, Shock, and Nora all lay equal claim to the reader's attention and interest.

The sum of Nabokov's major prose works in Russian — *The Gift*, *The Potato Elf*, *The Eye*, *Invitation to a Beheading*, *The Defense*, *Despair*, *Camera obscura*, *Mashenka*, *King, Queen, Knave*, and perhaps *The Event* and scattered other short stories such as *The Return of Chorb*, *Lik*, and *Spring in Fialta* — may be compared in this century only to the works of Bunin and Chekhov, but in all of Russian literature there are really only two prose writers against whose work Nabokov's should be measured — Gogol and Tolstoy.

Nine

✲ ✲ ✲ ✲

NABOKOV'S works of literary scholarship and criticism over the years comprise approximately four volumes. This estimate does not include his twenty monographs, articles, and reviews on lepidoptera — some of which are from forty to sixty pages in length and so would make a book in themselves; nor the many chess problems he composed for *The Rudder* and *The Latest News;* nor his collected lectures from Cornell, which will be published within the next few years and will then comprise a fifth volume of criticism. Fortunately, because Nabokov has always felt uneasy speaking in public without a prepared text, his lectures are all neatly typed out and will appear in essentially the same form in which they were originally presented. The four volumes that we now have include: the 1944 study *Nikolai Gogol* which appeared in the Makers of Modern Literature series; the two volumes of Pushkin commentaries accompanying Nabokov's 1964 Bollingen translation of *Eugene Onegin;* and approximately fifty reviews and essays, published primarily in *The Rudder* but also scattered through many other émigré journals and papers, which would collectively comprise a thickish volume.

The first article of any sort that Nabokov ever wrote was a short one, "A Few Notes on Crimean Lepidoptera," which appeared in a London entomological journal in 1920. His first literary article was the impressionistic survey of Rupert Brooke's poetry that appeared in 1922. Then, from about 1926 (that is, when he had already completed *Mashenka*) until 1931, Nabokov contributed reviews with some regularity (averaging about a review every two months) to *The Rudder*. These reviews, mainly of poetry, give a broad and trustworthy picture of émigré literature, and they will, with the reviews of Khodasevich, Weidle, Aikhenvald, Bem, Bitsilli, and Adamovich, be a necessary and sure guide to the future historian of Russian émigré literature.

Nabokov did not review Soviet literature, but he did write one article on the subject in 1930 which treats the general subject of "socialist realism," although — and this was intentional — without mentioning a single Soviet novel or writer. (Parodies of Sovietized Russians — Hermann in *Despair*, for instance — show that Nabokov did, however, read at least some Soviet novels.) The article *The Triumph of Virtue* (the very title mocks a typically Soviet publicistic phrase), advances the argument that in socialist realist fiction "we return to the very sources of literature, to simplicity still unconsecrated by inspiration," and Nabokov asks: "There is just one question I have — was there any point in mankind's having in the course of many centuries deepened and refined the art of writing books?" Some real writers remain, but the state, interested only in simple and "useful" literature, tells them: "Quiet, you talented sinners!" Socialist realist literature, according to Nabokov, is simply a very primitive form of moralistic sermonizing, and in the final account not a literature at all in any serious sense of the term, which is why "one does not [even] remember the writers' names."

Nabokov's reviews between 1926 and 1931 are tart and quick and tempered with a whimsical sort of mercy and humor. Reviewing a book of 250 sonnets by the minor poet Vladimir Dukelsky, he ponders the sad fate of the sonnet form: "I have had occasion to see centipede sonnets, sonnets consisting of ten lines, sonnets written in hexameter . . . The authors of these original productions have usually been ladies or very young high school students." He starts to cite and comment on one of Dukelsky's sonnets, explaining: "I omit the second stanza, but all the same it won't be any more comprehensible." Reviewing a pathetic little book of poetry by an obscure poet, Nabokov cites some absurd rhymes — such as *i ó* and *moevó* — which "would have stirred old Trediakovsky" (a prominent eighteenth-century poet dubbed the "dancing hippopotamus" of Russian verse). Another poet's verse is "very entertaining, tasteless, and yet not devoid of a certain coarse originality." Reviewing an epigone of Anna Akhmatova, he does away with the model as well as the imitator, referring to Akhmatova condescendingly as "a delightful poetess." Nabokov's attitude toward poetic symbolism is strongly conveyed in the strictures he passes on a collection of heavy-handed symbolic verse: "If he says 'door' or 'stone' or 'dawn' these are all symbols of something rather than simply a door, stone, or dawn. This is a fatal path!" But his acid touch is never applied indiscriminately, and so, typically, in reviewing one of the contributors to an almanac, Nabokov finds "eight very bad poems and one which is quite beautiful," or, in another review, he crushes the poetry of the younger poet Vladimir Dikson (who died two years later in 1929 at the age of twenty-nine), but he praises in equally strong terms three of Dikson's short stories.

The overall impression produced by the young Nabokov's criticism is that of carefree, cultivated independence. Among the prominent writers who felt Sirin's claws were Aleksei Remizov ("In Remizov you will find neither especial imagination, nor especial mastery") and — with greater justice — Marina Tsvetaeva, who was first a "poet of genius" and then a poet with "many flaws in her genius," but whose intensely nervous prose was described by him as an instance of "double-dyed vulgarity." A lesser victim was Irina Odoevtseva, but her husband was the major poet Georgy Ivanov, and that review, as we have seen, was the one that provoked a small tempest. There is but one instance in which Nabokov apparently let himself fall into an "anti-Establishment" stance which gravely affected his judgment. This occurred in his 1931 review of a volume of poems by one of the most talented of the young émigré poets, Boris Poplavsky. Poplavsky, who was also a most interesting novelist, art critic, and boxing writer, died in 1935, and was perhaps the brightest light in the "Adamovich group." This fact undoubtedly was not without its effect on Nabokov, and in fact at one point in the review Nabokov writes: "I will say only (as, by the way, the critic Adamovich likes to express himself) . . ." The book is almost dismissed out of hand: "Rarely, very rarely does poetry appear in Poplavsky's verse . . . I say 'almost,' because I do like the first poem in the book — it is amusing, low, but, just as it happens with Pasternak, somehow charming." To his credit, Nabokov drastically revised his opinion of Poplavsky in later years, and in *Speak, Memory* he wrote: "I did not meet Poplavsky who died young, a far violin among near balalaikas. *Go to sleep, O Morella, how awful are aquiline lives.* His plangent tonalities I shall never forget, nor shall I ever forgive myself the ill-tempered review in which I attacked him for trivial faults in his unfledged verse."

Nabokov was by no means a chronically negative critic; he wrote a number of extremely generous notices of important works, many of which received recognition nowhere else. He wrote warmly, for example, about the poetry of Korvin-Piotrovsky and also on Nina Berberova's novel of émigré life in rural France, *The Last and the First*. But his highest praise was reserved for the two men whose equals Nabokov was to become. In his first article on Khodasevich Nabokov wrote:

The special enchantment of Khodasevich's poetry consists in its bold, wise, shameless freedom plus its orthodox (that is, in a certain sense unfree) rhythm . . . In *A Ballad*, which is written in three-foot amphibrachic meter, Khodasevich has in my opinion attained the limits of poetic mastery . . . Khodasevich is a colossal poet, but I think that he is a poet not for everyone . . . He is a poet for those who can take pleasure in a poet without rummaging into his "world-view."

When Khodasevich died prematurely in 1939 at the age of fifty-three, Nabokov wrote a much fuller appreciation of him which appeared in *Contemporary Annals*. It began:

The most powerful poet of our time, a literary descendant of Pushkin in the path of Tiutchev, he will remain the pride of Russian poetry as long as the memory of Russian poetry still lives. His gift is the more striking because it developed to its fullness in the years when our literature was sinking into a torpor, when the Revolution had carefully separated poets into civic optimists and émigré pessimists, ruddy chaps over there and hypochondriacs here, which presents us with an instructive paradox: inside Russia there is an external command, while outside Russia the force is internal . . . In Russia even talent cannot save one; in the emigration only talent can save. No matter how difficult the last years of Khodasevich were, no matter how much he was tormented by our sterile émigré fate, no matter how much the long-time, sturdy indifference of people to him contributed to his extinction as a person, Khodasevich is saved for Russia — yes, and he himself was ready to confess, in bitterness and hissing jest, in the cold and gloom of his last days, that he occupied a special place: the happy solitude of a height inaccessible to others. I have no intention here of hitting anyone with a swing of the thurible: this or that poet of the current, still-emerging generation might also — how can one know — reach these heights of poetic art, if he is not ruined by life in that second-class Paris which swims about one with a slight list in tavern mirrors and which has nothing in common with the French Paris, solid and impenetrable. Feeling, as though in his fingers, his fleeting influence on the poetry created abroad, Khodasevich also felt a certain responsibility for it: he was more irritated than sad at its fate. Its cheap sadness seemed to him more a parody than an echo of his *European Night* where the bitterness, the anger, the angels, the aonization of the vowels were all real, unique, and not connected with the everyday moods which marred the poems of many of his semi-students.

The conclusion of the article is both an appeal for recognition of Khodasevich's greatness and a confession of perplexity that such an appeal should even be necessary:

I myself find it incredible that in this article, in this quick series of thoughts called forth by the death of Khodasevich, I take for granted the vague lack of recognition that surrounded him and enter into a sort of polemic with ghosts capable of disputing the enchantment and significance of his poetic genius. Fame and recognition are in themselves rather unreliable phenomena for which only death supplies the proper perspective. No doubt, there were more than a few people who, reading with curiosity the lead critical article in *Renaissance* (and the critical proclamations of Khodasevich, for all their intelligent symmetry, stand below his poetry, being somehow devoid of its throbbing and fascination), simply didn't know that Khodasevich was a poet. And there are probably those whom Khodasevich's fame after death will at first throw into perplexity. In addition to everything else he was not in more recent times printing his poems, and the reader is forgetful, while our critics, excitedly occupying themselves with fleeting contemporaneity, do not have the spare time or the occasion to reflect on what is important. However that may be, now all is over: a treasure which has been bequeathed to us stands on the shelf, on view for the future . . . Let us turn to his poems.

Nabokov's estimation of Khodasevich grew even more in succeeding decades, until, in his 1962 Introduction to the English
translation of *The Gift*, he referred to Khodasevich as "the greatest Russian poet that the twentieth century has yet produced."
This judgment is indeed a bold one (in this century Russian literature has been on the whole stronger in its poetry than its prose),
and I myself am hesitant to assert so unequivocally — as I can
rather confidently about Nabokov's own stature among Russian
novelists of this century — that Khodasevich stands above poets
such as Aleksandr Blok, Boris Pasternak, Innokenty Annensky,
Osip Mandelstam, and Fyodor Sologub. But, of course, any slight
excess in this judgment is fully justified by the fact that to this day
one of the great masters of Russian poetry is unknown or known
only by hearsay even to many cultured Russians who can quote by
heart and at great length poets like Blok and Mandelstam.

Nabokov's high regard for the other great poet of the emigration, Ivan Bunin, was necessarily reduced slightly by his growing
admiration for Khodasevich, although his respect for Bunin's
poetry (which he places above Bunin's prose) essentially remains.
In 1929 he wrote in *The Rudder:*

"The poems of Bunin are the best that has been created by the Russian
Muse for several decades . . . [*This is*] the voice of a poet who has no
equal from the time of Tiutchev . . . Every line of Bunin's is worthy
of being preserved . . . One grows giddy from these poems, and it is a
pity to disrupt the enchantment with a hollow exclamation of ecstasy
. . . Bunin's sonnets are the best ones in Russian poetry."

Although it is certainly true that the writing of criticism was
never more than an occasional diversion for Nabokov (in the 1930's
when his major novels were being written he stopped almost
altogether), his reviews always evidence that strict and rare sense
of "standard" as the term has been recently used by Stanley Edgar
Hyman. Because most literature in any language is bogus, a large
number of the reviews are naturally negative, but they are redeemed by the grace and good humor of their critical savagery. A
serious injustice was done to Poplavsky, and his good friend
Aldanov, who was one of Nabokov's strongest admirers among

leading émigré writers, was somewhat puzzled and slightly hurt by a 1936 review in which he was praised in an exceedingly odd manner. Nabokov called Aldanov's characters "caricatures in the positive sense of the term" and said of his language: "It's amazing — his words don't even cast shadows." But, apart from this one clear error and one instance of a somewhat capricious tone, the reviews stand with no need of revision — his little 1929 review of Kuprin is, I think, an almost perfectly balanced estimate of that writer — and they both focus firmly on the peaks of émigré literature and fix on many very minor but worthwhile figures whose names might otherwise have been totally lost from view. Reading through the reviews one may occasionally lose sight of Nabokov's constant seriousness behind his ever-present high spirits. There is one sentence which may stand as fully representative of Nabokov's lifelong attitude toward art and his insistence upon the sometimes painful standards of which both artist and critic must remain always conscious. In a 1927 review in *The Rudder* of an insignificant writer, Nabokov suddenly stops short in the midst of his terse devastation and says: "Pray God that these years of emigration do not pass in vain for the Russian Muse."

Apart from his 1937 Pushkin essay in *La Nouvelle Revue Française*, the next time Nabokov produced any quantity of criticism was upon his arrival in the United States. He wrote nine occasional reviews, most of them in the first half of the 1940's, in *The New Republic* and the New York *Times* Book Review. They represent a very mixed bag of titles — from a book by John Masefield to one about the Canadian Dukhobors — and one has reason to suppose that the books were assigned to Nabokov rather than personally selected by him. Two are of particular interest: the Sartre review and a 1944 *New Republic* piece, "Cabbage Soup and Caviar," on two anthologies of Russian literature: *A Treasury of Russian Life and Humor*, edited by John Cournos, and *A Treasury of Russian Literature*, edited by Bernard Guerney. Cournos is Nabokov's "cabbage soup" — he fiercely denigrates the quality of both the translations and the selections — but Guerney's effort is praised with but slight reservations as "the first Russian anthology ever published that does not affect one with the feeling of intense irritation produced by the omissions, the blunders, the flat, execrable English of more or less well-meaning hacks."

Nabokov's remarks on the Cournos anthology are of interest primarily because a selection in it provides Nabokov with the overwhelming temptation — a solitary instance — to go to work on some Soviet prose:

The number of contemporary second-class and third-class writers welcomed by Mr. Cournos greatly exceeds the necessity for their existence. I was particularly impressed by one gem. It is a story of a certain Alexander Poliakov, which Mr. Cournos introduces with the cry "How closely akin to life is Russian realism!" The story is about a dog which Russian soldiers take prisoner: " 'Well, let's give him a name,' said someone. From all sides came suggestions: 'Fascist,' 'Gangster,' 'Adolf,' 'Hitler,' 'Goebbels,' and so forth. 'None of these will do, boys,' Dormidontov interrupted his friends. His eyes flashed gayly as he drawled in a mock reproachful tone: 'Comrades, is it really proper to give such a name to a dog? Why insult an animal?' His words were drowned out in a loud burst of laughter [realism! humor!] 'Then what name shall we give him?' insisted the tankmen. 'Well,' said Dormidontov, 'we took the dog along with other German war materials. He's one of our trophies. Let's call him Trophy.' [paragraph] This suggestion was enthusiastically accepted. [paragraph] Several months passed [period]. Trophy became inseparable from the battalion. He quickly grew accustomed to his new name [I cannot stop quoting]. He was particularly attached to Dormidontov and when the jolly driver was away with his group, Trophy visibly missed him. All the tankmen became fond of the big pointer. They especially . . ." No, this is not a parody, this is a "true story" (*teste* Mr. Cournos), but it is curious how often stark realism and "simplicity" are synonymous with the tritest and most artificial literary conventionalities imaginable. The plot is so easy to deduce that it hardly needs to be hinted at. "The bold and intelligent pointer made three more trips with ammunition." As a matter of fact the bold and intelligent pointer had made — oh, many, many more trips than that in his steady course from magazine to magazine, in all countries, through all wars . . . Soviet literature, being human, never despised the oldest bourgeois cliché (the *avant-garde* touch being of course automatically supplied by political enlightenment), but I doubt whether the kindest Soviet critic would approve of this trash.

One would dearly like to hear Nabokov hold forth on such classics of socialist realism as, say, *The Tanker Derbent* or *Virgin Soil Upturned!*

Of note in his comments on the Guerney collection are some remarks on Aleksandr Blok:

The bulk of Blok's writings is a heterogeneous mixture of violas and vulgarity. He was a superb poet with a muddled mind. Something somber in him and fundamentally reactionary (remindful sometimes of Dostoevsky's political articles), a murky vista with a bonfire of books at the end, led him away from his genius as soon as he started to think. Authentic communists were quite right in not taking him seriously. His *Twelve* is a failure, and no wonder its strangely irrelevant end made one Soviet critic remark: "It was hardly worthwhile climbing our mountain to cap it (*nakhlobuchit'*) with a medieval shrine."

There have been no reviews and only a few critical essays — the introduction to *A Hero of Our Times* (1958) and a Russian-language introduction to a collection of Gogol's tales (1952) — in the 1950's and 1960's, but after *Lolita* there have been ample opportunities to satisfy eager reporters and interviewers. My favorite such salvo is the following exchange with a French reporter: "*Evtouchenko?*" "*C'est Aragon en petit . . .*" "*Dostoievsky?*" "*Un journaliste, comme Balzac . . . Camus est un romancier de troisième ordre.*" Explaining at greater length his feelings about Dostoevsky, Nabokov has said:

Non-Russian readers do not realize two things: that not all Russians love Dostoevsky as much as Americans do, and that most of those Russians who do, venerate him as a mystic and not as an artist. He was a prophet, a claptrap journalist and a slapdash comedian. I admit that some of his scenes, some of his tremendous, farcical rows are extraordinarily amusing. But his sensitive murderers and soulful prostitutes are not to be endured for one moment — by this reader anyway.

He has termed D. H. Lawrence a pornographer and spoken disparagingly of — to mention just a few — Gorky, Mann, and Faulkner. Comparing Hemingway and Conrad he said:

Hemingway is certainly the better of the two; he has at least a voice of his own and is responsible for that delightful, highly artistic short story, *The Killers*. And the description of the fish in his famous fish story is superb. But I cannot abide Conrad's souvenir-shop style, and bottled ships, and shell necklaces of romanticist clichés.

Nabokov's harsh opinions are a necessary corollary of his belief that "seldom more than two or three really first-rate artists exist simultaneously in a given generation." Among living American writers, he has praised Salinger and Updike, and Robbe-Grillet and Borges have also received his praise. On Nabokov, Nabokov has said: "I have a fair inkling of my literary afterlife. I have felt the breeze of certain promises. No doubt there will be ups and downs, long periods of slump. With the Devil's connivance, I open a newspaper of 2063 and in some article on the books page I find: 'Nobody reads Nabokov or Fulmerford today.' Awful question: Who is this unfortunate Fulmerford?"

Certainly Nabokov's greatest contempt is reserved not for a writer but for the founder of psychoanalysis, and a word has been set aside for Freud and Freudianism in almost all the English forewords to his Russian novels. In the Introduction to *The Eye* he wrote: "Freudians flutter around [my books] avidly, approach with itching oviducts, stop, sniff, and recoil. A serious psychologist, on the other hand, may distinguish . . ." In a more recent introduction, the tone has changed to that of faintly ironical sympathy: "After the dreadful frustrations Freudians have experienced with my other books, I am sure they will refrain from [seeing] a sublimation of the push-button power-feeling such as the manipulation of an elevator, up (erection!) and down (revenge suicide!)." In a 1966 interview on the National Educational Television network, when he was asked: "Mr. Nabokov, would you tell us why it is that you detest Freud?", the answer was: "I think he's crude. I think he's medieval, and I don't want an elderly gentleman with an umbrella inflicting his dreams upon me. *I* don't have the dreams that he discusses in his books. I don't see umbrellas in my dreams. Or balloons." It is, I think, generally assumed that Nabokov's anti-Freudian remarks are of fairly recent vintage and are the more or less expected sort of statement heard from such other writers as Shaw and Tolstoy after they have become world famous. Nabokov, no matter how amusing his comments on Freud may appear, is well acquainted with Freud's work (in English translations) and his quarrel with Freudianism actually dates back nearly forty years.

In 1931 Marc Slonim, the former editor of the Prague journal *Will of Russia,* published a Paris literary weekly newspaper *New Gazette.* It was very shortlived, and today the paper is extremely hard to obtain; but its five numbers contain a great deal of fascinating material which is essential for the student of Russian émigré culture. In a questionnaire about the achievements of modern Russian literature which the *New Gazette* put to various writers, mention of the works of Sirin is prominent. Gaito Gazdanov declared flatly that the younger generation of the emigration had produced only one real writer: Sirin. Kuprin called *The Defense* the most important Russian book of the preceding five years. Khodasevich cited three books: Bunin's *Life of Arsenev, The Defense,* and Olesha's *Envy.* In the fifth and last number of the *New Gazette* Nabokov printed an article entitled "What Must Everyone Know?" — a satirical treatment of the Freudian outlook.

The article is written as a mock sales pitch or platform speech by a representative from the Freudian delegation:

People had morality but they let it perish and buried it and wrote nothing on the tombstone. In its place there has appeared something new, and in its own way (to the great terror of the decrepit moralists) it has explained the behind-the-scenes reality of our sufferings, joys, and torments. Whoever once tries our shaving cream *Velveteen* will henceforth refuse all other brands. Whoever once views the world through the prism of *Freudism for All* will not regret it. Gentlemen, in an empty anecdote there is sometimes expressed a very deep truth. I present the following example: *Son:* "Daddy, I want to marry granny." *Father:* "Don't say silly things." *Son:* ". . . But why, papa, if you can marry my mother, can't I marry yours?" A trifle you say. But in it, in this trifle, is the entire essence of what we can learn about the complexes. This little boy, this pure and honorable little lad, whom the father (with his dull and rigid mentality) prevents from satisfying his natural passion will either hide his passion and be unhappy all his life (the Tantalus complex), or he will murder his father (the penal servitude complex), or, finally, he may somehow fulfill his desire in spite of everything (the happy marriage complex). Or let us take another example: a man, let us say, feels the onset of inexplicable fear upon encountering a tiger in the forest. How may we explain this fear? Psychoanalysis, gentlemen, provides us with a brilliant and simple answer: undoubtedly this person was frightened in early childhood by a picture of a tiger or by a tiger skin under mama's piano; this terror (*horror tigris*) has continued to live in him subconsciously, and then, as a full-grown man, the terror, as it were, burst into the open upon meeting a real beast. If he had a psychoanalyst with him in the forest, the psychoanalyst would have extracted from him that little trifling remembrance and explained in simple words to the tiger how he, the tiger, in his own youth tasted of human flesh which is how he became a man-eater. The result of the conversation is clear . . .

Gentlemen, you will know nothing of the intricate fabric of life if you do not accept one fact: sex governs life. The pen with which you write to your beloved or debtor represents the male organ, while the mailbox into which we drop the letter is the female organ. This is the way in which one should view everyday life. All children's games, for example, are based upon eroticism (it is especially necessary always to remember this). A little boy energetically whipping his top is a sadist; a ball (preferably of large diameter) is attractive to him because it recalls a woman's bosom; playing hide-and-seek is an emiratic (secret, obscure) urge to return to the mother's womb. This same Oedipal complex is reflected in certain of our common curses . . . No matter what you are concerned with, no matter what you are thinking of, remember that all our acts and actions, thoughts and reflections may be explained completely satisfactorily in the above manner. Try our patented product *Freudism for All*, and you will receive satisfaction. We have enthusiastic testimonials from many writers and artists, from three engineers, from pedagogues, from midwives, and many, many more. Its effect is instantaneous and pleasurable. Every modern man must acquire this. It's extremely interesting! Amazingly cheap!

Although he himself has never put the matter in quite this fashion, Nabokov appears to object to Freudianism as a kind of internal Marxism proceeding upon the assumption that the common is of greater import than the individual. It seems unlikely that Nabokov's views on Dostoevsky will gain any wide acceptance in the immediate future at any rate, but in the 1960's one can already clearly see that the corner has been turned regarding Freudianism in literature, and there are fewer and fewer important writers and critics who slavishly accept and practice the Freudian prescription — which, again, has nothing to do with a rejection of psychology or sexual questions in art. Nabokov has referred to himself as a "psychological novelist," and, judging from certain psychological terms in his fiction, it is evident that he has a knowledge of psychology.

Because of the stress which he places upon individualism in life and in art, it is to be expected that Nabokov does not much favor the notion of "influence" in literature. In the 1930 questionnaire on Proust in *Numbers* the questions were:

1. Do you consider Proust to be the most powerful spokesman of our epoch? 2. Do you see his heroes and the atmosphere of his chronicle in contemporary life? and 3. Do you consider that the peculiar features of the Proustian world, his method of observation, his spiritual experiment, and his style must necessarily have a decisive influence on world literature in the immediate future, particularly Russian?

Most of the writers replying, and there were French as well as Russian writers represented, wrote at some length on the importance and representativeness (or lack thereof) of Proust. The Sirin reply, however, was an acerb examination of the very terms of the question:

1. It seems to me that one cannot judge this: an epoch is never "ours." I don't know into what sort of epoch the future historian will place us and what its characteristics will be. I have a sceptical attitude towards those characteristics which are proclaimed by contemporaries. 2. Once again, it is difficult for me to imagine *en bloc* "contemporary" life. Each country has its own life, and each man has his own life. But there is something which is eternal. The depiction of this eternal is what is of true value. Proustian people have lived always and everywhere. 3. Literary influence is a dark and unclear thing. One may imagine, for example, two writers, A and B, completely different but both under a certain very subjective Proustian influence; this influence goes unnoticed by reader C inasmuch as each of the three (A, B, and C) has understood Proust in his own way. It happens that a writer has an oblique influence through another writer, or that some sort of complex blending of influences takes place, and so on. One may not foresee anything in this regard.

The writers whom Nabokov has translated into three languages are, with few exceptions, artists of the first rank. (As a very young man he translated Romain Rolland, which is somewhat amusing in view of his comments about Rolland in more recent years.) But they are not any guide to the influences present in Nabokov's art. Nabokov, for example, has never translated Gogol, but he has translated Supervielle, Tennyson, Lermontov, Goethe (an excerpt from *Faust* into Russian), and Yeats. There is one writer translated by Nabokov with whom he has a strong and clear affinity — Lewis Carroll. But Verlaine, Rimbaud, Shakespeare (excerpts from *Hamlet* and Sonnets XVII and XXVII), Tiutchev, and Pushkin can hardly be used to "explain" Nabokov, although, of course, one must know their works since allusions to them occur fairly frequently. Nabokov's translations are by and large of poetry, and, until recent years, they were done in poetic form. Nabokov has written that he now recalls these efforts with a moan, but this denial of the possibility of poetic translation in favor of the strictly literal "pony" frankly strikes me as being not unlike the harsh judgment of a religious convert upon his old faith. There is no particular justification for so totally denigrating the first method simply because it came before the one later chosen. Almost all novels written are terrible and worthless, but we preserve the genre to be used by real artists. Granted, there have been greater abuses perpetrated in poetic translations than in other forms of creative writing, and an innocent party (the poet being translated) is victimized, but superb poetic translations do exist.

It is really impossible, for example, to say that Sologub's Verlaine translations differ in any serious way from either the sense or the beauty of their models. Of course they are not "the same," but only a very naïve reader, it seems to me, would entertain such a notion about even a prose translation. Here is my literal version of a short Pushkin poem:

> *I thought my heart had forgotten*
> *Its ready capability to suffer;*
> *I said: "That which was,*
> *Can no longer be, can no longer be!"*
> *Past are the ecstasies and sorrows*
> *And the credulous dreams . . .*
> *But, now, they again throb*
> *Before the great power of beauty.*

And next to it, I submit the following poetic version by Sir Cecil Kisch:

> *I thought my heart had quite forgot*
> *Its ready strength to suffer pain.*
> *I said: "What once was, now is not,*
> *What has been, cannot be again!"*
> *The thrills of joy, the pangs of sorrow*
> *Have gone with dreams of texture light . . .*
> *But see — they throb upon the morrow*
> *Beneath the sway of beauty's might!*

The Kisch translation is far from exact and will not do for precise explication, but the important thing is that it will give a reasonably imaginative reader a sure sense that the original poem was written by a great poet.

Nabokov's own poetic translations do much the same. If Russians ever come to have a feeling for Rupert Brooke, it will be because of Nabokov's excellent renditions of his verse. His rendition of Hamlet's soliloquy is the best there is in the Russian language, and — I transfer it literally back into English — not very far from what Shakespeare wrote:

> *To be or not to be: now this is*
> *The question: whether it is better for one's soul to endure*
> *The slings and arrows of furious fortune*
> *Or, against a sea of misfortunes having taken arms,*
> *To finish with them.*
> *To die, to sleep;*
> *No more; and if sleep ends*
> *The soul's melancholy and the thousand anxieties,*
> *Inherent in us — such a consummation*
> *One cannot but wish.*

(I think it has not been noted in connection with *Lolita* that the last lines of the *Hamlet* soliloquy are: *"Nymph, in thy orisons / Be all my sins remember'd."*) A painful paraphrase of the world's greatest poetry? But any translation, whether literal or in freer poetic rendition, must be in the main a paraphrase. Words, and particuarly abstract words, have no flat and simple connotations. Thus, Nabokov has employed the proper and best Russian word for "consummation," *zavershenie*, but it does not even begin to approximate the many shades of meaning in the English word. *Zavershenie* happens to have become the counterpart in the Russian language of "consummation" in English, but it has its own quite distinct etymology and shades of association. Because Nabokov's Russian rendering of Hamlet's speech has an eloquence and poetry of its own (what a beautiful line *toskú dushí i týsyachu trevóg* is, even read phonetically without any knowledge of Russian) it has every right to be considered not an exact translation, but an accurate rendition and — to use a legalistic phrase in a poetic sense — a fair and full compensation for the damage inflicted.

In 1944 Nabokov published a book of excellent translations of Pushkin, Lermontov, and Tiutchev. In recent years, however, he has disowned his "poetic paraphrases" and steadfastly refused all requests to reprint or anthologize them. But the translations are in print and thus accessible to anyone who wishes to take the trouble to look them up. His decision has had far more drastic effect in regard to other poetic translations, which he used in his course lectures at Wellesley, Cornell, and Harvard, but never published. The most important of these translations are three poems by Khodasevich. Khodasevich's *Ballada* was translated by him under the title *Orpheus*. Here is my literal version of two stanzas from it:

> *Incoherent, passionate words!*
> *One cannot understand anything in them,*
> *But sounds are truer than meaning*
> *And a word is stronger than anything.*
>
> *And music, music, music*
> *Is woven into my song*
> *And narrow, narrow, narrow*
> *Is the blade that pierces me.*

And here is Nabokov's English translation of those same stanzas:

> *What a vague, what a passionate murmur*
> *lacking any intelligent plan;*
> *but a sound may be truer than reason*
> *and a word may be stronger than man.*

And then melody, melody, melody
blends my accents and joins in their quest,
and a delicate, delicate, delicate
pointed blade seems to enter my breast.

Do not these eight lines literally squirm with the translator's maggoty "from-oneselfers" (*otsebýatiny*)? The blade that is given a "point" which is taken for granted in the original; the bland "enter" in place of the far stronger "pierce"; the "seems to" where in Russian it *does;* the unwarranted "breast" (since the subject of the poem is poetic inspiration, the precise point of incision is quite as likely to be the mind or the soul, traditionally located in a Russian, according to one of Nabokov's scholarly notes, in the hollow of the throat). But enough of pedantry. For all its many liberties, Nabokov's translation is an excellent means of conveying to non-Russian readers the fact that Khodasevich *is* a great poet — together with something of the specific nature and character of his poetic genius. Even with Nabokov's high praise of Khodasevich, until and unless he permits the publication of his three translations (especially *Orpheus*), recognition of Vladislav Khodasevich as anything more than "evidently the best of the émigré poets" is deferred.

Beginning in 1955 Nabokov wrote a series of articles in both Russian and English. The Russian ones appeared in the New York journals *The New Review* and *Experiments*, the English articles in *Partisan Review* and the 1959 Harvard University Press collection *On Translation*. "The Servile Path" — the title of his article in the Harvard volume — conveys the substance of his argument. The idea of strictly literal translation with full scholarly and critical commentary — in compensation for the loss of poetry — was actually at the back of Nabokov's mind for many years, even while he was still doing poetic translations. In his review of the Guerney anthology, which includes a translation of the medieval Russian masterpiece *The Song of Igor's Campaign*, Nabokov wrote:

Although exquisitely worded, the translation of the celebrated *Lay of the Host of Igor* (presumed to have been composed by an unknown minstrel of unique genius at the end of the twelfth century) is not free from certain slips. Instead of the smooth, lovely Persian miniature that

Guerney makes of it, one would have preferred a really scholarly presentation of the thing, fattened on copious footnotes and enlivened by a thorough discussion of the various readings and obscurities which have been the distress and delight of Russian commentators.

Actually, Nabokov himself made a "readable" translation of the Igor Tale for pedagogical purposes in 1952. That version was entitled *The Discourse of Igor's Campaign*. In the Notes to his scholarly and more restrained 1960 translation, *The Song of Igor's Campaign*, Nabokov explained his discarding of the 1952 translation in the following way:

My object was purely utilitarian — to provide my students with an English text. In that first version I followed uncritically Roman Jakobson's recension as published in *La Geste du Prince Igor*. Later, however, I grew dissatisfied not only with my own — much too "readable" — translation but also with Jakobson's views. Mimeographed copies of that obsolete version which are still in circulation at Cornell and Harvard should now be destroyed.

The 1952 version is most helpful, however; by comparing it with the printed 1960 version, the superiority of the "servile" method in this instance is indisputable. There are two primary reasons why the Igor Tale lends itself so well to a more conservative treatment: in the first place, the epic is neither poetry nor prose — a metaphoric chronicle with certain poetic features is the closest possible description — and, secondly, the conception of literature in the Kievan period of Russian culture, usually dated from 1030 until 1240 (the Igor Tale was probably written sometime in 1187) was quite different from our modern understanding of literature. There is evidence that in the twelfth century, in writing which was not intended to be merely instructional, simplicity was not a virtue. The foremost literary genre was the sermon, and under Byzantine influence it attained a level of high sophistication and complexity in Russia. There is a high probability (one must generalize from rather limited evidence) that *The Song of Igor's Campaign* was not meant to be either "simple" or "natural" to its contemporary audience. Thus, in avoiding the "more readable" form of translation because of principles of translation and scholarly accuracy, Nabokov seems to me to have chosen a mode of expression exceptionally appropriate to render the literary tone that the epic may well have had when it was written.

The opening of the tale as rendered first in *The Discourse of Igor's Campaign* is: "Might it not become us, brothers, to start in an ancient style of speech the stern tale of Igor's campaign? Let us, however, start our song in a strain that would match the actual events of these times and not Bojan's artful fancies." In *The Song of Igor's Campaign* this opening has been translated in a way that is both more accurate and more eloquent: "Might it not become us, brothers, to begin in the diction of yore the stern tale of the campaign of Igor, Igor son of Svyatoslav? Let us, however, begin this song in keeping with the happenings of these times and not with the contriving of Boyan." One of the most celebrated and difficult lines of the epic (in the Old Russian *O Rus'skaya zemle, uzhe za shelomen'm' esi!*) was translated as "O Russian Land, you are already behind the skyline" in the 1952 text and as "O Russian land, you are already behind the culmen" in the 1960 version, which is a bold and very satisfactary improvement over the too simple "beyond the hill" of the Cross-Jakobson translation. Another of the most famous passages in the epic, the anonymous poet's quotation of his mysterious predecessor, the bard Boyan, was similarly refined in the later version, which now must be considered the best possible translation. The original translation was simply: "Of him the seer Bojan had pithily said in the tag: 'Neither guile nor skill can save man or bird from the Judgment of God'"; the more accurate and artistically satisfying 1960 translation is: "Of him vatic Boyan once said, with sense, in the tag: 'Neither the guileful nor the skillful, neither bird [nor bard], can escape God's judgment.'"

The sixty pages of footnotes and commentary accompanying the translation of *The Song of Igor's Campaign* constitute a full presentation of the best opinions and variant readings — the literature on the Igor Tale is mountainous — that scholarship has produced. Nabokov himself has made several new and appealing speculations, but the most striking innovation of his notes is the lively critical sense rarely if ever brought to bear on this work before. Nabokov's comments on the author of the epic are characteristic of him and include all that can or should be said on the subject:

It is pretty useless to deduce the life history and human form of a poet from his work; and the greater the artist the more likely it is for us to arrive at erroneous conclusions. It seems reasonable to suppose that our bard was a *druzhinnik*, a Kievan knight; but for all we know he might have been a learned monk taking a pagan vacation. We may suppose he was a courtier of Svyatoslav III of Kiev but it is just as likely that his home was Pereyaslavl in the Sula region or that he hailed from Kursk. He was evidently a keen sportsman with a fine knowledge of prairie fauna and flora and generally of the country from the Sein to the Azov Sea. It is possible that he took part in Igor's campaign or in some phase of it.

The justifications listed for Nabokov's choice of title (which is more a question of interpretation of the Old Russian than of translation into English) are most persuasive, and *The Song of Igor's Campaign* should replace the heretofore generally accepted *Lay of the Host of Igor*. The specific footnotes, readings, and the choices Nabokov makes from among previously disputed interpretations (Old Russian is *not* an easy language) constitute first-rate scholarship, and, equally important, the success of his translation and his articulated feeling for *The Song* as a work of art make the volume unique in the literature on the subject in any language.

Impressive as *The Song of Igor's Campaign* is though, it is a mere bauble in comparison with Nabokov's translation of and Commentary on Pushkin's *Eugene Onegin* in three thick volumes, the result of over seven years' labor, and thus, in size and time involved, the largest writing project in Nabokov's career. The *Eugene Onegin* was published in four volumes (the fourth is the Russian text and the index, itself of monograph length) by the Bollingen Foundation in 1964. In 1950 Véra Nabokov had casually suggested, in response to her husband's disgust at the rhymed paraphrases of *Onegin*, that he himself do a translation. Long before that Nabokov had tried his hand at a poetic translation of *Onegin*, and three stanzas from Chapter One appeared in the *Russian Review* in 1945. But Nabokov decided that an adequate verse translation was simply not possible, and, moreover, that the distortions of a verse translation would severely interfere with necessary commentaries.

Two essays on translating Pushkin were talked about and read much more widely than the Bollingen volumes themselves, and I begin my discussion of Nabokov's translation and Commentary with these articles. The first article — both appeared in *The New York Review of Books* — was by Nabokov attacking a poetic translation of *Onegin* by Walter Arndt that appeared shortly before Nabokov's own literal translation (April 30, 1964); the second (July 15, 1965) was an attack by Edmund Wilson on Nabokov's translation. Both articles provoked replies, counter-replies, letters, press commentary, and personal passions and loyalties. There are certain key questions having very little to do with Pushkin that should be commented on before we discuss Nabokov's translation and Commentary *per se*. The first thing to be said is that, in my opinion, Nabokov was wrong in attacking Arndt, or at least in attacking him in the way he did. One cannot but recognize and sympathize with a translator's natural vexation, after nearly a decade at work, at being confronted with another poetic translation. The vexation is compounded because there is evidence from the poetic versions he did print that Nabokov himself could have done the same thing slightly or even vastly better than Arndt did it. Be that as it may, Arndt did do the poetic version, and it is a remarkable achievement, recognized by the award of the Bollingen Prize for the best translation of poetry into English for that year.

There were numerous serious mistakes in the translation, and Nabokov dwelt on them at some length in his review; but these have been amended in a second printing so that now the main question — the poetic quality of the translation and the degree of liberty it takes — can be faced without side issues. There are many weak stanzas in the Arndt translation — and again, representative instances have been duly noted in Nabokov's article — but the translation as a whole stands high above the previous efforts, which are derided with perfect justice by Nabokov throughout the several hundred pages of his Commentary. In a note to his Commentary Nabokov wrote: "even worse than these is a new version, full of omissions and blunders, by Walter Arndt . . . which reached me after this Commentary was in press, and too late to be subjected to detailed comment." One simply cannot, ought not, say that the Arndt translation is *worse* than the other existing poetic translations.

Whereas Nabokov ought to have directed his fire at the desirability and feasibility of poetic translation, by detailed examination of a fairly or very successful example of the craft (depending on one's point of view), he instead attacked Arndt himself, with the result that the thrust of his basic argument was deflected. One had to feel either that Nabokov had not been very fair to Arndt or, judging by the article alone, that the Arndt translation was so obviously a bad translation that someone like Nabokov ought not to have wasted his time reviewing it. The point is that Nabokov could have granted at least some degree of merit in the Arndt translation and still made the same argument about the padding, strained rhymes, and so forth that must disfigure even a good poetic paraphrase. His comments would then have been both more effective and fairer to Arndt.

But the Arndt review was as nothing compared to the assault that Edmund Wilson mounted against Nabokov's translation. Answering Wilson some months later in *Encounter* (February, 1966), Nabokov wrote:

I am not sure that the necessity to defend my work from blunt jabs and incompetent blame would have been a sufficient incentive for me to discuss that article, had I not been moved to do so by the unusual, unbelievable, and highly entertaining opportunity that I am unexpectedly given by Mr. Wilson himself of refuting practically every item of criticism in his enormous piece . . . I am unaware of any other such instance in the history of literature. It is a polemicist's dream come true, and one must be a poor sportsman to disdain what it offers.

By this time recruits were being conscripted from all quarters. Robert Lowell, for example, was moved to write that "both common sense and intuition tell us that Edmund Wilson must be nine tenths unanswerable and right in his criticism of Nabokov."

What needs be said about the Nabokov-Wilson affair is that Nabokov is absolutely correct in his assertion that Wilson presented him with a polemicist's dream. Of all the comments by letter and article on the exchange, only four persons speaking with a knowledge of Pushkin in the original took Wilson's part: one of these diplomatically managed to praise both Wilson and Nabokov, another was a friend of Wilson's, and the other two were enemies of Nabokov — that is to say, no disinterested party took the part of Wilson. The most striking commentary on the whole affair came from a scholar of marked leftist sympathy who, on political and scholarly grounds, is no friend of Vladimir Nabokov's: is there, he asked, a serious literary journal in Europe that would have printed the Wilson piece as it was submitted?

Where Nabokov's Arndt review was initiated by genuine concern about Pushkin and translation and then somewhere along the way adopted the air of an *ad hominem* attack, Wilson's review seems (to me at any rate) to have begun in a spirit of highly personal challenge and then to have tried — unsuccessfully — to assume the form of disinterested, scholarly judgment. The "key" to Wilson's animus is found in the praise he gave in his opening paragraphs to Sartre's article on Nabokov! When Nabokov came to America Edmund Wilson showed him several kindnesses, and it was with the help of Wilson that *Bend Sinister* was published. But one notes an omission which is, I think, quite extraordinary: the man who is generally considered the dean of American criticism and whose life has been dedicated to bringing European culture to bear upon the American consciousness has scarcely written a word on the foremost writer of our times. Edmund Wilson has written about Nabokov twice: the first time was a review of his Gogol book which he praised as "one of the best volumes so far" in the Makers of Modern Literature series, but he ended his review with the incredible assertion that "in spite of some errors, Mr. Nabokov's mastery of English almost rivals Joseph Conrad's." And the second piece was his essay on the Pushkin translation. Beyond that Wilson has written a letter in praise of Nabokov to his publisher, a laudatory act but scarcely "criticism." Edmund Wilson stands by his own declaration apart from his age, and that intellectual remove is at once his virtue and his greatest weakness.

I wish to be fair. I do not want to suggest that Wilson's critical posture has been a consciously petty one. Wilson, I gather, does recognize that Nabokov is a great writer, but he simply has little empathy with *that sort of* (that is, "modern") greatness. This seems to be implicitly understood in Nabokov's remark made in passing in his first reply to Wilson's Pushkin piece: "I have always been grateful to him for the tact he showed in refraining from reviewing any of my novels." At the conclusion of his essay Wilson makes a few very general remarks about Nabokov's writing: "The principal theme of his work — from his early novel in Russian, *Mashenka,* to the English *Pnin, Lolita,* and *Pale Fire* — is the situation, comic and pathetic, full of embarrassment and misunderstanding, of the exile who cannot return." That generalization is absurd, but it must be excused because Edmund Wilson does not have a very extensive familiarity with Nabokov's writing. (A mutual acquaintance told me some years ago that he was astounded in discussing Nabokov with Wilson to learn that he had not even read *The Gift,* Nabokov's best Russian novel — it had not then been translated — and one of the few which was and still is easily obtainable in the Russian edition.) Wilson's statement that *The Real Life of Sebastian Knight* "still seems to me one of his best [novels]" is, of course, a perfect echo of Adamovich's praise of *The Exploit.*

It is to the great credit of Adamovich that, after Nabokov had become an English writer, he eventually re-evaluated the importance of Sirin's Russian *oeuvre,* and in his 1955 book of essays *Solitude and Freedom* selections from his writings on Nabokov are chosen in such a way as to exclude the niggling, carping tone that for so long characterized his writing on Nabokov, and to present instead a firm recognition of the fact that Nabokov is a major writer. This is no small change of opinion when one recalls how foolish Adamovich had been made to appear over the "Vasily Shishkov" poems. Edmund Wilson has been made to look equally foolish in the Pushkin controversy — at this writing this is apparent only to those who know Russian, but in time it will also be accepted even by those such as Robert Lowell and Robert Graves who leaped to Wilson's defense with no knowledge of Russian — and one wonders whether Wilson will be able, as Adamovich was, to arrive at a deeper and more careful view of Nabokov's art, whether or not his final judgment changes. I admire much that Wilson has written and, above all, his scope and reach. His main faults as a critic — his frequently strange taste, his superficial knowledge of the many languages and cultures about which he writes so authoritatively, and his tendency to oversimplify (a mirror image of the American academic's tendency to overcomplicate) — are the faults of the American intelligentsia writ large and thus present, often without many of his virtues, in almost all American critics, not excluding, I fear, this writer. Edmund Wilson has shown us directly what we must do and indirectly what we must not do. He is more and more frequently spoken of as "the American Sam Johnson," and there is some justice in this comparison. But, as regards Nabokov, Wilson has evidenced only the most frivolous side of his Johnsonian personality:

> Our perverse old писатель Vladimir
> Was stroking a butterfly's femur
> "I prefer this," he said
> "To a lady in bed,
> Or even a velvet-eyed lemur."

One hopes that this little limerick from *Night Thoughts* will not stand as Edmund Wilson's sole statement on the art of Vladimir Nabokov.

The indicative imbalance in Wilson's attack on Nabokov's Pushkin may be readily demonstrated graphically. Wilson's protracted essay was slightly over 165 column-inches long. Nabokov's translation is 345 pages long, while his commentaries in the two volumes are 1,087 pages in length. In other words, the translation is almost exactly *one-third* the length of the commentaries, and it is, moreover, made perfectly clear that the success of the translation is to depend in large part on the explication provided by the commentaries. Yet Wilson does not get around to the commentaries until the 115th of his 165 column-inches: "And now for the positive side. The commentary, if one skips the *longueurs,* does make very pleasant reading, and it represents an immense amount of labor . . ." And even in this conclusion Wilson wanders off into many other areas so that, finally, he devotes but ten per cent of his space to what is sixty-six per cent of Nabokov's work. What should have been appraised, for better or worse, at great length is passed off virtually in one sentence: "Nabokov has also studied exhaustively

Pushkin's relations with his Russian predecessors and contemporaries, and there is a good deal of excellent literary criticism."

There is only one item from the 1,087 pages of Commentary about which Wilson has anything to say, and it, too, is a derogation:

He underrates Pushkin's knowledge of English and quite disregards the evidence . . . Nabokov himself notes that Pushkin had English books in his library, but asserts that he could not read them. Of the most important evidence he says nothing at all. The volumes of Pushkin's notes and miscellaneous papers published by the Soviet government — *Tetradi Pushkina* and *Rukoyu Pushkina* [that must have been one of Mr. Wilson's *longueurs; Rukoyu Pushkina* is discussed — A.F.] — contain many extracts from English: passages of whole poems by Byron. Wordsworth, Coleridge, and Barry Cornwall, and a quotation from Francis Bacon. Mr. Nabokov does not seem to want to admit that Pushkin's competence in languages was considerable. These volumes contain passages, poems, and documents in French, German, Italian, Spanish, and Polish, and show that with Hebrew and Arabic he had at least got as far as the alphabets.

One would think that the very scope of that list of "copied-out" languages would give Mr. Wilson pause. In his *Encounter* reply Nabokov pointed out that the matter had been documented in one of his footnotes, which Wilson evidently also did not read, listing the many grotesque English misspellings of the name Childe Harold that Pushkin made. There is ample evidence, had Nabokov wished to go into the matter at greater length, that Pushkin's knowledge of English was certainly not anything more than very superficial. The only meaningful evidence in such a matter would be personal reminiscences of Englishmen who spoke with Pushkin in English (there are none), comments on works that Pushkin could have read only in English (there are none), and the active uses to which he put English in his writing. When one examines the twenty-volume Academy edition of Pushkin for its English phrases and expressions, the picture one gets of Pushkin's knowledge of English is quite amusing. Two examples will suffice. In its first appearance in print, Pushkin's play ("translated" from the non-existent English writer Chenston) had as its title in English *The caveteous Knigth*. (In manuscript it was "cuvetous.") Pushkin's other "English play," adapted from a work by the real eighteenth-century English author Wilson — I am sorry for the irony here — had as its English title — in the manuscript — *The city of the plaque*. As the form of the title shows, Pushkin worked from a French translation, and Nabokov's Commentary establishes this fact beyond any doubt. In addition to the misspellings, one should note the way Pushkin had of capitalizing English words, sometimes in the German manner and at other times in the French way. No further comment, I trust, need be made on Pushkin's knowledge of English or Wilson's authority to challenge Nabokov as a Pushkinist (every point he makes falls down in precisely the same manner). But above all, there is of course the unfortunate way in which two fine translations, a colossal work of scholarship, and poor Pushkin, too, have been buried beneath a mountain of polemicizing. I have devoted so much space to the whole business in the hope that it may be reduced hereafter (reviewers please take note) to its true importance, which, as regards Nabokov's artistic and scholarly career, is that of a turbulent footnote.

Nabokov's literal translation of *Onegin* does maintain the iambic meter, although he has since written that he would now ruthlessly expunge even that concession. It has an ascetic beauty and strength, and its faithfulness to what Pushkin actually said is both reassuring and refreshing to the Western reader, which means all of us who have read *Eugene Onegin* in Russian many times but without quite — often we did not even realize it — understanding certain lines and passages properly and fully. I cannot speak for the larger body of readers who have no direct knowledge of *Eugene Onegin*. However, several critics who do not read Russian but whose sensitivity to English usage I trust — John Updike and Conrad Brenner, for instance — have spoken of the translation with real enthusiasm and warmth, and so I take it that the translation is exceptionally effective, for those at least who do not get overly exercised beforehand at the thought that they are about to read a "pony." John Updike has written of it: "The translation itself, so laconic compared to the footnotes, with its breathtaking, pages-long, omitted stanzas whose lines are eerily numbered as if they were there, ranks with Horace Gregory's *Catullus* and Richard Lattimore's *Iliad* as superb, quirky, and definitive: a permanent

contribution to the demi-art of 'Englishing' and a final refutation,
let's hope, of the fallacy of equivalent rhyme." Actually, Nabokov's remarks in his Foreword to the translation make it quite
evident that the translation is meant primarily for those with a non-
native command of Russian: "In fact, to my ideal of literalism I
sacrificed everything (elegance, euphony, clarity, good taste, modern usage, and even grammar) that the dainty mimic prizes higher
than truth. Pushkin has likened translators to horses changed at the
posthouses of civilization. The greatest reward I can think of is that
students may use my work as a pony." With that goal stated and
attained, the "others" who derive benefit and pleasure from the
translation are an incidental gain.

In his discussion of the paraphrastic, lexical, and literal methods
of translation Nabokov gives examples of how the opening lines
might be rendered. First, perfectly lexically:

> *My uncle [is] of most honest rules[:]*
> *when not in jest [he] has been taken ill,*
> *he to respect him has forced [one],*
> *and better invent could not.*

Then, as a paraphrase:

> *My uncle, in the best tradition,*
> *By falling dangerously sick*
> *Won universal recognition*
> *And could devise no better trick.*

Finally, the preferred way, literally:

> *My uncle has most honest principles:*
> *when he was taken gravely ill,*
> *he forced one to respect him*
> *and nothing better could invent.*

To these I add Arndt's paraphrase:

> *Now that he is in grave condition,*
> *My uncle, decorous old prune,*
> *Has earned himself my recognition;*
> *What could have been more opportune?*

Nabokov's paraphrase is closer than Arndt's, but the difference between them is not that drastic, and Arndt's fourth line really is quite good. (Compare both these paraphrases with the same passage as done to death by Babette Deutsch:

> *My uncle's shown his good intentions*
> *By falling desperately ill;*
> *His worth is proved; of all inventions*
> *Where will you find one better still?*)

But why should either the Nabokov or the Arndt paraphrase be considered inferior — and they are — to Nabokov's literal translation?

The answer is to be found in the footnotes. Arndt's brief note to the first line in the Russian (the second line in his translation) informs us that "the original here alludes neatly but untranslatably to the well-known introductory line of one of Ivan Krylov's fables: 'An ass of most respectable convictions'." The information is concisely if sparsely given, but there is a painful "bump" in crossing from "decorous old prune" to the Krylovian echo in Pushkin's line. Nabokov's literal translation, in contrast, crosses smoothly over into an incredibly cool and verdant garden of information, poetry, and culture:

This is not a very auspicious beginning from the translator's point of view, and a few factual matters have to be brought to the reader's attention before we proceed. In 1823 Pushkin had no rivals in the camp of the Moderns (there is a tremendous gap between him and, say, Zhukovsky, Batyushkov, and Baratynsky, a group of minor poets endowed with more or less equal talent, insensibly grading into the next category, the frankly second-rate group of Vyazemsky, Kozlov, Yazykov, etc.); but c. 1820 he did have at least one in the camp of the Ancients: this was Ivan Krylov (1769–1844), the great fabulist.

In a very curious piece of prose . . . an "imagined conversation" between the author and the tsar (Alexander I, r. 1801–25), jotted down by our poet in the winter of 1824, during his enforced seclusion at Mikhailovskoe (Aug. 9, 1824, to Sept. 4, 1826), there occurs the phrase, spoken by the author: "*Onegin* Chapter One is being printed. I shall have the honor of sending two copies to Ivan Krylov for your Majesty's library" (since 1810 Krylov had been holding a sinecure at the public library of St. Petersburg). The opening line of EO is (as is known, I notice, to Russian commentators) an echo of 1.4 of Krylov's fable *The Ass and the Boor* . . . written in 1818 and published in 1819 . . . Pushkin, early in 1819, in Petersburg, had heard the portly poet recite it himself, with prodigious humor and gusto, at the house of Aleksei Olenin (1763–1844), the well-known patron of the arts. At this memorable party, complete with parlor games, twenty-year-old Push-kin hardly noticed Olenin's daughter Annette (1808–88), whom he was to court so passionately, and so unfortunately, in 1828 . . . but did notice Mrs. Olenin's niece, Anna Kern (Cairn), née Poltoratsky (1800–79), to whom at a second meeting (in the Pskovan countryside July, 1825) he was to dedicate the famous short poem beginning, "I recollect a wondrous moment," which he presented to her enclosed in an uncut copy of the separate edition of Chapter One of EO . . . in exchange for a sprig of heliotrope from her bosom.

Line 4 of Krylov's fable goes: "The donkey had most honest principles"; grammatically, "the donkey was a creature of most honest [honorable] rules." When told by the countryman to patrol the vegetable garden, he did not touch a cabbage leaf; indeed, he galloped about so vigilantly that he ruined the whole place, for which he was cudgeled by its owner: asininity should not accept grave tasks, but he errs, too, who gives an ass a watchman's job.

I have quoted the first footnote in its entirety, because one must see in its fullness the way in which the translation moves and lives. To refer to this sort of commentary in the way that Walter Arndt did (he was not without fault in the exchange) as "goading [*the reader*], with 'ardent stir' and 'in the blossom of glad hopes,' up a pyramid of footnotes every bumpy line or two, throughout a multi-volume trek [*without*] an inkling of the poetic impact which a verse translation, diluted and flawed as it must often be, can at least intermittently convey" is absurd. And it is no less absurd to suggest, as some who have obviously only leafed through the Commentary do, that there is something "Kinbotean" about them. They are rich with scholarship, and yet they move gracefully and intricately over a thousand-page expanse in just the manner of the cited note. Who is the closer to Pushkin's magic, the reader who has read Arndt's rhymed line and the two-line footnote to it or the one who has followed Nabokov's path? My own answer is clear — without in the least renouncing the excellence of Arndt's para-phrase — but the problem is not solved, for who else is going to be able to do this sort of thing? Over fifty years ago the great Russian Acmeist poet and Greek scholar Innokenty Annensky did something roughly analogous to what Nabokov has done when he translated Euripides in three volumes with copious notes and essays. It will probably be another half-century before a third feat of this sort is accomplished in any language by someone who is not merely an outstanding scholar, but also a great writer or poet. Are we to have no translations at all? Literal translations with just as many mistakes as the current rhymed versions and no compensating semblance of life? Even very bad translations can have happy issue, as Nabokov demonstrates conclusively in Pushkin's reliance on bad French translations. The literal translation and commentary raise a standard that had been all but forgotten, and, if there do not exist people sufficiently gifted and eager to do such work, that standard should at least help to raise the demands which we make upon our paraphrasts.

A good means of appreciating still more the beauty of the footnotes is to cite the best previous line-by-line Commentary on *Onegin* (and Nabokov is properly contemptuous of it) by N. L. Brodsky published in 1932. On that same opening line Brodsky says only:

An ironic adaptation of a line from Krylov's fable *The Ass and the Boor* (1819): "The donkey had most honest principles." A. P. Kern relates that Pushkin was present in 1819 in the home of the Olenins (in Petersburg) at an evening when I. A. Krylov read this fable (*Reminiscences of A. P. Markova-Vinogradskaya-Kern* in the collection of L. Maikov *Pushkin*, 1890, p. 235). There is an echo of Pushkin's line in the long poem Sashka by A. Polezhaev and in the long poem by the contemporary [Soviet] poet Vladimir Kirillov *On Childhood, the Sea, and the Red Standard*.

One may overlook — in view of the time at which Brodsky's book was published — the last slightly grotesque comparison and other similar moments throughout his book, but one is still struck by the enormous distance between Brodsky's compilation of "pertinent facts" and Pushkin's poem; even though Brodsky's book is written in Russian, it does not begin to have the proximity to Pushkin's poetry and world and the critical intelligence that Nabokov's has and which alone allows a commentary to stand at ease beside a poem such as *Eugene Onegin*.

Nabokov begins with introductory essays describing the text of *Onegin*, the *Onegin* stanza, the structure of the novel in verse, the history of the novel's appearance in print, its genesis, and Pushkin's epistolary references to *Onegin*. These essays, some of them dealing with quite technical matters, enable an attentive reader within a space of sixty pages to be fully "ready for" *Eugene Onegin*. They are, besides, tremendously amusing and lively. Here is a quotation from a Pushkin letter: "The obstacle is censorship, and this to me is no joking matter, for it is the question of my future fate, of the independence I need. In order to publish *Onegin* I am ready to . . . [my prudish Soviet sources expurgate an obscene phrase and a lewd proverb, which I cannot reconstruct exactly]. Anyway, I am ready to hang myself."

The question of precisely what languages Pushkin knew — which Wilson attempted to challenge Nabokov on — is actually of great importance in understanding *Eugene Onegin*. The notion that even Russians may not be adequately prepared to read Pushkin's masterpiece is an interesting or insulting one (depending upon whether one happens to be a Russian), but that is precisely what Nabokov demonstrates in an overwhelmingly convincing manner. For Pushkin did have a mastery of eighteenth-century French, and he was widely read in French literature even of the distinctly second-rate sort, and, as shown by the Russian spellings he gives names, he was almost wholly dependent upon French translations. Russian readers and Russian Pushkinists, too, have simply not had the French or the necessary knowledge of French literature of that time to deal adequately with this. As Nabokov describes *Onegin* in his introductory material:

Pushkin's composition is first of all and above all a phenomenon of style, and it is from this flowered rim that I have surveyed its sweep of Arcadian country, the serpentine gleam of its imported brooks, the miniature blizzards imprisoned in round crystal, and the many-hued levels of literary parody blending in the melting distance. It is not "a picture of Russian life"; it is at best the picture of a little group of Russians, in the second decade of the last century, crossed with all the more obvious characters of Western European romance and placed in a stylized Russia, which would disintegrate at once if the French props were removed and if the French impersonators of English and German writers stopped prompting the Russian-speaking heroes and heroines. The paradoxical part, from a translator's point of view, is that the only Russian element of importance is this speech, Pushkin's language, undulating and flashing through verse melodies the likes of which had never been known before in Russia.

Nabokov has gone deeper and farther into the secondary and tertiary materials which were either definitely or probably used by Pushkin than anyone before, and this is perhaps the greatest achievement of his Commentary, entitling him to stand beside the world's foremost Pushkinists, such as Boris Tomashevsky (whose opinions and scholarship are respected and used by Nabokov), Zhirmunsky (the absence of any mention of or commentary on his important 1924 book *Byron and Pushkin* is one of the very few puzzling lapses in Nabokov's work), Bondi, and Oksman. The only real efforts to plumb the French sources of Pushkin before Nabokov were modest and very tentative studies by Tomashevsky (in *A Pushkin Collection*, 1923) and Mansuy (in *Revue Bleue*, August, 1904). Tomashevsky concluded his *Pushkin — Reader of French Poets* with the assertion that French poetry was the measure against which Pushkin's poetry should be seen, but he was careful to state that his own statements on the subject were only hypotheses since an enormous amount of scholarship on thematic, lexical, stylistic, and compositional questions would have to be done before the matter could be satisfactorily resolved. After this, the question lapsed into abeyance, and although Tomashevsky did treat the theme with some thoroughness in a broader historical framework in his 1960 book *Pushkin and France*, Gallicisms in Pushkin's literary language and the question of French influences in *Eugene Onegin* remained untouched until Nabokov.

Nabokov has followed down so many French sources that to attempt to "review" his findings would be almost like trying to review a small-town telephone book, which indeed is what the index to Nabokov's *Eugene Onegin* is like. Yet the names and textual comparisons are always germane, never "dropped," and in the context in which they occur, never dry or dull. In just two pages Nabokov deftly and firmly traces the probable origins of

Pushkin's variant on the sonnet form in La Fontaine (and his popularity in Russia), Molière, and Malherbe. Frequently the comparisons with French writers are mere juxtapositions which enable the reader to see for the first time how much in the broad stream of French intellectual life and French art Pushkin really was. The ability to have found the hundreds of pertinent analogies, comparing, for example, two stanzas in Chapter Seven of *Onegin* with passages from Chateaubriand and Senancour, bespeaks not only a thorough knowledge of French literature, but also virtually total recall of what he has read. Even more important and subtle is the work Nabokov has done on Gallic influences in Pushkin's phrases and epithets. Thus, we learn that the line "having forgot the somber scapegrace" is close to the French *ténébreux* and derived from the type of *le beau ténébreux* (Amadis de Gaul) which was a fashionable term and model for young men in the late 1820's. We learn not only that "to a change of places" is a Gallicism, but also that the same Gallicism (*changement de lieu*) may be found in the play *Woe from Wit* by Pushkin's great contemporary Griboedov. And so it goes, through hundreds of pages. Pushkin's comments on writers he could not read in the original are traced back unerringly to the wretched French translation he read (giving a wildly distorted picture, for example, of Homer) or to the better translation and fashionable French literary sentiment which, for instance, caused Pushkin to rate Maturin's *Melmoth the Wanderer* higher than it deserves.

Also of enormous importance is the knowledge that Nabokov has of the specific weight of every Russian word during the period in which Pushkin wrote. Pushkin was a Russian poet of French inclination, and he was, in addition to that, a poet with one foot firmly in the Russian language of the eighteenth century. What this means is that much of Pushkin's poetic language had a faintly archaic air *at the time he wrote*. For modern readers of Pushkin, this quality of the language in which the great poet wrote has been, except for the most obvious archaisms, quite lost, and Pushkin's Russian has been accepted as the melodious and most pellucid of the time. Nabokov is able to spot the rich leather bindings on certain of Pushkin's words and phrases, and in his translation these are rendered by comparably obscure or archaic words, even to the extent of reproducing the weak line and unsuccessful word that occurs from time to time. This is in large degree the explanation for the many unusual words sprinkled throughout the translation that so astounded and disturbed Edmund Wilson, who wrote in answer to Nabokov's *Encounter* reply:

It is unfortunate — though not perhaps for Mr. Nabokov — that the readers of *Encounter* may not have seen my original article or the correspondence which followed it. A considerable part of the letter to *Encounter* has already appeared in the *New York Review*, and I have dealt there[!] with the questions it raises. I don't propose to recapitulate here . . . I do not, of course, object to the use of unusual words . . . But such words as those I cited in my review of the Nabokov *Onegin* make Pushkin appear grotesque, as he never is.

Nabokov's translation is never grotesque, and Pushkin's language was not "clear and simple." Pushkin made a polished and elegant monument out of the rough stuff of the Russian literary language of the eighteenth century, and the illusion of simplicity came later as Pushkin's fame and the distance in time grew. And again, all of this is fully documented with specific irrefutable examples in the commentaries. Nabokov responded to Wilson's criticism of his lexicon by saying:

Mr. Wilson can hardly be unaware that once a writer chooses to youthen or resurrect a word, it lives again, sobs again, stumbles all over the cemetery in doublet and trunk hose, and will keep annoying stodgy grave-diggers as long as that writer's book endures. In several instances, English archaisms have been used in my EO not merely to match Russian antiquated words but to revive a nuance of meaning present in the ordinary Russian term but lost in the English one . . . Some are mere signal-words whose only purpose is to suggest or indicate that a certain pet term of Pushkin's has occurred at that point. Others have been chosen for their Gallic touch implicit in this or that Russian attempt to imitate a French turn of phrase. All have pedigrees of agony and rejection and re-instatement, and should be treated as convalescents and ancient orphans, and not hooted at as imposters by a critic who says he admires some of my books.

Nabokov's wrestling with the English language in the process of doing his translation is, in fact, an echo and faithful reflection of the task Pushkin had in creating the Russian literary language in his poem.

Edmund Wilson's original attack concluded with a condescending psychoanalysis of alleged "inner needs" that caused Nabokov's work to take the form that it did: "Nabokov . . . is torn between the culture he has left behind and that to which he is trying to adapt himself . . . There is a drama in his *Evgeni Onegin* which is not Onegin's drama. It is the drama of Nabokov himself trying to correlate his English and Russian sides." There is drama in Nabokov's *Eugene Onegin*, but it is drama of quite a different sort. First, the drama of the full and essential restoration of the ties Pushkin had to French culture (paralleling the triple culture of Nabokov and proving that the label of "émigré" is just begging the question). And second, the drama tracing Pushkin's language and literary sources and analogues back into the Russian eighteenth century (this is somewhat similar to what Bitsilli, on a much smaller scale, did with Saltykov-Shchedrin and Sirin) thereby making much more specific the "Russianness" in his work. There is no more imposing work of scholarship on Pushkin in any language, and, long before the novels of Sirin and Nabokov are recognized in the Soviet Union, Soviet Pushkinology must come to terms with Nabokov's *Onegin*.

If there is anything which may be seriously questioned in the *Eugene Onegin* it is the two appendices, one on comparative prosody and the other on Pushkin's great-grandfather, Gannibal. In consulting an Ethiopian scholar on the attempt at historical reconstruction, I was told that the work stands and is a truly remarkable achievement for someone who is not himself Ethiopian and a professional student of that culture, but that there are certain minor faults that need to be corrected (for example, Ethiopians historically were and in fact still are often named after the towns in which they were born). The Notes on Prosody may be faulted for Nabokov's heavy reliance on the method of Andrei Bely who first made diagrammatic studies of half-stresses in Russian poetry to the total exclusion of fifty years of subsequent study of Russian versification, at least a minute portion of which ought to have been consulted. In a sense Notes on Prosody is written *ab ovo*, for

Nabokov writes of Bely: "When I was still a boy, I was greatly fascinated by Beli's admirable work, but have not consulted it since I last read it in 1919." In contrast to the Commentary, the prosody notes require a great deal of hard concentration from the reader. The notion of the scud does not seem to me either objectionable or difficult in itself, but the complexity with which it is applied and analyzed will perhaps be forbidding to some readers. The most fascinating aspect of the work for this reader is the way in which Nabokov crosses back and forth effortlessly between Russian and English verse (how many Englishmen, I wonder, can match his knowledge of poets such as John Dyer, Matthew Prior, and William Morris), dropping many intriguing literary judgments on the way.

As Pushkin's great contemporary, Gogol, stands in another world from the great poet, so Nabokov's *Nikolai Gogol* is quite a different sort of study than the *Eugene Onegin*. In the *Onegin*, Nabokov referred to it as a "frivolous book," which it is, of course, but I will not tolerate any attempt on Nabokov's part to read it out of his works. It is a joyful romp, half criticism and half artistic prose, essential to an understanding of both Gogol and of Nabokov. Beginning with Gogol's death, moving through numerous related diversions having to do with Gogolian themes or points about literature in general, ending with an imaginary conversation with his publisher in which the plots of various Gogol works are spelled out for the first time, *Nikolai Gogol* is one of the five or six existing examples of narrative criticism. And it is criticism most assuredly, for most of the things Nabokov says so gaily stand, with a slight change of voice and a slightly more restrained manner, as valid critical statements about Gogol's art. Gogol himself is taken to be the shadow of his books, and the biographical portrait which Nabokov gives of him is very close in many ways to the biography of Chernyshevsky. Gogol's fantastic art and his extraordinary literary non-characters are given firm (Nabokovian) substance, while the pathetic Gogol himself is made to emerge as a Gogolian character: "He was a weakling, a trembling mouse of a boy, with dirty hands and greasy locks, and pus trickling out of his ear. He gorged himself with sticky sweets. His schoolmates avoided touching the books he had been using." *Nikolai Gogol* is the first book which I would give to someone who knows no Nabokov. It is a fine — though admittedly iconoclastic — study of the essence of Gogol's literary genius, and because it is a wildly funny book of a truly Rabelaisian sort, it is eminently suited to prepare the reader for the slightly more conservative atmosphere of Nabokov's art.

Nabokov has from time to time indulged himself in historical fantasies of the "what if" sort. There is one that has frequently occurred to me as I write this book: what if Nabokov had written his *Nikolai Gogol* not in 1944, but in 1844? Would that more properly be the subject for a tale by Gogol or by Nabokov?

Ten

PERIODS in a writer's art should be determined first by the passage from "immaturity" or "apprenticeship" to "maturity." Sometimes this may be indicated quite simply on a calendar — Dostoevsky's return from Siberian exile — or in a name — Chekhonte to Chekhov. The first division is not at all clear in the case of Nabokov, however, and a plausible argument could be advanced for designating any year in the period between 1926 and 1932; Nabokov himself speaks of 1929, and since this is the year of *The Defense* and *The Potato Elf*, followed some months later by *The Eye*, 1929 probably is as good a year as any to speak of the "second period" in Nabokov's art. The later change from Sirin to Nabokov and from Russian to English, however, is a false division, a mere crease or ridge in a larger expanse. The second division that may be made in the mature writer's work — and in most cases none at all is required — depends upon questions of theme and structure. It is impossible to speak of a division in the art of Nabokov separating *Invitation to a Beheading* and *Bend Sinister* or *The Gift* and *The Real Life of Sebastian Knight.*

The "third period" in Nabokov's artistic career should be marked from about 1949 — two years after *Bend Sinister* — the time at which *Lolita* first began to assert itself as a novel in his imagination. *Lolita*, *Pnin*, and *Pale Fire* are novels which are in many ways wholly new departures, having only thematic similarities — it would be strange indeed if they did not — with previous finished Nabokov works. *Pnin* stands quite alone, and the pairing that one mentally makes of it with *Mashenka* is simply a matter of "tone." It is true that both *Lolita* and *Pale Fire* have their seeds in previous Russian works, but these works were, in the one case, unpublished and, in the other, uncompleted. And, as they finally emerged, they each acquired both a new country — America — and a new narrative form and scope. The first attempt that was later to become *Lolita* is well known from Nabokov's own Afterword to the novel, "On a Book Entitled *Lolita*," in which he speaks of and hastily sketches the 1939 short story that he was dissatisfied with and hence did not print, which gradually grew "the claws and wings of a novel." Quite unknown to his non-Russian readers, however, is the unfinished novel out of which *Pale Fire* grew.

This incomplete novel is *Solus Rex*. The first portion appeared in what was to be the last number (70) of *Contemporary Annals* in 1940, but with the journal's demise as France fell and Nabokov's transfer to America the continuation of the novel was abandoned. A second portion, under the title *Ultima Thule* — also written in France in 1939 — appeared in the American *Novy Zhurnal* (New *Review*) in 1942. (I include *Ultima Thule* in this discussion of *Solus Rex* — referring to it hereafter as the "second part" — because Nabokov himself confirmed *Ultima Thule* as part of *Solus Rex* in the 1963 German bibliography published by Rowohlt.) But Nabokov put aside this most complex undertaking while he set to the business of making himself as capable and accomplished a writer in English as he was in Russian. This novel remained and grew in Nabokov's mind over the years and this, together with the "Zoorlandian motifs" going back to 1931, gives *Pale Fire* a tacit seniority over *Lolita*, though chronologically of course it is seven years its junior.

Solus Rex cannot be profitably discussed in and of itself, but it provides a most instructive "commentary" when placed in juxtaposition to *Pale Fire* — even though the connection between the two parts of *Solus Rex* is as tenuous as that between John Shade's poem and Kinbote's Commentary in *Pale Fire*. *Solus Rex* and *Pale Fire* — and this cannot be stressed too strongly — do not coincide in specific characters or narrative structure; but the more subtle coincidences of theme and aesthetic logistics are so striking that one cannot help but see the strong link or, as Nabokov put it, "family relationship" between the two works. Indeed, there are sufficient grounds to suppose, on the basis of the two extant portions, that had it been completed, *Solus Rex* would have taken a form almost as unorthodox as *Pale Fire*'s. *Solus Rex* provides the happy service, even in its fragmentary state (72 printed pages in all), of openly treating certain themes that are central to both *Solus Rex* and *Pale Fire* but are partially hidden and refracted in the completed novel.

The first portion of *Solus Rex* is, as it were, the glorious saga of Zembla that *Pale Fire*'s Charles Kinbote (Botkin, Charles the Beloved, deposed ruler of that magical and unfortunate land) so wanted the poet Shade to write. The country — it is an island kingdom — and the language are not specifically named in *Solus Rex*, but reference is made to the disastrous political upheavals which have taken place there, and the language is beyond any doubt a non-identical twin of the Zemblan of *Pale Fire*, composed of a mixture of North Germanic and Slavic elements and vowel alterations common to the development of these two languages in the Middle Ages. Thus in *Solus Rex* the poetic lines "*sweet and opaque was the wave of the sea, and little girls drank from seashells*" are "*Solg ud digh vor je sage vel, ud jem gotelm quolm osje musikel*"; and the Zemblan lines "*Id wodo bin, war id lev lan, Indran iz lil ut roz nitran*" are Charles Kinbote's rendering of "*Had it lived long it would have been / Lilies without, roses within.*"

There are three kings in *Solus Rex*, and one, named Kr, rules as the result of a long court intrigue to do away with the depraved Prince Adolf, whose father, the previous ruler King Gafon, suffered from "quiet madness." There is no indication as to what happened to King Gafon, nor as to whether Adolf (or, in the first portion, Adulf) actually ascended the throne; we know only, from a reference to "poor Adolf" in the second portion, that the prince was not murdered, but escaped into exile instead. The king who is most fully described in *Solus Rex* is Kr, but it is obviously Prince (or King) Adulf who corresponds most closely to Charles the Beloved, "the self-banished king" of Zembla. And this similarity between Adulf and Charles leads to consideration of a most interesting and likely possibility about King Charles the Beloved's accounts of Zembla and Zemblan history.

Charles Kinbote is a madman. The general assumption that has been made about the kingdom is that it is but a figment of Kinbote's deranged imagination. But if one judges by the story of Prince Adulf and by the character of Kinbote, it becomes quite possible that Zembla both "actually exists" (which, in a work of fiction, it may so do — just as Ramsdale, New Wye, or any suchlike place exists) and, further, it exists in a consciously made-over version in the mad Kinbote's mind. There is therefore every likelihood that the reign and flight of Charles the Beloved did not occur precisely as he relates them: when Kinbote speaks, it is necessary for the reader to exercise care similar to that required with the narration of Hermann Karlovich in *Despair*. In this reader's judgment there are indeed two Zemblas — the thing itself and the tale as told — but they mirror each other's different insubstantialities, much as the "real" life of John Shade (which we cannot know) mirrors the artistic description of it in the poem *Pale Fire*.

When Kr, then a university student, first meets his cousin Adulf, the Prince — a frank and somewhat indolent lecher and pervert — good-naturedly justifies his behavior to Kr by saying:

Well, rumor is the poetry of truth. You're still a boy — and a rather handsome boy at that — and so there's much you don't understand now. I'll simply tell you one thing: all people really are depraved, but when the depravity occurs on the sly, when you hurriedly gobble up your jam in a dark corner till you are sick, or entrust your imagination with God knows what jobs — oh, that doesn't count, that isn't considered a crime; but when a man frankly and diligently satisfies the desire enforced by his demanding body — then people begin to trumpet about debauchery! And more than that: if in my case this legitimate satisfaction was reduced to one and the same monotonous device, public opinion would put up with this — I would at most have been rebuked for changing mistresses too often.

Kr's exposure to the Prince's unchecked perversion is part of a carefully prefigured plan by certain court figures to draw him into the circle of the revolutionary Humm and, without his knowledge of what is happening, establish him as king in Adulf's place. One part of the elaborate plot is the staging of a mock "mirror-like" trial in which an innocent and pure scholar, Dr. Onze, willingly lets himself be condemned for immoral acts which precisely duplicate those of Adulf, who cannot, of course, himself be brought to trial. The Prince seems not to notice the political parody, in spite of the fact that it is executed with the greatest precision, or, if he does, he gives no sign of it — his only reaction being vexation at not having been invited to take part in Dr. Onze's orgies: *"Que de plaisirs perdus!"* Onze is convicted, with the general approval of the press and the public at large, but old King Gafon, the nominal ruler, who understands what the trial is about and is as disturbed at his son's behavior as he is powerless to do anything about it, unexpectedly pardons the old scholar. The truly extraordinary and unexpected aspect of the whole trial is the attitude of the public toward Prince Adulf. Quite unexpectedly for the conspirators, the trial not only fails to bring Adulf into public disfavor, but even serves greatly to heighten his popularity, since the trial is erroneously seen by the masses as a delightful public spectacle proceeding with the gracious tacit consent of the good young prince. One should be careful then: as doubtful as his story is in other respects, Kinbote's sobriquet "Charles the Beloved" may not be fantasy.

Whatever speculations the story of Adulf gives rise to, however, evidence from *Solus Rex* can have no clearcut probative value in regard to *Pale Fire*. Charles Kinbote is the reader's sole source of information about Zembla, and we are ultimately left in the same position in which we found ourselves with Hermann Karlovich in *Despair*, unsure which, if any, of the many stories taking place represents the "true" version. The palace intrigue of which Kinbote tells in his Commentary ("A palace intrigue is a spectral spider that entangles you more nastily at every desperate jerk you try") is an attempt to make him renounce the delights of sodomy. His pederasty is the most outstanding characteristic he holds in common with Prince Adulf. This new information culled from *Solus Rex* ought not to be used to "unlock" *Pale Fire*, for what is not found between the covers of a novel does not exist as far as that novel is concerned. But the probability of "another Zembla" hidden behind Kinbote's arabesque account seems most helpful in reading the Commentary, even though that "real Zembla" can never be substantiated. The title that Kinbote wanted John Shade to use for his poem is *Solus Rex!*

The second portion of *Solus Rex* is set in France and concerns an entirely different cast of characters. It has only a few tendrils connecting it with the first part. The most important of these is the artist Sineusov, who is mentioned in passing in the first part, and is the narrator and protagonist of the second. Sineusov's wife has just died, and the chapter is in the form of a "letter" by the artist to his wife beyond the grave. There are two significant incidents related by Sineusov; one is told at great length and occupies the greater part of the chapter, while the other is a brief reference to something that happened while his wife was still alive. These incidents from *Solus Rex* throw strong light on the action of *Pale Fire*.

The first incident concerns Sineusov's art. During the period in which his wife was dying, Sineusov turned to the consolation of his art to ease the burden of pain. He is approached by a mysterious foreign poet who commissions him to do a series of illustrations to a long poem that he has written:

You remember, don't you, that strange Swede or Dane, or Icelander, the devil knows what he was, anyway, that lanky blond chap tanned an orange hue with the eyelashes of an old horse who introduced himself to me as a "well-known writer" and commissioned me for a fee, which delighted you (by that time you weren't getting out of bed and you couldn't speak, but you would write me amusing things with colored chalk on your little slate, such as how you most of all in life love "poems, wild flowers, and foreign money"), commissioned me, as I was saying, to do a series of illustrations to his long poem *Ultima Thule* which he had just finished writing in his own language. There was no possibility of my becoming intimately acquainted with his manuscript, of course, since French, the language in which we tortuously conversed, was known to him mainly by hearsay, and he was unable to convey his symbols to me. I was able to grasp only that his hero was some sort of northern king, unfortunate and unsociable; that in his kingdom, in the mist of the sea, on a melancholy and remote island, some political intrigues develop, murders, revolts, and a gray horse flies riderless over the heather in the mist. He was satisfied with my first *blanc et noir*, and we settled the subjects of the remaining drawings. But since he didn't come back the next week as he promised,

I phoned him at his hotel and learned that he had departed for America.

Nonetheless, even with his commission gone, Sineusov continues to work on his illustrations, and the island kingdom becomes a symbol of the grief he feels for his dying wife and "a sort of fatherland of my least expressible thoughts." (*Ultima Thule* — a term which was used by the ancients for the most remote and northernmost region, later became also a generalized abstract term for the farthest attainable point or degree, and hence it may serve as an approximate equivalent of both Zembla — "a distant northern land" — and its capital Onhava, which is Eskimo for "far-off place.")

This passage from *Solus Rex* is at once suggestive and perplexing, much like the stone fragment with an inscription in a completely unknown tongue which the archaeologist, to his chagrin, discovers can be decoded perfectly to mean two quite different things. On the one hand, there is the possibility that John Shade's long poem *Pale Fire* really belongs to the pen of the mad scholar Kinbote — in which case Kinbote's Commentary must be taken as — and, in fact, is (as I shall shortly show) — an integral "part" of the poem. On the other hand, Charles Kinbote and his Zembla might just as well belong to the pen of John Shade who has "taken" Kinbote from life and put him to his own artistic use, just as the artist Sineusov has appropriated a theme from a foreign stranger he barely knows. The connection between Shade and Kinbote and the primacy of Shade over Kinbote similarly demand some artistic fingerprint which is present in both poem and Commentary. It is helpful here to think of Picasso's *Mother* and *Guernica* or, for that matter, Nabokov's *A University Poem* and *Invitation to a Beheading* to realize that single authorship cannot always be determined by means of surface form.

The primary task then, before fixing upon either Shade or Kinbote as controlling author, is to establish the existence of a single shared thematic bond that will allow one to speak of *Pale Fire* as having the essential structural unity to be in fact the "monstrous semblance of a novel" that Charles Kinbote assures us he is seeking to avoid. The poem of John Shade has already been examined, and its central concern, as we have seen, is death. The Commentary of Charles Kinbote cannot be taken by itself in quite the same way as John Shade's poem, but it does seem to me that most of the critics of *Pale Fire*, while allowing the madness of the enterprise, have not in practice questioned the basic assumption that it is in some degree a commentary. The "pure" notes are almost all absurdities of either misinformation or wholly unnecessary information, such as the information given to Line 85 ("Who'd seen the Pope"): "Pius X, Giuseppe Melchiorre Sarto, 1835–1914; Pope 1903–1914." Nabokov told one interviewer that Kinbote's remarks on matters such as flora and fauna are all ludicrously inept, which is only, after all, commensurate with the quality of his remarks on literature (Kinbote's spelling of the title of Joyce's novel is *"Finnigan's Wake"*). The only portions of Kinbote's Commentary that fulfill his declared intention are those conveying essential information without his knowing it. Nabokov has declared that Kinbote does *not* know the source of John Shade's title for his poem, even though allusions to *Timon of Athens* are peppered throughout the Commentary. Kinbote at one point even goes to the trouble of Englishing a "Zemblan translation" of the relevant passage:

> *The sun is a thief: she lures the sea*
> *and robs it. The moon is a thief:*
> *he steals his silvery light from the sun.*
> *the sea is a thief: it dissolves the moon.*

The actual passage (from Act IV, Scene 3) is:

> *The sun's a thief, and with his great attraction*
> *Robs the vast sea. The moon's an errant thief,*
> *And her pale fire she snatches from the sun.*

The title *Pale Fire* itself presents, moreover, another most interesting point: it is incorporated in the poem's text, was supposedly not the title Kinbote was hoping for, and yet it has absolutely no relevance whatsoever to Shade's poem taken by itself, making sense only when applied to the constellation of author, poet, and mad scholar that constitutes the novel.

And even further, the title as it appears in the Shakespeare phrase is meant to refer not to the crude theft of Shade's manuscript by Kinbote, but to the less evident factor of the bonds and interplay of light and reflection between the novel's disparate bodies — again, Nabokov, Shade, and Kinbote. The manuscript "theft" is a put-up job, and this is the essential point — much more important than the source of the title (although, as we have seen, it is an extremely important clue) — a point that Mary McCarthy does not see when she asserts "that Kinbote has appropriated Shade's manuscript is clear to anybody, without reference to Shakespeare" (New York *Times* Book Review, July 10, 1966). Nothing, in fact, is less clear to someone who has examined in detail the poem and its Commentary.

The epigraph to the novel is as interesting as its title. It is taken from Boswell's *Life of Samuel Johnson:*

This reminds me of the ludicrous account he gave Mr. Langton, of the despicable state of a young gentleman of good family. "Sir, when I heard of him last, he was running about town shooting cats." And then in a sort of kindly reverie, he bethought himself of his own favorite cat, and said, "But Hodge shan't be shot: no, no, Hodge shall not be shot."

Now this curious little fragment presents several problems, not the least of which is deciding who posited it. Of the three candidates Kinbote is the least likely choice. Taken at its face, the epigraph seems to refer somehow to the assassination of Shade by mistake. And this requires that the eminent poet John Shade be cast as Hodge. This is absurd. The epigraph in fact makes sense only when it is seen as a statement by Nabokov about the novel, or a statement by Shade about Kinbote, who must live to write the Commentary: " . . . no, no, Kinbote shall not be shot." The reader who is willing to march through Boswell's biography in search of it will find (on page 1,038 of the Modern Library edition) that the remark about the cat Hodge occurs on the same page as a remark by Boswell about a work that was to be written by Johnson on the Boswell family, based on papers to be furnished by Boswell. This plan, Boswell informs us, was soon put aside in favor of other projects, which strongly suggests that the epigraph does indeed have something to say about *Pale Fire* as a whole, should it be thought that the epigraph is simply a whimsical bit of nonsense signifying nothing about the novel.

It hardly need be pointed out that Boswell's remark about the dropped project does not suit itself to the purposes of Kinbote who is determined against all evidence to find "his" story in Shade's poem. The epigraph, like the title, is unsuited for either poem or commentary, but it makes perfect sense for the novel as a whole.

The most cogent argument for the essential unity of poem with commentary are the rejected draft portions of the poem which Kinbote cites and which, if they are Shade's, would prove — in direct contradiction to the poem itself — that the old poet was indeed on the verge of writing a poem about Zembla. In discarded variants for lines 70 and 130 there is a goodly portion of Kinbote's story as he himself tells it:

> *Thus that northern king,*
> *Whose desperate escape from prison was*
> *Brought off successfully only because*
> *Some forty of his followers that night*
> *Impersonated him and sped his flight.*

It is conceivable that John Shade might have used the fantasies of his boring and intrusive neighbor in a poem, but there is no logical reason to suppose that such themes could have an integral place in *this* poem. There again we have a choice as to the author of the Commentary: Charles Kinbote speaking in the voice of "John Shade," or John Shade dropping back into his first voice (the craggy poet) within the context of the phantasmagoria of Charles Kinbote (the second voice). The primary author — even without Nabokov's acknowledgment that Kinbote really does not know what is going on in Shade's poem — must be John Shade.

In all, considerably less than a quarter of what Kinbote writes is even ostensibly concerned, much less actually connected, with the Shade poem. The rest falls into two categories: Kinbote's conversations with Shade, and Kinbote's account of his miraculous escape from Zembla and the subsequent hunt for him by the Extremist assassin Jakob Gradus. Both these themes are to a great extent concerned with death, and this is the unifying bond between the poem and the commentary — in a word, the subject of *Pale Fire*.

Kinbote is by his own constant avowal a deeply devout Christian. In a long religious conversation with Shade, Kinbote asserts: "I know also that the world could not have occurred fortuitously and that somehow Mind is involved as a main factor in the making of the universe. In trying to find the right name for that Universal Mind, or First Cause, or the Absolute, or Nature, I submit that the Name of God has priority." But, as Mary McCarthy correctly points out (*The New Republic*, June 4, 1962), the religious conversations are of no real significance, and given its primary concern, the novel is remarkably free of any religious symbolism. Kinbote's religious fervor seems in fact to be one of the madman's whimsical pretenses. He has another secret, greater even than Zembla, and at one point he tells Shade: "As soon as your poem is ready, as soon as the glory of Zembla merges with the glory of your verse, I intend to divulge to you an ultimate truth, an extraordinary secret, that will put your mind completely at rest." A very similar "ultimate truth" figures most prominently in *Solus Rex*.

As John Shade's death is the necessary conclusion to his poem — and, being planned from the very first line, that death must be a literary device — the Commentary vacillates between Kinbote's fear of murder and his impulse to commit suicide. In a delightfully comic twist, Kinbote's "Christianity" is used to justify self-destruction:

When the soul adores Him Who guides it through mortal life, when it distinguishes His sign at every turn of the trial, painted on the boulder, and notched in the fir trunk, when every page in the book of one's personal fate bears His watermark, how can one doubt that He will also preserve us through all eternity? So what can stop one from effecting the transition? What can help us to resist the intolerable temptation? What can prevent us from yielding to the burning desire for merging in God? We who burrow in filth every day may be forgiven perhaps the one sin that ends all sins.

In that same note to Hazel Shade's suicide ("But then it is also true that Hazel Shade resembled me in certain respects," Kinbote has commented mysteriously in an earlier note) there is a detailed disquisition on the various ways in which one may destroy oneself, and he decides that the ideal death is from an airplane:

Your muscles relaxed, your pilot puzzled, your packed parachute shuffled off, cast off, shrugged off — farewell, *shootka* (little chute)! Down you go, but all the while you feel suspended and buoyed as you somersault in slow motion like a somnolent tumbler pigeon, and sprawl supine on the eiderdown of the air, or lazily turn to embrace your pillow, enjoying every last instant of soft, deep, death-padded life, with the earth's green seesaw now above, now below, and the voluptuous crucifixion, as you stretch yourself in the growing rush, in the nearing swish, and then your loved body's obliteration in the Lap of the Lord.

The "*shootka*" is not a "little chute" but, in Russian, a "joke" or "trick," either of which is a precise definition of the Zemblan's "life story" as he narrates it. Kinbote's arrival in America, it will be recalled, was by parachute, and when he escapes from Zembla the Extremists "naturally assumed" he would go only by airplane, but he fools them by going overland instead.

Kinbote's last words are addressed to the question of his own suicide, which he has been contemplating throughout his Commentary, and here a strange thing happens — the clown's voice changes, and at just this moment he speaks to us in a voice not unlike Humbert Humbert's alter ego, Clare Quilty:

Many years ago — how many I would not care to say — I remember my Zemblan nurse telling me, a little man of six in the throes of adult insomnia: "*Minnamin, Gut mag alkan, Pern dirstan*" (my darling, God makes hungry, the Devil thirsty). Well, folks, I guess many in this fine hall are as hungry and thirsty as me, and I'd better stop, folks, right here. Yes, better stop. My notes and self are petering out. Gentlemen, I have suffered very much, and more than any of you can imagine. I pray for the Lord's benediction to rest on my wretched countrymen. My work is finished. My poet is dead. "And you, what will *you* be doing with yourself, poor King, poor Kinbote?" a gentle young voice may inquire. God will help me, I trust, to rid myself of any desire to follow the example of two other characters in this work. I shall continue to exist. I may assume other disguises, other forms, but I shall try to exist.

One cannot be sure.

Kinbote closes with the assertion that, whatever the future may hold for him, some day "a bigger, more respectable, more competent Gradus" will find him. Kinbote maintains that Gradus is an assassin of the "regicidal organization" called the Shadows, and also that he is a bungler who cannot get anything done by himself. But we also know that "*grados*" is Zemblan for "tree," and so, in a topsy-turvy way, Gradus has completed *his* assignment too: the Shade has been felled by a tree, which, in turn, obligingly fells itself to complete the metaphor. And, in addition to the connection that has been noted by Mary McCarthy between the name Gradus and mirrors — that *gradus* is the Russian for "degree," and one of his many pseudonyms is Degree, thereby connecting the name with both mercury for mirrors and the inexorable advance of fate — there is also the strong suggestion of *Gradus ad Parnassum*, which affirms the author's passage into art.

Two important anagrams should also be considered in connection with the name Gradus. A Zemblan named Sudarg of Bokay is "a mirror maker of genius," and his name — without the "of" — is an anagram of Jakob (in Russian, Yakov) Gradus. In his notes Kinbote gives the birth and death dates for Gradus, but in the case of Sudarg he specifies "life span not known." Secondly, Gradus and Sudarg are incomplete anagrams of *gosudar'*, which, depending upon whom one is addressing, means "Lord, Your Majesty, Sire, Sir." Although the "mirror maker of genius" has great delegated power, his title of *gosudar'* is to be understood in the more humble, modern corruption of the term. Kinbote is correct, for once, when he says that Gradus is only an agent — he is the windowpane that leads to eternity, to art, to all unearthly realms — but what Kinbote doesn't realize is that he has nothing to fear from Gradus because he is already on the other side of the false azure in the windowpane. His mirror of death lies in his past, in Zembla, land of semblances.

That Shade is the intended victim is made evident by the perfect synchronization of Gradus' advance on him. Gradus sets out on the very day that Shade begins his poem and "steadily marching neared in iambic motion, crossing streets, moving up with his valise on the escalator of the pentameter, stepping off, boarding a new train of thought," Gradus arrives just in time to "complete" *Pale Fire*. The line of vision and reflection that orders the novel may be represented graphically (see accompanying illustration), with the "windowpane" — the central image in all of *Pale Fire* (*"in the false azure of the windowpane"*) — representing the glass and mirror toward which both Shade and Kinbote look and in which "reality" becomes "art."

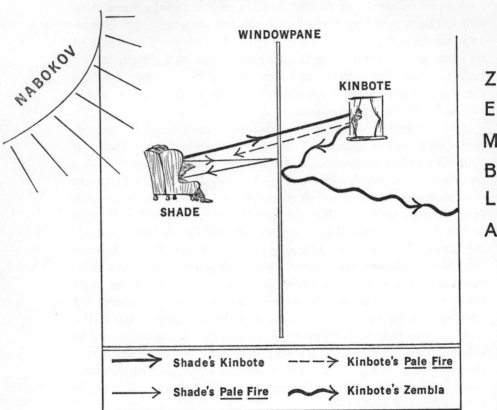

Shade peers at himself (his poem) in the reflection of the windowpane and also at Kinbote who, with only intermittent and distorted glimpses of his creator, Shade, in that same glass, for his part sees, reflected (and distorted) in the windowpane, mainly the fabulous and deadly kingdom of Zembla behind him. Kinbote does not belong in Nabokov's long chain of *doppelgängers*, or, if one chooses to see him in that way on the basis of Shade's hints of moments of madness, he is the most astounding of them all, far surpassing Felix, the double who isn't really a double. In creating Kinbote as the reflection that flies on after his (artistic) death, Shade more than substantiates his own speculation: "Life is a great surprise. I do not see why death should not be an even greater one." And one recalls how the hero of another Nabokov novel speculates that "the hereafter for all we know may be an eternal state of excruciating insanity."

The complex relationship of the disparate parts of *Pale Fire* may be seen more sharply by analogy with the major episode of the second portion of *Solus Rex*. After he has completed his work on the no longer necessary illustrations to *Ultima Thule* (supplementary troops for the Zemblan army, by the way, come from "Thule"), the artist Sineusov turns to the only other expedient he now sees open to him to go beyond his grief. Those who do not have the gifts of imagination and art usually resort to various forms of dubious spiritualism and professional nonsense, but it happens that Sineusov has an old casual acquaintance named Adam Falter about whom he hears a remarkable story very shortly after his wife's death. Falter, whom Sineusov remembers as an essentially ordinary and even slightly vulgar man, one night suffers a fit in the little hotel where he is staying. Falter's screams are so unnatural that they seem like those of "a woman in the throes of labor, but a woman with a man's voice and a giant in her womb," and they finally seem to lose all connection with any human personality. The door to Falter's hotel room is locked, and when the hotel manager finally finds the key to open it, the screaming has ceased. Falter, sweating and in his pajama bottoms, refuses to make any comment about what happened to him; he merely steps out of the room, urinates profusely down the stairs, and then returns to his room and goes to sleep.

From that time on, although there are occasional difficulties with the police over some of his street antics, Falter is a more or less quiescent madman. The sudden onset of his madness does, however, draw the interest of a well-known Italian psychiatrist who happened to have been visiting someone in Falter's hotel. The psychiatrist is far and away Nabokov's wittiest gibe at Freudianism. He is a kind of *ur*-Freudian who believes that:

All psychic illnesses may be explained by the patient's subconscious memory of his ancestors' misfortunes, and if the afflicted person is suffering from, say, megalomania, then, in order to cure him completely, it is necessary only to determine which of his ancestors was a power-hungry failure and explain to his great-grandson that the ancestor has died and is at peace for evermore, although in complex cases one has to resort to practically a theatrical presentation, in costumes of the epoch, depicting the ancestor's specific sort of death, and the ancestor's role is played by the patient.

And so, of course, "the details about Falter-père were unnecessary to him." But the promised hilarity never comes to pass, for the psychiatrist suffers a heart attack and dies in the course of an interview with Falter:

Probably, it had something to do with hypnotism, since Falter later assured the investigator that he had let it slip against his will, and that he was not quite himself . . . and when finally these troublesome queries bored him, he explained that he had by chance solved the "riddle of the world," and that he had yielded to his elaborate persuasions and told the solution to his inquisitive interlocutor who dropped dead from surprise.

The story is promptly taken up by the press, and that is how it finally comes to the attention of Sineusov, who, because he does happen to know Falter and thus can believe that what he says may not be the usual cheap fakery, plans to see if he can scientifically or logically verify the madman's experience. This attempt parallels John Shade's three-hundred-mile drive to talk to Mrs. Z to verify his own mystical experience, and the conversations that Sineusov has with Falter are strikingly similar to the theological and philosophic exchanges of Shade and Kinbote. It would seem that in *Pale Fire* Nabokov has combined with heightened skill and precision the three narrative threads in *Solus Rex:* the mysterious kingdom, the artist's quest for the "ultimate truth," and the madman in art in whom that truth resides. Both works have as their basic idea the depiction of wholly separate narrative worlds in whose precise conjunction, as in astrology, fate is played out. And that interaction is the chief reason why Kinbote's Commentary cannot be considered as something which has been "glued on" (the phrase is

Mary McCarthy's) to Shade's poem. Just as the noises that Hazel
Shade heard in the barn were, in Kinbote's judgment, "an outward
extension or expulsion of insanity," the figure of Kinbote is that
same "outward extension" of insanity in relation to John Shade.
(Those sounds, by the way, are really a warning to John Shade not
to go to the Goldsworth house.)

In *Solus Rex* Sineusov has little luck with Falter. Falter reacts to
him as though he had last seen him not years ago but just yesterday,
and at the same time he shows not the slightest warmth or interest
in him. They have a long intellectual sparring session in which
Falter talks freely enough, but refuses to allow himself to go to
"the Italian precipice" again — to avoid more difficulties with the
authorities. He merely leads Sineusov on and then stops:

Take any commonplace truth, say, that two angles equal to a third are
equal to each other — does this assertion include such statements such
as that ice is hot or that there are stones in Canada? To put it in
different words, any given little truth does not contain any other
related truths, and this is even more true of those which belong to
other areas and levels of knowledge or cognition. What would you say
then about a truth which contains in it the explanation and proof of all
possible mental affirmations? One may believe in the poetry of a wild
flower or the power of money, but neither of these beliefs foreordains
faith in homeopathy or the necessity to destroy antelopes on the
islands of Lake Victoria; but when one has learned what I have — if
one can call this learning — one has obtained the key to absolutely
all doors and boxes in the world, only I have no reason to use it.

During their long discourse Falter sometimes merely turns aside
questions ("Does God exist?" "Cold."), and sometimes he wanders
into complex statements. One is struck by the way in which both
Sineusov *and* the madman Falter make statements which have
direct correspondence to statements which Shade makes in his
poem. Thus Falter, for example, says: "Every man is mortal; you
(or I) are a man; this means that perhaps you are *not mortal*.
Why? Why because any selected man by virtue of that very fact
ceases to be *every*. And together with that, you and I are all the
same mortal, but I am mortal in a different way than you are"; and
in lines 213–214 of *Pale Fire:* "*A syllogism:* other men die; but I/
Am not another; therefore I'll not die." And Sineusov's statement:

"The terror which I experience before the thought of my future unconsciousness is equal only to my repulsion before the imagined putrefaction of my body" has its echo in Canto Three (lines 523–524) of *Pale Fire:* "*I'm ready to become a floweret/ Or a fat fly, but never, to forget.*"

When Sineusov, still trying to prod Falter into some sort of meaningful statement, compares life to some sort of confused foreword with the main text still to come, Falter replies: "Skip the foreword, and you've got it!" — a statement which means nothing to Sineusov, but which in retrospect has great meaning for us. And it also, to draw yet another textual comparison with *Pale Fire*, brings to mind Shade's "Man's life as commentary to abstruse/ Unfinished poem. *Note for further use*" (lines 939–940), which, if read as an anagrammatic formulation (man's life as abstruse commentary to unfinished poem), is another confirmation — the poem itself, after all, is hardly "abstruse" — of the complicated orbital paths that comprise the novel. The real irony of the title *Pale Fire* is that, fine as Shade's poem is, it is pale beside the mad and wonderful work of art and distortion that whirls dervishly around it — just as the artist's life must be pale before his art.

In the end Falter's remarks strike Sineusov as being as deft as those of any streetcorner sophist — which is just what the artist had been hoping to avoid in talking to his old acquaintance; Sineusov says as much to Falter, and Falter pardons himself by saying that, after all, sophistry is his sole defense, but, all the same, he has let slip two or three words that showed "a little corner of the truth" in the course of his nonsense. There Sineusov's letter to his wife and *Solus Rex* end, but I think that I have found those "two or three words" in their twenty-page conversation, and I have given my reader a chance to discover them, too, with a great deal less difficulty. Falter's casual "the poetry of a wild flower or the power of money" repeats in slightly varied form the jest of Sineusov's dying wife which she made when the mysterious foreign poet commissioned the artist to illustrate *Ultima Thule* ("Most of all in life I love poems, wild flowers, and foreign money"). This poem in a strange language, as the title of the chapter also indicates, is evidently the "map" Sineusov requires to chart and unravel his own life.

And Kinbote's Zembla — apart from what *he* thinks it is — is also a mapping of man's subconscious. Nabokov's whole *oeuvre*, but *Pale Fire* above all, is overwhelming proof that the subconscious does not exist only in Freud's vision of it. Kinbote's Zembla is a homosexual fantasy, but especially striking is the fact that this subterrane has absolutely no connection with the John Shade we know from the poem. The Freudian understanding of the unconscious requires "apertures" through which the conscious is subtly prompted. There is, when one thinks of it, a valid psychological connection with John Shade after all. *Pale Fire* depends centrally on mirroring, and just as one's image is reversed in a mirror, so it is quite logical that a poet who is unquestionably "sexually normal" should have an inverse subconscious world in which perversion runs rampant.

The sexual perversity of Zembla does not signify only itself. It is a poetic coefficient of death, which comes when the surface of the mirror is broken. As Kinbote crosses the mountains to escape from Zembla, he recites to himself, in both German and Zemblan, the opening lines of Goethe's poem *The Erl-King* in which a sinister fairy king or wood spirit continually beckons to a terrified child riding in his father's arms on horseback. The poem combines perfectly the images of perversion and death, and is indeed a strange poem to be reciting as one goes into exile; Kinbote either does not notice or does not say, but in the last line of *The Erl-King* the child lies dead in his father's arms. Another fairly obvious portent of death (it was a standard stage effect of both Russian and French Decadent writing) is the journey through the secret underground passage with his boyhood "pal" Oleg: "Oleg walked in front: his shapely buttocks encased in tight indigo cotton moved alertly, and his own erect radiance, rather than his flambeau, seemed to illume with leaps of light the low ceiling and crowding walls. Behind him the young Prince's electric torch played on the ground and gave a coating of flour to the back of Oleg's bare thighs." On this little excursion into the bowels of Zembla, the boys listen to the sounds of what they take to be a coarse heterosexual peasant couple (in reality it is two actors rehearsing in the theater through which Kinbote will escape many years later), and it is upon their return that the boys lock themselves up together "in a manly state and moaning like doves."

Kinbote's first, "real" bride is little Fleur — a liaison forced upon him by her scheming mother, who guards the door of their bedroom at night and "snores stentoriously in her lair." Kinbote tells us that "our Prince was fond of Fleur as of a sister, but with no soft shadow of incest or secondary homosexual complications," which is to say, she does not succeed in fulfilling her mother's instructions to get herself deflowered by Charles. Fleur's primary virtue in the Prince's eyes is that "she did not seem to mind when he abandoned her for manlier pleasures." Fleur is really something of a girl-boy, but, even so, Charles can only "dislike her less" than other women, and — one of the superb lines in the novel — "the sight of her four bare limbs and three mousepits (Zemblan anatomy) irritated him."

The extensive "historical background" supplied by Kinbote, particularly in his Index, is evidently the fulfillment of the remarkable *ur*-Freudian theory of the Italian psychiatrist of *Solus Rex*. Thus Kinbote's (at least partially) heterosexual father is described as "kind and gentle," but, except for some snapshots of his death which cause the Prince to have nightmares, he does not matter much, and his surname is The Vague. Uran the Last, who reigned in Zembla only one year, from 1798 to 1799 (and whose name means Queer the Last), is described as "an incredibly brilliant, luxurious, and cruel monarch whose whistling whip made Zembla spin like a rainbow top." Poor Uran was "dispatched one night by a group of his sister's united favorites." In contrast, heterosexual Thurgis the Third ("surnamed The Turgid") has a very long and dull reign, while his mistress, the celebrated actress Iris Acht, is "strangled in her dressing room by a fellow actor." Queen Yaruga meets Hazel Shade's fate, "drowned in an ice-hole with her Russian lover during traditional New Year's festivities."

The political spectrum of Zemblan life is divided into shades of sexuality, and a man is "a Zemblan patriot" in Kinbote's Index (which is not "glued on" either, but has a definite role in the novel and an independent life of its own) when he is both perverse and constant. There are some exceptions, most notably the "heterosexual man of fashion and Zemblan patriot," Count Otar, whose patriotism seems to consist of having taken little Fleur as his teen-age mistress. But almost all the Zemblan patriots have doubles who are traitors, and for this reason *Pale Fire* has a greater profusion of doubles than any other Nabokov work. Thus Kinbote's throne page is a "man of fashion and Zemblan patriot," but his "cousin" (whose first name is an anagram of the page's) is an "experi-mentalist, madman and traitor." The family name of the throne page and his cousin is Mandevil, and this would seem to contain a rather obvious duality; in fact, the name refers to *another* and extremely important duality: Bernard de Mandeville (1670–1733) is a minor English poet — of French origin — who wrote an ex-tensive commentary to one of his own poems; and Jean de Mande-ville is a fourteenth-century author of a popular book describing his visits to countries where he had not in fact been! Two other important twins in *Pale Fire* are Nodo and Odon — "No, do" and "Oh, don't" — whose names themselves mirror their roles. Odon is the pseudonym of Donald O'Donnell "world-famous actor and Zemblan patriot" who is Kinbote's intimate and helps him to escape abroad; while his half-brother Nodo — he is the son of "a Zemblan boy impersonator" — is the "despicable traitor."

The trick names, anagrams, and little Russian jokes that sprout like mushrooms throughout *Pale Fire* are, in turn, useful and amusing. But they are also dangerous and distracting, and the most ample basket of Nabokovian mushrooms will not describe the forest. The little puzzles and tricks, like mushrooms, have their place in the fictional landscape, but only *after* the forest and its fantastic lakeside distortion have been fully studied and enjoyed. And even for the reader who cares for nothing but mushrooms, one cannot hope to do a reasonably decent job of collecting and unraveling unless one possesses all of Nabokov's languages. Perhaps this is the real justification for all these seemingly excessive literary ruses and clues.

Howard Nemerov once noted that Eliot forced poets and other literate Americans and Englishmen to acquire at least a cursory knowledge of Italian to read Dante, and, in the same way, Nabo-kov seems bound to make his readers learn his own exotic "Zemblan" — the Russian language. Two little examples will suffice — Gerald Emerald, the teacher of freshman English at

Wordsmith College where Shade and Kinbote also teach, is (in Miss McCarthy's article) "slowly recognized to be" Izumrudov, who is the superior officer of Gradus in the Shadows and gives Gradus the death order. But the reader who knows even enough Russian to use a Russian-English dictionary has it at once: *izumrud* means "emerald" in Russian. Kinbote, of course, assures the reader that though the name Izumrudov appears to be Russian it actually derives from the Eskimo Umruds, and even *this* joke takes some Russian to appreciate fully: in Russian, "from the Umruds" would be *iz Umrudov!* A second good illustrative instance of the way in which Russian aids the reader are the names of the three lakes near the Wordsmith campus in one of which Hazel Shade takes her life: Omega, Ozero, and Zero. These are Indian names, Kinbote tells us, which were garbled by the early settlers. In fact there is only one lake, or *ozero* (the Russian word for lake), which corresponds to the glass between Shade and Kinbote, and hence is neatly set between the other two O-ish obeli (Omega and Zero), signifying the possibilities after death: nothing and everything (omega, the final letter of the Greek alphabet, is, of course, a symbol of infinity).

But, granting the absolute necessity that those who accept Nabokov as a great writer learn *some* Russian and affirming the enormous pleasure of being able to read Nabokov in the fullness of his linguistic amplitude, I wish to assert firmly that Nabokov should not be given over to the pedants and the puzzle-solvers. The — to borrow a phrase — "MAIN STRUCTURE" *can* be perceived by the good reader, and I take as confirmation several articles and reviews in scattered American journals and newspapers — some only a few paragraphs long — in which the writer conveyed that he or she saw what was "going on" in *Pale Fire*.

The danger of the tricks and allusions in *Pale Fire* is that the clever reader is very likely not to be satisfied with the essential finds — Kinbote's name, Zembla, Pope's *Essay on Man, Timon of Athens* — and be misled by the still cleverer Nabokov into missing the point of the whole thing. This, I think, was what happened to Mary McCarthy in her excellent article on *Pale Fire*, which I do not mean to denigrate, for there are — together with a few suspicious-looking fungi enthusiastically thrown in — some superb mushrooms in her basket. She was the first to get the Pope allusion to Zembla (John Shade is the author of a book on Pope), and she wisely and carefully examined the text of Pope's *Essay on Man* and found that it contains not only the reference to Zembla, but also the source of the Zemblan "Extremist" party. Her most perceptive discovery — and I am deeply grateful to her for it — is the source of Hazel Shade's name which is taken from *The Lady of the Lake* ("in lone Glenartney's hazel shade"). The reader of this book who is by chance not acquainted with Miss McCarthy's essay (*New Republic*, June, 1962; and, in a revised form, *Encounter*, October, 1962) is strongly urged to read it.

One very important trick in *Pale Fire* is John Shade's "Word Golf," amiably taken up by Kinbote. Kinbote gives his best scores as: "hate-love in three, lass-male in four, and live-dead in five (with 'lend' in the middle)." Mary McCarthy plays the game with the following results: "hate-love in three (hate-late-lave-love), lass-male in four (lass-last-mast-malt-male), live-dead in five. If you play Word Golf with the title words, you can get pale-hate in two and fire-love in three — or pale-love in three and fire-hate in three." And this prompts Miss McCarthy to choose love as the theme of the novel: "Love is the burden of *Pale Fire*, love and loss . . . The sense of loss in love . . . binds mortal men in a common pattern — the elderly couple watching TV in a lighted room, and the 'queer' neighbor watching *them* from his window." "Live-dead in five (with 'lend' in the middle)" is possible: live-line-lene-lend-lead-dead. Life and death are at the center of *Pale Fire*, with love and sex merely decoy or secondary motifs — poetic metaphors of the primary theme.

An excellent example of the pleasurable but essentially irrelevant sport of mushroom-picking in *Pale Fire* is the fine survey article on all the Nabokov novels available in English by R. H. W. Dillard, which appeared in *The Hollins Critic* (June, 1966) of Hollins College, Virginia. Although the article devotes less than two pages to *Pale Fire*, Dillard seems to me to be one of that handful of critics who may be said to be more or less "at home" in the novel. Dillard also demonstrates his understanding by means of Word Golf. (The real meaning, by the way, of the constant play of the colors green and red in *Pale Fire* is not to be found within some Freudian or political context, but, rather, in Word Golf — the golf green and the red flag over the hole [madness] into which Shade drops his putt.) Dillard takes the first word of Kinbote's Foreword (*Pale*) and the last word of his Index (land), and on the basis of the four words pale-pane-lane-land introduces suitable passages from *Pale Fire* to unlock the novel. Dillard's comments about the novel, however, do not depend upon such gamesmanship. He knew what he was looking for and got his ball to the right place (not into the hole, but on the green at least) by putting it into his pocket and going there.

The name Kinbote is one of the book's important puzzles. We are told by Kinbote that in Zemblan it means "regicide," and we may find mention in the Commentary of a certain V. Botkin, "American scholar of Russian descent." Kinbote also tells us — falsely — in that note that the "king-bot" is the "maggot of extinct fly that once bred in mammoths and is thought to have hastened their phylogenetic end"; in fact, the bot is the larva, often parasitic in sheep and horses, of the bee-sized insect called the botfly, and this progression from internalized embryonic form to an insect buzzing round the "parent" animal is yet another verbal allegory — in all but proportion — of *Pale Fire*. Botkin also reminds us of the Shakespearean dagger ("a Danish stiletto" in Kinbotese), and we are probably safe in taking "V. Botkin" to be the secondary Nabokovian agent who was the "real" person out of whom Shade fashioned Kinbote or Kinbot (another variant). But the matter, again, can be carried quite as far as one wishes and is able, even beyond the intention of the author himself. Botkin — it is a fairly common Russian name — is the name of a nineteenth-century Russian literary critic (perhaps best known now for his friendship and correspondence with Turgenev). The direct anagram of Botkin in Russian is *nikto*, the Russian for "nobody." Botkin has, it will be seen, the same superfluous "b" — the Russian is *zemlya* and means "land" — we find in the Popean Zembla ("*Nova Zembla, poor thing, with that B in her bonnet*," Nabokov wrote in one of his early English poems). And finally (I have a few more up my sleeve, but there is no need to prolong the trick) a Botkin, as Chairman of the United Russian Organizations, was the signatory of the official expression of grief on behalf of the Russian community in exile which appeared after the assassination of Nabokov's father in 1922. But none of these three particular things, Nabokov informs me, was on his mind when he wrote *Pale Fire*.

Nabokov once said that his ideal readers consist of "a lot of little Nabokovs," and *Pale Fire* is a structure whose general plan and pattern are so brilliant, so perfect, that the reader who follows after Nabokov long enough can — like those butterflies that mimic the patterns of other butterflies he is so fond of referring to — indeed continue on as a "little Nabokov" without in any way destroying or distorting the pattern (the usual danger of academic overreading) or even the "universal or ultimate truth" that seems to me to be present in this breathtakingly simple and endlessly complex novel. The realization that the anagram of Botkin is my own invention and discovery is a source of greater amazement to me than solving the most difficult of the author's own puzzles. *Pale Fire* is like Nature herself, and though our knowledge about it may increase tenfold, the essential mystery will remain intact.

Above Shade and Kinbote, the poem and the Commentary is Nabokov himself, who is the most important of the three artists, and who imposes his own pattern upon *Pale Fire* without in any way impinging upon the separate designs of the poet Shade and the madman-artist he has created. This aspect of the novel is clearest and most serenely open and obvious when seen in the perspective of Nabokov's entire artistic career. To repeat, I think it safe to say that there might have been a good deal less bafflement over *Pale Fire* if such earlier Russian Nabokov novels as *The Defense* and *The Gift* had been translated into English prior to 1962; and there would beyond any doubt have been a great deal less if some of the articles by Nabokov's most appreciative Russian critic, Vladislav Khodasevich, had appeared in English translation. It was Khodasevich who very early in Nabokov's writing career declared that his sole thematic concern is art, and that he writes only about artists — failed artists, aspiring artists, mad artists, every conceivable kind of artist — but that he does this in allegorical form, choosing as his protagonists chess players, homosexuals and murderers. I would have the reader of Nabokov always bear in mind this wise and simple observation — though it doesn't *always* apply. Khodasevich expressed the hope that Nabokov would some day write about a writer *as such*, and this, of course, is precisely what he did in *The Gift*, whose serial completion Khodasevich did not live to see. There are two entirely distinct "works-of-art-within-the-work-of-art" in *The Gift:* the poems of Fyodor Godunov-Cherdyntsev and the hilarious "biography" of Chernyshevsky, also written by him. It is most interesting in connection with an examination of *Pale Fire* to consider the example of the two voices of Godunov-Cherdyntsev, both so absolutely different, yet both coming from the same character.

The primary pattern — that is, the form as opposed to the theme — of *Pale Fire* is a complete and precise portrayal of the artist and his creation. We have the artist, Shade, and we have his creation, another artist who happens to be mad and whose work orbits about Shade in a complete circle, Foreword to Index. It seems sometimes as if the huge moon (with its glitter and size, it is a "moon" only in the sense that Greenland is an "island") must both control and bind the pale and staid planet, but this is merely the natural astronomy of literature: Flaubert is not nearly "as large" as Emma Bovary, who now has a separate existence of her own and whirls dazzlingly around her creator (in spite of his assertion that he was she!) and even the giant Tolstoy is small beside his Anna Karenina. This, in art, is an elemental truth: as the work comes closer and closer to true greatness, the protagonist and the novel as a whole must challenge and then finally eclipse, in varying degrees, the creator.

In the case of Nabokov it has become accepted practice to speak of Humbert Humbert, Hermann Karlovich, Smurov, Luzhin, and Kinbote as being "semi-autobiographical portraits" of their author, but there is little consideration of the enormous diversity within the huge gallery of Nabokov's eccentrics, nor do many of the people inclined to pass such autobiographic judgments (always without personal knowledge of the author) ever stop to consider such characters as Godunov-Cherdyntsev and John Shade. When we say Salinger is Holden Caulfield, or Nabokov is in some way Humbert Humbert or Charles Kinbote, we make a statement that is both evasive and all but precludes confrontation with the novel as a work of art. This, too, is an elemental truth. In the relationship between John Shade and Charles Kinbote, Nabokov has given us the best and truest allegorical portrait of "the literary process" that we have or are likely ever to get, and the Shade-Kinbote relationship also happens to be a completely fictional but very apt paradigm of Nabokov's relationship to his own various fictional worlds. There *are* complex ties of reflection, gravity, transmutation, and patterns of thought between Shade and Kinbote, and in the end we must admit that we can recognize but not fully understand them any more than we can understand the ties between a real author and his real work of art. With a printed book in hand, we usually have at least the author's name on the cover, but Nabokov complicates matters within the book by forcing his reader to find and understand what he demonstrates in full view but does not name. In *Pale Fire* the two distinct lines of Nabokov characters, suitably represented by Godunov-Cherdyntsev and Hermann Karlovich, have been joined for the first time.

There is, as always happens in complex mirroring, the danger that by approaching the problem incorrectly the various aspects of the novel will be seen in an inverted and meaningless way. This happened in Page Stegner's 1966 book on Nabokov's five English novels, *Escape into Aesthetics* (it appeared after the completion of the present book to which only this short commentary has been added), in which Stegner, while guessing at the Shade-Kinbote tie, opts for Kinbote as the primary author, with no real basis for the choice apart from the unquestionably greater color and flourish in the madman. But this is very much like having Chiron invent Caldwell and then having them both team up to invent John Updike and *The Centaur;* or Chichikov invent Gogol; or any of hundreds of such possible reversals that have a certain quaint charm when presented as conscious whimsy, but are less than satisfactory as serious critical propositions.

There are many compellingly logical reasons to place John Shade before Charles Kinbote. A sane man may invent an insane character, and we call him an artist; an insane man who invents a perfectly sane character is also an artist, but *ipso facto* no longer insane in the way that Kinbote is. What sort of an Alice would the Mad Hatter make for us? The Stegner reading of *Pale Fire* reduces the novel at best to the description of a rare type of madness, and, for all practical purposes, it leaves the reader with an enormous and rather pointless joke for its own sake, something which Nabokov has never done, although his criticists have long tried to force this claim about Nabokov's perverse characters. Positing Kinbote as prime author (in addition to the fact that it contradicts all the many secret notes left throughout the novel) is, in a sense, just as confusing as the apparently obvious idea that Kinbote and Shade are quite separate.

After Nabokov's master plan, one wants to consider other, secondary themes that have figured in his prose since he first began to write. Robert M. Adams (who picks up several of the difficult trick names of minor characters and places) in a short but very interesting review of *Pale Fire* in *The Hudson Review* in 1962 uses the elegant formula applied to *Lolita* by John Hollander in *Partisan Review* (*Lolita* as a love affair with the Romantic novel) and subsequently changed by Nabokov himself to read: ("*Lolita* as a love affair with the English language"). Adams tries to apply this to *Pale Fire*, which he sees as being about "a perverse love for an impossible princess, the English language; the essential experience is that of mental alienation." One hesitates to accept this well-meant hermit crab of a *mot* in the way that it is put, but Adams has all the same succeeded in housing three of the most important minor motifs of *Pale Fire* in the shell discarded by Hollander and Nabokov. They are: perversity, love for an impossible princess, and alienation. (How *Pale Fire*, which utilizes five languages and literatures, can be a love story about the English language frankly puzzles me; about language in general, it is most certainly.) The most fascinating of these themes, because it has been such a furiously rocked hobbyhorse of American literature in the 1960's, is alienation. Alienation is simply a "given" for Nabokov, another way of expressing the individuality he sees in even the most obtuse people and characters. This is the reason why even his "doubles" assert their own individuality. It is in fact amusing to apply the classical Marxian notion of alienation to Nabokov's art. According to Marx, alienation occurs in culture at the historical moment when men can no longer recognize and identify themselves with their own work. But *Pale Fire* is precisely a demonstration of how the artist's satisfaction is greater in direct proportion to the separation he can effect between himself and his creation —

henceforth to be known as Nabokov's Law. John Shade, too, is "alienated" in a certain sense, but he is also an artist, and the title of his book on Pope is *Supremely Blest*. Alienation, for Nabokov, exists both in nature (in man's separation from the hereafter) and in man (in the human proclivity toward abandonment of oneself to deceptively alluring but fatal roles). Hence, it is Kinbote — not merely mad, but also supremely confident — who may be spoken of as truly "alienated."

The theme of impossible love is present in Kinbote's love for his Queen Disa, Duchess of Payn. It is, really, no different from — to choose the farthest possible example in time and style — the powerful but unconsummated love of Ganin in *Mashenka*. Mashenka had told Ganin he could do what he wanted with her, but they never actually made love, and their romance was cut short by the Revolution. Ganin has the unexpected opportunity to see Mashenka again, but he realizes that the best and most beautiful part of their relationship is finished and perfect, and he does not take advantage of his opportunity. Compare this with Kinbote's relationship with his Queen Disa of Great Payn and Mone. (The last part of her name needs no explanation, but Disa itself, although Kinbote gives us the information in scrambled form, is from the Zemblan *paradisa*, which, with the English prefix *para-*, gives the name two readings.) Kinbote had to marry Disa to produce an heir, but their prerevolutionary (pre-Zemblan revolution, that is) marriage was never consummated: "In the beginning of their calamitous marriage he had strenuously tried to possess her but to no avail . . . He farced himself with aphrodisiacs, but the anterior characters of her unfortunate sex kept fatally putting him off. One night when he tried tiger tea, and hopes rose high, he made the mistake of begging her to comply with an expedient which she made the mistake of denouncing as unnatural and disgusting."

As a result of such occurrences, Disa goes abroad to live ("for reasons of health" the Zemblan people are told), returns to Zembla, and then, after the King's lapses back into "manly Zemblan customs," abroad once more. After the revolution Disa remains faithful and wants Kinbote to live with her, but he is in danger from the Shadows and leaves her to live in America. As Ganin had two Mashenkas in his mind — one idealized and resplendent, the other an ordinary wife of a very vulgar émigré — so Kinbote has two Disas — Disa and para-Disa. It is the para-Disa of his mind that Kinbote adores, and she is, in a manner of speaking, a homosexual's homosexual fantasy. Kinbote's torment and longing is hopelessly fixed by a past admission to her that he does not love her: "Everything had changed, everybody was happy. And he absolutely had to find her at once to tell her that he adored her, but the large audience before him separated him from the door, and the notes reaching him through a succession of hands said that she was not available; that she was inaugurating a fire; that she had married an American businessman; that she had become a character in a novel; that she was dead." Disa of Great Payn and Mone is one of the great gambols in *Pale Fire;* and yet, it is at the same time an exact analogue (reversed in a mirror, of course) to Ganin's love for Mashenka and fully as moving as Shade's love for his difficult daughter Hazel.

In the shadow of its more obvious and in many ways more complicated and deceptive twin *Lolita,* it has not been generally noticed that *Pale Fire* is the Nabokov book most centrally concerned with sex. The sexuality in *Pale Fire* happens to be pederasty, but again it merely takes the proper positioning of a mirror to translate this into the perversion of Humbert Humbert, or the potentialities inherent in all sexual practice or fantasy. Nabokov's artistic usage of perversion has been frequently commented on. There is no need to pause over the opinions that attribute the perversion to Nabokov himself, but many critics have seen in the theme an artistic expression of the natural scientist's human coldness and impersonality as he affixes the butterfly's thorax to his board with a pin. Or, the same thing expressed in a slightly more charitable form, it is seen as a kind of affection peculiar to the scientist. Mary McCarthy, for example, has written: "Nabokov's tenderness for human eccentricity, for the freak, the 'deviate,' is partly the naturalist's taste for the curious. But his fond, wry compassion for the lone black piece on the board goes deeper than classificatory science or the collector's choplicking."

Nabokov's chops are not even slightly damp, and he certainly does not view his art as a display board of curiosities. One of the harshest portraits in *Speak, Memory,* and one in which Nabokov's deep personal abhorrence is not at all concealed, is of the boy whom he calls Dietrich, who collected photographs of executions and dreamed of attending an American electrocution. And when Humbert Humbert finally has the repulsive Clare Quilty cornered, Quilty tries desperately to dissuade him from murder with a promise of "The in folio de-luxe *Bagration Island* by the explorer and psychoanalyst Melanie Weiss, a remarkable lady, a remarkable work — drop that gun — with photographs of eight hundred and something male organs she examined and measured in 1932 on Bagration, in the Barda Sea, very illuminating graphs, plotted with love under pleasant skies — drop that gun — and moreover I can arrange for you to attend executions, not everybody knows that the chair is painted yellow." This confusion about the motivation of the objective observer and the artist derives from an admixture of repulsion and morbid interest on the reader's part. The passages which I have just cited are as clearly a statement of "what the author thinks" as anything Nabokov has written. The joy and passion of the natural scientist, properly understood, are independent but not exclusive of moral feeling. We are putting an exceedingly odd question when we ponder whether Tolstoy *approved* of Anna, and it is odder still to declare, in however well-meant a way, that Nabokov *approves* of or is "fascinated by" characters such as Humbert and Kinbote. It is precisely because the natural scientist and the artist are not obligated, as a function of their investigation, to pass moral judgment upon the objects of investigation that a man may study snakes without particularly *liking* them, and that Nabokov can use certain forms of perversion for artistic purposes to which they are admirably suited without abdicating or compromising in any way his private judgment (which he has expressed on numerous occasions) of them.

Frank Kermode has written that Kinbote's homosexuality is "a metaphor for the artist's minority view of a bad world." I am not so sure that Nabokov views ours as a "bad world," but it is certainly true that Nabokov very often uses perversion metaphorically. As an inversion or direct opposite, homosexuality provides a perfect negative image with which to project normal feeling. The subtle and brilliant way in which Queen Disa is used to signify, just as Mashenka did, the necessarily frustrating, inconclusive, and guilt-ridden emotions involved in actual love and in the more abstract and vague love we feel for our native land shows how far and how boldly Nabokov can reach for his artistic metaphors. Even Fate (Gradus) may be a sexually impotent pervert who, when his role has been fulfilled, attempts to castrate himself. And perverse sexuality by its very nature satisfies one of the most basic precepts of comedy from the time of Aristophanes: the world turned on its head, tragedy and pain softened (but not lessened) by the presence of the absurd and the ludicrous.

Pale Fire is a serious work of art and also one of the eight masterpieces of the novel in this century (Nabokov is the only author who has written *two* of them!), and the burden of my discussion has quite naturally been addressed to the novel in a tone which these convictions require. But, by way of a final comment on *Pale Fire*, I should like to remind the reader who may have forgotten or been too confused to notice in the first place that this serious and perfect novel radiates a humor on every page that is anything but pale, right down to the notes in the Index telling us of Kinbote's "contempt for Prof. H. (not in Index)" and "MARCEL, the fussy, unpleasant, and not always plausible central character, pampered by everybody in Proust's *À la Recherche du Temps Perdu*." One may always say — someone, at any rate, has — that "Nabokov is too funny, indeed even too brilliant for his own good," but if we are to turn our backs on an artist on democratic grounds such as these, then, to paraphrase something someone else said, there is no point in writing novels, poems, commentaries to them, or anything else at all.

Eleven

✼ ✼ ✼ ✼

olita is Vladimir Nabokov's greatest novel, but it is also, of course, his most controversial work. The theme and the novel itself require no defense, but I hope that my reader may now have in mind several considerations about Nabokov's purposes in this work that may not have occurred to him before.

The flickerings of the theme that was finally to become *Lolita* came to Nabokov in September, 1939, when he chanced to read a little filler item in a French newspaper about an ape "who, after months of coaxing by a scientist, produced the first drawing ever charcoaled by an animal: this sketch showed the bars of the poor creature's cage." Unfortunately, Nabokov's recollection about precisely where he read the article is somewhat vague. In his Afterword to *Lolita* Nabokov spoke of the time as being "late in 1939 or early in 1940," and only recently Nabokov discovered another copy of the original Russian story, which he thought had been destroyed, dated October–November, 1939, thereby confirming that the time has to be September or perhaps early October. The newspaper, he thought, was *Paris-soir* ("somewhere in the middle of a page"), but when I failed to find it — which does not mean that it isn't there — he thought of three other Parisian newspapers that he occasionally also read at that time, but which also failed to produce the desired *entrefilet*. It was a time when other bestialities consumed almost all the newspaper space, and the animal stories are mainly about the evacuation of dangerous zoo animals so that they would not be let loose in the event that bombs fell on the zoos; one kind man had invented a gas mask that could be worn by dogs; but that is all I was able to find. Even the question of the precise zoo is unsettled — in the *Lolita* Afterword Nabokov thought it was the Jardin des Plantes, but some years later he told an interviewer that it had been the Zoo de Vincennes. My somewhat sheepish inquiry to the Director of Parisian Zoos did not solve the problem either — none of their older employees could recall the incident. It is true, of course, that "such humdrum potterings are beneath true scholarship," but I am saddened by my failure to unearth this finest needle in all the news stacks I have searched; it does exist and will, I trust, be found sometime.

My concern to locate this story does not lie in mere pedantry, nor, taken in its historical context, is this inspiration for *Lolita* frivolous or meaningless, as some have thought it to be. The notions of man being essentially an invisibly caged animal and of art itself as a kind of beautiful caging can be followed throughout Nabokov's writing. Thus, to cite but one instance, he writes in *The Exploit* of Martin's Uncle Heinrich: "It happened that in Uncle Heinrich's menagerie — and everyone has his own menagerie — there was among other things even one of those beasties which the French refer to as *noire*, and Uncle Heinrich's black beasty was: the Twentieth Century." And perhaps the French usage, as found in Pushkin's letter, of monkey or ape (*sapajou*) to signify a lecher may have flashed in Nabokov's mind as he read his newspaper. His impulse was thus to create a portrait of a man imprisoned in passion, but not in "blind passion" (we remember Albinus Kretschmar); this man was to draw the bars of his own cage which would be of different dimensions than the real ones of prison. In a printed conversation that he had with Alain Robbe-Grillet, Nabokov said that for him *Lolita* was really *"Un certain problème que je voulais résoudre, je voulais trouver une solution économe et élégante, comme dans les problèmes d'échecs où il y a certaines règles qu'il faut suivre. C'était un problème très difficile: il fallait trouver l'idée, les personnages, l'inspiration aussi, le petit frisson."* This "problem" which Nabokov sought to resolve, and which actually preceded any specific theme or characters, would appear to be threefold in nature. First, the protagonist as victim of his own or someone else's passion (Franz in *King, Queen, Knave*, Kretschmar in *Laughter in the Dark*) had to be joined with the protagonist-artist (Hermann in *Despair*, Smurov in *The Eye*) who controls and conveys the story. This synthesis, which presented a challenge far more difficult than it might appear at first glance, required in turn that, while the narration would reside with the protagonist, the course of the narrative itself had to proceed according to inexorable rules; hence Nabokov's comment that he had in mind something like a chess problem proceeding according to strict rules. In such a synthesis, moreover, the hero's game must be both won and lost, as indeed it is in *Lolita*. And finally — but this likely occurred to Nabokov only after he had read the newspaper — there was the challenge and delight of allegorically resolving a theme (love) in terms of its extreme and seemingly mutually exclusive opposite (lechery). This, at any rate, is the way in which I reconstruct the basic problem of the novel, although, to judge by the original Russian story he wrote but did not publish, the formulation probably did not reach this level of complexity until sometime after 1950. *Lolita* is, to a much greater degree even than *Pale Fire*, a meeting ground and perfect blending of all the major themes in Nabokov's art, and every bit as complex and simple as *Pale Fire*.

The basic story that was to become *Lolita* was in Nabokov's mind as early as 1936 or 1937. In Chapter Three of *The Gift*, Zina's unpleasant stepfather tells Fyodor a story which is obviously about himself:

Ah, if only I had a tick or two, what a novel I'd whip off! From real life. Imagine this kind of thing: an old dog — but still in his prime, fiery, thirsting for happiness — gets to know a widow, and she has a daughter, still quite little — you know what I mean — when nothing is formed yet but already she has a way of walking that drives you out of your mind — a slip of a girl, very fair, pale, with blue under the eyes — and of course she doesn't even look at the old goat. What to do? Well, not long thinking, he ups and marries the widow. Okay. They settle down the three of them. Here you can go on indefinitely — the temptation, the eternal torment, the itch, the mad hopes. And the upshot — a miscalculation. Time flies, he gets older, she blossoms out — and not a sausage. Just walks by and scorches you with a look of contempt. Eh? Do you feel here a kind of Dostoevskian tragedy? That story, you see, happened to a great friend of mine, once upon a time in fairyland when Old King Cole was a merry old soul.

This basic "Dostoevskian" plot becomes an artistic problem only when, as in *Lolita*, the action moves beyond the seduction. Imagine if you will, the Marquis de Sade not merely having his sex objects, but having also to live with them.

Lolita is a novel of prisons. Humbert Humbert is in prison as he writes the book. Lolita herself, most obviously, was Humbert's prisoner, but he, too, was hers, as, in quite a different way, he was also the prisoner of Lolita's mother Charlotte during their brief marriage. Beneath the neon smiles of their vacancy signs, the motels at which Humbert and Lolita stay in their flight across America are transient prisons: "WE WISH YOU TO FEEL AT HOME WHILE HERE. ALL EQUIPMENT WAS CAREFULLY CHECKED UPON YOUR ARRIVAL. YOUR LICENSE NUMBER IS ON RECORD HERE. USE HOT WATER SPARINGLY. WE RESERVE THE RIGHT TO EJECT WITHOUT NOTICE ANY OBJECTIONABLE PERSON." Most of all, Humbert is a prisoner of his past, the idyllic and brutally disrupted childhood romance which he is sentenced to attempt to repeat in his grotesque longing for nymphets. Nymphets themselves are eventually imprisoned in the excessive flesh of maturity ("the coffin of coarse female flesh in which my nymphets are buried alive"). When Lolita escapes (is kidnapped) from Humbert with Quilty, it is because she has been momentarily transferred from the captivity of Humbert to that of a provincial American hospital where she is guarded from him by an imperious young nurse. And at the end of the novel Humbert imprisons and executes Quilty in his own house, after having carefully removed all the keys from the doors beforehand so that the prisoner cannot lock himself away from his executioner.

The natural correspondent to these various cagings is chess, the game of cell-like squares. *Lolita* is not a chess game in fact, but it does utilize the playing of chess at several points, and the action of the novel frequently suggests a chess simile. One of the important articles on *Lolita*, written in French by Edmond Bernhard (*L'Arc*, No. 24, 1964), is devoted to this problem, and I shall merely list very briefly the most important chess themes as gathered by Bernhard. (Serious chess players are advised to consult the article itself, which includes extraneous but extremely interesting comparisons of certain moments in *Lolita* with famous chess games;

Bernhard's literary comments, though somewhat mannered, are also of considerable interest.) There are three actual chess games in the novel. Before his first marriage, in Europe, Humbert plays chess with his future father-in-law while his fiancée stands at her easel nearby working on a silly cubist painting. The second game occurs in America when Humbert plays chess with his friend, the homosexual Gaston Godin, while Lolita, paralleling the first game, dances on the upper floor: "My mournful and pompous adversary rubbed his head as if he had confused these far-off sounds with the stupefying and frightful attacks of my Queen." In the third game, also played with Gaston, Humbert receives a telephone call in the middle of the game from Lo's piano teacher complaining about her absence from her lessons. It is the first clue that Humbert has had that something is wrong, and it immediately finds reflection in the chess game: "I saw suddenly, across the fog of my disarray, that he could take my Queen."

Bernhard makes an effort to speak of the entire work as a match, which frequently leads to strained analogy: to see Lolita as a "pawn" promoted to Queen after Charlotte's death does not coincide with Humbert's vision of her — although certainly the marriage is a tactical move; the chess references, though, are sometimes most helpful in explaining the forward tempo of the plot. Humbert's initial fault is, like "premature use of the Queen," a beginner's error, and so he is thrown into the thick of play before he is really ready for it. The death scene with Quilty is compared to a King blocked by his own guard — proposing in vain a series of exchanges, which amount to all his powers, for the opportunity of slipping out of his own fortress. Humbert keeps "Chum" the murder weapon in a chess box given him by Gaston, and the poem he gives Quilty to read before shooting him contains a play on chess terminology ("because you took advantage of my disadvantage . . . ").

Important as the stylized figurations are in the novel, however, *Lolita* depends primarily upon a vivid realistic portrayal of the major characters. When F. W. Dupee writes that *Lolita* is about "a real wolf howling for a real Red Riding Hood," he is only in the main correct, for it is remarkable how well Nabokov has succeeded in diverting the attention of his readers from the at times very dubious reality of his wolf, little girl, and entire fable.

The primary cause of Nabokov's dissatisfaction with his original 1939 short story was not uneasiness over its daring theme, but what he felt was its failure to achieve an effectively realistic base for his tale. The story, entitled *The Magician* (*Volshebnik*), turned out to be somewhat longer than Nabokov had remembered it in his *Lolita* Afterword — fifty-four typed pages. The nymphet is a twelve-year-old French girl, and this, Nabokov told Robbe-Grillet, was the reason why the story had not succeeded: he did not know any French children of that age. One of the few "research tasks" he undertook to write *Lolita*, he told an Ithaca newspaper reporter, was a protracted series of local bus rides, during the course of which he carefully took note of the peculiarities and character of American teenage jargon. However much Lolita may differ from the "typical American teenager" in other respects, she speaks in an American idiom whose purity has seldom been equaled in modern American literature.

There are certain vague similarities between *The Magician* and *Lolita*, but there are also enormous differences in the respective plots. *The Magician* is narrated in the third person, and after the protagonist marries the little girl's mother, the mother, who has been seriously ill, dies of natural causes. Curiously, it is the magician who at the end of the story dies by hurling himself under the wheels of a truck.

The first encounter of the magician — his name is Arthur — with the little girl occurs at the Tuileries Gardens where he watches her playing:

A girl of twelve (he determined age with an unerring eye), dressed in a violet frock, was moving step by step her roller skates, which did not work on the gravel — lifting each in turn and bringing it down with a crunch — as she advanced at a kind of Japanese tread, through the striped rapture of the sun, toward his bench. Later (as long as that "later" endured) it would seem to him that right then, at one glance he had taken her measure from head to foot: the animation of her reddish-brown curls which had been recently trimmed, the lightness of her large vacant eyes which somehow brought to mind a semi-translucent gooseberry, the gay warm color of her face, her pink mouth, just barely open so that her two large front teeth were resting lightly on the cushion of her lower lip, the summer tan of her bare arms with sleek fox-like little hairs running along the forearms, the vague tenderness of her still narrow but already not at all flat chest, the movement of the folds in her skirt, their short sweep and light fall back into place, the slenderness and glow of her careless legs, the sturdy straps of her roller skates. She stopped in front of the amiable woman sitting beside him who, turning to rummage in something which she had by her right hand side, found and held out to the little girl a piece of chocolate on a piece of bread. Chewing rapidly, she undid the straps with her free hand, shook off all the heaviness of steel soles on solid wheels — and, descending to us on earth, having straightened up with a sudden sensation of heavenly nakedness which took a moment to grow aware of being shaped by shoes and socks, she rushed off.

The sexual advance upon the nymphet does not occur in *The Magician* until what would be, in print, the next-to-last page of the story. They are at an inn together shortly after the death of the girl's mother:

"Is this where I sleep?" the little girl asked indifferently, and when, struggling with the shutters so to further close the slits between them, he answered, yes, she looked at her cap which she was holding in her hand and limply tossed it onto the broad bed.

"Well," he said after the old porter who had lugged in their suitcases had left, and there remained only the beating of his heart and the distant shiver of the night, "Well . . . Now to bed."

Unsteady in her drowsiness, she stumbled against the edge of the armchair, and, then, simultaneously sitting down, he drew her to him by encircling her hip; she, arching her body, grew up like an angel, strained all her muscles for a moment, took still another half-step, and then lightly sank down in his lap. "My darling, my poor little girl," he murmured in a sort of general mist of pity, tenderness, and desire, observing her sleepiness, fuzziness, her wan smile, fondling her through her dark dress, feeling the stripe of the orphan's garter through its thin wool, thinking about her defenselessness, her state of abandonment, her warmth, enjoying the animated weight of her legs which sprawled loose and then again, with an ever so light bodily rustle, hunched themselves up higher — and she slowly wound one dreamy tight-sleeved arm around the back of his neck, immersing him in the chestnut odor of her soft hair.

The setting, of innocence and angelic semi-acquiescence, has a much graver aspect than the similar scene in *Lolita* in which Humbert is himself "seduced" by the unvirginal little nymphet.

Nabokov took note of newspaper imitations of his theme during the time he was writing the novel and included some in it — thus Humbert is interrogated by a meddling woman, who, he thinks to himself, must be asking: "Had I done to Dolly, perhaps, what Frank Lasalle, a fifty-year-old mechanic, had done to eleven-year-old Sally Horner in 1948?" and this refers to an actual case of a Philadelphia mechanic who took an eleven-year-old Camden girl to Atlantic City. In *Lolita* Nabokov takes a mad obsession and follows it through to its even madder consequences. But then the strangest thing of all happens — Humbert falls in love with Lolita, not the Dolly Haze who satisfied the obsessive dream of his childhood, but the real one for the violation of whom he murders Quilty — the embodiment of all Humbert's lecherousness. Thus Humbert, who did not deflower Dolly and who is in prison for murder rather than child molestation, is concerned in the book he writes with two things — his human failure toward Lolita and his very real love for her, which has nothing to do with sex. Dolly, however, has not been completely broken by her relationship with Humbert. At the book's end she is steadfastly attached — married to a devoted if unexciting mechanic. (Her death, however, in giving birth to his child does seem both fated and natural, and it recalls Nabokov's 1934 story *The Beauty*, in which the heroine also dies in childbirth very shortly after her long overdue marriage.) Humbert has the means to soften his own guilt toward Lolita, but it is not his intention to rationalize what he has done. When Humbert addresses the "gentlemen of the jury," he has himself in the dock: "Sometimes . . . Come on, how often exactly, Bert? Can you recall four, five more such occasions? Or would no human heart have survived two or three? Sometimes (I have nothing to say in reply to your question), while Lolita would be . . ."

It does not seem to me to have been widely noticed that one must speak of two Humbert Humberts in *Lolita*, and this may in fact be the sense behind the lugubrious double name. There is the one everyone knows — lecher and debaucher of small children.

But there is also the one who, when he confronts Clare Quilty, calls himself Dolores Haze's father. This Humbert not only murders this image of his darkest self — which is, after all, comparatively easy — but he then retraces everything that has happened to him (the writing of the book is an exact parallel to the second journey in pursuit of Quilty and Lolita) and mercilessly cauterizes himself at every kumfy kabin in which he abused Lolita and deprived her of her childhood. Humbert Humbert would smile at the suggestion, but he has honestly faced everything he did and did not do and thereby cleansed himself of his unclean past; although he himself denies it, he has been "cured." The murder he commits is seen by him to have been morally necessary, both in itself and so that he, the other Humbert, could live to give his Lolita refuge and immortality in art. For the rest, however, there is no possibility of mercy in his own eyes: "Had I come before myself, I would have given Humbert at least thirty-five years for rape, and dismissed the rest of the charges." Whereas the novel opens with an incantation of "Lolita, light of my life, fire of my loins," it ends with a declaration of pure love: "That husband of yours, I hope, will always treat you well, because otherwise my specter shall come at him, like black smoke, like a demented giant, and pull him apart nerve by nerve."

The Foreword to the novel by John Ray, Jr., Ph.D., is in large part a joke ("*Lolita* should make all of us — parents, social workers, educators — apply ourselves with still greater vigilance . . ."), but one should not be taken in — there are several very serious things said in this Foreword. They come either from Nabokov himself or Humbert (as one critic has noted, John Ray, Jr., equals JR Jr.), and one of these statements is probably the truest single sentence statement about *Lolita* that could be made:

If, however, for this paradoxical prude's comfort, an editor attempted to dilute or omit scenes that a certain type of mind might call "aphrodisiac" (see in this respect the monumental decision rendered December 6, 1933, by Hon. John M. Woolsey in regard to another, considerably more outspoken, book), one would have to forego the publication of *Lolita* altogether, since those very scenes that one might ineptly accuse of a sensuous existence of their own, are the most strictly functional ones in the development of a tragic tale tending unswervingly to nothing less than a moral apotheosis.

Lolita is, as Lionel Trilling has said, about love, and its morality is a natural corollary of its concern. It "has no moral in tow" simply because, given the nature of Humbert's sin, his gain must occur at the price of the loss that can have no counterbalance.

There is one other point that should be touched upon in discussion of the novel's "erotic content." There exists in the Russian literary tradition a much clearer differentiation between popular pornography and the serious use of sexual themes than is found in English or even in French literature. D. H. Lawrence is closer in intent and spirit (and here the word "pornographic" must be used) to Artsybashev, Verbitskaya, and Nagrodskaya than he is to Dostoevsky (the famous suppressed chapter of *The Possessed*), Leskov (the powerfully and evilly erotic *Lady Macbeth of Mtsensk Province*), Sologub, Kuzmin (a Russian Firbank), Rozanov (whom Lawrence so derided), Kuprin, or any of the revolutionary writers such as Pilnyak and Babel in whose works realistic scenes of extreme sexuality were included. In émigré literature occasional erotic passages and themes continued to occur in the works of serious authors such as Bunin and Korvin-Piotrovsky, and this was accepted without any special outcry. The exception was a work entitled *The Splitting of the Atom* by Georgy Ivanov, which, judging by its title and theme, seems to have been intended as "a Russian answer" to Henry Miller's *Tropic of Cancer* — the American can always go home, but the Russian does not have that option — and which includes, among other things, a not particularly appealing description of necrophilia. There was a partial "conspiracy of silence" in the Russian émigré press about *Splitting of the Atom* which was said to have been initiated by a letter signed "a Russian mother" and sent to various editors; Nabokov himself referred derisively to the book in print, but Vladislav Khodasevich, somewhat more fairly, I think, noted in *Renaissance* in 1938 that the book had intrinsic merit which was marred and obscured by its excesses of pornography.

There was scarcely any reason then for Nabokov to think of his modest short story as in any real sense "daring" or "shocking," and it may be reasonably speculated that *Lolita* itself would not have caused quite the sensation had it appeared in the emigration in 1939 — given the eminence that Nabokov had by then achieved and the presence of critics such as Bitsilli, Khodasevich, and Varshavsky — that it was to cause slightly less than twenty years later in America as "an underground Parisian novel." Of course one does not want to pretend that *Lolita* is an innocent idyll, but I think that the original plot of *The Magician* in which the molestation is only attempted — and that at the very end of the story — does show clearly that Nabokov's primary concern is not with the particular subject so much as with the psychological and artistic problems inherent in it. Two of Nabokov's early short stories also treat sexual themes in a manner that deliberately stops short of the protagonist's desired goal. *A Fairytale* (1926) is an unassuming and almost disarmingly simple little fable about sexual desire. Fyodor Sologub wrote many tales in this manner (one of the best of them for example, *The Queen of Kisses*, is about a queen who disrobes and offers herself to all her subjects), but there is no question of influence here inasmuch as Nabokov has read very little of Sologub's prose and values Sologub primarily as a poet. A timid little man named Erwin has made a ritual as he travels to and from work every day of "selecting a harem" for himself from among the women he sees from the window of his trolley-car seat. Once he had summoned up the nerve to approach a woman whom he took to be a prostitute, but he had erred in his judgment, and since then he has avoided women except for his harmless trolley fantasies. Then one day in a café, after he has just made a mental choice through the window, a woman sitting opposite him says aloud: "That can be arranged." She explains to the surprised Erwin that she is the devil.

The devil, in the guise of Madame Ott (curiously, one of the alternate pseudonyms Humbert informs us he considered was Otto Otto), tells Erwin that she has been attracted by the rare combination of timidity and fierce desire in him, and that he may select himself a harem between noon and midnight the next day. Madame Ott allays all of Erwin's doubts and fears: he will not be required to sacrifice his soul for this pleasure, a much more commodious place of assignation with his chosen women than his meager little room will be provided, and he may choose as many women as he wishes so long as the final total number is odd. And this, as it must in any fairytale, proves his undoing, for in a rush to achieve his odd number just before the time is up he by mistake selects as his thirteenth choice the same girl who was also his first choice, and this time she reproaches him in the same way as the woman he had once taken to be a prostitute. Erwin's twelfth choice is a nymphet; he might have had his harem had he not chosen her. Instead, Erwin and Madame Ott chat familiarly and indifferently, like two office workers, and go their separate ways. *A Fairytale*, by the way, as is indicated at one point, is a partial imitation of E. T. A. Hoffmann.

A Dashing Fellow (in Russian, *Khvat;* the story is undated but was probably written sometime between 1935 and 1937) is a much more serious treatment of the same problem of moral duty versus sexual desire that faces Humbert. A traveling salesman, a Russian émigré named Konstantin, meets a somewhat pretentious but very friendly German actress on a train; he himself has a more than slightly fanciful vision of the "estate" his family used to have in Russia, and he and the actress get on very well together, as she readily agrees to Konstantin's proposal that he get off the train with her and spend the night at her apartment. The actress goes out to buy some food with money he has given her, and while she is gone someone comes and leaves a message for her that her father is dying. When she returns, Konstantin tries to hustle her to bed, but she is more interested in eating, and Konstantin has "an awkward, messy, and premature spasm." He tells her that he is going out to get some cigars, but heads instead for the station where he has checked his bag and leaves the town. He considers sending her a note about her father, but then decides that she will find out sooner or later anyway, and that there would probably have been an unpleasant scene if he had stayed to tell her. The narrative viewpoint plays a very important role in *A Dashing Fellow* — the narrator is Konstantin himself, and the story is told in a nonchalant first person plural: "What an old rag she was! No, we only like little blondes — we'll have to keep that in mind from now on. This train is packed full, and it's hot. We're somehow not feeling our usual self — one can't say whether it's hunger or fatigue. But when we have eaten and had a good sleep, life will get better again, and the American instruments in the gay café Lange told me about will start to play. And, in several years, we'll die." Moral judgment in *A Dashing Fellow* obviously resides with the reader, and this story provides, I think, a good measure of how earnest and morally involved, for all his wit and raillery, Humbert Humbert really is.

The story of *Lolita*'s publication, as is well known, concerns a non-existent novel, invented by hasty publishers' readers, which is somewhat more simplified and considerably more explicit than the one which Nabokov in fact wrote. The work on *Lolita* was completed in 1954, and in submitting the novel to various American publishers Nabokov at first, on the advice of a friend, took the cautionary step of stipulating that the book was to appear anonymously, but very shortly afterward he came to feel "how likely a mask was to betray my cause" and so made the decision to sign his name to the book. The reaction of the publishers who saw the book was a compound of fright and incomprehension, and as a result of this, *Lolita* was submitted to the infamous Olympia Press in Paris. This decision was in certain respects a tactical error almost as serious as the abandoned decision not to sign the novel. The Olympia Press (it was later hounded out of France by the de Gaulle government), which was headed by Maurice Girodias, can indeed claim some very prominent publishing credits, including works by Durrell, Beckett, Donleavy, and Genet, but Girodias himself, I presume, would not deny that the *sine qua non* for books published by Olympia was their sexual content. Moreover, Girodias' business ethics — about which Nabokov has written in *The Evergreen Review* (February, 1967) — were no more above reproach than most of the books he published. In an article which he wrote detailing his early dealings and subsequent dispute with Nabokov ("*Lolita*, Nabokov, and I," *Evergreen Review*, September, 1965), Girodias states quite frankly: "I sensed that *Lolita* would become the one great modern work of art to demonstrate once and for all the futility of moral censorship, and the indispensable role of passion in literature." Nabokov had no interest in using his novel to lead a crusade against censorship — Girodias reports that Nabokov explicitly stated that he would be deeply hurt if the novel were to obtain a *succès de scandale* — and it is quite obvious, too, that Girodias and Nabokov had somewhat different conceptions about the nature and role of passion in literature. But by the very fact of appearing under the imprint of the publisher of *White Thighs* and *The Sexual Life of Robinson Crusoe*, Nabokov's novel — probably the most chaste book ever printed by Olympia — could scarcely help but have a *succès de scandale*.

All things considered, however, the book had a relatively swift and happy victory over its at first unpromising history. *Lolita*, in spite of the high value Girodias placed on the novel, was not treated any differently than any one of the steady run of Olympia titles, and in the first year after its publication it sold poorly and received no reviews. But then Graham Greene named *Lolita* as one of the best books of the year in an interview in the London *Times*. Greene's pronouncement aroused great controversy, but also stimulated the interest of many important and respected critics and writers who, with few exceptions, were quick to recognize the enormous importance and non-pornographic nature of the novel. Girodias continued to have trouble with the French censorship (in 1957 he published a curious little book of assorted documents, letters, and materials relating to the general topic of censorship under the title *L'Affaire Lolita*), but in an unexpected demonstration of good sense and judgment the U.S. Customs Bureau made the decision to release confiscated copies of the Olympia *Lolita* to their owners, which meant in effect that the book was free to be published in America with no danger to author or publisher.

The possible "objections" to *Lolita* were countered most cogently by V. S. Pritchett writing in *The New Statesman*:

I can imagine no book less likely to incite the corruptible reader; the already corrupted would surely be devastated by the author's power of projecting himself into their fantasy-addled minds. As for the minors, the nymphets and schoolboys, one hardly sees *them* toiling through a book written in a difficult style, filled on every page with literary allusions, linguistic experiment and fits of idiosyncrasy.

Pritchett also makes a very telling point about the object of all the outcry over Lolita:

The book ends with a murder which makes our "respectable" murder mongers and classy writers of sadistic thrillers (never threatened with prosecution) look like the fakers they are. Being comic, Mr. Nabokov's murder is horrible. Murder is. By what perversion of moral judgment does society regard murder as "clean" and sex as "dirty" as a subject?

My own favorite reactions to *Lolita* are, first, the review in the distinguished American Catholic magazine *Commonweal* which states firmly: "It has been said that this book has a high literary value; it has much more; a style, an individuality, a brilliance which may yet create a tradition in American letters," and, placed right beside it, the reaction of a certain Adolf Eichmann who, given a copy of the novel to read in his cell in Jerusalem, declared: *"Das ist aber ein sehr unerfreuliches Buch"* ("That is quite an offensive book").

The primary means by which the reader of *Lolita* is separated from the narrator's passion are the vulgarity and shallowness which, Humbert confides, are very often found in the true nymphet. (This term, by the way, was indignantly claimed by French critics as belonging to their language: *nymphette* occurs as far back as the seventeenth century in such poets as Ronsard; what they failed to note, however, is that Ronsard is mentioned in the novel.) Dolores Haze is no idealized little water maiden: she is "the Lolita of the strident voice and the rich brown hair — of the bangs and the swirls at the sides and the curls at the back, and the sticky hot neck, and the vulgar vocabulary — 'revolting,' 'super,' 'luscious,' 'goon,' 'drip'— *that* Lolita, *my* Lolita." In the course of their cross-country trip her passion for comics, soda, chewing gum, and other Americana will prove to be the only means Humbert has to keep her acquiescent to his amatory needs. When, after he has already had intercourse with her, Humbert tells Lo that her mother is dead, Humbert's consolatory gesture to her is an orgy of trinkets and gadgets. As F. W. Dupee has so correctly noted, this ritual of bribe and banter is in essence an extreme parody of the "normal" man's form of collusion with his child:

"It would take hours of blandishments, threats and promises to make her lend me for a few seconds her brown limbs in the seclusion of the five-dollar room before undertaking anything she might prefer to my poor joy . . . Mentally, I found her to be a disgustingly conventional little girl. Sweet hot jazz, square dancing, gooey fudge sundaes, musicals, movie magazines . . . She it was to whom ads were dedicated: the ideal consumer, the subject and the object of every foul poster."

It almost seems at times as if Humbert is determined not even to allow the irrational command of beauty to suggest itself as a partial explanation for what he has done, or perhaps he wishes to flaunt the constancy of his love, even while he is bribing her, even when he has lost her, and "even if those eyes of hers would fade to myopic fish, and her nipples swell and crack, and her lovely young velvety delicate delta be tainted and torn — even then I would go mad with tenderness at the mere sight of your dear wan face, at the mere sound of your raucous young voice, my Lolita." There has been much written about Humbert's nympholepsy as a kind of perverted idealism. The French critic Denis de Rougemont attempted to see a Tristan and Isolde pattern in the novel, but had to admit finally that Lolita is no Isolde and that the novel is, at best, a *"Tristan manqué."* Humbert himself exercises his scholarly skills in what purport to be historical asides ("Among Sicilians sexual relations between a father and daughter are accepted as a matter of course . . . I'm a great admirer of Sicilians, fine athletes, fine musicians, fine upright people, Lo . . ."), but many of the comparisons he makes are not really applicable — Beatrice was eight when Dante saw her, but he himself was nine, and there was never any actual romance between them — and many that are applicable such as Swinburne and Baudelaire (both writers Nabokov knows well) and Dowson are not mentioned. The most outstanding literary forebear to Humbert's situation is the marriage of Edgar Allan Poe to a girl child, and Humbert does make numerous references to this. The historian of literature knows, however, that Poe married his child bride primarily to tighten his rather strange and neurotic ties to her guardian aunt. If *Lolita* were indeed modeled on the life of Poe (as at least one article has tried to maintain), Humbert would marry Lolita in order to be closer to her mother Charlotte!

Lolita is not the elaboration of either a literary myth or a Freudian myth. F. W. Dupee is perfectly correct again in stating that the Humbert-Lolita relationship is presented in such a way so as to make the usual Freudian interpretation of fathers wanting to sleep with their daughters "ridicule itself out of existence." But *Lolita* does unfold according to a subterranean sexual myth of its own, which is only indirectly connected with nymphets and which is far more complex than the usual Freudian stereotypes. In the second part of *Lolita* in particular the book's mythic or fairy-tale aspect emerges to challenge and at times overpower, only to withdraw again, the novel's realistic base.

Humbert's passion is a consuming ideal, but it is important to remember that, quite apart from society's norms (which may vary from age to age and country to country), it is beyond any doubt a *perverse* ideal. The specific psychological character of Humbert's perversion is very close to homosexuality, though Humbert is not (repeat: *not*) in fact a homosexual. At one point early in the novel Humbert tells the reader about one of several occasions on which he lapsed into insanity and spent some time in a sanatorium: "I discovered there an endless source of robust enjoyment in trifling with psychiatrists; cunningly leading them on; never letting them see that you know all the tricks of the trade . . . By bribing a nurse I won access to some files and discovered, with glee, cards calling me 'potentially homosexual' and 'totally impotent.' "

Humbert claims that the basic appeal of a nymphet is the perilous indefiniteness of her form, and he even wishes to see in nymphets a third sex. The nymphet is indeed a female caught at that moment in her life — from age nine to fourteen — when her sexual development has begun, but during which time she in many respects resembles a young boy much more than a mature woman. Moreover, the true nymphet cannot be picked from a large group of girls by any such simple outward sign as mere prettiness, and Lolita's tomboyish personality and manner of dress lead one to suspect that *this* is the true criterion by which nymphets are determined. Since the nymphet herself is evidently a form of sexual displacement for Humbert, it is only natural, when he is in her presence in the Haze house but has not possessed Lolita, to double his displacement. "What I had madly possessed was not she, but my own creation, another, fanciful Lolita — perhaps more real than Lolita . . . The child knew nothing. I had done nothing to her. And nothing prevented me from repeating a performance that affected her as little as if she were a photographic image rippling upon a screen and I a humble hunchback abusing myself in the dark." There are many such statements hinting at or clearly suggesting masturbation in the first half of the novel: "Little did the good lady dream that one morning when an upset stomach (the result of my trying to improve on her sauces) had prevented me from accompanying her to church, I deceived her with one of Lolita's anklets."

Humbert's dreams of Lolita, interestingly, are mingled with the images of the "real" women he has married, Valeria and Charlotte: "She did haunt my sleep but she appeared there in strange and ludicrous disguises as Valeria or Charlotte, or a cross between them. That complex ghost would come to me, shedding shift after shift, in an atmosphere of great melancholy and disgust, and would recline in dull invitation on some narrow board or hard settee, with flesh ajar like the rubber valve of a soccer ball's bladder." This, too, brings to mind Disa and para-Disa from *Pale Fire*, but here the second image of Lolita is an admixture of normal womanliness and the aversion that the pervert both feels in himself and senses in others about himself. In all of the mature women with whom Humbert has lived there are either plausible suggestions of nymphancy (Valeria, for example, although she is quite plump, has cultivated certain childish mannerisms that were enough to charm Humbert), or else (as in the case of the female scientist in the Arctic expedition, or the neighborly and willing Jean Farlow) Humbert is quite impotent. Charlotte Haze possesses the nymphet herself, but, implausible as Charlotte is in that role, Humbert even manages — he must, after all, have intercourse with her — to espy traces of Lolita in Charlotte. Taken at its face value, Humbert's abandoned urge to drown Charlotte while they are swimming in a local lake is simply a desire for clear access to Lolita, but Humbert's real wish reaches much farther than that — to the destruction of all mature women. He has done horrible things to Valeria; he is spared by fate from actually murdering Charlotte as he planned; and when he is called in to the Beardsley School for a conference by Miss Pratt, who is concerned about Dolly's morbid *dis*interest in sexual matters ("She is still shuttling between the anal and genital zones of development"), the thought flashes through his mind: "Should I marry Pratt and strangle her?"

There is, however, one mature woman (and Humbert tells us she is precisely twice Lolita's age) who is an exception to this pattern, and she is the second most important female character in the novel. This woman is Rita, the drunken divorcée whom Humbert picks up in a bar shortly after he has lost Lolita and who occupies only six pages in the novel. Nonetheless, those few pages span a period of time exactly matching the time — two years — that he lived with Lolita, and it is with Rita that his love for Lo moves beyond perversion and the second Humbert moves downstage at last in the novel. We know that Rita is smallish, but Humbert does not mention that she has any of the essential attributes of a nymphet. The key to her success with Humbert is her ability to make no demands of or on him. "She was so kind, was Rita, such a good sport, that I daresay she would have given herself to any pathetic creature or fallacy, an old broken tree or a bereaved porcupine, out of sheer chumminess and compassion." It is precisely compassion rather than passion that Humbert requires, and Rita, who is herself an outcast, is able to give him everything freely: companionship, sex that keeps him out of mischief, sympathy, and approval of his intention to find and kill the man who has stolen his Lolita. She even leaves him as painlessly and naturally as she first joined him, and Humbert addresses his warmest words to her: "There is no earthly reason why I should dally with her in the margin of this sinister memoir, but let me say (hi, Rita — wherever you are, drunk or hangoverish, Rita, hi!) that she was the most soothing, the most comprehending companion that I ever had, and certainly saved me from the madhouse." Once Rita and Humbert awaken in their hotel room to find a strange man sleeping on the edge of Rita's bed. The man is completely amnesiac, and they drop him off at the local hospital on their way out of town after having named him "Jack Humbertson." The "isolation from his personal past" of Jack Humbertson serves two functions — it is a sign or shadow of what has happened to Humbert, and it initiates a chain of actions that will take him back to The Enchanted Hunters, where he first stayed with Lolita, and set the stage for another journey, his last meeting with Lolita, and his revenge upon his past.

Humbert's perversion is characterized by a constant dissociation from the sexual act and also by voyeurism and the fear that he is being watched by others. The essential component of joy in making love to a nymphet, Humbert informs us, is the very distance in ages between the man and his nymphet; a nymphet cannot be a nymphet to a boy who is even approximately her own age. This distance in time and, until Lolita, the inaccessibility of nymphets is a transposed equivalent of voyeurism. In a light mood Humbert asks us to imagine the spectacle that would be presented if all the pigment were to drain from the outer walls of motel cabins, and he himself hallucinates that the same thing will happen to him as he makes love to Lolita. By means of his "urgent and well-paid request," he learns from Lolita all the "incredible details" of her friend Mona Dahl's affair with a marine, just as earlier, at Charlotte's urging, he tells us, he traded fictionalized accounts of his past mistresses for the hilarious details of Harold Haze's sexual practices with Charlotte. Humbert compares the sex act to an epileptic fit several times — "that leaping epilepsy."

Proper understanding of the function of dissociation in *Lolita* is essential in understanding the role and place of the mysterious Clare Quilty in the novel. Just who is he? As his very name indicates ("*Qu'il t'y* [*mène*]" means "that he [take] you there"), Quilty is both the way in which Humbert has led Lolita astray and the possible further depths to which Humbert's perversion could lead him. Clare Quilty's role, as his name also shows, is both clear and obscure. Ostensibly he is a well-known American playwright who shares Humbert's passion for nymphets. He meets Lolita when she is given a role in one of his plays, eventually steals her from Humbert who tracks him down and subjects him to "my so-called mercy." But Quilty is also Humbert's perverse *alter ego*, the most prominent piece of the full field of opposing chess figures whose dark standard is perversion. It is when the game moves into its crucial phase and Quilty and Humbert track each other in turn that the realistic pretense of *Lolita* is dropped, and the novel becomes either a madman's fantasy or an artist's surrealistic rendering of a deadly, sexual chess match. Like Rita, Quilty has a comparatively minor role in the novel (one of the achievements of the movie version of *Lolita* was the way in which Quilty's prominence in the narrative was heightened, even if this was done primarily to increase the part for the star who had the role), but the reader who pays careful attention to Quilty's appearances must, in the end, question the entire realistic basis of the story.

The secondary forces of Quilty's pieces include Humbert's friend and fellow chess player Gaston Godin, Gustave Trapp (Humbert's father's queer cousin whom he remembers from childhood), and such minor figures as Lolita's classmate Kenneth Knight, who exhibits himself at every opportunity and whom, in his imagination, Humbert has Charlotte accuse of having violated Lolita. Godin knows all the little boys in the neighborhood, and he feeds them chocolates with real liqueurs in the Oriental basement den he has built, where one sloping wall is adorned with pictures of such people as André Gide, Nijinski ("all thighs and fig leaves"), and one Harold D. Doublename, who Humbert informs us is "a misty-eyed left-wing professor at a Midwestern university."

Quilty is Humbert's other half in the most literal sense of the term, as we see when we compare Humbert's estimate of the distance he has covered in his travels with Lolita (about 27,000 miles) with the run, given in a "biographical note" from *Who's Who in the Limelight* much earlier, of Quilty's play *Little Nymph*, which traveled 14,000 miles. The contest that is the novel is a struggle — chess game if you will, but only in a loose sense — between the related forces of perversion and nympholepsy and those of normalcy and love. Humbert does win the seemingly impossible struggle by transforming the symbol of his perverse passion into an object of actual love. This transference necessitates the annihilation of his old self and the loss of his nymphet who was so closely tied to that old self. As Rita loved Humbert in spite of all, the supremely perverse Quilty, who even tries to make Lolita take part in the filming of stag movies, is adored by Lolita. And, like so many of Nabokov's heroes before him, Humbert's love for Lolita can only be realized in her absence, in the pain and purity of memory and of art. For he can never make the real Lolita forget what he has done to her.

The foregoing discussion of *Lolita*'s underlying sexuality should in itself bring to mind the true literary forerunner and partial model for Nabokov's masterpiece. It is Proust's *Remembrance of Things Past*, and there is an excellent long article — one of the best written on *Lolita* of the many I have read — comparing *Lolita* with Proust's novel in close detail. The article, by Octavio Mello Alvarenga, is written in Portuguese; its title is *"Proust e Nabokov: Aproximações,"* and it appeared in the Brazilian journal *Revista do Livro* in June, 1960.

The similarity between the two works that Alvarenga calls attention to is, of course, that between the pairs Lolita and Humbert and Albertine and Marcel. Both Lolita and Albertine are held prisoner, and both attempt to run away from their captors. Humbert does not at first question Lolita's purity, but when she becomes his paramour, her kisses make him suspect her of lesbianism, just as Marcel comes similarly to suspect Albertine. Both Marcel and Humbert are seduced, and both are subject to fits of intense jealousy; they each enjoy considerable financial power over their lovers, in spite of which they are each deceived behind their backs. After Albertine dies her lesbianism is confirmed, and in their last meeting Lolita tells Humbert that she really loves not him or her husband Dick but the perverse Quilty. As Lolita had a predecessor in the Annabelle of Humbert's youth, Albertine too had one in Gilberte. And finally, both *Remembrance of Things Past* and *Lolita* are told in the first person singular, and memory is the primary motive force in each. The clear intent behind all or most of these parallels is attested to, as Alvarenga points out, by Humbert's passing remark that his story could be called *Dolorès Disparue; Albertine Disparue* was Proust's title for two volumes (1925) of his masterpiece.

There are also many striking differences between the two novels, and Alvarenga carefully notes many, but not all, of them. (The limitations of Alvarenga's fine piece are that it does not consider *Lolita* at all outside the context of its stated comparison, and does not move beyond its listing of particulars to compare and contrast the two works in any larger way, but this is criticizing Alvarenga for not doing something which his very interesting article did not intend to do.) Proust's novel proceeds at a deliberately and beautifully slow pace, the aim of which is poetic contemplation, whereas

Lolita is a whirlpool of journeys and chases. Albertine is very much a mirage or photographic image from the past; Lolita, on the other hand, although she technically belongs in the past, is completely vital and alive in the novel. Lolita is far less willing to please than is Albertine, and perhaps less treacherous, too.

But the most important difference of all, which Alvarenga does not note, is the tremendous difference in narrative forthrightness between the two works. To write about homosexuality, Proust adopts what Stanley Edgar Hyman has so aptly dubbed "the Albertine Strategy." In place of Albertine we must always read Albert, for *Remembrance of Things Past* is, above all, a glorification of homosexual love. It is a covert novel, and its primary weaknesses are the coyness and archness that must necessarily accompany this artistic approach. *Lolita*, however great the complexity of its patterns and underlying causes, is a perfectly overt novel: Lolita is a girl-child, and Humbert Humbert is driven by a very heterosexual, if perverse, passion to possess her. The *real* stakes in the game, of course, are quite another question again, but this does not impinge on the main action of the novel, which should be and has been taken to be the tragic story of a man's passion and love for a nymphet. The greatness of Nabokov's novel, I believe, lies primarily in the extraordinary fullness and subtlety with which the subconscious and the conscious, the realistic and the fantastic play themselves out in perfect harmony.

The second great difference between *Remembrance of Things Past* and *Lolita* is the daring and abrupt breakthrough of Nabokov's hero into normalcy. Humbert warns his reader that he would be a knave to claim that he has been cured of his mania, but, even if the passion for nymphs remains within him, "never did I dwell now on possibilities of bliss with a little maiden, specific or synthetic, in some out-of-the-way place." A new emotional order has emerged in Humbert, and it is at just this turning point that he asserts: "This book is about Lolita," a statement which can never be accepted in the way we speak of *Anna Karenina* as being "Anna's book." Humbert is the narrator, but he is far from being the omniscient stage manager of all that happens in the book and to him personally.

The assault of Humbert upon the dark side of his own past in the person of Quilty ("my brother") is explained by Alvarenga as being a symbolic murder of Lolita whom he wants to kill, but cannot because of his love for her. Quilty, in his opinion, corresponds to Lolita. I will grant that the murder of Quilty in place of Lolita is a possibility that comes readily to mind on the plane of everyday probability, but that is not the plane on which Quilty moves in the novel, and Humbert does not give a single indication that he has ever considered killing Lolita. When Humbert first learns the name of Dolly's husband and assumes that he must be the one who stole her from him, he takes Chum and practices firing into an old sweatshirt, "rehearsing the death of Dick Skiller" (who lives on Killer Street). In the French translation of *Lolita* Quilty, to turn the puzzle back on the French, is once rendered as Kilt. As he leaves Lolita to go in search of Quilty, Humbert says: "Then I pulled my automatic — I mean, this is the kind of fool thing a reader might suppose I did. It never even occurred to me to do it."

There is a 1935 Nabokov short story, *An Episode from Life*, in which a husband does murder his former wife, but the difference is that in the story the murder is totally unexpected, whereas in *Lolita* to kill Lolita would be the most banal "Frankie-and-Johnny" conclusion, and it would be quite contrary to the declared feeling of Humbert's entire narrative. Again, we have no evidence in the novel of conscious fabrication on the part of Humbert, or, for that matter, of a subconscious hatred of her. She is the most beautiful, the almost-redeeming flower of his perversion, and Humbert never has the urge — as Marcel has toward Albertine — to break off his relationship with her:

I looked and looked at her, and knew as clearly as I know I am to die, that I loved her more than anything I had ever seen or imagined on earth, or hoped for anywhere else. She was only the faint violet whiff and dead leaf echo of the nymphet I had rolled myself upon with such cries in the past; an echo on the brink of a russet ravine, with a far wood under a white sky, and brown leaves choking the brook, and one last cricket in the crisp weeds . . . but thank God it was not that echo alone that I worshipped. What I used to pamper among the tangled vines of my heart, *mon grand péché radieux*, had dwindled to its essence: sterile and selfish vice, all *that* I canceled and cursed. You may jeer at me, and threaten to clear the court, but until I am gagged and half-throttled, I will shout my poor truth.

This passage is commended to the reader for especially careful consideration, for I believe it to be one of the crucial passages in the novel.

The murder of Quilty is a ghoulishly comic dream, and not a murder as much as a partial suicide or auto-assassination. After Humbert practices killing Dick Schiller, and after he has left Dolly, he himself puts on the bullet-riddled sweatshirt. When he enters Quilty's castle, he is wearing a black suit and a black shirt, the color of the enemy forces. As he first enters and looks around, Humbert sees a number of used drink glasses, the only clue, undecipherable, that was present when Jack Humbertson made his appearance; Humbert himself "had overdone the alcoholic stimulation business." Quilty, wearing a purple bathrobe "very like one I had," confronts Humbert — and we think of Gaston Godin again — "in the Oriental parlor." The first question he puts to Humbert is an apparently obvious but actually very subtle challenge of identity: "Now who are you?"

As they spar verbally, Quilty makes every possible effort to confuse the question of both his own and Humbert's true identity. When Humbert accuses him of kidnapping Dolly Haze, Quilty cries out in protest: "I did not! You're all wet. I saved her from a beastly pervert. Show me your badge instead of shooting at my foot, you ape, you. Where is that badge? I'm not responsible for the rapes of others. Absurd!" When Quilty lurches out of his armchair to try to get Chum away from Humbert, for a brief moment they do become one again: "He was naked and goatish under his robe, and I felt suffocated as he rolled over me. I rolled over him. We rolled over me. They rolled over him. We rolled over us."

In possession of Chum once again Humbert gives Quilty a neatly typed poem to read aloud before he shoots him. It is his death sentence, and also Humbert's declaration of innocence:

> *Because you took advantage of my inner*
> *essential innocence . . .*
> *because of all you did*

because of all I did not
you have to die

The dream murder of the beastly pervert Quilty is the final fulfillment of another dream of impotence and murder that had long
haunted him: "Sometimes I attempt to kill in my dreams. But do
you know what happens? For instance I hold a gun. For instance I
aim at a bland, quietly interested enemy. Oh, I press the trigger all
right, but one bullet after another feebly drops on the floor from
the sheepish muzzle. In those dreams, my only thought is to
conceal the fiasco from my foe, who is slowly growing annoyed."
When Humbert fires his first bullet at Quilty, there is in fact a
"paralyzing" moment during which he thinks that "it had merely
trickled in and might come out again," but Quilty has inherited his
impotence as well as his guilt ("You see, I had no fun with your
Dolly. I am practically impotent, to tell the melancholy truth"),
and the rest of the shots he fires do find their nebulous mark.

Clare Quilty, with his "strange feminine manner," is at last
brought to beg for his life, but, since he has no life apart from
Humbert's will, the question of "life and death" is only a convention that Humbert observes with himself.

Ghosts and phantoms do not die easily, and as he pumps bullet
after bullet into him Humbert understands that "far from killing
him I was injecting spurts of energy into the poor fellow." At one
bullet Quilty rises "like old, gray, mad Nijinski, like Old Faithful,
like some old nightmare of mine." As is appropriate to the farce
they are enacting, Quilty greets every shot with mimicry, a fake
accent, a joke. He suffers as Punch suffers (Humbert has called
him that), and he bleeds the blood of Blok's Pierrot — a black
Pierrot, of course — cranberry juice. Quilty is quite literally a "semi-
animated, subhuman trickster who had sodomized" his darling, and
seven or eight bullets cannot exterminate him as well as a simple
theatrical curtain: Humbert threads his way out through the
enemy ranks (guests have dropped in while the murder is in
progress and are helping themselves to Quilty's liquor), whereupon Quilty collapses in a heap at the top of the stairs.

But Quilty is much more than the dubious incarnation of Humbert's sinister side (when Quilty is no more, Humbert drives

without fear on the left-hand side of the road not, as some have thought, because he is "beyond the law," but because he has no more to fear from his sinister double). Quilty is also, like Charles Kinbote, the repository of certain essential clues about other aspects of the novel that Nabokov wishes to give the reader but cannot very well put in the mouth of Humbert himself. While Humbert is being seduced by Lolita in The Enchanted Hunters, Clare Quilty is there, too, writing his *The Enchanted Hunters* in which Lolita will play and meet the playwright. Humbert, turning Freud on his head, advances the interesting and appealing idea that "it is not the artistic aptitudes that are secondary sexual characters as some shams and shamans have said; it is the other way around: sex is but the ancilla of art." And, with that in mind, we examine the plot of Quilty's *The Enchanted Hunters:* "[They] went through a complete change of mind in Dolly's Dell, and remembered their real lives only as dreams or nightmares from which little Diana had aroused them, but a seventh Hunter (in a *green* cap, the fool) was a Young Poet, and he insisted, much to Diana's annoyance, that she and the entertainment provided (dancing nymphs, and elves, and monsters) were his, the Poet's, invention . . . The play's profound message [was] that mirage and reality merge in love."

Precisely. And thus not only is the novel defined, but we are shown how even *Lolita* may be read according to Khodasevich's formulation about Nabokov's art. One would not have thought that a stranger allegory of the artistic process than the murder in *Despair* could be found, and yet lust and child-molestation as a tale representing the tragic pain and entrancing beauty of art and the tremendous price it exacts are just that. Or, if we read Quilty's play as an exact critical prescription, then all of *Lolita* becomes as fantastic a world as that of *Invitation to a Beheading*. The fatal hotel room at the Enchanted Hunters is a panoply of mirrored surfaces whose many reflections seem to take away the reality of the room that is held within them. *Lolita*, like all of Vladimir Nabokov's art, is no less mirrored, but it can claim pre-eminence among all his other novels because its central reality remains ever firm and vibrant, even while its diabolically artful reflections play around it.

There remains only a brief footnote for the future. Nabokov has four major projects at hand or under way. One — his lectures on Russian and European literature at Cornell — has already been mentioned. The second is a short book on butterflies. The third, recently completed, is a Russian translation of *Lolita* undertaken, Nabokov has said, because, when he imagined the distant future time when a Russian translation of the novel might be done, "I saw that every paragraph could lend itself to a hideous mistranslation." This translation, which reminds us again of his unbroken tie to his native language, will likely prove of great importance for further study of *Lolita*. Slight changes of phrasing and the reworking of puns and other verbal effects have been of great interest and importance in many of Nabokov's English translations of his Russian novels, and now, for the first time, one of his English novels will have its own "double" to be studied and compared.

But by far the most important forthcoming work is a new novel now in progress. Its title is *Ada* and is to be in large degree an artistic expression and exploration of the precise meaning of time. Time has occupied an important place in almost all of Nabokov's major fiction, although it has most often been contained within the context of the theme of memory. In *The Gift* Fyodor tells Koncheyev:

Our mistaken feeling of time as a kind of growth is a consequence of our finiteness which, being always on the level of the present, implies its constant rise between the watery abyss of the past and the aerial abyss of the future. Existence is thus an eternal transformation of the future into the past — an essentially phantom process — a mere reflection of the material metamorphoses taking place within us . . . The theory I find most tempting — that there is no time, that everything is the present situated like a radiance outside our blindness — is just as hopeless a finite hypothesis as all the others.

Two minor English short stories, *Time and Ebb* (1944) and *Lance* (1952), are in large part concerned with the nature of time. In *Time and Ebb* a memoirist writes about the time before the "stupendous discoveries" of the 1970's, which are evidently connected with time and immortality:

Elementary allobiotic phenomena led their so-called spiritualists to the silliest forms of transcendental surmise and made so-called common sense shrug its broad shoulders in equally silly ignorance. Our de-nominations of time would have seemed to them "telephone" numbers. They played with electricity in various ways without having the slightest notion of what it really was — and no wonder the chance revelation of its true nature came as a most hideous surprise (I was a man by that time and can well remember old Professor Adams sobbing his heart out on the campus in the midst of a dumbfounded crowd).

Lance is a story that mocks "science fiction," but all the same allows it a certain unintentional crude verisimilitude:

Now if one is perfectly honest with oneself, there is nothing extraor-dinary in the tendency to give to the manners and clothes of a distant day (which happens to be placed in the future) an old-fashioned tinge, a badly pressed, badly groomed, dusty something, since the terms "out of date," "not of our age," and so on are in the long run the only ones in which we are able to imagine and express a strangeness no amount of research can foresee. The future is but the obsolete in reverse.

As Nabokov has described his new novel it is to be a scholarly sort of essay on the nature of time in which the metaphors and similes (without which, according to Nabokov, it is very difficult to speak of time at all) gradually start to live and assume the guise of a story, after which they start "to bleed and fall apart," trailing off into the same recondite essay with which the novel begins. This then will be — what one would have thought impossible after *Pale Fire* — another entirely new departure, and will also mark the elevation of a secondary motif in Nabokov's fiction to the level of a primary concern.

Twelve

IN PLACE OF A BIBLIOGRAPHY

❋ ❋ ❋ ❋

THE complete works of Vladimir Nabokov (with the exception of letters) would, if collected, comprise something between thirty and thirty-five ample volumes. And, if such a Complete Works were to be published with facing English or Russian texts where necessary, the project would grow to well over fifty volumes. Although such a project would require at least a decade and many tens of thousands of dollars to complete, I view it as an urgently needed scholarly undertaking awaiting one of our more ambitious university presses.

As matters stand now, unfortunately, there is not a library in the world that possesses a collection of all that Nabokov has written. Harvard University's Widener Library contains the largest collection, and although it lacks numerous Sirin books, it possesses the only almost-full microfilm run of *The Rudder* (compiled from the partial holdings in several European libraries with only a few lacunae remaining), the Paris paper *Latest News*, and a complete set of *Contemporary Annals* and *Russian Annals*. The New York Public Library and the Library of Congress also have sizable Nabokov collections, and the University of Helsinki Library, which was a copyright library for Russian publications in Tsarist times, has maintained an enormous Russian collection. There is, in addition, a very good collection of émigré publications at the Hoover Institute Library at Stanford University in Palo Alto, California.

I have used as a base for this bibliography of Nabokov's writings the excellent bibliography compiled by Dieter E. Zimmer, published by Rowohlt Verlag in 1963 and republished in revised form in 1964. The Zimmer bibliography gives all the Russian titles and first lines in transliteration, as well as in German translation, together with a complete listing of all translations of all Nabokov works. I decided not to proceed in this way because the Zimmer bibliography is available and can be referred to by those who need the Russian titles and translation information, and because such a complicated listing would have rendered *this* bibliography enormously difficult to read. With the addition of over eighty items not in the Zimmer bibliography at all, together with corrections and fuller entries, this compilation contains over three hundred additional listings (such as first lines from all poetry collections) — and is still not complete. I feel, however, that it has approached the ninety-eight or ninety-nine per cent mark and lists, I hope, everything of importance. Missing are a handful of early poems and translations, an occasional piece or two from the *Cornell Sun,* and probably a few poems and reviews from the later years of the Paris *Latest News.* I shall be most grateful to those who are able to supply any corrections or additions.

In the listing below, works originally written in English or translated into English are preceded by an asterisk.

COLLECTED POETRY

A Verse Brochure. St. Petersburg, 1914. Privately printed. This little brochure-printing of a single poem ("in a violet paper cover") has evidently been lost, barring the discovery of an old family album or trunkful of papers somewhere in Leningrad. Nabokov remembers that it had a motto from *Romeo and Juliet.*

Poems. St. Petersburg, 1916. Privately printed.
  Spring
  In Church
  Easter
  Happiness
  "Our boat is almost motionless"
  "To one in love call the carnations"

"Beyond the forest with a parting smile"
"Eternally young are my sorrows"
"Laughs the color, and laughs the line"
"No pride and no power has sorrow"
Summer Night
"In July paradise showed me its rich reflection"
"Do you recall that day? To nature, dying"
A Caress
Autumn
"You, only you I promise I shall love"
An Autumnal Poem
*Stained Glass
An Autumnal Song
"The autumn day like an old Bacchante"
"A chrysanthemum trembles in grief"
"Big lindens, reeling, sang"
"Autumn has spread its webs"
Winter
"Mauve smoke above the rooftop snow"
"Without hope I waited"
"Dancing ever more softly"
"Grasshopper sonorously echoes grasshopper"
"I await you tenderly"
"My poor heart until the pale of day"
Colloque Sentimental
To the Capital
"Do you recall — in the park, midst the languor of night"
"By the Neva's palaces I roam, not glad"
"The velvet night enveloped us in shadow"
A Dream
"I recall how obsessively sweet"
"Hyacinths with their passionate fragrance"
Our Star
Lunar Reverie
Moonlight
"How the lips burn! Our speeches we bring to an end"
"You remember my lips growing mute"
"That night I could but sob with rapture"
"The gods of autumn have shrouded the city"
"Over humans that luminous evening was brooding"

"Softly wept the willows . . . In the misty lake"
"The plucked forget-me-not he carelessly discarded"
"Beauty! Beauty! In it is mysteriously blended"
"There's something I failed to perceive, and there's somewhere a
    loss"
"When in the dark my hand meets yours"
*"I want so much, I want so little"
"It happens that clouds race in the blue"
"Whisper that word to me, that wondrous word"
Contrast
Two Moments
"Lips tender as sunbeams"
"Come sit closer to me. We'll remember together"
"I shall shed tears at the dread hour of torment"
"Chords of music like waves, and the specter of parting"
"Enough, farewell! I do not need an answer"
"How strange to look back after parting"
"Lilies I want not, innocent white lilies"
"If sometimes one spends the whole day"
"With all my strength I strive to happiness"
*A Summer Day (a prose poem)
"On your threshold I wait, into the future soaring in fancy"

Two Paths. An almanac of poems by Andrei Balashov and V. V. Nabo-
    kov. Petrograd, 1918. This collection contains eight poems by
    Balashov and twelve by Nabokov.
"The dark-blue wallpaper"
"The fields float by, the marshes pass"
Sonnet ("I have returned to my forgotten love")
"Rain has flown by and burnt out in its flight"
"Admiring the tumultuous clouds"
"Dissolved is the thunderstorm, clear the sky"
"With rain and wind the birches wrestle"
Autumn
Sonnet ("A cloudless firmament, and not a sound")
"I'm fond of unfamiliar railroad stations"
"Everlasting terror. The black quagmires"
"Of the wise and the wicked I've nothing to ask"

The Empyrean Path. Berlin, 1923.
    Dedication (To the Memory of My Father)
    To the Poet

"Live. Do not murmur, do not number"
"Vibrate, my faithful verse; hover, remembrance"
"When from the heavens onto this wild shore"
An Elegy
Two Ships
"The almond at the crossroads blossoms"
"O night, I'm yours! All evil is forgotten"
"You'll come in and sit down, silent"
"Here, in this *dacha* garden, we were happy"
Birch Tree in the Vorontsov Park
The Nut Tree and the Birch
After the Thunderstorm
"What redolence of lime and lilac"
The Staircase
"You will forget me as you will this night"
The Lake
"What am I thinking of? Of falling stars"
"And I beheld: the vaults of heavens darkened"
Sun of the Sleepless (translation from Byron)
Moonlit Night
The Great Bear
"Far from the shore, in the sea's shimmer"
The Poet
The Cranes
"When my belated light past midnight I extinguish"
"Radiance kindles aloft"
"We were enclosed within a ball of crystal"
"If my verse whirls about, if it flies, if it quivers"
Autumn Dance
The Little Shoe
"The cypresses that stand on guard"
"You are asking too much, far too much you are asking"
"The fairy's daughter has drowned in a dewdrop"
"In the sky you're a delicate cloudlet"
On a Swing
The New Year
To Iu. R. ("Like you, I from my boyhood days")
Morning
"Upon a brilliant cloud reposing"
The Scythian

"I have been in the country of Remembrance"
"That marvelous thrill of our meeting"
The Bee
Peter in Holland
Russia
"My love for this life is a frenzied love"
Cypresses
"Still I am mute, and gaining strength in silence." According to
  Nabokov, this poem, composed in March, 1919, was the last one
  which he wrote on Russian soil.
Istanbul
"I wander about in the garden and brood"
"What is it that my heart must have"
Catkin Week
The Water Nymph
"The clouds break up. The diamonds of the rain"
"So simple my dreaming, so joyful a dream"
In Memory of a Friend
"A simple song, a simple sadness"
The Blizzard
"The sky sweeps along, palpitating and blazing"
Autumn ("And again as in those sweet years")
To M.W.
"A chime, and like a dewy rainbow"
"Be with me more limpid and more simple"
Winter
"My friend, I am sincerely sorry"
Spring
"The little marquise knows"
Death
Drops of Paint
  He Who Forgives All
  Joie de vivre
  Midday in the Crimea
  Blades of Grass
  The Artist
  Apple Trees
  River Lily
  In the Forest
  Inspiration

La Morte d'Arthur
Decadence
Bearers of the Cross
A Kimono
Meretrix
*Dostoevsky
The Airplane
Napoleon in Exile
Childhood (a long poem)
Angels. This is, to me, the least interesting of all Nabokov's longer
   poems, and thus I have omitted it from consideration in Chapter
   Four of this study.
Seraphim
Cherubim
Thrones
Kingdoms
Forces
Powers
Beginnings
Archangels
Guardian Angel
The Crimea (a long poem)
Dream at the Acropolis
Wanderings
"A pale-bluing vapor hangs over the earth"
Football
"Lost forever, forever my own"
Motion
Telegraph Poles
Chestnut Trees
"In flowing drowsiness I like"
"I chanced to brush against your airy garments"
Une Romance
Swallows
Cena Domini ("Pensive hour of the austere supper")
"She has long gone away, she has long since forgotten"
To M. Sh.
"Who will drive me"
Peacocks
In Paradise ("Greetings, Death! And my winged companion")

"The ciliary little springs keep ticking"
The Forest
The Return
The Poet ("Joy and anxiety, he knew")
Autumn ("Here's Fall. With an ethereal carillon")
Imitation of the Ancients
Lawn Tennis
The Butterfly
The Cyclist
"Inspiration is the ardent passion"
"A monkey in a sarafan"
"Armless dwarf in a dress coat"
To an Italian Girl
On Calvary
"My rapture, the clouds and the glittering waters"
"I can't without tears"
Homeward
Birches
The Poets ("Well what! In years of din and stench")
Biology
To V. Sh. [*not* Shishkov] ("If the wind of fate, for the fun of it")
The Poor Artist
Clouds
The Feast
White Heaven
Horses
The Mirror
Night
La Belle Dame Sans Merci (translation from Keats)
The Drunken Knight
"I think of her, that little girl, so distant"
The Feather
"In a dim little church we have crowded"
To My Mother ("You'll tell people: the time has now come")
Rus
Life

The Cluster. Berlin, 1923.
    "Who will go out at morn? The ripe fruit who will notice?"
    "Weighed down by stifling drowsiness"
 *"There's liberty in solitude"

"From shine to shade, from shade to shine"
"I'm looking seaward from a marble temple"
"Mists of night sleep, coating of dusty languor"
"A maple leaf upon black velvet"
"We, the young ones, the winged, are few"
On the Anniversary of Dostoevsky's Death
On the Death of Blok
To Ivan Bunin
"When, still bedimmed, we saw each other first"
"About you I daydreamed so long ago, so often"
Sonnet ("A spring-time wood I see in fancy. Wait")
"Let me daydream. You're my first anguish"
"Her soul, like an extraordinary light"
"When you want I shall go away"
"O bright voice, slightly tinged with sadness"
"All the windows you opened, the curtains you drew"
"At full moon, in the drawing room, dusty and sumptuous"
"O love, you are bright, you are winged"
Eyes
"However dismally and densely"
*Easter (1922)
"Be silent, don't stir up your soul"
Tristram
"You see my signet ring? For stars, for precious stones"
"All I recall is piny fragrance"
Christmas ———
Viola tricolor
In the Menagerie
Moths
In the Train
The Express
"How often, how often in a fast train"

Poems collected as "Poems 1924–1928" in *The Return of Chorb: Stories and Poems*. Berlin, 1930.
"For happiness the man in love can't sleep"
The Quiet Sound
Bricks (a poem about a boy's footprints on ancient bricks, recalling a similar passage in *Lolita*)
The Mailbox
A Charming Season

The Snapshot
The Airplane
The Train Accident
Yuletide
The Execution
The Guest
La Bonne Lorraine
Anniversary
Lilac
To Iu. Aikhenvald: The Pilgrim
A Vision in a Dream
A Passer-by with a Christmas Tree
The Shadow
The Sun
Dreams
The Room
The Mother
Spring
*In Paradise

Poems 1929–1951. Paris, 1952.
   "I recollect your coming. Swelling tones"
   Evening in the Wasteland. This excellent 1932 poem appeared originally in *The Latest News* divided into four separate poems. The poem is structurally intended to move in four parts toward its concluding line: "*You haven't changed since the time of your death,*" a line which is addressed, according to Nabokov, to a dead friend. The personal quotient of this particular poem renders commentary on it somewhat difficult, and it is to be hoped that Nabokov himself will in some connection find occasion to make some further statement about it.
   How I Love You
   "At sunset, by that same bench"
   L'inconnue de la Seine. This poem was one of the ones annotated "from F.G.Ch." when it first appeared in *The Latest News*.
   "What happened to my memory during the night?"
   "You and I so believed"
   The Poets ("From the room to the hallway the candle progresses"). This 1939 poem addresses itself in part to Nabokov's decision to abandon the Russian language as his means of literary expression

("the silence of love").

"Will you leave me alone, I implore you!" This poem and the one before are signed "Vasily Shishkov."

Fame (a long poem)

A Parisian Poem (a long poem)

*"No matter in what battle piece depicted" (translated into English by Nabokov in *Modern Russian Poetry*, edited by Markov and Sparks)

About Rulers (". . . The historian dies from boredom: / After every Mamai just another Mamai . . .")

To Prince S. M. Kachurin (a long poem)

"It was a day like any other. My memory dozed"

Poems. New York, Doubleday, 1959.

The Refrigerator Awakes

A Literary Dinner

A Discovery

The Poem

An Evening of Russian Poetry (a long poem)

The Room. This poem about a poet who dies in a cheap hotel room, which is then occupied by another poet — the author of the poem — is a poetic treatment of the main theme of Nabokov's prose and *Pale Fire* in particular: the relationship between the artist and his creation. The concluding stanzas of the poem are — *"Perhaps my text is incomplete./ A poet's death is, after all,/ a question of technique, a neat/ enjambment, a melodic fall./ And here a life had come apart/ in darkness, and the room had grown/ a ghostly thorax, with a heart/ unknown, unloved—but not alone."*

Voluptates Tactionum

Restoration

The Poplar

Lines Written in Oregon

Ode to a Model

On Translating *Eugene Onegin*

Rain

The Ballad of Longwood Glen (a long poem)

Pale Fire. New York, Putnam, 1962. A long poem serving as an integral portion of the novel *Pale Fire.*

UNCOLLECTED POETRY

ODD JOURNAL GROUPINGS AND MISCELLANY

For convenience, in certain but not all cases, some poems that were subsequently included in collections are listed here as they originally appeared in journals or almanacs.

In 1915 young Nabokov, with his father, signed the famous guest book — the Chukokkola — of the well-known critic and children's poet Kornei Chukovsky, to which most outstanding Russian artists from Blok to Pasternak contributed. Young Nabokov's contribution, signed "son of the foregoing," was a poem that has never appeared in print.

The Zimmer bibliography lists one poem as having been published in *The Messenger of Europe* in 1916 (this poem is one of those from the 1916 book), and also a more generalized entry "poems in *The Messenger of Europe* and *Russian Thought* 1915–16." A most careful check of these numbers, however, has failed to reveal any Nabokov poems for these years.

Spolokhi (Northern Light). A Berlin art and literary almanac in which several Sirin poems appeared, only one of which, "My Calendar," (in issue No. 2) was not collected.

Russkaya Mysl' (Russian Thought). Prague and Berlin. Poems in Nos. 1, 2, 3–5, and 6–8.

Zhar-Ptitsa (Fire-Bird). Berlin. Poems in Nos. 1, 4, 5, 7, 11 (*"And those who came to God's paradise from earth"*), and 12 ("Shakespeare").

Raduga (Rainbow). An almanac of poems for children, edited by Sasha Chyorny. Berlin, 1921 (?), which included "The Fairy's Daughter," "The Penguin," "I dream that I'm a dwarf."

Gryadushchaya Rossiya (The Future Russia). Paris, 1920. "Funeral Services," "The Blizzard," "After the Storm." This excellent but very short-lived journal, edited by Aleksei Tolstoy and Mark Aldanov, was the forerunner of *Contemporary Annals.*

NEWSPAPERS AND MAJOR JOURNALS

"How alluring my North is in Spring!" *The Rudder,* April 10, 1919.

Quiet Fall. *The Rudder,* December 10, 1920.

Remembrance. *The English Review,* 1920.

"While in the mist of dubious days"; "How long since o'er the snowy quay." *Contemporary Annals,* No. 7, 1921.

"I've traveled, O Lord, around your world." *The Rudder*, May 14, 1921.

Petersburg. *The Rudder*, July 17, 1921.

Peacocks. *The Rudder*, August 11, 1921.

The following few poems were found in the very early stages of my research in the limited *Rudder* holdings of the New York Public Library. Unfortunately, the dates are not recorded because the top edges of the paper had often cracked away, but the poems themselves have been Xeroxed and may be ordered from the Library. There are: three poems which have been mutilated by cracking of the paper; "The Apparition of Joseph"; "The Cross-Bearers"; and "Where are you little wind of April."

On the Death of Aleksandr Blok. *The Rudder*, August 14, 1921.

The Shrine (two poems). *The Rudder*, December 4, 1921.

Autumn Leaves (three short poems). *The Rudder*, December 7, 1921.

By the Fireplace; "A simple song, a simple sadness"; Night. *The Rudder*, December 22, 1921.

Russia. *Contemporary Annals*, No. 11, 1922.

"Do you know my faith?" *The Rudder*, June 22, 1922.

To I. A. Bunin. *The Rudder*, September 18, 1922.

To I. A. Bunin. *The Rudder*, October 1, 1922.

Mushrooms; At a Village Cemetery. *The Rudder*, November 19, 1922.

A Snowy Night; The Knight's Betrothed. *The Rudder*, December 3, 1922.

The Beetle. *The Rudder*, December 17, 1922.

The Legend of the Old Woman in Search of a Carpenter. *The Rudder*. December 24, 1922.

To My Native Land. *The Rudder*, April 8, 1923. ("Let me live and seek the Creator in creation")

"When I, along a diamond staircase." *The Rudder*, April 29, 1923.

Hexameters (four short poems). *The Rudder*, May 6, 1923.

The Leopard. *The Rudder*, May 10, 1923.

The Storm. *The Rudder*, June 10, 1923.

The Meeting. *The Rudder*, June 24, 1923. (This poem has an epigraph from Blok.)

Song. *The Rudder*, July 29, 1923.

Provence. *The Rudder*, September 2, 1923.

My Native Land; The Deer. *The Rudder*, September 23, 1923.

Leningrad. *Nash Mir* (*Our World*), No. 1, 1924.

The Sheep. *Our World*, January 4, 1924. (A Christmas poem)

The Apparition. *The Rudder*, January 27, 1924.
The Wanderers. *The Rudder*, March 2, 1924.
Cubes. *The Rudder*, March 10, 1924.
The Window. *The Rudder*, March 23, 1924.
"While wandering in an untended garden." *The Rudder*, April 3, 1924.
"You do not know how terrifying." *The Rudder*, April 18, 1924.
An Automobile in the Mountains. *The Rudder*, April 20, 1924.
The Boxer's Girlfriend. *Our World*, May 11, 1924.
Saint-Petersburg. *The Rudder*, June 1, 1924.
Death. *The Rudder*, June 18, 1924.
The Guest. *The Rudder*, July 6, 1924. ("In deceit there is sense and sweetness!")
About Angels. *The Rudder*, July 20, 1924.
Prayer. *The Rudder*, August 24, 1924. (A poem to the Russian language)
The Albatross (translation from Baudelaire). *The Rudder*, September 3, 1924.
Exodus. *The Rudder*, October 26, 1924.
Three Chess Sonnets. *Our World*, November 30, 1924.
The Land of Poems. *The Rudder*, December 7, 1924.
To My Native Land. *The Rudder*, December 25, 1924.
The Skater. *The Rudder*, February 5, 1925.
Berlin Spring. *The Rudder*, May 25, 1925. ("My unusual destitution/ in a foreign land I prize/ . . . /They perceive, thank God, that I shall give superiority/ over all to my wild road,/ to my golden poverty"—these lines now strike Nabokov as "Emily Dickinson-ish.")
Exile. *The Rudder*, June 14, 1925. (A poem speculating on what Pushkin might have been like in exile)
The Dream. *The Rudder*, June 30, 1925.
Paradise. *The Rudder*, July 26, 1925.
The Summit. *The Rudder*, September 19, 1925.
The Path. *The Rudder*, December 13, 1925.
The Skijump. *The Rudder*, January 24, 1926.
Ut pictura poesis. *The Rudder*, April 25, 1926.
A University Poem. *Contemporary Annals*, No. 33, 1927. (A long poem)
Native Land. *The Rudder*, June 15, 1927.
The Chess Knight. *The Rudder*, October 23, 1927.
The Ticket. *The Rudder*, June 26, 1927.
The Islands. *The Rudder*, March 25, 1928.

The Wasp. *The Rudder*, June 24, 1928.

To Russia. *The Rudder*, July 1, 1928.

Tolstoy. *The Rudder*, September 16, 1928. (A poem written on the 100th anniversary of Tolstoy's birth)

The Cinema. *The Rudder*, November 10, 1928.

Stanzas on a Knight. *The Rudder*, February 2, 1929.

"For traveling at night I do not need." *The Rudder*, August 11, 1929.

Aerial Island. *The Rudder*, September 8, 1929.

To the Muse. *The Rudder*, September 24, 1929.

Snow; To an Unborn Reader. *The Rudder*, February 7, 1930.

Uldaborg: Translation from the Zoorlandian. *The Rudder*, May 4, 1930.

Poems. *Rossiya i Slavyanstvo* (*Russia and Slavdom*). Paris, No. 100, October, 1930.

The Formula. *The Rudder*, April 3, 1931.

The Awakening; To Grapefruit. *Contemporary Annals*, No. 47, 1931.

The Night Journey (from the Calmbrood poem). *The Rudder*, July 5, 1931. (A long poem)

The Madman. *Poslednie Novosti* (*The Latest News*), Paris. ("how dear to me/is the glum snigger of an enemy!")

The Appeal. *Contemporary Annals*, No. 70, 1940. (A Vasily Shishkov poem)

"Inspiration, a rose-colored sky"; "Once it had been easier, simpler"; "My youthful solitude"; "Blinking, a fiery eye." *The Latest News*, July 31, 1932. These poems constitute the larger poem later known as "The Evening of the Wasteland" of the 1952 collection.

*The Softest of Tongues. *The Atlantic Monthly*, December, 1941.

The Water Nymph. *Novy Zhurnal* (*The New Review*), No. 2, 1942. (A conclusion to Pushkin's unfinished poem)

*Exile. *The New Yorker*, October 24, 1942.

*"When he was small." *The Atlantic Monthly*, January, 1943.

*Dream. *The Atlantic Monthly*, September, 1946.

Irregular Iambs. *Opyty* (*Experiments*), No. 1, 1953.

Seven Poems. *The New Review*, No. 46, 1956.

*"What is the evil deed I have committed" (imitation of Pasternak); "There are such moments: it can't be, you mutter." *Vozdushnye Puti* (*Aerial Ways*), No. 2, 1961. The Pasternak parody has been translated by Nabokov in *Modern Russian Poetry*.

*"Spell 'night.' Spell 'pebbles.' " *The New York Review of Books*, April 28, 1966. This poem appears to have issued from an unused note card from material for *Pale Fire* (read to an interviewer):

"Naive, nonstop, peep-peep twitter in dismal crates late, late at night, on a desolate frost-bedimmed station platform."

NOVELS AND COLLECTED SHORT STORIES

Mashenka (Mashen'ka). Berlin, 1926. A 1928 German translation of this novel exists under the title *Sie kommt — kommt sie?* The title character does not actually appear in the novel, but the hero of the novel relives in memory his romance with Mashenka.

King, Queen, Knave (Korol', dama, valet). Berlin, 1928. The Russian translation of the Andersen fable from which this novel takes its title may be found in *The Rudder* (February, 1927). A German translation of this novel is currently in print as *Konig, Dame, Bube* (Rowohlt, 1959) and an American edition with many revisions is being prepared.

*The Defense (Zashchita Luzhina). Berlin, 1930. English translation, Putnam's, 1964. ("Some curious additional information might be given if I took myself more seriously.")

The Return of Chorb (Vozvrashchenie Chorba): Stories and Poems. Berlin, 1930.

Port (1924)
Bachmann (1924)
Well-Being (1924)
The Return of Chorb (1925)
Letter to Russia (1925)
Christmas (1925)
Guidebook to Berlin (1925)
A Fable (1926)
*The Passenger (1927). English translation, *The Quarter*, London, 1933(?).
Terror (1927)
*The Potato Elf (1929). English translation, *Esquire*, December, 1939.
The Catastrophe (1927)
The Storm
The Doorbell

**The Scoundrel. English translation as "An Affair of Honor," *The New Yorker*, September 3, 1966.

*The Eye (Soglyadatai). *Contemporary Annals*, No. 44, 1930. English translation, New York, Phaedra, 1965.

The Exploit (Podvig). Paris, 1932. Now being translated into English.

Camera obscura. Paris and Berlin, 1932. English translation, *Camera obscura*, London, 1936. The American translation of the novel was substantially altered and retitled *Laughter in the Dark* and published in 1938.

Despair (Otchayanie). Berlin, 1936; English translation, London, 1937. The novel was altered and slightly enlarged in its 1966 English translation (New York, Putnam).

The Eye (a novella and twelve short stories). Paris, 1938.

 *The Eye (1930)

 The Offense (1931)

 Goosefoot (*Lebeda*) (1932)

 *Terra incognita (1931). English translation in *The New Yorker*, May 18, 1963.

 The Meeting (1931)

 A Dashing Fellow

 The Busy Man (1931)

 *Pil'gram (1930). English translation as "The Aurelian" in *Nabokov's Dozen*

 Perfection (1932)

 The Beauty (1934)

 An Event from Life (1935)

 Notification (1936)

Invitation to a Beheading (Priglashenie na Kazn'). Paris and Berlin, 1938; English translation, New York, Putnam, 1959.

The Gift (Dar). New York, 1952; English translation, New York, Putnam, 1963. The novel's first appearance was in the Paris *Contemporary Annals*, 1935–36, but without the fourth chapter, which was deleted by the editors.

Solus Rex. An unfinished novel, the first portion of which appeared in *Contemporary Annals*, No. 70, 1940, and the second, under the title "Ultima Thule," in *The New Review*, No. 1, 1942.

The Real Life of Sebastian Knight. Norfolk, Conn., New Directions, 1941.

Bend Sinister. New York, Henry Holt, 1947.

Lolita. Paris, Olympia, 1955; published in America in 1958 and in England in 1959.

Spring in Fialta and Other Stories (Vesna v Fialte i drugie rasskazy). New York, 1956.

 Lips to Lips (*Usta k ustam*) (1931?)

 The Admiralty Needle (1933)

 The Kinglet (1933)

Heavy Smoke (1934)

In Memory of L. I. Shigaev (1934)

Recruitment (*Nabor*) (1935)

The Circle (1936)

*Cloud, Castle, Lake (*Oblako, ozero, bashnya*), 1937; English translation in *Nabokov's Dozen*, 1958.

*Spring in Fialta (1938)

The Annihilation of Tyrants (1938)

*Visit to a Museum (1938). English translation, *Esquire*, March, 1963.

Vasily Shishkov (1939). This story is incorrectly dated 1940 in this collection; it appeared in *The Latest News* in 1939.

*Lik (1939). English translation, *The New Yorker*, October 10, 1964.

Ultima Thule (1940)

Pnin. New York, Doubleday, 1957; London, 1957.

Nabokov's Dozen. New York, Doubleday, 1958. Nine of the stories in this collection appeared in an earlier volume, *Nine Stories* (Norfolk, Conn., New Directions, 1947).

The Aurelian. Originally published in 1930 under the title "Pil'-gram."

Cloud, Lake, Castle (1938)

Spring in Fialta (1938)

Mademoiselle O (from *Speak, Memory*)

The Assistant Producer (1943)

"That in Aleppo Once . . ." (1943)

A Forgotten Poet (1944)

Time and Ebb (1945)

Conversation Piece (1945). Originally titled "Double Talk" in *Nine Stories*.

First Love (from *Speak, Memory*)

Signs and Symbols (1948)

Scenes from the Life of a Double Monster (1950)

Lance (1952)

Pale Fire. New York, Putnam, 1962; London, 1962.

Nabokov's Quartet. New York, Phaedra, 1966.

Visit to a Museum (1938)

Lik (1939)

The Vane Sisters (1959)

An Affair of Honor

UNCOLLECTED SHORT STORIES

The Fight (*Draka*). *The Rudder*, September 26, 1925.
The Razor (*Britva*). *The Rudder*, February 19, 1926.
The Magician (*Volshebnik*). (1939, unpublished).

(Several of the story listings in the Zimmer bibliography are, in fact, excerpts from novels, and "Story," from the Paris *Latest News*, March, 1934, is the story "The Circle.")

DRAMA

The Wanderers (*Skital'tsy*). *Facets II* (Grani II), 1923. A pretended translation of the first act of a non-existent eighteenth-century English play by the imaginary playwright Vivian Calmbrood.
Death (*Smert'*). A verse-drama in two acts. *The Rudder*, May 20, 24, 1923.
The Grandfather (*Dedushka*). A verse-drama in one act. *The Rudder*, October 14, 1923.
Agaspher (*Agasfer*). The poetic accompaniment to a staged symphony. The Prologue appeared in *The Rudder*, December 2, 1923.
The Pole (*Polius*). A verse-drama in one act. *The Rudder*, August 14, 16, 1924.
The Tragedy of Mister Morn (*Tragediya gospodina Morna*). A five-act play in verse. A précis and excerpts from the play appeared in *The Rudder*, 1925.
The Man from the USSR (*Chelovek iz SSSR*). A five-act play. This play was staged in Berlin in 1926. Only the first act appeared in print in *The Rudder*, January 1, 1927.
The Event (*Sobytie*). A dramatic comedy in three acts. Staged in Paris (1938), Warsaw, Belgrad, and New York (1941). Printed in *Russian Annals* (*Russkie Zapiski*), April, 1938.
The Waltz Invention (*Izobretanie Val'sa*). A drama in three acts. *Russian Annals*. November 1938; English translation, New York, Phaedra, 1966.
Lolita. Screenplay for the 1962 film of the novel. "Another project I have been nursing for some time is the publication of the complete screenplay of *Lolita* that I made for Kubrick. Although there

are just enough borrowings from it in his version to justify my legal position as author of the script, the final product is only a blurred skimpy glimpse of the marvelous picture I imagined and set down scene by scene during the six months I worked in a Los Angeles villa. I do not wish to imply that Kubrick's film is mediocre; in its own right it is first-rate, but it is not what I wrote. A tinge of *poshlost'* is often given by the cinema to the novel it distorts and coarsens in its crooked glass. Kubrick, I think, avoided this fault in his version, but I shall never understand why he did not follow my directions and dreams." (From an interview with Herbert Gold in a forthcoming issue of *Paris Review*.)

MEMOIRS

Conclusive Evidence. London and New York, 1951. Prior to the book's appearance the separate chapters appeared in slightly different form in *The Atlantic Monthly* (January, 1943); *The New Yorker* (January 3, 1948; March 27, 1948; June 12, 1948; July 31, 1948; September 18, 1948; January 1, 1949; April 9, 1949; December 10, 1949; February 11, 1950; April 15, 1950); *Partisan Review*, 1951; *Harper's* (January, 1951).

Other Shores (*Drugie berega*). New York, 1954. This is not a translation but a varied and slightly expanded version of *Conclusive Evidence*. It has a purposefully weird and useless "index."

Speak, Memory. First published in 1951 as *Conclusive Evidence*. The 1966 edition is an expanded version including most of the additional material in *Other Shores* and some wholly new material, such as a brief biography of Nabokov's father.

TRANSLATIONS

Poems by Rupert Brooke. *Facets*, 1922.

Romain Rolland, *Colas Breugnon* (*Nikolka Persik*). Berlin, 1922.

A sonnet by Ronsard. *The Rudder*, July 31, 1922.

Seumas O'Sullivann (two poems). *The Rudder*, 1922. Available from the New York Public Library.

Translations of Verlaine, Supervielle, Tennyson, and Yeats. (Unlocated.)

Lewis Carroll, *Alice in Wonderland* (*Anya v strane chudes*). Berlin, 1923. (The first Russian translation of *Alice* was done by Allegro-Solovieva in 1909.)

Translations of Byron, Keats, and Baudelaire. *The Empyrean Path*, 1923.

Shakespeare, Sonnets XVII and XXVII. *The Rudder*, September 18, 1927.

Alfred de Musset, *La Nuit de mai*. *The Rudder*, November 20, 1927.

Alfred de Musset, *La Nuit de décembre*. *The Rudder*, October 7, 1928.

Arthur Rimbaud, *Le Bateau ivre*. *The Rudder*, December 16, 1928.

Shakespeare, two excerpts from *Hamlet:* Act IV, Scene 7, and Act V, Scene 1. *The Rudder*, October 19, 1930.

Shakespeare, Hamlet's monologue, Act III, Scene 1. *The Rudder*, November 23, 1930.

Goethe, The Prologue to *Faust*. *The Latest News*, December 15, 1932.

Bal'mont. An (unpublished) re-translation back into English of Konstantin Bal'mont's wretched but famous translation of Edgar Allan Poe's *The Bells*. This "translation back" was done about 1940 at the request of Rachmaninoff, who had set Bal'mont's version to music prior to the 1917 revolution, but later found Poe's original not at all suited to the music he had written for Bal'mont.

Pushkin. Translations into French. *La Nouvelle Révue française* and *Cahiers du journal des poètes*. Brussels, 1937.

Pushkin. "Mozart and Salieri" (in collaboration with Edmund Wilson.) *The New Republic*, April 21, 1941.

Three Russian Poets: Translations of Pushkin, Lermontov, and Tiutchev. Norfolk, Conn., New Directions, 1944.

*Three poems by Afanasi Fet. *The Russian Review*, Vol. III, No. 1.

*Pushkin. Rhymed paraphrases of three stanzas from *Eugene Onegin*. *The Russian Review*, Vol. IV, No. 2.

The Song of Igor's Campaign. New York, Random House, 1960; London, 1960.

*Pushkin, *Eugene Onegin* (4 vols. with Commentary). New York, Bollingen Series, Pantheon Books, 1964; London, 1964.

Lolita (in Russian). New York, Phaedra, 1967.

CRITICAL AND SCHOLARLY WORKS AND LETTERS

"Cambridge." *The Rudder*, October 28, 1921.

"Rupert Brooke." *Facets I*, 1922.

Review of poems by Sergei Krechetov. *The Rudder*, December 17, 1922.

The Enchanted Nightingale, a fable by Richard Dehmal (review). *The Rudder*, March 30, 1924.

"The Russian River." *Our World*, September 14, 1924.

Odes and Hymns by Aleksandr Saltykov (review). *The Rudder*, October 1, 1924.

Poems by A. Bulkin (review). *The Rudder*, August 25, 1926.

Sonnets by V. Dukel'sky (review). *The Rudder*, November 3, 1926.

Review of poems by Sergei Rafalovich. *The Rudder*, January 19, 1927.

Review of three books of poetry by D. Kobyakov and E. Shakh. *The Rudder*, May 11, 1927.

"New Poets" (V. Dikson, D. Gusev, R. Arkadin, L. Shlossberg, Iu. Galich, G. Pronin). *The Rudder*, August 31, 1927.

A chess review of "Capablanca and Alekhin" by A. Znosko-Borovsky. *The Rudder*, November 16, 1927.

"Jubilee" (a political article). *The Rudder*, November 18, 1927.

Review of almanac *The Architect* (*Zodchi*). *The Rudder*, November 23, 1927.

Poems by Andrei Blokh (review). *The Rudder*, November 30, 1927.

Collected Poems by V. Khodasevich (review). *The Rudder*, December 14, 1927.

Review of books of poetry by Raisa Blokh and Maryam Stoyan. *The Rudder*, March 7, 1928.

Review of books of poetry by B. Bozhnev and D. Knut and the book *The Poem, Poetry, and Poetic Criticism*. *The Rudder*, May 23, 1928.

Omar Khayyam in the translations of I. Tkhorzhevsky (review). *The Rudder*, May 30, 1928.

An Anthology of Lunar Poets (review). *The Rudder*, June 6, 1928.

"Two Slavic Poets," a review of N. Beskid and J. Kasirovic. *The Rudder*, October 10, 1928.

Reviews of books of poetry by N. Snesareva-Kazakova and V. Pozner. *The Rudder*, October 24, 1928.

The Star Above Stars by A. Remizov (review). *The Rudder*, November 14, 1928.

"In Memory of Iu. Aikhenvald." *The Rudder*, December 23, 1928.

Review of *Contemporary Annals*, No. 37. *The Rudder*, January 30, 1929. ("It is better to be silent about the two poems by Adamovich. This subtle and sometimes brilliant literary critic writes absolutely undistinguished poems.")

Review of *The Will of Russia*, No. 2, 1929. *The Rudder*, May 8, 1929.

Selected Poems by Ivan Bunin (review). *The Rudder*, May 22, 1929.

Wives by A. Damanskaya (review of a book of poems). *The Rudder*, September 25, 1929.

Review of *Literary Review. Contemporary Annals*, No. 70, 1940.

Collection of short stories *Elan* by A. Kuprin (review). *The Rudder*, October 23, 1929.

Isolde by Irina Odoevtseva (review of a novel). *The Rudder*, October 30, 1929.

*Reply to a questionnaire on Proust. *Chisla* (*Numbers*), No. 1, 1930.

"The Triumph of Virtue," *The Rudder*, March 5, 1930.

Review of *The Will of Russia*, Nos. 7–8, 1930 (review). *The Rudder*, October 15, 1930.

Beatrice by V. Korvin-Piotrovsky (review). *Russia and Slavdom*, No. 98, October, 1930.

"Autour de Maiakovsky." *Les Nouvelles littéraires*, Paris, July 12, 1930. A group letter on the death and artistic inadequacies of Mayakovsky. However, Nabokov had no role in the preparation of the letter, and his name was in fact added to the list of signatories through a misunderstanding.

Review of a book of poems *Black and Azure* by A. Ladinsky and an anthology *Crossroads 2. The Rudder*, January 28, 1931.

*"What Must Everyone Know?" *The New Gazette*, No. 5, 1931.

Flags by B. Poplavsky (review of a book of poems). *The Rudder*, March 11, 1931.

The Last and the First by Nina Berberova (review of a novel). *The Rudder*, July 23, 1931.

The Cavern by M. Aldanov (review of a novel). *Contemporary Annals*, No. 61, 1936.

"*Pouchkine ou le vrai et le vraisemblable*." *La Nouvelle Revue Francaise*, March, 1937.

"On Khodasevich." *Contemporary Annals*, No. 69, 1939.

*"Diaghilev and a Disciple" (a review of a biography by Serge Lifar). *The New Republic*, November 18, 1940.

*Review of the Georgian epic *The Knight in the Tiger's Skin. The New Republic*, November 25, 1940.

*"Mr. Masefield and Clio." *The New Republic*, December 9, 1940.

Slava Bohu: The Story of the Dukhobors by J. Wright (review). *The New Republic*. January 13, 1941.

**Mr. Shakespeare and the Globe* by F. Williams (review). *The New Republic*. May 19, 1941.

*"The Art of Translation," *The New Republic*, August 4, 1941, and reply to a letter pointing out a misquotation in "The Art of Translation," *The New Republic*, December 22, 1941.

The Silence of the Sea by Hilaire Belloc (review of a collection of essays). New York *Times* Book Review, November 23, 1941.

"The Great Russians and Their Influence." Three public lectures (unpublished) delivered at Wellesley College. 1941.

*"What Faith Means to a Resisting People." Remarks at a symposium published in *The Wellesley Magazine*, April, 1942. "The splendid paradox of democracy is that while stress is laid on the rule of all and equality of common rights, it is the individual that derives from it his special and uncommon benefit. Ethically, the members of a democracy are equals; spiritually, each has the right to be as different from his neighbors as he pleases; and taken all in all, it is not perhaps an organization or a government or a community that we really have in mind when we say 'democracy' but the subtle balance between the boundless privileges of every individual and the strictly equal rights of all men. Life is a state of harmony — and that is why I think that the spirit of democracy is the most natural human condition . . . Democracy in its inner sense is not politics, or party regulation, or things like that. A Russian democrat of the old days, and an American or an English one, despite the differences in forms of government in their respective countries, could meet with perfect ease on a common and natural basis — which basis is so familiar to democrats that it almost escapes definition. Democracy is humanity at its best, not because we happen to think that a republic is better than a king and a king is better than nothing and nothing is better than a dictator, but because it is the natural condition of every man ever since the human mind became conscious not only of the world but of itself. Morally, democracy is invincible. Physically, that side will win which has the better guns."

*"Cabbage Soup and Caviar." A review of two anthologies of Russian literature edited by B. Guerney and J. Cournos, respectively. *The New Republic*, January 17, 1944.

Nikolai Gogol. Norfolk, Conn., *New Directions*, 1944.

*"On Learning Russian." *The Wellesley Magazine*, April, 1945. "A Russian vowel is an orange, an English vowel is a lemon. When you speak Russian your mouth ought to distend laterally at the corners, vowels being expressed by a horizontal line from cheek to cheek, rather than by a vertical one from chin to nose, as in

English. You can, and should, speak Russian with a permanent broad smile, which is a very difficult feat in English where the mouth forms a proximo-distad-directed oval to say O. Compress its poles, inflate its sides and you get the Russian equivalent. I strictly avoid the humorous touch when dealing with my classes, but such-like explanations, which are merely meant to stress the anatomical differences between the two languages, oddly enough provoke a ripple of laughter, when all I ask for is a bland smile of the Cheshire cat type . . . However exasperating the impredictable quality of Russian grammar may seem, the thing must be seen through. The conjuror's patter of the Berlitz school is not, in my opinion, a good introduction to the Russian language, and generally speaking I must admit to feeling a great deal of disgust for any leveling or over-simplification. Brains must work the hard way or else lose their calling and rank. The loaves of knowledge do not come nicely sliced. All you get is a stone-strewn field to plough on an exhilarating morning. Incidentally and apart from totalitarian regimes, the most despicable invention of our times is Basic English."

*"The Place of Russian Studies in the Curriculum." *The Wellesley Magazine*, February, 1948. "Between 1820 and 1920 Russia produced one of the greatest literatures we know . . . There is a certain unique quality about Russian literature, a quality of truth not rubbed in, of imagination controlled by dignified truthfulness, which has had an ennobling influence on the world literatures, but which, to be fully understood and appraised, calls for a knowledge of the workings of the Russian creative mind (or I would prefer to say, workings of a creative mind in Russian), which, in turn, calls for a sound knowledge of the language." It is worth noting, I think, that in over fifteen years of teaching in America, Nabokov never once wrote an "academic" article or even a review.

*"Sartre's First Try." The New York *Times* Book Review, April 24, 1949.

Introduction to a Russian-language edition of Gogol's short stories. New York, Chekhov Publishing House, 1952.

*"Problems of Translation: *Onegin* in English." *Partisan Review*, 1955.

"Notes of a Translator I." *The New Review* (*Novy Zhurnal*), New York, No. 49, 1957.

"Notes of a Translator II." *Experiments* (*Opyty*), No. 8, New York, 1957.

*Introduction to English translation of Lermontov's *A Hero of Our Time*. New York, 1958.
*"The Servile Path." From *On Translation,* edited by Reuben Brower. Cambridge, Mass., Harvard University Press, 1959.
*Foreword and Commentary to *The Song of Igor's Campaign.* New York, Random House, 1960.
*Letter. *The Times* (London), May 30, 1962.
*Letter. *Encounter,* September, 1962.
Letter. *Russkaya Mysl'* (*Russian Thought*), Paris, October 8, 1963.
*"Pounding the Clavichord," a review of Walter Arndt's translation of *Eugene Onegin. The New York Review of Books,* April 30, 1964.
*Commentary to *Eugene Onegin* (in 4 vols. with translation). New York, Bollinger Series, Pantheon Books, 1964.
Notations to prison letters of V. D. Nabokov. *Aerial Ways IV,* 1965.
*Letter. *New Statesman.* January, 1965.
*Letter. *New Statesman.* April 23, 1965.
*First reply to Edmund Wilson's attack on translation of *Eugene Onegin. The New York Review of Books,* August 26, 1965.
*"A Cautionary Letter for the benefit of my learned friends." *The New York Review of Books,* January 20, 1966.
*Reply to My Critics. *Encounter,* February, 1966.
*Letter. *Encounter.* April, 1966.
*Reply to a letter from Robert Lowell and reply to a review of "Notes on Prosody" (Vol. III of *Eugene Onegin* translation and Commentary). *Encounter,* May, 1966.
*Letter. *The Sunday Times* (London), January 1, 1967.
*"*Lolita* and Mr. Girodias." *Evergreen Review,* February, 1967.
Letter. *Encounter.* February, 1967.

*Forewords to English works and English translations of Russian works include: *Lolita* (Afterword), *The Defense, Despair, Invitation to a Beheading, The Gift, The Eye, Bend Sinister* (Introduction for Time-Life Books edition), *The Waltz Invention,* and *Nabokov's Quartet* and *Speak, Memory* (revised).

*ARTICLES ON LEPIDOPTERA

"A Few Notes on Crimean Lepidoptera." *The Entomologist* (London), Vol. 53, 1920.
"Notes on the Lepidoptera of the Pyrénées Orientales and the Ariège." *The Entomologist,* Vol. 64, 1931.

"On Some Asiatic Species of Carterocephalus." *Journal of the New York Entomological Society*, Vol. 49, 1941.

"Lysandra cormion, a New European Butterfly." *Journal of the New York Entomological Society*, Vol. 49, 1941.

"Some New or Little-Known Nearctic Neonympha." *Psyche, Journal of Entomology*, Vol. 49, 1942.

"The Female of Neonympha maniola Nabokov." *Psyche*, 1943.

"The Nearctic Forms of Lycaeides Hüb." *Psyche*, Vol. 50, 1943.

"Notes on the Morphology of the Genus Lycaeides." *Psyche*, Vol. 51, 1944.

"Notes on Neotropical Plebejinae." *Psyche*, Vol. 52, 1945.

"A Third Species of Echinargus Nabokov." *Psyche*, Vol. 52, 1945.

"A New Species of Cyclargus Nabokov." *The Entomologist*, Vol. 81, 1948.

"The Nearctic Members of the Genus Lycaeides Hübner." *Bulletin of the Museum of Comparative Zoology at Harvard College*, Vol. 101, 1949.

"Remarks on F. M. Brown's *Measurements and Lepidoptera*." *The Lepidopterists' News*, Vol. 4, 1950.

A Field Guide to the Butterflies of North America by A. Klots (review). New York *Times* Book Review, 1951.

The Female of Lycaeides argyrognomon sublivens Nabokov. *The Lepidopterists' News*, Vol. 6, 1952.

On some inaccuracies in *Klots' Field Guide. The Lepidopterists' News*, Vol. 6, 1952.

Review of Audubon's *Butterflies, Moths and Other Studies*, compiled and edited by A. Ford. New York *Times* Book Review, December 28, 1952.

Butterfly Collecting in Wyoming. *The Lepidopterists' News*, Vol. 7, 1953.

Migratory species observed in Wyoming, 1952. *The Lepidopterists' News*, Vol. 7, 1953.

Comments on Lycaeides argyrognomon in Wisconsin. *The Lepidopterists' News*, Vol. 7, 1953.

Note on types of *Plebejus (Lysandra) cormion* Nab., p. 288 of *Speak, Memory* (revised).

MISCELLANEOUS

The following epigram on the poet Georgy Ivanov was composed by Nabokov in the mid-thirties. Because it was found unsigned in the album of Vladislav Khodasevich, it has been falsely attributed to Khodasevich. The epigram turns on the Russian use of the common names Ivanov and Petrov in the sense of Jones and Smith. The sense of it is that a particular "Johnson" (that is, Georgy Ivanov) is automatically assumed when a "magazine scoundrel" is referred to.

> "Takogo net moshennika vtorogo
> Vo vsey sem'e zhurnal'nikh shulerov!"
> "Kogo ty tak?" "Ivanova, Petrova,
> Ne vsyo l' ravno . . ." "Postoy, a kto zh Petrov?"

> "No greater crook exists among the sharpers
> Of the whole magazine fraternity!"
> "Whom are you cursing so?" "Oh, Johnson, Smithson,
> What do I care . . ." "But Smithson — who is he?"

Chess problems and crossword puzzles. *The Rudder* and *The Latest News*, 1920–1940.

*Interview. *New York Post*, August 6, 1958.
*Interview. *Newsweek*, November 24, 1958.
*Interview. *Louisville Courier-Journal*, January 25, 1959.
*Letter. *Life*, July 6, 1959.
*Interview with Alain Robbe-Grillet. *Arts* (Paris), October, 1959.
*"A Conversation with Vladimir Nabokov," *Twentieth Century* (London), December, 1959.
"A Meeting with the Author of *Lolita*." *Russkaya Mysl'* (*Russian Thought*), Paris, February 7, 1961.
Interview. *Nice-Matin*. April 3, 1961.
*Letter. *Esquire*, June, 1961. "My wife never worked as a milliner, nor in any other shop, and anyway could not have made that trite and silly remark . . . Finally, let me quote . . ."
*Letter. *Playboy*, July, 1961.
*Interview. New York *Herald Tribune*, June 1, 1962.
*Interview. *Victoria Colonist* (British Columbia), July 15, 1962.
*Interview from BBC Bookstand program. Reprinted in *The Listener*, November 22, 1962.
Interview. *Tribune de Lausanne*, September 1, 1963.
*Interview. *National Observer*, June 29, 1964.
*Interview. *Life*, November 20, 1964.
*Interview. *The Twelfth Anniversary Playboy Reader*, Chicago, 1965.
*"Why Nabokov Detests Freud." Excerpts from a National Educational Television interview, New York *Times* Sunday Theater Section, January 30, 1966.
Interview. *Die Zeit*, November 1, 1966.

*"Nabokov," *Vogue*, December, 1966.   Article by Penelope Gilliatt.
*Interview. *Saturday Evening Post*, February 18, 1967.
Letters. *Saturday Evening Post*, March 25, 1967.
Interview with Alfred Appel, Jr., in *Wisconsin Studies in Contemporary Literature*, Spring, 1967.   "I would say that imagination is a form of memory. Down, Plato, down, good dog. An image depends on the power of association, and association is supplied and prompted by memory. When we speak of a valid individual recollection we are paying a compliment not to our capacity of retention but to Mnemosyne's mysterious foresight in having stored up this or that element which creative imagination may use when combining it with later recollections and inventions. In this sense, both memory and imagination are a negation of time."
Interview with Herbert Gold in a forthcoming issue of *Paris Review*. "*Poshlost'* speaks in such concepts as "America is no better than Russia," or "We all share in Germany's guilt." The flowers of *poshlost'* bloom in such phrases and terms as "the moment of truth," "charisma," "existential" (used seriously), "dialogue" (as applied to political talks between nations) and "vocabulary" (as applied to a dauber). Listing in one breath Auschwitz, Hiroshima, and Vietnam is seditious *poshlost'*. Belonging to a very select club (which sports *one* Jewish name — that of the treasurer) is genteel *poshlost'*. Hack reviews are frequently *poshlost'*, that is, simple, but it also lurks in certain highbrow essays . . . Of course, everybody has his *bête noire*, his black pet, in the series. Mine is that airline ad: the snack served by an obsequious wench to a young couple — she eyeing ecstatically the cucumber canapé, he admiring wistfully the hostess. And, of course, *Death in Venice*."

Concluding Remarks

⌘ ⌘ ⌘ ⌘

AS A comparison between the bibliography and the relevant chapters of my study shows, only representative examples of Nabokov's poetry have been dealt with. There is a need for a detailed metrical and thematic study of Nabokov's poetry, including all of his many youthful poems of secondary merit. In the area of criticism and scholarship, one would like to see comparative studies of Nabokov and Poe, Nabokov and Proust, Nabokov and Dostoevsky, and Nabokov and Sologub. There is a need for a thorough and scholarly compilation of all the revisions and slight changes in the translations of Nabokov's Russian works into English, and also for a dictionary of all literary references and parodies in Nabokov's art. If this book does nothing else, I hope it will render impossible the meaningless and harmful division of Nabokov's art into "Russian works" and "English works."

For the reader who wishes to delve further, I can recommend only individual essays (there is one other book-length study, *Escape into Aesthetics* by S. Page Stegner, published in 1966): Conrad Brenner on *The Real Life of Sebastian Knight*, Frank Kermode on *Bend Sinister*, John Updike and Robert M. Adams on *The Defense*, Stanley Hyman on *The Gift* and *Despair*, Howard Nemerov on the short stories, Simon Karlinsky on *The Event*, Mary McCarthy on *Pale Fire*, and, of course, there are many fine essays on *Lolita*. A special Nabokov issue of the *Wisconsin Studies in Contemporary Literature*, which will have appeared shortly before this book is published, will have an excellent and quite complete bibliography of all the English essays and newspaper reviews of Nabokov's work, compiled by Jackson Bryer. The special issue of the French journal *L'Arc* (No. 24, Aix-en-Provence) contains worthwhile articles. The four best general surveys in English of Nabokov's writing are probably those of F. W. Dupee (*The King of the Cats*), Conrad Brenner (*The New Republic*, June 23, 1958), R. H. W. Dillard (*The Hollins Critic*, Vol. 3, No. 3, Hollins College, Virginia) and Alfred Appel, Jr. (*The New Republic*, January 14 and 21, 1967). In Russian the best easily obtainable articles on Nabokov are those by Vladislav Khodasevich (*Literary Articles and Memoirs*), Vladimir Varshavsky (*The Unnoticed Generation*), and Georgy Adamovich (*Solitude and Freedom*); these three books are readily available in inexpensive editions from any of a number of Western outlets for Russian publications, and they are the three books best suited to give someone who reads Russian but knows little about émigré literature and culture a proper grounding in the subject. Another important survey article on Nabokov in Russian is that of Nina Berberova in the New York *Novy Zhurnal* (No. 57), and a 1967 Russian reprinting of *Invitation to a Beheading* (Editions Victor, Paris) has a fine general introduction, translated from English into Russian by Julian Moynahan. Unfortunately there is no historical survey of émigré literature in English or any other Western European language. (There is, for that matter, only one such history in Russian, but to my mind the taste and manner of its discussion and literary judgments are more than questionable.) Another useful book (also published in an inexpensive edition and readily obtainable) is *In the West*, a comprehensive anthology of émigré poetry edited by Yury Ivask. Happily, a book in English on Russian émigré literature by Vsevolod Setchkarev is now in progress, and it promises to be a scholarly event of major importance.

I am indebted in many small and large ways to the six people who read *Nabokov: His Life in Art* in manuscript. Four of these readers were strict and attentive; two, permissive and attentive. The strict readers were Vsevolod Setchkarev, one of the handful of those with a substantially full knowledge of Nabokov's writing in three languages, Erik Wensberg, founding editor of the Columbia University *Forum* and a truly remarkable sounding board, Mrs.

Joyce Olesen of Little, Brown, and Audrey Field. But since I as often as not chose to stand with my intermittent eccentricities of style and judgment (these are matters a critic must be willing to test, but also know how to guard), not even my "strict" readers are to be held accountable for such infelicities and errors as may still remain.

My two permissive readers were Véra and Vladimir Nabokov. Having once decided to aid my work by answering questions and supplying certain materials and information which I could not otherwise obtain, they were steadfastly unconcerned with the opinions I chose to express. This complete freedom from any restraints together with such generous aid is something, I think, quite extraordinary if not unprecedented in the uneasy history of the relations between writer and critic.

I should like to close with two citations which I rejected as epigraphs to begin this book. It seems to me, though, that they do have a fitting place here, at its conclusion. The first is from a letter by John Constable: "One ambition I *will* hold fast. I am determined never to deserve the praise of S ——, H ——, C ——, D ——, W ——, R ——, etc. etc. etc." The second is the opening sentence of an article on Nabokov: "To approach Nabokov's novels with anything less than complete humility is not only an act of arrogance but of foolishness."

Appendix

❋ ❋ ❋ ❋

Some sample excerpts from Nabokov's Russian poems quoted or referred to in this study:

The description of how the following fragment was composed appears on page 37. Nabokov has said that this little prerevolutionary poem was the first formulation of the idea that occurs in the chapter on versification in *Speak, Memory*.

Воздух живителен, влажен, душист,
Как жимолость благоухает!
Кончиком вниз наклоняется лист
И с кончика жемчуг роняет.

Excerpt from *St. Petersburg* (pages 46–47):

Таких, как я, немало. Мы
блуждаем по-миру бессонно
и знаем: город погребенный
воскреснет вновь; все будет в нем
прекрасно, радостно, и ново —
а только прежнего, *родного*
мы никогда уж не найдем . . .

Poem from *The Cluster* (pages 72–73):

Есть в одиночестве свобода,
и сладость — в вымыслах благих.
Звезду, снежинку, каплю меда
я заключаю в стих.

И еженочно умирая,
я рад воскреснуть в должный час,
и новый день — росинка рая,
а прошлый день — алмаз.

In Paradise or *To My Soul* (page 81):

Моя душа, — за смертью дальной
твой образ виден мне вот так:
натуралист провинциальный,
в раю потерянный чудак.

Там в роще дремлет ангел дикий, —
полупавлинье существо . . .
Ты любознательно потыкай
зеленым зонтиком в него,

соображая, как сначала
о нем напишешь ты статью,
потом . . . Но только нет журнала,
и нет читателей в раю.

И ты стоишь, еще не веря
немому горю своему . . .
Об этом синем, сонном звере
кому расскажешь ты, кому?

Где мир и названные розы,
музей и птичьи чучела?
И смотришь, смотришь ты сквозь слезы
на безымянные крыла . . .

Excerpt from *A University Poem* (page 84):

Живой душой не правит мода,
но иногда моя свобода
случайно с нею совпадет:
мне мил фокс-трот, простой и нежный . . .
Иной мыслитель неизбежно
симптомы века в нем найдет —
разврат под музыку бедлама;
иная пишущая дама
или копеечный пиит

о прежних танцах возопит;
но для меня, скажу открыто,
особой прелести в том нет,
что грубоватый и немытый
маркиз танцует менуэт.

Excerpt from *Fame* (page 94):

Оттого так смешна мне пустая мечта
   о читателе, теле, и славе.
Я без тела разросся, без отзвука жив,
   и со мной моя тайна всечасно.
Что мне тление книг, если даже разрыв
   между мной и отчизною — частность?
Признаюсь, хорошо зашифрована ночь,
   но под звезды я буквы подставил
и в себе прочитал чем себя превозмочь,
   а точнее сказать я невправе.

Excerpt from *A Parisian Poem* (page 96):

А мосты — Это счастье навеки,
счастье черной воды. Посмотри:
как стекло несравненной аптеки
— и оранжевые фонари.
А вверху — Там неважные вещи.
Без конца. Без конца. Только муть.
Мертвый в омуте месяц мерещится.
Неужели я тоже? Забудь.
Смерть еще далека (послезавтра я
все продумаю), но иногда
сердцу хочется «автора, автора!»
В зале автора нет, господа.

Copyright Acknowledgments

❊   ❊   ❊   ❊

In Place
of an Index

This Index is purposely abbreviated and is meant for the use of re-readers only.

The phrase "In Place of," which has proved so convenient in labeling the Foreword, Bibliography and Index in this particular book, is a time-honored convention for labeling forewords in all but the most scholarly Russian works.